AF361539

Allama Prabhu and the Shaiva Imagination

SUNY series in Hindu Studies

Brian Collins, editor

D. R. NAGARAJ

Allama Prabhu

and the
Shaiva Imagination

Edited and Translated from the Kannada by

N. S. GUNDUR

SUNY
PRESS

First published by Permanent Black, 'Himalayana', Mall Road, Ranikhet Cantt, Ranikhet 263645, INDIA, for the territory of SOUTH ASIA. perblack@gmail.com

First SUNY Press edition 2026. Not for sale in South Asia.
Cover design: Anuradha Roy
Published by State University of New York Press, Albany
© 2026 Girija Nagaraj and Amulya Nagaraj for all material by D. R. Nagaraj
© 2026 N. S. Gundur for the translator's introduction, translation of vachanas, and related editorial apparatus
All rights reserved
Printed in the United States of America

No part of this book may be used or reproduced in any manner whatsoever without written permission. No part of this book may be stored in a retrieval system or transmitted in any form or by any means including electronic, electrostatic, magnetic tape, mechanical, photocopying, recording, or otherwise without the prior permission in writing of the publisher.

Links to third-party websites are provided as a convenience and for informational purposes only. They do not constitute an endorsement or an approval of any of the products, services, or opinions of the organization, companies, or individuals. SUNY Press bears no responsibility for the accuracy, legality, or content of a URL, the external website, or for that of subsequent websites.

EU GPSR Authorised Representative:
Logos Europe, 9 rue Nicolas Poussin, 17000, La Rochelle, France
contact@logoseurope.eu

For information, contact State University of New York Press, Albany, NY
www.sunypress.edu

Library of Congress Cataloging-in-Publication Data
Names: Nagaraj, D. R., author | Gundur, N. S., editor, translator.
Title: Allama Prabhu and the Shaiva imagination
Description: Albany : [State University of New York Press], [2026] |
    Includes bibliographical references and index.
Identifiers: ISBN 9798855807295 (hardback) | ISBN 9798855807325
    (PDF) | ISBN 9798855807318 (epub)
Further information is available at the Library of Congress.

for

CHINMAYI

Contents

Acknowledgements

I have borrowed words, ideas, and strength from many minds and institutions.

The New India Foundation (NIF), which enabled this translation by offering me a fellowship (2022), is a great source of hope for intellectual achievements in our country through knowledge production. I am indebted to its trustees, Niraja Gopal Jayal, Srinath Raghavan, Manish Sabharwal, Rahul Matthan, Nandan Nilekani, and Ramachandra Guha. The last-mentioned eminent historian, whose admiration for D.R. Nagaraj brought us together over frequent cups of coffee at Koshy's in Bangalore – where he used to meet Nagaraj – read the Translator's Introduction carefully, adding value to it with his comments.

Cooking this book with Rukun Advani was a time of great recognition and joy. While I deem it an intellectual feat to be published by Permanent Black, it has been an even greater honour to earn Sheldon Pollock's endorsement. Many thanks to Prithvi Datta Chandra Shobhi, my prajna, for enabling all this.

Comments from Srinath Raghavan, who read the drafts thoroughly, have stuck within me as a pedagogical imperative. Along with Rivka Israel, he is there in every line of this book, and Rivka's sharp editorial eye left this text clean.

The entire process was seamlessly facilitated by the ever-energetic Yauvanika Chopra, who gave way to an equally active Sanchita Kapoor at the NIF.

My heartfelt thanks to the eminent writer Vivek Shanbhag, whose trust in my capabilities keeps me going. He introduced me to the Nagaraj family. I am grateful to Girija Nagaraj, and to Amulya and Anoop, for giving access to the handwritten manuscript, and for useful conversations.

I should express my gratitude to the NIF fraternity and its various language experts – Tridip Suhrud, Harish Trivedi, Jatin Nayak, Arupjyoti Saikia, and A.R. Venkatachalapathy; and fellow NIF awardees – Rahul Sarwate, Richa Kumar, Srikar Raghavan, Venu Madhav Govindu, Srinivas SV, Indira Chowdhury, Dinyar Patel, Akshaya Mukul, and Manoj Mitta, among others.

I am grateful to my teacher, Professor C.R. Yaravintelimath, on whose translation of Allama's vachanas, I could refashion my own. While my conversations with Devu Pattar and G. Veerabhadragoudru strengthened my literary scholarship, Dr Manjunath Hiremath lifted my heart in the most dispirited times.

When this book was in its final stages, I lost *avva*, my wonderful mother, but gained a foster parent in Nithyananda B. Shetty, who sides with the powerless. I owe to him my interest in Kannada literature and culture; he stayed with me throughout the project.

I am grateful to my colleagues in the Department – Dr Shivalingaswamy H.K., Dr Kiran S.N., and Dr Monbinder Kaur – for creating a conducive workplace environment; which is not to forget the affectionate Lingaraju and Basavaraju. Thanks are also due to former colleague Dr Ashwin Kumar A.P., whose conversations provoked me to think differently.

Madhava Chippali brought to my notice the NIF's fellowship advertisement. Sundar Sarukkai, who inspires my thinking, read the manuscript and made valuable suggestions. I am indebted to Dr D.V. Paramashivamurthy, Dr Nanjundaswamy, and Shashidhar Todkar for sharing books on vachana studies with me.

I must particularly remember the help of several Kannada scholars whose discussions shaped my translation. I have lost count of the number of calls with which I troubled vachana scholar O.L. Nagabhushana Swamy, and the cultural critics Rajendra Chenni and Rahamath Tarikere. Likewise, I am grateful to C.N. Ramachandran, Krishnamurthy Hanur, K.V. Akshara, Venkataramana Aithal, Shriram Bhat, Basavaraj Kalgudi, Shivanand Kanavi, Mrinal Kaul, Vikram Visaji, Tharakeshwar V.B., Mahendra M., Mahantesh Patil, and Bhimashankar Biradar for their inputs.

A special word of thanks to Kamalakar Bhat, N. Manu Chakravarthy, Chandan Gowda, Vijayakumar M. Boratti, and Shrikanth B.R., all of whom went through the draft and offered valuable suggestions. In each of them I saw reflections of Nagaraj's intellectual depth.

Thanks are due to Agrahara Krishnamurthy, Nataraj Huliyar, and M.S. Ashadevi for helping me to understand Nagaraj's mind and language. Professor Richard Polt (Heidegger scholar, Xavier University, Cincinnati) and Susan Germein (of the Western Sydney University) keep inspiring me through email discussions.

My heartfelt thanks to Yogendra Yadav, Shankar Ramaswami, Amulya Purohit, Amrita Mehta, Asim Siddique, and Venkat and Sachin who eagerly waited for this book to be completed.

I am greatly indebted to a group of research scholars on our campus who toiled with me and deserve to be thought of as co-translators of this work. A big thank you is due to Amar, Dhanush, Varun, Gangadhara, Shridhara, Sathisha, Mathapati, Harshavardhan, Mohankumar, Shivakumar, Ranganatha, Puneeth, Prabhukumar, Rangaswamy and Aravind. Dr Pavanagangadhara, Dr Yagnasri, and Veerendra Yadav helped me with their critical appreciation.

Basavaraj Sindhur, my well-wisher, has keenly awaited this book, while the love and affection of mestru C.K. Narayanaswamy Reddy, Sankranti, and Prasanna Kumar's families took care of our social well-being. Ravi, demonstrating the Aristotelian notion of friendship as recreating each other, brought depth to the bonding.

More than I, my family, eager to hold this book in their hands, endured my slow and steady slogging. While my children Sumeru and Nittila pushed me along asking, "How many chapters have you finished, Appa?", my wife Chinmayi, to whom I dedicate this book, wanted only the best to come out of this delayed process. My only legacy for them is what the vachanakaras advocate: kayaka realised in arivu.

I am an absent-minded professor, and it is therefore mandatory on my part to miss out some important names; if you are among them, I hope it will suffice to say that you are very much there in my heart and mind.

ಶಿಲೆಯೊಳಗಣ ಪಾವಕನಂತೆ

ಉದಕದೊಳಗಣ ಪ್ರತಿಬಿಂಬದಂತೆ,

ಬೀಜದೊಳಗಣ ವೃಕ್ಷದಂತೆ

ಶಬ್ದದೊಳಗಣ ನಿಶ್ಶಬ್ದದಂತೆ,

ಗುಹೇಶ್ವರಾ ನಿಮ್ಮ ಶರಣಸಂಬಂಧ

Shileyolagana pavakanante
Udakadolagana pratibimbadante,
Bijadolagana vrukshadante
Shabdadolagana nishyabdadante,
Guheshwara, nimma sharanasambandha.

Guheshwara,
Your bond with sharana is like
Fire within the stone, reflection in the water
Tree within the seed, silence within the sound.

Translator's Introduction

My Own Way of Saying Things

Preamble

D.R. NAGARAJ (1954–98), one of India's foremost cultural critics and public intellectuals, wrote mainly in Kannada. Known to the Anglophone world for his insightful writings on the Dalit movement, as well as more specifically B.R. Ambedkar's fractious relations with M.K. Gandhi preceding the Poona Pact (1932), Nagaraj's essays in English have been compiled in two volumes, *The Flaming Feet and Other Essays: The Dalit Movement in India* (1993; 2nd edn 2010) and *Listening to the Loom: Essays on Literature, Politics and Violence* (2012).[1] His last monograph, *Allamaprabhu mattu Shaiva Pratibhe*, published posthumously in 1999, is a classic critical work in Kannada presented here in English translation as *Allama Prabhu and the Shaiva Imagination*.

In this work Nagaraj develops certain arguments about the twelfth-century Shaiva mystic Allama Prabhu and Indian intellectual history by examining Allama's vachanas and life narratives in the larger context of Indian darshanas. Allama figures in the Kannada cultural imagination as a prominent vachanakara in the company of, among others, Basavanna, Akkamahadevi, Sonnalige Siddharama, and Chennabasavanna. They are considered the architects of the twelfth-century Vachana and Sharana tradition in

---

[1] Both these have been edited and introduced by Prithvi Datta Chandra Shobhi and published by Permanent Black. *The Flaming Feet* (1993) is the only English work that Nagaraj published within his lifetime. Its second edition (2010), edited by Chandra Shobhi, includes all of Nagaraj's essays on the Dalit movement in India. *Listening to the Loom* (2012) comprises Nagaraj's English essays on these themes, along with some Kannada writings translated into English by Chandra Shobhi.

the Kannada-speaking regions, most of which now lie in the state of Karnataka. Diverse darshanas, religious sects, and schools of thought in premodern India comprise the context that Nagaraj examines, while his own modern cultural politics and impressive familiarity with contemporary ideas are the bedrock of his sharp and highly provocative analysis of Allama.

While Nagaraj's work on Allama shows the significant contribution of the Kannada critical tradition to Indian intellectual history, it is undeniably challenging and complex, and therefore not the easiest of works to read. Partly, this is explained by Nagaraj's untimely death, which meant that the Kannada manuscript did not benefit from his editing, revision, or polishing; in fact he left it relatively raw, with many repetitions and unconnected thoughts that he would normally have taken care of.[2] Moreover, this work belongs to the period in his life when Nagaraj's thought processes and writing style had grown more dense and ambitious. His own immersion in the Kannada tradition and scholarship, particularly relating to vachanas, can seem at times to assume a familiarity with them that his readers do not in fact possess. The consequence – especially for those new to Nagaraj's writing – is that his style can seem riddled with sudden intertextual jumps. And yet, for all these difficulties, the book stands as Nagaraj's magnum opus, replete with profound and penetrating reflections. This introduction aims to provide readers with the larger picture and familiarise them with the author, his text, and their contexts.

Nagaraj's Intellectual Journeys: How Did He Arrive at Allama?

Kannada literary criticism was not quite a 100-year-old practice when Nagaraj came on the scene as a critic in his late twenties.[3]

---

[2] However, the publisher Akshara Prakashana did a good job putting the manuscript, which was in disarray, into a more or less coherent whole, thanks to the efforts of Venkataraman Aital and Ki. Ram. Nagaraja. See Nagaraj, *Allamaprabhu mattu Shaiva Pratibhe.*

[3] See Raghavendra Rao, *Shatamanada Sahitya.*

Earlier critics, his intellectual predecessors, were mostly writers of the Navodaya period – creative writers, poets, and scholars.[4] His contemporary Kirtinath Kurtkoti (1928–2003) – the literary critic who in Kannada truly extended what Gramsci thought of as "the function of an intellectual" – was a critic whom Nagaraj greatly admired and respected.[5] While several scholars following Kurtkoti produced literary criticism, it was Nagaraj who changed the course of the Kannada critical tradition; in fact, I see Kurtkoti and Nagaraj as the two eyes of Kannada literary criticism.[6] Nagaraj, insofar as he evolved from a literary critic into a cultural theorist, is especially interesting for bringing a special blend of interdisciplinary scholarship to Kannada critical practice, this being very evident in the present book. Placing Nagaraj within the history of Kannada literary research, the Kannada scholar Nithyananda B. Shetty describes him as an inaugurator of a new model of literary and cultural studies in Kannada because he uses the insights of Western theory to engage with knowledge systems embedded in the life of local communities.[7] Later, Nagaraj also looked at Western theories with suspicion, but there is no doubt that he demonstrated how literary criticism could be a criticism of the world, and how its tools could additionally be used to analyse non-literary phenomena and wider spheres of life. Through what he himself thought of as a decolonising project, he showed new possibilities for non-Western post-

---

[4] Literary historians roughly divide modern Kannada literature into "movements", such as over the Navodaya period (renaissance of Kannada literature, early twentieth century); Pragatisheela period (progressive movement, 1940s); Navya period (modernist period, 1950s to 1970s); and Dalita-Bandaya period (protest and subaltern movement, late 1970s and 1980s). For more on these modern Kannada literary periods, see "Pradhana Sampadakara Matu", in Honnusiddartha, ed., *Samagra Kannada Sahitya Charitre*, vol. 1, pp. 22–5. For a detailed discussion on modern Kannada literary trends, see Rao, *Hosagannada Sahitya*.

[5] For Nagaraj's critical appraisal of Kurtkoti as a critic, see Nagaraj, "Kannadada Kirtige", pp. 281–4. For English translations of select writings of Kurtkoti, see Kurtkoti, *Courtesy*.

[6] Gundur, "Nagarikate".

[7] Shetty, *Marganveshane,* p. 184.

colonial scholars to engage with the world on their own terms: it is in fact for this reason that *Allamaprabhu mattu Shaiva Pratibhe* is exemplary.

Affectionately known as DR or DRN, Nagaraj was born on 20 February 1954 to Ramaiah and Akkayyamma, who belonged to the Devanga caste (weavers by occupation). The initial "D" refers to his home town Doddaballapura, and "R" to his father Ramaiah, a schoolteacher.[8] Nagaraj grew up with five brothers and a sister, moving to Bangalore for higher studies and completing an MA and then a PhD in Kannada at Bangalore University. He married outside his caste: he met his wife Girija while teaching at Bangalore University. Diabetes ruined his health, and perhaps he neglected himself, being busy with his reading and writing. He died of cardiac arrest in Bangalore on 12 August 1998 at the age of forty-four, survived by his wife, daughter Amulya, and son Anup.

Nagaraj was exposed to the culture of books while in his village school. His interest in literary humanism was apparent in his pre-university days when he made Matthew Arnold's *Sohrab and Rustum* (1853) accessible to his classmates by translating it into Kannada. His intellect took firmer shape in Bangalore, where friends and mentors, the Central College Library, bookshops, and the then-famous Government Arts College (which he joined for his bachelor's degree) formed Nagaraj's learning milieu. Agrahara Krishnamurthy, his friend at the Arts College, affirms that the Central College Library was Nagaraj's most favoured haunt.[9]

Doddaballapura firmly in the past, Nagaraj was now smitten by Socialism and Marxism through the ideas of E.V. Ramaswamy "Periyar" and Marx.[10] A Communist Party worker, Shankar Lala-

---

[8] Huliyar, *D.R. Nagaraj*, p. 11. I have heavily borrowed biographical details and episodes in Nagaraj's intellectual development from this book. Huliyar, Nagaraj's research student, also provides eyewitness social and intellectual profiles of P. Lankesh, the famous Kannada writer, as well as D.R. Nagaraj: see Huliyar, *Inti Namaskaaragalu.*

[9] Krishnamurthy, "Matige Avakashavideyandare", n.p.

[10] Nagaraj, *Vasanta Smriti*, pp. 5–6.

pur, introduced him to the active politics of communism. Dr Siddalingaiah (1954–2021), a Dalit poet and later his colleague at Bangalore University's Kannada Department, was Nagaraj's close friend from college days. Siddalingaiah's autobiography, *A Word with You, World* (2013), portrays Nagaraj as also his mentor.[11]

In his Introduction to Nagaraj's *The Flaming Feet and Other Essays*, Chandra Shobhi gives an account of Nagaraj's involvement with the Dalit movement in Karnataka during the 1970s.[12] Nagaraj was, he says, the most talented literary critic and political commentator in the new class of writers and activists, most of whom were Shudras and Dalits. As a leading theoretician of the Dalita-Bandaya movement in Karnataka, Nagaraj coined the slogan "Khadgavagali Kavya, Janara Novige Midiva Pranamitra" (Let Poetry Become [a] Sword, the Dear Friend Who Responds to the Pain of the People).[13] Unlike the standard-issue Marxist of those days, however, Nagaraj was undogmatic, reflective, and self-critical, never hesitant to change his intellectual positions as his ideas and understanding expanded. Chandra Shobhi is correct to point out that *The Flaming Feet* shows a shift in Nagaraj's intellectual journey from declaring "Let Poetry Become a Sword" towards a more inclusive politics.[14]

In his short introductory book *D.R. Nagaraj* (2022), Nataraj Huliyar refers to a diary that DRN maintained in the second year of his MA.[15] Huliyar suggests from his reading of the diary that "if novelists like Lawrence, Hemingway, and Shivaram Karanth seem to have drawn the attention of this young intellectual in his twenties towards fiction writing, thinkers and critics like Georg

[11] Siddalingaiah's autobiography in Kannada *Orukeri* is in two parts, and the English translation combines these. See Siddalingaiah, *A Word with You*, p. 105.

[12] Chandra Shobhi, "Introduction", in Nagaraj, *The Flaming Feet*, pp. 1–17.

[13] Ibid., pp. 6–7.

[14] Ibid., p. 7.

[15] Huliyar mentions these unpublished documents as being in the possession of Nagaraj's friend Agrahara Krishnamurthy, a Kannada writer and former Secretary, Sahitya Akademi. See Huliyar, *D.R. Nagaraj*, p. 144.

Lukacs, Jean-Paul Sartre, [Christopher] Caudwell and others drew him towards literary criticism and theory."[16] Moreover, the influence of Freud, Derrida, Foucault, and Said is quite evident in his thinking. Huliyar also observes the fact that Nagaraj was a Shudra boy who grew up in Bangalore's literary milieu influenced by the ideals and ideas of the Samajvadi Yuvajana Sabha (SYS, the Young Socialist League), the JP (Jayaprakash Narayan) movement, and communism. As a college student his private ambition was to become a philosopher, and his immersion in Western and Indian philosophies is most evident in the present book.[17]

Over his time in the university Nagaraj mastered Kannada literature but found his knowledge of English wanting, and so devoted more time to reading in that language. He is the rare example of a Kannada teacher of his generation forging his mind in the bilingual smithy of Kannada and English.[18] I was told by Chandan Gowda — sociologist, writer, and Nagaraj's family friend — that Nagaraj, despite being really a Kannada teacher, found his way to acquiring scholarship in English through two Bangalore friends, Siddhartha and T.G. Vaidyanathan (TGV). Siddhartha, a social activist who ran the Institute for Cultural Research and Action — which brought out Nagaraj's first edition of *The Flaming Feet and Other Essays* — often gifted English books to Nagaraj. Vaidyanathan, a highly regarded

[16] Ibid., p. 14.

[17] Nagaraj's close friend Agrahara Krishnamurthy, in a conversation with me, remembers that, once, in a hostel room, Nagaraj asked him what he wanted to become, to which Agrahara replied he wanted to become a short story writer; in turn, he asked Nagaraj the same question and Nagaraj said he wanted to become a philosopher.

[18] As elsewhere in India, bilingualism (Kannada and English) has shaped the Kannada critical tradition, and there is a tradition of English teachers in Karnataka who have, by virtue of their bilingualism, contributed to Kannada literature and criticism. For the contribution of English teachers to Kannada literature, see Kurtkoti, *Hejjenu* — a festschrift for G.B. Sajjan (an English teacher). However, Nagaraj's bilingual scholarship was an exceptional intellectual asset quite unique in the Kannada world. For more on the bilingual intellectual, see Guha, "The Rise and Fall", pp. 36–42.

film and literary scholar who taught at Bangalore University, very likely introduced Nagaraj to Western literary thought and theory, and guided him into the tradition of critical textual reading.[19] Possibly this intellectual debt led Nagaraj to dedicate his first book of criticism on modern Kannada literature, *Amruta mattu Garuda* (Nector and Eagle, 1983), to TGV.

Nagaraj's friend Manu Chakravarthy, also a literary critic, believes *Amruta mattu Garuda* is deeply informed by its author's interest in social justice. Consequently Marxist thought – via Lukacs, Althusser, and the Frankfurt School – underpins Nagaraj's analysis of Kannada poets, novelists, and literary texts in the essays that comprise the book.[20] In it, Nagaraj's study of modern Kannada writers – including Kuvempu, Shivaram Karanth, D.R. Bendre, Masti Venkatesh Iyengar, and G.S. Shivarudrappa – follows the method of textual analysis based on a fine-grained understanding of literary genres.

Nagaraj owed as much to the Kannada Department at Bangalore University, headed by his teacher and research supervisor G.S. Shiva-rudrappa, "GSS" (1926–2013) – who was Kuvempu's disciple as well as a noted poet – as to the intellectual milieu he inhabited in the city. GSS organised conferences and invited scholars to the department, which exposed Nagaraj and other students to the intellectual climate of the time. Nagaraj joined the department as a research assistant and became a reader early in his career. His doctoral dissertation, supervised by GSS and published as *Shakti-Sharadeya Mela: Studies in Modern Kannada Poetry* (1987), is an interdisciplinary exploration of the thematic concerns – bhumi (earth), kala (time), kama (desire/sex), and samaja (society) – of the major modern Kannada poets. In the womb of modern Kannada poetry Nagaraj finds several historical struggles, the onslaught of colonial experiences, and the structures of modernity that have affected Indian sensibilities.

---

[19] See Ashok, "D.R. Nagaraj", p. 374.
[20] Chakravarthy, "Amruta mattu", p. 8.

In the ensuing decades Nagaraj's thought found home in *Sahitya Kathana* (1996) and *Samskruti Kathana* (2001), outstanding collections of essays that Kannada readers have much appreciated. In the former, he seeks liberation from centuries-old intellectual constructs, which he calls vikalpas, borrowing the term from Buddhist thought. This project of liberation involves three tasks. The first is to find liberation from the idea that Western civilisation is the measure of mankind's progress; this involves a decolonising agenda – to address contemporary problems we must examine the colonial experience that has distorted our understanding of the past. Second, we need to counter the idea that Shudras and subalterns do not have an autonomous cultural life. Third, we must do away with the binary thinking that has distinguished between canonical and popular forms of expression, such as folk forms, to the detriment of the latter.[21] Methodologically, two convictions frame the essays in this anthology: first, all forms of knowledge are narratives; and second, concepts in literary studies can illuminate other systems of knowledge, so that one can enter all domains of knowledge through literary criticism and theory – hence the title *Sahitya Kathana* (The Narrative of Literature). Accordingly, the essays go beyond the literary to take up cultural and political issues such as nationalism, the nation-state, progress and development, science and technology, colonialism, cinema, and so on as their objects of study. For all this, when examining this variety Nagaraj stands firmly within the terrain of literary studies.

Nagaraj contributed extensively to the periodicals, journals, and little magazines of his time, such as *Kannada Prabha*, *Lankesh Patrike*, and *Ninasam Matukate*, among others. *Samskruti Kathana*, edited by Agrahara Krishnamurthy, consists of ninety-five such essays by Nagaraj and two interviews with him published in journals. This posthumously published book contains essays ranging from Marxist, Ambedkarite, and Dalit thought to environment-

---

[21] Note how Nagaraj discusses the folk epic *Manteswamy Kavya* in relation to mainstream literary canons in ch. 5 of the present book.

alism, Kannada-ness, life portraits, brief travelogues, and other issues. By examining contemporary developments in the political and socio-economic spheres, several essays in this collection reflect on what constitutes a good life for Kannadigas.

Scholars have often emphasised Nagaraj's distinction as a writer who throughout employed the Marxist dialectical method,[22] and as one who used metaphors extensively in critical practice.[23] The sociologist Chandan Gowda draws our attention to Nagaraj's faith in Critical Intuitionalism – where imagination and intuition are sources of creativity and knowledge.[24] Chandra Shobhi, a social historian, describes his method as narrative imagination: "[I]n his literary criticism, as well as his political and cultural writings, he retained and displayed the sensibilities of an epic poet who understands the significance and influence of narratives . . . His secret ambition, I suspect, was to be the *pauranika* of Indian civilization."[25] In my view, Nagaraj is a radical reader of texts and cultures. He was neither an archivist nor a field worker but a thorough textualist very accomplished in the interpretation of texts. Interpretive skill is the heart of his method for, like Abhinavagupta's method of sankalananusandhana, which he elaborates on in this book, Nagaraj assembles ideas to then weave intertextual connections between them, and by an astute arrangement of his material arrives at a compelling narrative. I will return to his analytical method later.

Early in his career, a stint with the Centre for the Study of Developing Societies, New Delhi, and visits to the Indian Institute of Advanced Study, Shimla, gave Nagaraj national exposure. His appointment in 1997 as Visiting Professor in the Department of South Asian Languages and Civilizations at the University of Chicago was "gratifying and important since Nagaraj was seen to

---

[22] Amur, "D.R. Nagarajara".

[23] Ashadevi, "Baudhika Nekara", p. xii.

[24] Gowda, "The Wonder".

[25] Chandra Shobhi, "Introduction", in Nagaraj, *Listening to the Loom*, pp. 1–2.

have replaced the great Kannada writer and scholar A.K. Ramanujan."[26] There, Nagaraj perhaps began to think differently about
Kannada literary culture, being engaged with Sheldon Pollock's
research programme on literary cultures in history. His essay entitled "Critical Tensions in the History of Kannada Literary Culture", one of the best theoretical pieces on its subject, is the result
of Nagaraj's collaboration with Pollock.[27] Outside the Kannada
world, Nagaraj now interacted and made friends with scholars and
thinkers of diverse streams, most notably Sheldon Pollock and
Ashis Nandy.[28] Arjun Appadurai was reported as saying that "Nagaraj had the potential to be another Ambedkar,"[29] while Ramachandra Guha commends *The Flaming Feet* as one of the works that
profoundly transformed the way he himself looked at the world.[30]
Nagaraj was yet to bring about innovative breakthroughs in Kannada, so, in a sense, he died in harness, making "Nagaraj" an unfin-
ished intellectual project.

It was during the early 1990s that Nagaraj's intellectual journey
took a significant turn as he began to explore Indian texts and traditions. While his students and various scholars have described this
as a postcolonial turn in his career, Nagaraj himself explained it
through the concept of vismruti – i.e. cultural amnesia.[31] The ideas

---

[26] Ibid., p. 4. Nagaraj, Ananya Vajpeyi writes, "landed like a missile on the
Hyde Park campus . . . exploding our usual methods of Indology and phi-
lology, anthropology and literary criticism, area studies and political theory."
Vajpeyi, "Let Poetry", p. 114.

[27] Nagaraj, "Critical Tensions", pp. 323–82.

[28] "When we lost D.R., we lost a beloved friend and scholar as well as a
visionary of the global political": Pollock and Breckenridge, "In Honor of
D.R. Nagaraj", p. xiv. Nagaraj wrote an Introduction to Ashis Nandy's col-
lected essays, *Exiled at Home*: see Nagaraj, "Introduction". Nandy wrote the
Foreword to the second edition of *The Flaming Feet and Other Essays*: see
Nandy, "Foreword".

[29] See Chandra Shobhi, "Introduction", in Nagaraj, *The Flaming Feet*, p. 2.

[30] Guha, "Contending Visions".

[31] Nagaraj wanted to develop this idea in a book he had planned, to be titled
"Recreating Each Other", which did not see the light of day. However, for more

of Said and Fanon had not, at the time, made a big impression on Kannada thinkers. Writers, including Nagaraj, U.R. Ananthamurthy, and Kirtinath Kurtkoti, had been thinking about what later began to be fashioned as a postcolonial agenda, though not with the same conceptual vocabulary. It was Nagaraj who made postcolonialism a form of radical politics in Kannada's intellectual sphere through the concept of vismruti. The translation scholar and critic Tharakeshwar observes that Nagaraj did not merely apply postcolonial theory to the Kannada archive but also made a critical intervention in the process.[32] Unlike other critics of modernity and colonialism, Nagaraj went into the intellectual moorings of India's past through his study of Indian texts and thinkers. His involvement with "Akshara Chintanamale", a monograph series that covered diverse thinkers from Nagarjuna to Ashis Nandy, Kumarilabhatta to Ananda Coomaraswamy (among many), testifies to his postcolonial praxis.

The start of the 1990s saw the socio-economic fallout of the implementation of the Mandal Report, the fall of the Babri Masjid and the rise of new Hindu communalism, economic liberalisation, and the collapse of the Soviet Union: among related developments, these formed the backdrop of the "vismruti" discourse among Kannada thinkers and in other Indian regions.[33] Nagaraj felt the need to explore Indian traditions to combat intellectual amnesia, his big idea being to problematise the simplistic classification of the Vedic and the non-Vedic as binaries, and to revitalise a plurality of traditions and non-Vedic darshanas by regaining the cultural memory of non-Vedic darshanas.[34] The result was the "Akshara Chintanamale" series that he began to edit for the publisher Akshara Prakashan. This press published all his critical writings (except *Samskruti Kathana*),

---

on the historical backdrop of this notion in relation to Nagaraj, see Huliyar, *Inti Namaskaaragalu.*

[32] Tharakeshwar, "D.R. Nagaraj mattu Vasahatottara", p. 115.

[33] Ibid., p. 122.

[34] Huliyar, *Inti Namaskaaragalu*, pp. 114–15.

and he was a frequent visitor at an annual event in the small town of Heggodu, the Samskruti Shibira (Culture Course).[35] The Akshara Chintanamale, which later became the "D.R. Nagaraj Nenapina Akshara Chintanamale", comprises sixteen-odd monographs on Indian thought and thinkers, each prefaced with a critical introduction. It is worth quoting the stated aim of the series to show Nagaraj's distinctive engagement with postcolonial thought and politics:

> A peculiar kind of forgetfulness (vismruti) engulfs societies. It is a terrible tragedy for societies to forget their ways of thinking, responding, and feeling. With the advent of colonialism, India suffered a kind of amnesia. We forgot the structures of thinking embedded in our society and looked to the West. Western ways of thinking hardly help us properly grasp our problems. The "Akshara Chintana" series aims to overcome this intellectual amnesia.
>
> Thoughts that serve as neither a mirror nor a lamp are not useful. The series presents alternative thoughts in critical idioms that help us confront contemporary problems. It searches for new ways of thinking quite different from those in established, hegemonic, and dominant systems of thought, and also aims to understand dissenting alternatives in the West. This series will publish texts on individual thinkers and works, movements, schools of thought, translations, original writings, and commentaries. This is an ambitious project that seeks to explore the universe through Kannada.[36]

This project dealing with vismruti invited an immediate response from writers, had a far-reaching impact on Kannada scholarship, and gave an impetus to Kannada cultural studies. Nagaraj's *Allamaprabhu mattu Shaiva Pratibhe* appeared as part of this larger project, germinating as early as 1993, though traces of it exist in Nagaraj's thinking even earlier than that date. The book was shaped

---

[35] At Heggodu, K.V. Subbana (1932–2005) and his Ninasam Theatre were culturally vital, vibrant, and inescapable. They influenced Nagaraj's worldview quite significantly.

[36] Titled "Akshara Chintana", this statement (the translation is mine) appears in all books of the series. For example, see Nagaraj, "Akshara Chintana".

by the ideological horizons of its time as much as by Nagaraj's distinguished cultural politics. It was a time when Kannada intellectuals had begun to think about developing a poetics native to their world in order to understand their past and literature on its own terms. Embedded in this ideological environment, Nagaraj's politics had begun to build on existing Indian literary theory. He says in the second chapter of this book:

> I would like to explore Allama's vachanas through concepts internal to Shaiva poetics . . . [This] is also an attempt to untangle a particular problem that has been bothering me the past few years, and I would like to address it here through Allama. It concerns the importance of interpreting a body of work – created in a specific cultural space and time – using the methods and ways of understanding available in the field to which the body of work belongs. To put it clearly, this involves a process of understanding intellectual decolonisation.
>
> I raise this issue in the context of studying Indian cultural, literary, and historical processes as a whole. For the last hundred years, attempts at studying these processes have been largely shaped by the West, be they Liberal Positivist or Marxist or Subaltern Studies methods.

So Nagaraj came to Allama as a means to develop the tools for critical study in an Indian context. To understand how Nagaraj achieves his aim and what he does with Allama, it would be helpful to explore the Shivasharana phenomenon and the place of Allama in Kannada's cultural imagination.

The Shivasharana Phenomenon in the Kannada World

The twelfth-century medieval Kannada world of Allama and shivasharanas – devotees of Lord Shiva – is a complicated phenomenon, difficult to access and recognise as verifiable history.[37] It is a world

[37] Premodern India largely related itself with the past through myths and purana narratives. Colonial modernity introduced historical consciousness and since then these narratives began to be seen as historical testimonies, which is

that has come down to us mostly through hagiographical and mythical imaginings, and rather partly as historical record. I call it a phenomenon to emphasise that we are not even sure of many of its facets that purport to be facts; what we know is what has been represented. Definitive pronouncements about the Shivasharana phenomenon rely as their primary source on the archive of vachanas, which are short free-verse compositions that express the worldview of shivasharanas (devotees, who are therefore also known as vachanakaras). The Vachana movement is primarily perceived as a religious uprising and is also known as the Lingayat or Virashaiva movement.

Apart from the vachana archive, which does not provide sufficient information about the lives and times of vachanakaras, we have to resort to inscriptions, kavyas (literary narratives), and puranas (mythological texts) to reconstruct what can ultimately only be an imagined story of the Sharana phenomenon. What is possible is a more empirically grounded historical account of how successive generations have *represented* the lives and works of shivasharanas, but not authentic histories of these figures themselves.[38] A related issue in getting to grips with this phenomenon is that while a practical criticism approach to the vachanas is not problematic, understanding them as utterances embedded in their social milieu is more difficult.[39] As Jonardon Ganeri puts it, the intellectual historian of premodern India typically faces a problem when invoking historical context to make sense of texts, because "When

---

problematic. Kirtinath Kurtkoti discusses this idea in Kannada contexts in some of his essays. For example, see Kurtkoti, "Itihasada Bhaya"; Kurtkoti, "Itihasada Berugalu"; Kurtkoti, "Itihasada Artha"; Kurtkoti, "Itihasada Atikramana"; Kurtkoti, "Prastavane"; Kurtkoti, "Purana, Itihasa mattu Kadambari".

[38] I owe this distinction to Prithvi Datta Chandra Shobhi who, in a conversation with me, reiterated that we cannot write authentic biographies of Basavanna or Allama; instead we can reconstruct the history of their representation and the way their lives and thoughts are re-created in others' works.

[39] In fact, the "practical criticism" method as originally advocated by I.A. Richards in the 1920s recommended reading texts as anonymous, without regard to authorial identity and biography.

it comes to India, it's all text and no context." Skinner's insistence
on biographical, social, political, and literary context to help understand particular documents and pronouncements does not
work in the Indian case.[40] The situation is one of confusion worse
confounded because vachanas are not stable entities; they have been
composed and recomposed repeatedly. Therefore, my account here
of vachanakaras, and of Allama and his times, borrows from myths,
legends, and historical accounts of premodern and modern times
in an attempt to understand how Kannada culture has imagined
Allama and the Shivasharana phenomenon, shunning all pretence
at the futile attempt to show how they really existed. I have worked
more as a humanist scholar with my own biases and preferences, not
as a social scientist setting out to establish the actual lineaments of
the world under scrutiny.

What is kept alive in Kannada cultural memory as the Sharana,
the Vachana, or the Virashaiva/Lingayat movement is a phenomenon which originated in the twelfth-century medieval South Indian city of Kalyana, now a town in the Bidar District of North Karnataka. Medieval Kannada encompassed several kingdoms – from
the Chalukyas to the Vijayanagara Empire – that patronised Kannada language and literature. Kalyana was the capital of the Chalukya and Kalachuri dynasties from the tenth century to the twelfth.
This period witnessed intense political turmoil, and towards the
end of the twelfth century the Chalukyas of Kalyana fought battles against their feudatories. After the death of the Chalukya king
Tailapa III, the Chalukya feudatories – Seunas in the north, Kaka-
tiyas in the east, Hoysalas in the south, and Kalachuris in the west –
declared their independence. The Kalachuri king Bijjala II (1130–
1167), whose ancestors came from Central India, captured Kalyana
in 1162, and the Kalachuri dynasty ruled the Deccan Plateau until the 1180s. The Sharana or Vachana phenomenon is said to have
originated in Kalyana during the reign of Bijjala II.

---

[40] Ganeri, "Contextualism in the Study", p. 553. See also Quentin Skinner's
well-known methodology essay, "Meaning and Understanding in the History
of Ideas". Also see his essays on methods in intellectual history: Skinner, *Visions*.

It is generally agreed that Basavanna (1131–96), who held an important official position in the Kalachuri court at Kalyana, led a movement against the prevailing orthodox practices.[41] According to some accounts he renounced his brahminhood and formed a dissenting community of sharanas who protested against the conservative and dogmatic social order of the time, heralding a new way of life called Virashaivism. Scholars like S.C. Nandimath assert that Basavanna was not the founder of Virashaivism; it had existed before him, but he upheld its cause, which had been weakened: "Virasaivism, as revived in the 12th century, may not be exactly identical with that existing before, although it professes to be identical with the old form and in all probability retained the cardinal doctrines unbroken. The outstanding feature of the revived Virasaivism is its zeal for social reform."[42] However, the social scientist K. Ishwaran argues that Basavanna was the inaugurator of the Lingayat movement because, though he borrowed ideas from his predecessors, he transformed them into Lingayat concepts, values, orientations, and doctrines.[43] A practising Lingayat and leading vachana scholar, M.M. Kalburgi, makes a clear distinction between "Virashaivism" and "Lingayat", asserting the status of Basavanna as the founder of Lingayat dharma as a religion specific to Kannada.[44]

[41] There are disagreements among scholars about Basavanna's place and year of birth, the places where he lived, and accounts of his personal life. Scholars have worked out the date 1131 after researching Virashaiva Puranas and inscriptions. See Malwad, "Basavannana Kala". P.B. Desai's book remains the earliest historicist re-creation of Basavanna. See Desai, *Basaveshvara and His Times*. As noted earlier, historicising medieval India is difficult. The difficulties of establishing authentic documentation of a twelfth-century life are given credibility by similar difficulties even in the present. I myself, born in the late 1970s, have two names, one given by my parents and another by a village accountant; and two dates of birth, one assigned by my schoolteacher and another that I later discovered after consulting my mother – who had her own calculation based on the panchanga almanac.

[42] Nandimath, *A Handbook of Virasaivism*, p. 5.

[43] Ishwaran, *Speaking of Basava*, p. 2.

[44] YouTube, "M M Kalburgiyavaru".

Nagaraj, in this book, does not engage with these originary debates: he uses "Virashaivism" and "Lingayat" interchangeably and believes, as evident in the first chapter, that Virashaivism had its originary matrix (mulamatruke) in pre-existing Shaiva darshanic streams; and that Virashaivism — as mentioned in this book's second chapter — emerged from the womb of declining Uttarapatha Shaiva sects. Shaivism, a dominant religion, had in the process of proliferating split into sects such as the Kalamukha, Pashupata, Kapalika, and Srotriya.[45] Virashaivism took shape at a time when Shaiva sects such as the Kalamukha and Kapalika were degenerating.[46] The Kalamukha sect of Shaiva ascetics was prominent in the Kannada region before Virashaivism, and scholars believe that Kalamukha mathas (monasteries) were later turned into Virashaiva mathas.[47]

Before the twelfth century, the Kannada region had already witnessed the rise and fall of Buddhism and Jainism. Nearly seven decades before the twelfth-century Virashaiva event, Ramanuja (eleventh and twelfth centuries) had heralded what is known as Vishishtadvaita in South India, especially in the Tamil region, and in some parts of the southern Kannada region. The Dvaitism of Madhva-charya (thirteenth century) in the Kannada-speaking coastal area later gave a new turn to Hinduism. In the wake of the Vishistadvaita of Ramanuja, the Shaktivishistadvaita of Basavanna and other shivasharanas, and the Dvaitism of Madhvacharya, even Jainism, though a strong presence in the region, suffered a great setback.[48]

---

[45] Hiremath, "Sri Basavesvara", p. 283. Farquhar classifies Shaiva sects into Pashupata Shaiva and Agamic Shaiva, and includes Virashaivism in the latter. See Farquhar, *An Outline*, pp. 190–1. However, there are different opinions about this classification of Shaiva sects and their nature and scope. See Hiremath, *Mahaayatre*, p. 86.

[46] Note the criticism of other Shaiva sects in several vachanas. For an English translation of Chennabasavanna's vachana, which gives a picture of Shaiva sects such as the Pashupata, Kalamukha, Kaula, etc., see Hiremath, "Sri Basavesvara", p. 283.

[47] For more on Virashaiva mathas, see the various articles in Yeresime, ed., *Dasoha Siri*.

[48] Settar, "Bharatiya Hinneleyalli", pp. 32–61.

The sociology and theology of the Virashaiva/Lingayat sampradaya will long continue as material for studies within history of
religion; as of now, given the diversity of vachanas and the ways
they have come down to us, we can merely be more or less sure that
this sampradaya replaced the traditional religious and spiritual
culture by putting forward the practice of ishtalinga, because of
which it is called Lingayat.[49] "Lingawanta" is a term used for one
who wears the ishtalinga, the aniconic image of Shiva, on the
body.[50] This sampradaya places faith in kayaka (physical work and
therefore care of the body too, as evident in some vachanas) and
dasoha (humble service, such as serving food to others). However,
this Shaiva way of life has never been monolithic and shows a
history of fluid and dynamic practice. In fact no religious darshana
has triggered as much controversy as Virashaiva or Lingayat darshana in contemporary times.[51] It is important to observe that the
vachanakaras themselves hold diverse views on worship of the linga
and related practices.

So, it may legitimately be asked what, at its core, is the Sharana
or Vachana phenomenon? In the twelfth-century scheme, the
sharana who wears the ishtalinga is a Shaiva devotee who has sur-
rendered himself to the trinity of guru, linga, and jangama.[52] The

[49] Today Lingayats, also known as Virashaivas, are a dominant community
in Karnataka. Scholars and contemporary intelligentsia make subtle distinctions between Virashaiva and Lingayat. For more on this issue, see ch. 12 in
Mahadevappa, *Primer of Lingayatism*. However, I use the terms Virashaiva and
Lingayat interchangeably. Likewise, vachanakara, sharana, and Virashaiva.

[50] In modern times, the terms Lingayat and Virashaivism have become mark-
ers of caste, though they are actually sampradayas (traditions and practices).
There are about ninety-nine castes in this particular sampradaya. The deployment of "Lingayat-Virashaiva" as caste marker makes them the dominant community in Karnataka, comprising about 17 per cent of the total population,
thus determining the fate of electoral politics in the state.

[51] Other than intellectual debates, it has created social and political con-
troversies. For example, the Congress leader Siddaramaiah's political cam-
paign during the 2018 Assembly election used the divide between Virashaiva
and Lingayat.

[52] Virashaivas follow eight principles, known as ashtavaranas – guru, linga,

antithesis of the sharana, who is committed to shivabhakti (devotion to Shiva), is the bhavi – one who does not wear the linga and doesn't follow shivabhakti.[53] Some leading sharanas, Manu V. Devadevan argues, emphasised the significance of labour (kayaka) and held to their professions. He points out that most sharanas had their profession prefixed to their names, such as Madivala (washerman) Machayya, Madara (cobbler) Channayya, Nuliya (ropemaker) Chandayya. Among them, true renunciation was possible even without actually renouncing worldly life.[54]

The sharanas, who participated in the movement for socio-religious reform in the city of Kalyana, often responded to the world through the compositional form called the vachana, which means both utterance and spoken promise, implying action in accordance with speech. Before Basavanna, Jedara Dasimaiah and his contemporaries had perfected a genre called sulnudi, meaning wise speech, this being a precursor of the vachana form. In a brilliant piece entitled "Critical Tensions in the History of Kannada Literary Culture", Nagaraj, while showcasing the changes that the vachanakaras brought about in the Kannada literary tradition, captures the coming into being of the vachanakaras:

> One of the most important problematics of the history of Kannada literary culture is the emergence of radically new epistemes – the core notions about the social and cultural order – and the reformations of the epistemes over time. A dramatic instance of such emergence occurred in the twelfth century, when an entirely new communicative form ap-

---

jangama, padodaka, prasada, vibhuti, rudrakshi, and mantra. Guru (teacher) is believed to be a form of Shiva, who initiates the bhakta and shows the path of moksha (liberation). Linga symbolises the formless Shiva, which is worshipped by the bhakta on his palm. He/she wears it on the body all the time. Jangama (literally, ever-moving) is a principle followed by ascetics who are also called jangamas. They move from place to place preaching ethics, bhakti, and knowledge. For more on this, see Nandimath, *Karnataka Dharma-galu*.

[53] Within the Virashaiva doctrine, the meaning and significance of the concept of sharana is deeper than the current usage. See Yaravintelimath, *Vachana Lexicon*, pp. 763–5.

[54] Devadevan, *A Prehistory of Hinduism*, p. 40.

peared, along with a new religious practice. The movement is popularly referred to by this literary form, which was named, with disarming simplicity, the *vacana* (which means utterance, statement, discourse; an author in the genre was called *vacanakara*, maker of *vacana*). It is often also called the Virasaiva movement, in acknowledgement of the religious group that adopted the *vacana* as one of its principal genres.[55]

More than 200 vachanakaras have been identified so far. The online archive Vachana Sanchaya – the most helpful source for these compositions – documents more than 20,000 vachanas composed by 249 different vachanakaras, 218 of them male and 31 female. The fact that most vachanakaras came from non-Vedic backgrounds and diverse social segments of the populace, especially from the lower artisan castes, has led most scholars to perceive the Sharana phenomenon as an anti-caste movement. However, some readings of the vachanas contest such a conclusion.[56]

[55] Nagaraj, "Critical Tensions", pp. 346–7.

[56] The research programme of S.N. Balagangadhara, author of *Heathen in His Blindness*, largely argues that caste as a system was a colonial construct. (Note Nagaraj's referencing of it in ch. 2.) Dunkin Jalki, who works with this research programme, argues that vachanas hardly talk about the caste system. See Jalki, "Vachana Sahityavu"; also see Jalki, *Vachanas as Caste Critiques*. However, O.L. Nagabhushana Swamy seems to argue that we tend to reconstruct the past in accordance with our present interests and needs. Therefore, different ages have emphasised different aspects of vachanas. For example, in the 1970s vachanas were read as social texts, as anti-caste propagations. The anti-caste stance was not distinctive in relation to vachanas alone; all schools that presented alternatives to Vedic thought have addressed the caste problem. See Swamy, *Vachana Prashnottara*, pp. 44–5. Further, he is of the view that vachanas are records of how to lead a good life – the kinds of life practices that can ensure the welfare (kalyana) of individuals and the community. See Swamy, *Vachana Prashnottara*, pp. 71–2. Also note that, at the beginning of the twentieth century, vachanas were read as religious texts; later, with the development of Kannada Studies in education, they began to be read as literary texts. Following E.D. Hirsch's distinction between meaning and significance, we can say that the meanings of vachanas are different from their significance; we may not be sure about their meanings, but their significance for contemporary Kannada self and culture is important. The meaning of a text does not change over time, but the significance of the text does change over time. For more on meaning and significance, see Hirsch,

Each vachana ends with an ankitanama, this being a signature name somewhat akin to a pen name but referring to the chosen deity rather than to the vachanakara. In Basavanna's compositions this ankitanama is Kudalasangamadeva; in Akkamahadevi's it is Chennamallikarjuna; in Allama's it is Guheshwara; and so on. According to the vachana scholar O.L. Nagabhushana Swamy, the ankitanama, which is the name of the ishtadaiva (chosen god), is used as a signature in the vachanakara's compositions. But also, apart from using these names as imprints, many vachanas are addressed and dedicated to these ishtadaivas. As Kurtkoti points out, the variously named Shivas adored by these vachanakaras may conceivably not be the Vedic Shiva at all; moreover, even Allama's Guheshwara is different from Basavanna's Kudalasangama.[57]

Returning to the story of twelfth-century Kalyana: Basavanna and his followers, being committed to shivabhakti (devotion to Shiva) and shivatattva (the Shiva principle), aspired to establish the shaiva way of life (shivachara) through their discourses. As some narratives testify, the city of Kalyana became a meeting place for shivasharanas – Akkamahadevi from Udutadi, Allama from Balligavi, Siddharama from Sonnalige (today's Solapur in Maharashtra state) – and were said to have deliberated there on the sharana way of life in the anubhavamantapa.[58] In his mahamane – the site of spirituality contrasting the royal power of Bijjala's court – Basavanna patronised the community of shivasharanas who were, at the time, called jangamas (devotees of Shiva).[59]

"Meaning and Significance Reinterpreted". When we deal with past texts, we need to pay attention to what Gadamer calls "the fusion of horizons" (achieving understanding between the reader in a particular historical context and the text). See Gadamer, *Truth and Method*.

[57] Kurtkoti, *Kannada Sahitya Sangati*, p. 73.

[58] According to Manu V. Devadevan, "Akka Mahadevi's meeting with Basava and Allama Prabhu at the anubhava mantapa is not known from any source before the 15th century." See Devadevan, "Introduction", p. xviii. For more on the historicity of anubhavamantapa, see Uttangi, *Anubhava Mantapada*.

[59] The notion of "jangama" has undergone a sea change. As a concept in

According to descriptions in many premodern narratives, Allama, a wandering mendicant (jangama), arrives at the mahamane where Basavanna accepts him as his guru and makes him preside over the shunyapita (throne of the void). Among vachankaras, if Basavanna has the honorific "anna" (elder brother), and Akkamahadevi "akka" (elder sister), Allama is addressed as "prabhu" (Lord, in the sense of Master to all).

The story that has come down to us is that the socio-religious intervention of Basavanna and the shivasharanas was the cause of social unrest in Kalyana. As they imagined a new social order, which is at times described as an egalitarian society, the sharanas came into conflict with the conservative sections of society, and specifically with King Bijjala. We are not sure of Bijjala's social identity, nor whether he followed Virashaivism or Jainism.[60] Girish Karnad's play *Tale-danda* (1990), which is based on historical research, represents the intercaste marriage between Brahmin Madhuvarasa's daughter and Pariah Haralayya's son as triggering the problem in Kalyana.[61] King Bijjala blinded Madhuvarasa and Haralayya for this pratiloma ("lower"-caste man marrying "higher"-caste woman) marriage, upon which some Virashaivas killed Bijjala. As most accounts testify, the fall of Kalyana resulted in a dispersion of the sharanas from the city. Basavanna left for Kudalasangama, Allama and Akkamahadevi moved towards Srisailam, Chennabasava and other sharanas towards Ulavi. These places are now Lingayat pilgrim centres keeping the memory of the twelfth-century Sharana phenomenon alive. Over the last eight centuries a variety of interpretations and accounts have

---

Virashaiva theology, "jangama" is a dynamic concept, denoting certain principles and one who follows those principles. In the famous vachana of Basavanna, it is understood as a moving entity as opposed to the static, connoting the principle of change, resisting rigidity and dogma, etc. In the contemporary Virashaiva/Lingayat context, it has become a marker of caste identity that refers to the priestly class which conducts rituals, such as Virashaivas'/Lingayats' initiation into linga and their death rites.

[60] See Venkannaiah, "Bijjalanu Jainane?", pp. 108–14.

[61] Karnad, *Tale-danda*. English translation 1993.

attempted to capture the Sharana phenomenon, but it remains an enigma.

Allama in the Kannada Cultural Imagination: Premodern Narratives

So far, I have recounted a brief, quasi-mythical, quasi-historical account of the Shivasharana phenomenon to which Allama belonged. Now let me turn to understanding the image of Allama in the Kannada cultural imagination. As noted earlier, we have the history of Allama's representations in Kannada from the twelfth century to the present, and it is centrally through these that I will interpret the Allama phenomenon.

While several inscriptions have been found that refer to Basavanna, only four mention Allama: a seventeenth-century copper inscription of Anandapuramath dated to 1660; the Jodidasenahalli inscription dated to 1686; the Chikkahejje inscription (date unknown), and a stone inscription of 1158 erected in front of the Siddheshwara temple in Siddhapura village of Dharwad taluk.[62] Though scholars use inscriptions to trace the historicity of sharanas, these are not in themselves sufficient for the purpose.

Then, there are eighty vachanas that record the name "Allama". However, we cannot assume that the Allama represented in all these vachanas is by his contemporaries, for some of them may be compositions of a later date, meaning that the image of Allama in many of the vachanas may be the result of constructions arrived at by later generations. Given this combination of difficulties – inadequate historical sources and vachana references that cannot be accurately dated – Nagaraj's argument in this book is cogent: we need to take a different approach to understanding the medieval Kannada world, its figures, authors, and texts. I would concur that the fixity and singularity of modern categories – such as a historical figure, an author, an authentic text, an ur-text – make them of little help in

---

[62] Kalburgi, *Shashangalli Shivasharanaru*, pp. 74–5.

comprehending aspects of the premodern world in which the relevant body is a collective. Instead of trying to see Basavanna, Allama Prabhu, Akkamahadevi, and other such figures as authentic historical authors, it is useful to perceive them as sampradayas (lineages; traditions). Chamarasa declares in his *Prabhulingalile* (fifteenth century) that he wishes to narrate the noble path of the Allama sampradaya: "I shall in fit measure narrate, / In amenable tongue, for everyone's delectation / Allama Prabhu's *tradition* of the true path of grace."[63] The insistence here is on the idea that existence can transcend the boundaries of individual physical life by animating the sense of continuity between past and present in the popular imagination. The sensibility nurtured thereby is a capacity to see not only temples and holy places as the celebrations of a living tradition but also toru gadduges (symbolic tombs). In Karnataka, for example, besides Allama's temple in Gugal (Raichur District), more than ten Allama gadduges are worshipped, including those at Savalagi, Kodekallu, Madihala, Terdala, and Basavakalyana.[64]

In premodern Indian culture, texts were in the nature of a growing organism, somewhat like Wikipedia in our time: possibly, any competent authority could add to them and reshape them, rendering these premodern figures the authors of a field – akin perhaps to Marx and Freud, the makers of discursive fields.[65] Historically, vachanas were not recorded artifacts, as they tend to seem now because they have been frozen by contemporary print culture. They were dynamic and open and have filtered down over successive generations after several processes of recomposition, often through oral transmission and sometimes as scripts on palm leaves. In the latter case, since no colophon providing the production history of what is called vachana kattu (the bundle of leaves) is available, it is difficult

---

[63] Chamarasa, "Selections from *Prabhulingaleele*", emphasis added, p. 14. For the declaration of authorial intent, see Chamarasa, *Prabhulingalile*, p. 19.

[64] Vrushabhendraswamy, *Kannada Sahityadalli*, p. 26. Obviously, Allama was not in fact buried at these various locations – no more than deities were physically resident in the temples where they are worshipped.

[65] Foucault, "What Is an Author?"

to precisely pinpoint the antiquity of written vachanas. Scholars are fairly sure only of some that were written during the fourteenth and fifteenth centuries.[66] Before the print era, variations during the process of copying were more or less inevitable.

It is also important to keep in mind the fluidity and flexibility of vachana ontology. Until the twentieth century we had no compilations of vachanas in any individual name (as author), but rather generically or thematically organised compilations such as sthala vachanas, stotra vachanas, bedagina vachanas, etc. The classification and compilation of vachanas on the basis of individual authors is the result of modern literary and scholarly practice in the age of print capitalism. As Foucault says, the notion of author is a function, it helps us to classify things.[67] Currently we can, as mentioned earlier, identify more than 20,000 vachanas, but given our understanding of their composition and survival over the centuries we can be certain that not all of them were composed during the twelfth century. Some will have been lost, new ones will have been added, and some edited or recomposed: each age authored and re-authored them.

We do not have a definitive transmission history, either, of these vachanas. The strongest likelihood is of initial oral forms in popular memory and subsequent written forms. In this process the existing vachanas were altered and new compositions in the names of past shivasharanas added. This is clear from the existence of different versions of the same vachana, which scholars call patantara (textual variations). Sometimes the same vachana carries the ankitanama of two different vachanakaras. We cannot view these as interpolations either, because that presupposes an original text, or a devavani (God's text) which may not be changed by mortals.[68]

With this understanding of premodern authorship and textuality, we move on to the image of Allama as imagined in this cul-

---

[66] Shivanna, *Virashaiva Hastaprati*; for more on Kannada manuscripts, see Hiremath, *Kannada Hastapratigalu.*

[67] Foucault, "What Is an Author?"

[68] I owe this idea to my discussion with O.L. Nagabhushana Swamy.

ture. In Chapter 5 of the present book, "Life Narratives of Allama: Three Models", Nagaraj argues that Allama became a subject for diverse narratives among the poets who came after him. He says accounts of Allama's life after the twelfth century fall into three categories of narrative: the literary model of Harihara and Chamarasa; the spiritual model of the *Shunyasampadanes*; and the folk Shaiva narrative model – the *Manteswamy Kavya*. There are, in addition, Virashaiva Puranas and Sharana hagiographies in which the story of Allama is recounted. However, I will confine myself to Nagaraj's three narrative models so as to understand the nuanced arguments he builds around them.

Seven decades after the vachanakaras, Harihara was the first poet to include their life narratives in his *Ragalegalu*, this being the term for hagiographic stories of Shiva's saints.[69] By convention all sharana ragalegalu begin with a "framing story, in which Siva actively sends his attendant from Kailasa down to earth so that he may serve as the god's earthly voice for the Saranas' stories."[70] Like-wise, Prabhudevara ragale (The Story of Allama Prabhu) begins in heaven, where Shiva notices Nirmaya, one of his entourage of ganas (attendants), gazing at a surasati (a female attendant in heaven). He sends them both to earth so that they may erotically cavort and then return to heaven. Nirmaya is then reborn as Allaiah on earth to Nagavasadipati and his wife at Balligavi.[71] He grows up as Allama and becomes an expert mrudanga player (i.e. a percussionist) serving at the Goggeshwara temple. Meanwhile the surasati is reborn on earth as Kamalate to Dhanadatta and his wife, also at Balligavi. When Kamalate, beautiful and wise, visits the temple, she is attract-ed by Allama's charm and his talent with playing the mrudanga.

---

[69] Harihara, *Hariharana Ragalegalu*; for an analysis of Harihara's *Ragalegalu* in English, see Ben-Herut, *Śiva's Saints*.

[70] Ben-Herut, *Śiva's Saints*, p. 52.

[71] For more on Allama's birthplace, see Kalburgi, "Allamaprabhuvina Janmagrama". Further, according to Manu V. Devadevan, "Allama's dates are not known, but it is certain that he was active in the fifth and sixth decades of the 12th century." See Devadevan, "Introduction", p. xix.

On seeing the beautiful Kamalate, Allama forgets his mrudanga and Shiva, and is completely captivated by her. They long for each other, so Kamalate's friends arrange for them to meet, and they enjoy life as a couple. And this coupling is both erotic pleasure and the pleasure of Shiva worship.

Kamalate, destined to return to heaven, falls sick, suffers a high fever, and dies. A broken-hearted Allama sits alone and depressed, scratches the earth with his toes, and comes upon traces of a golden cupola. Digging deeper, he begins to see a complete dome. When news of this reaches the king, he orders an excavation, and they discover an old Shiva temple. Nobody wants to risk entering the ruined temple except Allama: since he has lost his beloved Kamalate, why worry about losing his own body? Entering the temple he finds a saint, Animisha, engrossed in yogic meditation. Soon, Allama's own spiritual transformation begins. His carnal desires disappear and Shiva-jnana (knowledge of Shiva) takes birth within him. He begins to praise Shivayogi, finds a linga on his palm, and comes out with the blessings of Guheshwara. Thus, Allama, having transformed himself from a worldly lover into a spiritual seeker and mystic, guides Basavanna in Kalyana and suggests that Siddharama – another noted Sharana, a fellow vachanakara – undertake penance in order to escape from kaliyuga. Allama himself finally disappears in a plantain grove in Srisailam. In heaven, Shiva hears his story and blesses the former Nirmaya.

This plot appears with varying details in the narratives that follow Harihara. Though each of them focuses on different aspects of Allama's life and extends the plot – depending upon the specific ideological environment of each – the theme of Allama rising above worldly erotic pleasure, which is maye (illusion), remains central to his life narratives. Symbolically, the narratives enact the triumph of spirit over body and intellect over materiality; and they teach the importance of understanding (cognition) and bayalu (literally, an open field, denoting the void, formlessness, and "place without placeness").

The next text to deal with Allama is Raghavanka's *Siddharama*

Charitra. Raghavanka (late twelfth and early thirteenth centuries), believed to be Harihara's nephew, is best known for his magnum opus entitled *Harishchandra Kavya*. According to scholars, he fashioned the shatpadi mode (the hexameter verse form) in kavya, following Harihara's ragale tradition.[72] His *Siddharama Charitra* portrays the making of the twelfth-century Sharana, Siddharama. Sandhi (section) 9, stanzas 37 to 45 in this text deal with a conversation between Siddharama and Allama. Allama is described as courageous and an incarnation of linga; when he – possessing the radiance that emanates from one who has worked wonders for people – comes to Sonnalige, his discourses shape the understanding and ways of shivajnana in Siddharama.[73]

In the preface to *Tale-danda*, his play on the Sharana upheaval, Girish Karnad says: "It becomes inevitable for every Kannadiga to return, like a tongue that returns again and again to a painful tooth, to the victories and agonies of that period."[74] In fact, no phenomenon in Kannada cultural history has been as frequently revisited as the time of the twelfth-century Sharana. A great moment of such revisiting occurred during the Vijayanagara Empire (fourteenth to seventeenth centuries), at a point when twelfth-century Kalyana became an inspiration for later poets. In his *Shiva-tattva Chintamani*, Lakkanna Dandesha (fifteenth century), a minister and military commander in Devaraya II's empire, calls Vijayanagara "Vijayakalyananagari", his intention being to suggest Vijayanagara as the replication in his own day of the glory that was Kalyana of the twelfth-century Sharanas.[75] According to Kannada scholars, the Sangama dynasty (1336–1485) of the Vijayanagara Empire patronised Virashaivism and its compositions. In particular, the reign of Devaraya II (1424–46) – the monarch also popularly known as Praudhadevaraya – saw the start of a new vachana archive, namely the Virashaiva Puranas, narrating the lives of shivasharanas and providing commentaries on the vachanas. The *Shunya-*

---

[72] Rama Rao, "Upodghata", p. 5.
[73] Ibid., pp. 246–7.
[74] Karnad, "Lekhakana Nudi".
[75] Paramashivamurthy, "Prastavane", p. 109.

sampadanes – works that comprise the quintessence of Virashaiva philosophy through episodic narratives of Allama's encounter with other sharanas – were also composed during this period.

We can thus see Allama's story evolving. Allama episodes appear as interludes in Virashaiva Puranas composed between the fifteenth and seventeenth centuries: Bhimakavi's *Basava Purana*,[76] Lakkanna Dandesha's *Shivatattva Chintamani*, Singiraja's *Singiraja Purana*, Shadaksharadeva's *Basavaraja Vijaya*, Virupaksha Pandita's *Chennabasava Purana*, and Siddhananjesha's *Gururaja Charitra* being prominent among them. Whether the twelfth-century vachanas reached this period in oral form or also in script has been a matter for speculation. According to an expert in vachana studies, Veeranna Rajur, in the Vijayanagara period vachanas were kept alive in Lingayat mathas (Virashaiva monasteries) through daily recitation as well as by making written copies and rearranging them.[77] So, in this period another genre of vachana literature emerged, which involved the compilation and reorganisation of vachanas according to shatsthalas (six states in the quest for enlightenment), and producing commentaries on them.[78]

In the early fifteenth century Mahalingadeva edited and commented on Allama's vachanas in works like *Shatstala*, *Mishrashatstala*, and *Ekottarashatastala*. Following him, Jakkanarya (fifteenth century) separated swara-vachanas from ekottarashatastala and wrote commentaries on the vachanas. Kallumathada Prabhudeva (fifteenth century) classified vachanas into sixteen sthalas in his *Lingalila Vilasa Charitra*, while Karastalada Virannanodaya (fifteenth century) curated Allama's vachanas in *Lingasutrada Vachana*. Gubbiya Mallanna (fifteenth century) authored *Ganabashita Ratna Mala*, and Maggeya Mayideva (fifteenth century)

---

[76] Bhimkavi's *Basava Purana* is a Kannada recomposition of the Telugu poet Palkurike Somanatha's *Basava Purana*.

[77] Rajur, *Vachana Samshodhane*, p. 3.

[78] The six states being bhakta sthala (the devotee state), maheshwara sthala (the state of steadfast faith), prasadi sthala (the state of grace), pranalingi sthala (the state of pranalinga), sharana sthala (the state of surrender), and aikya sthala (the state of union).

rendered and commented on Allama's shatsthala vachanas in *Prabhugeeta*.[79]

These authors are, by and large, known as Viraktas, and in this league Chamarasa (fifteenth century), who is said to have worked under the patronage of Praudhadevaraya, produced a full-length life narrative, *Prabhulingalile*, with Allama as the protagonist. He develops Allama's story as a lile (a play), telling the tale of Allama's encounter with other sharanas and saints and how he influenced them. Chamarasa is considered one of the nuronduviraktaru – 101 renouncers – of the Vijayanagara period. Viraktas were a group of militant Shaiva ascetics in the city of Vijayanagara who were believed to have been sent to the earth from Kailasa to protect and spread Virashaiva devotion.[80] They were wandering ascetics who renounced material life for the cause of Shivabhakti.[81] Their contribution to Virashaivism during the fifteenth century lies in collecting, rearranging, and compiling vachanas and producing Shaiva narratives. According to Prithvi Datta Chandra Shobhi, "political, institutional, and sectarian motivations propelled the Viraktas, leaders of the Kannada Śivabhakti tradition in this period, to undertake a well-orchestrated project of framing the voices of the twelfth-century devotees in social and political terms that would resonate with new contexts of the fifteenth century."[82] The fact that Chamarasa was a Virakta is key to understanding his portrayal of Allama in *Prabhulingalile*. In one out of a couple of legends about why Chamarasa wrote this work, Mukunda Peddi, a Vaishnava, criticised Allama's bedagu vachanas and his erotic relationship with

[79] This is available in both English and Kannada. See Maggeya Mayideva, *Prabhugeeta*.

[80] The contemporary usage of virakta refers to the monastic order known as Virakta mathas, adhering to Basavanna's philosophy understood as an anti-Vedic stand. This spiritual order is often perceived as an alternative to another monastic order, panchapeetha, which does not consider the Basavanna order as its basis.

[81] For more on Viraktas of Vijayanagara, see YouTube, "The Viraktas of Vijayanagara".

[82] Quoted in Ben-Herut, *Śiva's Saints*, p. 9.

Kamalate.[83] The idea of an ascetic like Allama succumbing to maye (illusion) sparked controversy in medieval Kannada thought. Nagaraj suggests Chamarasa may have written *Prabhulingalile* in response, portraying Allama as a spiritual seeker – this portrayal being unlike that by Harihara, who had no qualms narrating Allama's erotic love for Kamalate. Chamarasa's Virakta sensibility could have been a compelling factor in portraying Allama as an ascetic who conquers maye.

The Prologue to *Prabhulingalile* states the purpose and significance of narrating Allama's miracles, after which each stage of Allama's life is portrayed over twenty-five cantos called "gatis". Though, like Harihara, Chamarasa frames his narrative in Kailasa, the abode of Shiva, his Allama is not Nirmaya, cursed by Shiva to be reborn on earth. He was born on earth at Balligavi of Banavase, a divine child, to parents called Sujnani and Nirahankari. (The former name signifies virtuous knowledge and the latter absence of pride.)

According to Kirtinath Kurtkoti, Harihara's Allama is a man so consumed by infatuation for Kamalate that he is transformed into an ascetic by the depth of his suffering for her loss and his incidental encounter with Animisha. In contrast, Chamarasa's Allama is born a yogi, a human embodiment of Shiva. Harihara's is a human story whereas Chamarasa's is a spiritual account.[84] *Prabhulingalile* offers an image of Allama as a destroyer of maye and seeker of truth. Among the Allama life narratives, this work occupies an important place as the first available comprehensive account of Allama Prabhu, its importance being evident from its translation into Telugu, Tamil, Marathi, and Sanskrit.[85]

Allama's life became a further event in Kannada cultural history when five versions of the *Shunyasampadane* were produced. In

---

[83] Bedagu vachanas are riddle-like compositions. For more on them, see fn. 70 in ch. 1 of this book.

[84] Kurtkoti, "Chamarasana Prabhulingalile", p. 186.

[85] Chamarasa, *Prabhulingalile* (in Sanskrit, Tamil, and Telugu); and Chamarasa, *Leela* (Marathi).

chronological sequence these are (1) Shivaganaprasadi Mahadevaiah's *Shunyasampadane* (early fifteenth century), which has
been abridged into English;[86] (2) Kenchaveerannodeya's *Shunyasampadane* (late fifteenth century), which is no longer extant;
(3) Gummalapurada Siddhalingadevara's *Shunyasampadane* (early
sixteenth century); (4) Guluru Siddhaveerannodeyara's *Shunyasampadane* (early sixteenth century), also available in English translation;[87] and (5) Halegeyarya's *Shunyasampadane* (sixteenth century).[88] What is interesting about the *Shunyasampadanes* is that the
same theme, under the same title, is handled with distinguishable
differences by the different authors, who each develop their own narrative – a most rare example of so many renditions of a single devotional account.

All these narratives borrow from their predecessors and change
the material, adding and subtracting episodes to suit their respective purposes. It is generally accepted that the first shunyasampadanakara, Shivaganaprasadi Mahadevaiah, set the template on
which the others reworked the material. Nagaraj discusses in
Chapter 5 how the context in which the *Shunyasampadanes* were
produced may have shaped their plots and motifs. He believes they
were the products of an institutional imagination, meaning they
were produced when Virashaivism was trying to reinvent itself as an
institutional religion. Institutional necessity required the power of
texts, and these *Shunyasampadanes* turned Virashaivas into a textual
community. According to Brian Stock, a textual community is a
community whose life, thought, sense of identity, and relations
with outsiders are organised around an authoritative text.[89]

[86] See Shivaganaprasadi, *Shoonyasampadane*.

[87] Gooluru Siddhaveeranna Wodeyar, *Sunyasampadane*, 5 vols.

[88] According to R.C. Hiremath, the last *Shunyasampadane*, which generally
goes under the name of Halegeyarya, was actually composed by Kenchaveerannodeya, and it is Halegeyarya's version that is not extant. See Thipperudraswamy, *Shunyasampadane*, p. 30. Scholars have reached a consensus that they
are the same.

[89] See Stock, *The Implications of Literacy*. Nagaraj discusses this process in
ch. 5 of the present book.

The number of chapters in the various *Shunyasampadanes* varies from nineteen to twenty-one. Here I will reproduce the gist of Shivaganaprasadi Mahadevaiah's and Gummalapurada Siddhalingadevara's *Shunyasampadanes* because Nagaraj makes frequent references to them. All the *Shunyasampadanes* begin with Prathamopadesha (the first lecture) which describes Allama as virashaivachara prathamanayaka (the foremost leader of Virashaivism), and the composition of the *Shunyasampadane* as a "narrative of Allama's encounter with sharanas like Basava and Chennabasava by arranging independent vachanas of the shivadvaita order in the form of dialogues."[90] While Harihara and Chamarasa narrate the story of Allama, the supreme achievement of the *Shunyasampadanes* is to have arranged the vachanas into a narrative of the story of Allama's significant encounters.

As in other narratives, here too Nirmaya, a consort of Shiva, is sent to the earth to resuscitate virashaivachara (Virashaiva practice). Interestingly, the Allama–Kamalate episode is not elaborated upon in the *Shunyasampadanes*, as it is in Harihara's *Prabhudevara Ragale*; in fact, Allama's worldly life with Kamalate comes to a quick end in the *Shunyasampadanes*. After conquering maye, Allama comes across Animisha, who makes him realise that there is no separation between guru and disciple, and initiates him into spirituality. After obtaining the linga from Animisha, Allama achieves spiritual mastery through shatsthala, the six-fold spiritual stages. Thus, Allama becomes a wandering mendicant narrating the nuances of Shivadvaita and the mirage of maye to those he meets. Subsequent chapters of the text give a vivid picture of Allama's encounters with Muktayakka, Siddharama (Siddharamayya), Basavanna, Chennabasavanna, Marulushankara, Mahadeviakka, and others.

Over his encounters with Muktayakka and Siddharamayya, Allama seeks to elevate their spiritual endeavours towards attaining shivatattva. In the chapter that follows, Allama arrives at Kalyana along with Siddharamayya. They are impressed by the spiritual and

[90] Shivaganaprasadi, *Shivaganaprasadi Mahadevayyana*, p. 73 (my translation).

material opulence of the city. But when Basavanna, immersed completely in worshipping ishtalinga, sends his attendants to receive them, Allama expresses displeasure and stays outside. Finally, Basavanna himself comes to receive Allama and Siddharamayya, and in the exchange between Allama and Basavanna the former makes the latter realise that the living jangama is more important than the act of worshipping linga. In the next chapter, while continuing his teaching, Allama spots Marulushankaradeva lying in a heap at Kalyana. Allama shows the spiritual power within this neglected figure, who is mistakenly reckoned a simpleton by the people of Kalyana, including Basavanna. The next two chapters describe Allama's spiritual debates with Basavanna, Chennabasavanna, and Madivala Machayya.

The question of Siddharamayya's lingadikshe (initiation into the fold) takes up most of the subsequent chapter, particularly so in Gummalapurada Siddhalingadevara's *Shunyasampadane*. Though Allama has brought Siddharamayya to Kalyana to seek an understanding from Basavanna on various forms of linga, such as karasthala linga (linga on the palm), Basavanna, Chennabasavanna, and other sharanas refuse to admit and accept Siddharamayya as he has not been initiated into wearing a linga on the body. Allama defends Siddharamayya, saying he has attained a true understanding of Shiva, and, given that Shiva is one with him – transcending the boundaries of internal and external – why should he need a separate ishtalinga? However, all the sharanas support Chennabasavanna and make Siddharamayya take lingadikshe. This section has generated debate among modern scholars, including Nagaraj, who theorises on the episode in Chapter 5.

In subsequent chapters the narrative extends to describe the spiritual ideals of sharanas such as Molige Marayya, Nuliya Chandayya, and Gattivalayya, illustrating the integration of kayaka (work) and linga (the divine symbol) in daily life. An episode centred on Akkamahadevi, who renounces worldly life and argues with Allama about the significance of her nudity, further explores the themes of purity, identity, and spiritual transcendence.

As Allama sets out on a tour from Kalyana, the *Shunyasampadanes* give a vivid account of his wanderings across east, south, north, and west. At Kalyana they imagine an institution called anubhavamantapa (hall of experience) where Allama, on the shunyasimhasana (throne of the void), is expected to preside over discussions on spiritual matters. Finally, Allama returns to Kalyana in the guise of a vagabond. By this time Kalyana has changed from a spiritual arena into a palace of opulence and luxury. The sharanas here, lacking all sensitivity and refinement, are unable to recognise Allama, a jangama who has assumed the appearance of an uncouth vagrant. While Basavanna recognises Allama, the other sharanas ridicule the jangama's filthy attire. However, Allama agrees to ascend the throne of shunya and Basavanna begins to offer puja, which delays the offering of food to the devotees (sharanas, also referred to as jangamas) assembled in Basavanna's house. The impatient devotees now depart and boycott Basavanna and Allama. A debate ensues between Basavanna and Allama regarding offerings of food to devotees. Basavanna accepts the spiritual supremacy of Allama but convinces him of the importance of offering food to devotees.

In the final chapters Allama encounters Goraksha, a siddha who has perfected his body through yogic discipline. Their debate highlights the futility of relying solely on the body's strength, with Allama demonstrating the value of spiritual strength over physical prowess. Finally, all the sharanas disperse – Allama goes into the plantain groves of Srisailam. The shunyasampadanakaras end the narrative by saying that it represents the exalted teachings of a great teacher, Allama, and the noblest Virashaiva thought. Those who listen to it will attain liberation.

Choosing the sense of the word "spirit" – as in the phrase "letter and spirit" – the spirit of the *Shunyasampadanes* is to restore shivachara to the earth.[91] However, scholars like Basavaraja Kalgudi have argued that the stated purpose of the *Shunyasampadanes* has

---

[91] For critical essays on the *Shunyasampadanes*, see Nugadoni, ed., *Shunyasampadanegalu*. For a critical analysis of the *Shunyasampadanes* in English, see Michael, *The Origins of Vīraśaiva*.

not been realised within the content of the narrative.[92] There is also Blake Michael's view that the *Shunyasampadanes* do not offer any single ideal form for Virashaivism.[93] Be that as it may, they do represent a technical triumph in the history of Kannada literature for creatively adapting the existing corpus of vachanas to form a narrative. It is interesting to note that the shunyasampadanakaras created narratives that followed neither the epic tradition that flourished before them nor long bhakti narratives of the Harihara type. They wove the existing vachanas into their prose narratives in the form of dialogues. Vachanas as dialogic short compositions serve the narrative structure – based on Allama encountering different sharanas and debating with them – very well.

There are other interpretations: scholars like Rahamath Tarikere argue that the philosophical aspiration of vachanas is different from that of the narrative in the *Shunyasampadanes*.[94] Kirtinath Kurtkoti says that by embedding vachanas in their narrative the *Shunyasampadanes* turned them into a literary phenomenon. In his view the vachanas, the expressions of shivasharanas, may have lost the meanings their composers gave them, but these expressions have remained in our cultural memory awaiting newer interpretations and meanings.[95] The *Shunyasampadanes* are one such attempt to interpret the vachanas through their protagonist Allama.

It is very difficult to speculate why the Allama story is called shunyasampadane, i.e. the attainment of nothingness, or void. O.L. Nagabhushana Swamy argues that the shunyasampadanakaras found the idea of shunya at the heart of the vachanas and Allama a true representative of this idea. By connoting the attainment of shunya, these stories describe Allama and his interlocutors as attaining shunya, the absolute state.[96] Be that as it may, it remains

---

[92] Kalgudi, "*Shunyasampadanegalu*", p. 23.

[93] Michael, *The Origins of Vīraśaiva*, pp. 58–9.

[94] Tarikere, "*Shunyasampadane* mattu", p. 127.

[95] Kurtkoti, "Shunyasampadane", pp. 237–8. Note Hirsch's distinction between meaning and significance as explained in fn. 56. Kurtkoti here seems to observe the "significance" of vachanas for shunyasampadanakaras.

[96] Swamy, "Shunyasampadanegalu", p. 73.

very difficult to demonstrate the validity of this argument with textual evidence.

We must now turn to what is known as pamara parampare, i.e. folk imagination. Folk culture in Kannada is as rich as its so-called "mainstream" counterpart, and its engagement with the twelfth-century Sharana phenomenon is interesting. Two folk epics, the *Male Mahadeshwara Kavya* and the *Manteswamy Kavya*, have a critical rendezvous of sorts with Kalyana. They narrate the legends of Mahadeshwara and Manteswamy, respectively. Like Manteswamy, Male Mahadeshwara from the south visits the north – which, in the narrative, is Kalyana.[97] Nagaraj discusses the intertextual connections between the *Shunyasampadanes* and the *Manteswamy Kavya*, the protagonist of which is a reincarnation of Allama.

According to scholars, the *Manteswamy Kavya* emerged in the Mysore region as a counternarrative to Virashaivism. Like Male Mahadeshwara, Manteswamy is a fifteenth-century historical figure who became a legend. He may be described not just as a subject of the folk epic but a parampare, i.e. a religious folk tradition mostly revered by subaltern communities. Like Allama's gadduge, there are toru gadduges (symbolic tombs) of Manteswamy at various places in Karnataka, especially in the Mysore region. The performers of the *Manteswamy Kavya* belong to the Nilagara community of southern Karnataka. This tradition has generated its own clan, often known as okkalu – the community of Manteswamy's disciples. Since this is an oral epic that has come down to us from premodern times, the documentation of the *Manteswamy Kavya* in our own time has taken different forms, each with a specific purpose in mind.[98] The Dalit poet Siddalingaiah remembers Nagaraj having directed a serial called *Dharege Doddavaru* (The Great One on the Earth), another nomenclature for Mante-

---

[97] For an English translation, see Prasad, *Male Madeshwara*.

[98] For example, Venkatesh Indvadi edited a version that is specifically produced as a reading text. See Indvadi, *Manteswamy Kaavya*. So far there are seven versions of this kavya. Ambalike Hiriyanna's documentation aims at studying the oral epic by way of documentation. See Hiriyanna, *Manteswamy Epic*.

swamy.[99] In the present book Nagaraj uses for his analysis the text of this work edited by H.C. Boralingaiah.[100]

In this version, the story of Manteswamy is divided into nine chapters. The first, "Jagattu Srushtiya Salu" (Lines on the Creation of the World), tells the creation myth.[101] This is followed by the very famous "Kalyana Pattanada Salu" (Lines on the City of Kalyana), where Manteswamy tests Basavanna and other sharanas in Kalyana. The Nilagaras (performers) consider Manteswamy greater than Basavanna and the other sharanas. In their rendition, they refer to Kalyana as adi Kalyana (primordial Kalyana), not the historical Kalyana. According to H.S. Shivaprakash, the author of a play called *Mateswamy Katha Prasanga* (1993) based on the Manteswamy story, the twelfth-century vachanakaras replaced the stavaralinga (static linga) with the ishtalinga (chosen linga in the mind); however, the latter also became static in due course, which the Manteswamy parampara critiques.[102]

When Manteswamy visits Kalyana, the jangamas there do not allow him to enter the city as he does not wear a linga (the static symbol), nor is there any vibhuti (sacred ash) on his forehead. Manteswamy responds by making the lingas worn by these jangamas disappear. When they begin to search for their lingas, Manteswamy reveals them in his pot, which the jangamas hesitate to touch. Manteswamy tells them to go away with their man-made static lingas. Shivaprakash interprets this to mean that "the aim of linga upasane (worship) is to be enlightened within. The linga in the temple, which rejected the enlightenment inside, became a static linga."[103] Therefore, this folk epic virtually reminds the sharana culture of its now-forgotten understanding of linga. This in the main is how scholars read the *Manteswamy Kavya* — as a critique of

---

[99] Siddalingaiah, "Udghatana Bashana", p. 12.

[100] Boralingaiah, *Manteswamy*.

[101] For an English translation of this part, see Ramachandran, "Creation Myth".

[102] Shivaprakash, "Manteswamy Parampare", p. 46.

[103] Ibid., p. 47.

fifteenth-century Virashaivism, which had by this time become an institutionalised practice far distanced from its early ideals.

The rest of the *Manteswamy Kavya* is all about guru Manteswamy searching for, obtaining, and initiating shishyas (disciples). Accordingly, each chapter is devoted to a particular shishya – Rachappaji Salu, Boppagoudana Salu, Kempachari Salu, Phalaradayyana Salu, Kalipurushana Salu, Siddappaji Salu. Salu, which literally means "line", refers to an episode or chapter. The narrative ends with mangalarati (epilogue). This text yields itself to a reading which sees the personification of Allama in Manteswamy, and to how Manteswamy takes on the spirit and image of Allama. Nagaraj makes an interesting interpretation of this aspect in the fifth chapter.

Many other works on Allama were produced during the premodern period.[104] I have not discussed them all as the purpose here has been to supply background information for Nagaraj's treatment of Allama's life narratives in the fifth chapter. However, in essence we may say that no other twelfth-century Sharana captured the medieval imagination as thoroughly as Allama.

Modern Studies on the Vachana Tradition and Allama

I have divided my understanding of the vachana phenomenon and Allama's representations in the Kannada cultural imagination into premodern and modern approaches.[105] For convenience, I take colonial modernity or European imperialism in India as the dividing line between the two periods, although this sharp division is a map, not a territory.[106]

---

[104] Yalanduru Hareeshwara's *Prabhudevara Purana*; Rachayya's *Prabhulinga Leeleya Sangatya*; Parvatesha's *Prabhudevara Sangatya*; Marirachavattisha's *Prabhunatana Taravali*. For more, see Rajur, "Prastavane".

[105] For more on periodisation, see Chakrabarty, "The Muddle of Modernity".

[106] I borrow this concept from Alfred Korzybski's dictum that the map is not the territory, i.e. the world as represented pictorially is not the world itself.

The epistemology of colonial modernity had changed the ways in which we have looked at premodern texts, traditions, and practices, and what has come to be known as postcolonial theory has grappled with the problems arising out of this epistemological change. Accordingly, modern engagement with the vachana tradition began a new era in the social and intellectual life of vachanas.[107] Chief among the different forms of modern engagement with the vachana tradition has meant textualising the vachanas – collecting, editing, and printing them. Vachanas were performative practices but became objects of study, research, and translation into English. Apart from novels and plays about vachanakaras, performative traditions of singing vachanas began in the modern period. The engagement of Company theatre performances with the vachana tradition is an interesting aspect of change in this domain. Finally, during the "cassette age", 1980s onwards, vachanas began to be sung as lyrics and gained mass popularity, and now in the twenty-first century they are part of a new area of studies, the digital humanities.

Print capitalism, in a sense, rediscovered the vachanas by opening up different ways of engaging with them. The renowned vachana scholar M.M. Kalburgi divides the print history of vachanas into three stages.[108] The first stage, between 1880 and 1920, was when stray attempts were made to publish vachanas.[109] The second stage, between 1915 and the 1950s, began with Fa.Gu. Halakatti, who is known as vachana pitamaha (the father of vachana text and dis-

[107] Vijayakumar M. Boratti's research largely deals with the social and intellectual life of vachanas in colonial Karnataka. For more, see Boratti, *The Discovery of Vachanas*.

[108] Kalburgi, *Vachana Sahitya Prakataneya*. Vijayakumar M. Boratti traces the history of vachana publication to 1874, when Mangalore's Basel Mission Press published eleven vachanas in *Lingatism Examined*. For more on the complex history of vachana publication before Halakatti, see Boratti, "Praprathama Vachana".

[109] Early works were produced by European scholars and bureaucrats like C.P. Brown and Wurth. Brown wrote a commentary on the Telugu *Prabhulingalile*. For more, see Boratti, *Hiriyara Hiritana*, p. 34. For more on the work on Allama in the modern period, see Boratti, "Adhunika Itihasakke".

course) in the modern period.[110] And the third stage, between the 1960s and 1980s, may be described as a period of institutionalisation of Vachana Studies when universities and mathas (Lingayat monasteries) began to publish vachanas and other Lingayat texts. The third stage's extension, during the 2000s and after, could be described as the time when vachanas have become digitised objects. For example, https://vachana.sanchaya.net/ is a rich archive which includes close to 21,000 vachanas, designed to suit the needs of common reader and scholar alike.

What was needed at the beginning of the modern period (nineteenth and twentieth centuries) was the production of a tradition — of narratives and continuity in language and literary culture. The process of nation-building in India and its linguistically organised states (such as Kannada/Karnataka state), went hand in hand with the creation of a national literary tradition as well as the various vernacular traditions, such as the Kannada literary tradition. The emergence of Kannada Studies as a discipline and the writing of Kannada literary histories thereafter produced the Kannada literary canon. Following E.P. Rice's *A History of Kanarese Literature* (1921), R.S. Mugali, Professor of Kannada, wrote *Kannada Sahitya Charitre* (a history of Kannada literature) in which a chapter, "Basava Yuga" (The Age of Basava), discusses the twelfth-century vachanas and Virashaiva narratives as part of Kannada literary culture.[111] Earlier, R. Narasimhacharya produced a three-volume *Karnataka-Kavi-Charite*, which chronologically documents Kannada poets from earliest times. The first volume records details of most vachanakaras.[112] As part of this process, especially thanks to print culture, vachanas began to be read in schools and colleges, securing their place in the Kannada literary canon. Scholars and researchers in higher education began to produce annotated anthologies of vachanas and other texts for academic research. English education,

---

[110] For more on Halakatti's contribution, see Boratti, *The Discovery of Vachanas*.

[111] Mugali, *Kannada Sahitya*.

[112] Narasimhacharya, *Karnataka-Kavi*.

print culture, increases in literacy, the spread of nationalism and
sub-nationalism – all these contributed to construct the Kannada
literary past as a form of knowledge. It was the expansion and proliferation of this circulatory domain of transmission alongside a
discursive field of scholarship that shaped the vachana trajectory
in modern Karnataka.

Two institutions played an important role in the production
of vachanas as forms of knowledge. While the Lingayat mathas
acted as publishing houses of vachana literature and Virashaiva or
Lingayat culture, the establishment in 1949 of Karnatak University
at Dharwad, a region dominated by Lingayats, provided a major
platform for Vachana Studies.

The production of the vachana archive began with an early
generation of scholars in the twentieth century, with research continuing into the twenty-first. One method of investigating vachana
culture followed the Western mode of interpretive studies.[113]
Others worked on historicising the vachanas, reading them ideologically, etc. In turn, it has been remarked that historical consciousness and translations shaped Kannada modernity.[114] Historicising was in fact the most sought-after intellectual tool for Kannada
scholars in the twentieth century. (I will discuss translations in a later
section.) Most scholars, including M.M. Kalburgi and P.B. Desai
(author of *Basaveswara and His Times*), busied themselves trying
to date the various vachanakaras and discover historical details
about them.[115] Ideological readings then suggested the vachanas
were historical sources – for the anti-caste movement, for example.
If the Dalita-Bandaya movement of the 1970s brought socially
marginalised vachanakaras to the fore, women scholars – quite

---

[113] For example, Chidanandamurthy, *Shunyasampadaneyannu*; Thipperudraswamy, *Vachanagalalli*; Thipperudraswamy, *Shunyasampadane:
Vivaranatmaka*; Bhoosnurmath, *Śūnyasaṃpādeneya Pāramarśe*.

[114] Kurtkoti, "Prasthavane", p. 22.

[115] Desai, *Basaveswara and His Times*; Kalburgi, *Shashangalli Shivasharanaru*; Kalburgi, "Allamaprabhuvina Janmagrama". These are a few examples of attempts at understanding vachanakara historicity.

early from Jayadevitayi Ligade to later Shailaja Udachan, Jayashree Dande, Vijayashree Sabarad, Meenakshi Bali, Shivagangamma Rumma, Sabita Bannadi, and several others – looked at the vachanakaras most productively. Nagaraj's student M.S. Ashadevi produced *Belakiginta Bellage*, which examines Kannada vachanakartis through a feminist lens in the context of medieval female mysticism.[116]

It is because of their enigmatic or elusive nature – what Lacan called *objet petit a* (the unattainable object of desire) – that the vachanas seem to have been so frequently revisited and appropriated over the centuries. Questions about their authorship, their semantic contradictions, and their transmission via modifications have grown into epistemological challenges and made them the object-cause of desire – to reread and reinterpret.[117] Interpretations of the vachanas have appeared in anthologies, doctoral theses, monographs, and articles, and in two important commentaries.[118] However, Kannada scholarship produced no substantial work theorising vachanas in the hermeneutic mode until Nagaraj's *Allamaprabhu mattu Shaiva Pratibhe* (1999). No work before put forward

[116] See Ashadevi, *Belakiginta*. Among women vachana poets, Akkamahadevi has obviously attracted the attention of women scholars. See Imrapur, *Akkamahadevi;* Bannanje, *Akkamahadeviya;* Also for a recent novel on Akkamahadevi, see Anupama, *Belaginolagu.*

[117] Employing Lacan's notion of *objet petit a*, Catherine Belsey explains that enigmas and elusive elements – whatever is not resolved in texts – puzzles readers and makes them often revisit them. See Belsey, "Attention to Language", p. 3.

[118] For example, for an anthology of Allama's vachanas, see Allama Prabhu, *Allamana Vachanagalu*; on the critical interpretation of the *Shunyasampadanes*, see Michael, *The Origins of Vīraśaiva*; for social and cultural analysis of the Lingayat and vachana tradition, see Schouten, *Revolution of the Mystics*; Narayana, *Vachana Sahitya*, and Kalgudi, *Anubhava Samskrutika*; for critical interpretations of Allama's vachanas, see Nugadoni, ed., *Allamaprabhuvina Vachanagalu.* Two examples of commentaries are Divakara, *Vachanashastrarahasyavu*, and Immadi Shivabasavaswamigalu, *Allamaprabhudevara Teekina.*

theoretical propositions and bold hypotheses on vachanas and vachanakaras.[119] Nagaraj changed the social and intellectual meaning of vachanakaras and their trajectory by exploring Allama.

Nagaraj's Allama

Nagaraj chooses a single vachanakara, Allama, and attempts to situate him in three intellectual contexts: the medieval Shaiva intellectual world, the bhakti tradition, and the mystical tradition. This expansion in framing enables him to reconstruct an Allama who can be related not merely to his fellow vachana poets but also to the Kashmir Shaiva philosopher Abhinavagupta, and the poet-mystic Gorakhnath. And his close reading of Allama's vachanas presents Shaiva bhakti as not solely lodged in shringara rasa, but also as a mode of expression seeking to explore the limits of language when attempting to communicate an understanding of the divine. He takes ninety-odd vachanas of Allama and a couple of life narratives but does not merely explicate them and reconstruct Allama's life story. What he does is problematise the historiography of Indian philosophy by showing how figures like Sarahapada, Allama, and Bhima Bhoi have been kept outside the Indian philosophical tradition because they practised their philosophy through metaphors and images in local languages (bhashas). In some ways, Nagaraj's enterprise is comparable to the work of British Marxist historians such as Raymond Williams, Christopher Hill, and E.P. Thompson, who saw culture and thought as composite, being practised in different yet closely linked ways by thinkers, poets, and writers unnecessarily separated by categories such as "literature", "political history", and "social thought".[120] Nagaraj's dissolution of

[119] S.M. Vrushabhendraswamy's *Kannada Sahityadalli Allamaprabhu* had earlier provided a descriptive account of Allama's representation in Kannada literature, but it hardly attempted a hermeneutical study of Allama's compositions, not to mention any attempt to theorise. See Vrushabhendraswamy, *Kannada Sahityadalli.*

[120] Raymond Williams' *Culture and Society* (1958), E.P. Thompson's *William Morris* (1959), and Christopher Hill's *Milton and the English Revolution* (1977)

such boundaries happens by trying to build an alternative literary theory with the help of Shaiva poets, showing how the vachanakaras, particularly Allama, put forward their own poetics. In this sense his reading of the vachanas, by making intertextual references in particular to the Kashmir Shaivism of Abhinavagupta and other tantric sects, though contestable, is a landmark in the history of Vachana Studies. Additionally, his unravelling of the cultural politics of Allama's life narratives – the *Shunyasampadanes* and the *Manteswamy Kavya* – provides deep insights into Virashaiva/Lingayat religion and the formation of Kannada literary culture.

The major themes that Nagaraj explores in seven chapters, and the analytical methods he employs to explore them, are as follows: in the first chapter, "A Historical Survey of Shaiva Darshanas", Nagaraj demonstrates how, in his *History of Indian Philosophy*, Surendranath Dasgupta gets vernacular traditions such as the Sharana movement and figures like Basavanna wrong.[121] For Nagaraj the root cause of this kind of misunderstanding lies in translating desi; when dissenting desi religious traditions like the Virashaiva movement – which happen to be recorded in desha bhashas (regional languages) – are accessed through Sanskrit translation, they are likely to be misunderstood because a radical change has taken place in their meaning. Further, Nagaraj's assumption is that religious dissent and rebellions do not emerge from nowhere but the very womb of the originary matrix (mulamatruke) against which they have rebelled. For example, according to Nagaraj the Virashaiva movement emerged from inside Shaivism. As he notes in Chapter 2, it was because the Shaiva philosophy of Uttarapatha degenerated that the Virashaiva movement emerged from within that locus.

This leads Nagaraj to distinguish between desi Advayavadis like Allama, Narayana Guru, and Shishunala Sharif (among others), and Marga Advaitins like Shankaracharya. They differ not only

---

remain among the best-known works in this intellectual tradition which fuses biography, literary studies, political history, and social thought.

[121] Dasgupta, *A History of Indian Philosophy*, vol. 5.

in their methods of articulation but also in their engagement with social power structures. While the former resorted to figurative language (laghu) and narrative modes, the latter used rigorous concepts (ghana) and stuti kavya (eulogy). Allama's innovation, in Nagaraj's assessment, lies in an unconventional mixing of laghu and ghana. While Marga Advaitins take a conservative stance on caste and varnashrama, Desi Advayavadis adopt a rebellious stance.

Further, while drawing our attention to the complex relationship between Brahminical sects and Shramana sects – how they share certain common elements, learn from and influence each other – Nagaraj explains the process of Brahminical darshanas undergoing self-constriction (atmasankochikarana) by leaning towards rigid conventionalism; at the same time dissenting philosophical streams, not only from Shramana traditions but also from within the Brahminical fold, resisted this rigidification. In this respect Nagaraj's Allama, who has mastered Buddhist thought, does not consider sansara and nirvana different: he differs from Advaitins and, in line with Buddhist pratityasamutpada (interdependence), views everything as connected. And like the Buddhists Allama believes that the mind creates maya (illusion).

In the second chapter, "Foundations of Shaiva Poetics", Nagaraj articulates his decolonising agenda by a deployment of the Allama legend. As noticed earlier, this book is the result of Nagaraj's phase as a postcolonial critic committed to keeping Western theories at a distance for a nuanced understanding of Indian cultural production. Accordingly, in this chapter he tries to enter the expanse of Allama's vachanas through concepts internal to Shaiva mimamse. While exploring the foundations of Shaiva poetics, he places Allama alongside poets and philosophers of the Shaiva imagination such as Abhinavagupta (the Kashmir Shaiva philosopher and proponent of rasa theory), Sekkizhar (author of the Tamil work *Periyapuranam*), Harihara (author of *Ragalegalu*, the narratives of Shaiva devotees), Basavanna and Akkamahadevi (vachanakaras), and various others. He suggests Allama's Shaiva sensibility is different from all of these others. In Allama's advaya all realities merge, and for him there is no distinction between Shiva and the poet. This is the originality in the nature of Shaivadvaya imagination and it follows that Allama can be viewed as a poet-philosopher rejecting the bhakti sensibility which makes a distinction between the bhakta and Shiva.[122] Using the concept of Shaiva mimamse, Nagaraj also terms Allama a nimilana poet – one in whose work paradoxes and differences disappear.

Throughout his book Nagaraj has in mind the larger context of Kashmir Shaivism and its tantric sects, especially in relation to Abhinavagupta (975–1075), a leading exponent of Trika Shaivism and "absolute non-duality".[123] Though Abhinavagupta and Allama are advayavadis, Nagaraj recognises Allama as an anxious (atankita) mystic and Abhinavagupta as a mystic of bliss (ananda).[124] Like Abhinavagupta, Allama is devoted to the notion of shivananda (the bliss of Shiva), but his perspective on how to reach and capture this state is antithetical to the ways of Shaiva tantrism. In a similar spirit, to further bring out subtle differences between these two philosophers, Nagaraj is reminded of the Danish philosopher Søren Kierkegaard, in whom he finds a blend of both Harihara's dvaita and Allama's advaya. Kierkegaard, he says, oscillates between dvaita and advaya sensibilities.

Nagaraj perceives Shaivism's Uttarapatha as left-wing and Dakshinapatha as right-wing, and conceives Allama as belonging to neither. Allama not only opposed the world of mantradevates in Uttarapatha but also the external rituals of Shaivism in general. If Shakti is a female principle in Shaivism and in tantrism Shakti worship is a path of sadhana, in Allama shakti is not a female principle. By reading a vachana (no. 589), Nagaraj demonstrates that Allama conceives Shiva as the dynamic spirit and shakti as the

---

[122] Also see, Youtube, "Webinar with Dr. Manu Devadevan".

[123] Kashmir Shaivism, a non-dualist branch of Shaivism, came into prominence in the region after 850 CE. It included cults which go by the name of Tantric, where the practitioner pursues the power manifest in Shakti and Shiva. For an overview of Kashmir Shaivism, see Internet Encyclopedia of Philosophy, "Kashmiri Shaiva Philosophy".

[124] For more on this, see YouTube, "Is there a Philosophy of 'Joy-full-ness'?"

consciousness, and both are a single person. Shakti is not a female principle (note the gender marker in the vachana).

In the third chapter, "Towards a New Poetics", while placing Allama in relation to pan-Indian philosophical systems, including Kashmir Shaivism, Nagaraj reconstructs the poetics of vachanas, especially Allama's poetics, and theorises the formation of premodern Kannada literary cultures. Following Pollock's framework, he argues that vachanakaras heralded a new literary paradigm called the regional vernacular (pradeshika desi) in contrast to the cosmopolitan vernacular (vishwatmaka desi) of early Kannada writers like Srivijaya of *Kavirajamarga*, Pampa, and Ranna (among others).[125] If Pampa, etc., wrote vastuka kavya in an epic mode influenced by Sanskrit literature, the twelfth-century vachanakaras rejected it and refashioned the varnaka mode through the vachana genre.[126] If vastuka poetry expands (vikasa, unfoldment), Allama's sankocha (contraction) mode in the vachanas can pack elaborate philosophical arguments within a few lines – "since it compresses a large mass into an atom, it has an explosive quality."

[125] Nagaraj was also associated with Pollock's project on the exploration of literary cultures in history and contributed a posthumously published article, "Critical Tensions in the History of Kannada Literary Culture", to Pollock's edited volume, *Literary Cultures in History: Reconstructions from South Asia*, which is dedicated to Nagaraj and Norman Cutler. On the Sanskrit cosmopolis and vernacular literary cultures, see Pollock, *The Language of the Gods*.

[126] Vastuka and varnaka are two kinds of poetic practices in classical Kannada poetry. According to *Kannada Kaipidi*, the poetry that follows the poetic and prosodic features of Sanskrit poetic practices are called vastuka and poetry that does not follow the model of Sanskrit poetry is called varnaka. See Puttappa, *Kannada Kaipidi*. For a detailed discussion, see Bhatt, "Vastuka-Varnaka". In his translation of Allama's vachanas, H.S. Shivaprakash translates vastuka and varnaka as objective poetry and subjective poetry. See Shivaprakash, *I Keep Vigil of Rudra*, p. 52. They can also be called thematic poetry (vastuka) and descriptive poetry (varnaka). However, Nagaraj is using vastuka in the sense that poets like Pampa chose themes from epics like the *Mahabharata*, or from the Jain Puranas, weaving larger narratives around these predominantly in the form of vritta and kanda (metrical stanzas).

Nagaraj suggests that Allama developed a unique counter-poetics by standing against the rasa theory, which reigned supreme in the cosmopolitan vernacular and the Sanskrit cosmopolis.[127] In his vachanas Allama offers a critique of Abhinavagupta's rasa theory, taking issue with shringara-based bhakti poetry not only of the Sanskrit tradition but also of contemporaries like Akkamahadevi and Basavanna who try to humanise the divine. Allama, in this estimation, strongly disagrees with the "desiring-fancying-feeling" encountered in bhakti poets who desire, fancy, and feel the divine.

Allama does not articulate his critique in the philosopher's mode of maxims or propositions, but through images and metaphors. However, it seems apparent that, to an extent, Nagaraj imposes meanings on to these images and metaphors to reconstruct Allama's critique. For example, he interprets Allama as responding to the shringara rasa whenever he is on the subject of ogara (food), kama, the experience of Guheshwara, memory, language construction, and so forth. But there is in fact no unambiguous evidence of any such critique by Allama in the vachanas; Nagaraj's view is more in the nature of a plausible inference. In a similar spirit, he reads Allama's phrase "pomp of the words" as a critique of extensive verbiage in vastuka and bhakti poetry. In this way, Nagaraj's method of informed inference (or, in the inflated language of current scholarship, a "hermeneutics of suspicion") unravels underlying motives and an ideological impetus resonating as a subcurrent in the vachanas. Nagaraj's method looks not just for what Allama's words say (mean) but what they do (perform) – the performative act, for example, of critiquing shringara rasa.

The fourth chapter presents Allama's theory of kaya – the physical body. Here, Nagaraj begins with the assumption that in his vachanas Allama indirectly converses and debates with others. These interactions take place within the poetic tradition (especially the Kannada poetic tradition) as well as with other philosophical traditions: Allama is seen to critique both. One of Allama's prominent

---

[127] For Rasa theories, see Pollock, *Rasa Reader*.

debates in this chapter is about Kaula (Uttarapatha) tantrism's celebration of the body and its belief that sexual intercourse can be transformed into a spiritual experience – as set out in Abhinavagupta's tantric tradition. Nagaraj's reading demonstrates that by comparing the body to a plantain grove Allama shows the body's limits and thus confronts the elders of Shaiva traditions.

This chapter abounds in Allama's comparison with Abhinavagupta and pan-Indian Shaiva traditions. If the latter may be described as a philosopher of "bodily prosperity", the former is the poet who doubts it. Nagaraj's Allama is distinguished by his ability to convert philosophical debates into poetry and historical personalities into tattvas; he possesses kavi-pratibhe (the individual talent of a gifted poet) and does not require kavi-sankalpa (poetic ability obtained through hard work and practice). Thus, as a poet Allama could hear more than his contemporaries and he, like Shive (the female form of Shiva), commands the power to perform the higher sankalananusandhana – i.e. make connections between distinct sounds and blend them into palpable wholes. In the ears of ordinary mortals sounds enter without penetrating their minds, hence they cannot achieve sankalananusandhana. Though poets in general and to an extent possess the power of reaching sankalananusandhana, they do not hear all the whispers that arise in the world. Allama is unique in this respect. And finally, by reading those of Allama's vachanas that deal with the theme of "linga falling down", Nagaraj draws our attention to symbol-centric religious violence in history (the falling linga referring to a violent act). Since Nagaraj's Allama places Guheshwara linga beyond the horizon of time, epoch, and history, violence cannot be inflicted on linga.

A comparative study of Allama's life narratives in the fifth chapter, and practical criticism of his vachanas in the sixth chapter, are among the high points of the book. In Chapter 5, which offers a comparative analysis of Allama's life narratives through the three models (literary, spiritual, folk) mentioned earlier, Nagaraj provides deep insights into the politics of narrativisation, the institutionalisation of religion, the formation of textual communities, and the nuances of an oral epic as a counternarrative. In his estimate, while Harihara's work devotes time to the Allama–Kamalate affair, the *Shunyasampadanes* are narratives of the institutional imagination produced under the pressures of Virashaivism's dire need to develop into an institutionalised religion. Nagaraj also reads the *Shunyasampadanes* as playing a decisive role in shaping Virashaivas as a textual community. Accordingly, they try hard to reconcile their protagonist Allama (who is against any sort of institutionalisation) with the institutional demands of restoring Shivachara on earth. Here Nagaraj employs the Foucauldian idea of intellectual genealogies to trace the transformation of concepts such as ishtalinga and jangama from the twelfth century to the time of the *Shunyasampadanes*.

Another perspective, as earlier noted, is to read a folk-narrative, the *Manteswamy Kavya*, as a counternarrative to the *Shunyasampadanes*. Nagaraj suggests the character of Allama has been grafted onto Manteswamy and the two blended into a composite. A comparative analysis of the two texts sees in the *Manteswamy Kavya* a critique of Virashaivism, the city of Kalyana, and sharana figures like Basavanna and others as portrayed in the *Shunyasampadanes*. Nagaraj's sympathy is with the *Manteswamy Kavya*, for despite its literary merit, the politics of literary history keeps it outside the literary canon.

Chapter 5 is also significant in another way. Whereas cultural studies formulate rigid binaries between the Western and the non-Western, or the Semitic and the non-Semitic, by arguing the politics of cultural difference, Nagaraj draws our attention to cultural similarities and the fluid nature of religious identities. While the "revealed word" in Semitic religions forms the laws that guide the everyday social life of the community, Vedic religion has apausheya shruti, which functions as the "revealed word", and the accompanying shastras provide the laws.

In the sixth chapter, via practical criticism of thirty-eight-odd vachanas of Allama, he discusses the major themes and motifs in them. Through a historicist and intertextual reading Nagaraj explains what Allama is doing in and through these vachanas. Examining one of Allama's vachanas (no. 50), for example, he demonstrates Allama turning the social hierarchy upside down by attributing a superior position to outcastes and an inferior one to upper castes. Likewise, by discussing a vachana (no. 1004) that deals with the theme of linga falling, Nagaraj reads in it the history of symbol-centric violence in India, from the historical bloodshed of Jainas and Shaivas to the communal violence of Babri Masjid/Ramjanmabhumi. Thus, God's death, community discipline, pralaya (deluge), engagements with elders of the Shaiva tradition, and anti-Veda thought feature as themes here. Additionally, Nagaraj examines how entities like the sun, water, the goddess Lakshmi, and animals work as metaphors in Allama. He shows that, unlike conventional bedagu poets, Allama does not create metaphors to suggest unchanging essence; his portrayals of the cat, for instance, change from one vachana to another.

In the final chapter, Nagaraj attempts to problematise the writing of literary history by critically surveying premodern literary culture through the lens of Allama. His Allama is here impatient with the literary practice of poets reproducing what the tradition has set out for them to do in the manner of a flock of parrots: the possibilities and limits of poetic endeavour, he suggests, have been prescribed along sanctified templates, and the process of scribing and erasing done by canonical literary cultures which have rubbed out mystic and folk poetry. Nagaraj reconceptualises the notion of Marga-Desi, a decisively important category that scholars use while understanding premodern Indian literary culture. Desi here refers to the local, regional, non-Sanskrit, etc., and marga to transnational and cosmopolitan, mostly Sanskrit-based. In a non-essentialist and relativistic way, Nagaraj defines Marga-Desi as a dynamic process in the history of Indian intellectual culture.[128] He demonstrates how Allama is neither margi nor desi but simultaneously both. Though this is the shortest chapter, it contains the

---

[128] For Nagaraj's views on this, see YouTube, "D.R. Nagaraj Sandarshana".

seeds of brilliant thought, opening up the possibility for further work on the formation of literary cultures.

Nowhere within the book does Nagaraj specifically discuss the title of his book, leaving much room for interpretation. He takes the notion of pratibhe from Indian literary thought and extends it to the Indian darshanas (philosophical schools).[129] In Indian poetics, both the reader (receiver) and the poet (creator) are on an equal footing, they are sahridayas (sharing a temperament).[130] But the poet possesses the unique ability to create a world of his own – the talent is called pratibha, translatable into English as imagination.[131] David Shulman's *More than Real: A History of Imagination in South India* draws our attention to the theory and praxis of the imagination in premodern South Asia. One of the meanings of imagination here is the ability to visualise, to see. In this respect, Nagaraj's Allama is darshanika, a veritable seer. According to Shulman, in Sanskrit poetics pratibha also means "illumination" or, more literally, "counterradiance" – "a visionary, luminous mode".[132] This seems in line with Nagaraj's Allama, who is nothing if not luminous.

We could interpret "Allama" and "Shaiva Imagination" as Allama in the world of the Shaiva imagination, or Allama as the Shaiva imagination, Allama as extending the Shaiva imagination, or Allama illuminating the Shaiva imagination. There is also Nagaraj's description of Allama as vyaktivishista pratibhe – one whose creative talent is highly individualistic. According to Kirtinath Kurtkoti, pratibhe involves the ability to create new meanings out of words; it is not just the ability to create new experiences, but also to transform life experiences to suit one's own ends.[133] In this respect, Naga-

---

[129] Note Nagaraj's conviction that the conceptual tools of literary criticism and theory can be used to analyse and understand any other domain of knowledge. See Nagaraj, "Munnudi", p. 9.

[130] For a simple explanation of this notion, see Hiriyanna, "What to Expect of Poetry?"

[131] Rao, *Adhunika Kannada Sahitya*, p. 45.

[132] Shulman, *More than Real*, p. 81.

[133] Kurtkoti, *Da.Ra. Bendre*, pp. 38–9.

raj's Allama has a different pratibhe. He is a poet and the creator of a new literary culture as well as he who has transformed the Shaiva sect.

So much for speculation on the title; of greater import is the substance of the achievement. In this respect, what seems most notable is that, in the absence of authentic archival material on medieval culture, Nagaraj resorts to Abhinavagupta's hermeneutic method, sankalananusandhana, to build his arguments. In Abhinavagupta, "*sankalana* means effecting congruous and suitable connection of distinct sounds and *anusandhana* means blending them in a definite, meaningful whole."[134] Nagaraj understands this as a hermeneutic method of weaving the whole–part relationship. In other words, it is a method of assembling diverse ideas to build arguments, which enables Nagaraj to read a variety of texts and facilitate a dialogue between different traditions. Accordingly, Nagaraj's perspective on Allama weaves together Shaiva philosophers, including Shankara, Abhinavagupta, Sri Ramana Maharshi, Sekkizhar, Bheema Bhoi, Sri Narayana Guru, and Buddhist philosophers like Sarahapada and Nagarjuna. And, as noted, he draws connections between premodern and modern, Vedic and non-Vedic, folk and classical, Western traditions and Indian, desi and marga, all within a highly contrapuntal reading of twelfth-century vachanas. This is the work of a literary critic who expands into a desi philosopher in the process of revealing the spirit of the philosopher-poet Allama.

Nagaraj is throughout aware of the paucity of empirical contextual evidence outside the texts he is reading. Therefore he makes it clear that his readings are in the form of hypotheses and speculation; he is not formulating any grand theory of the Shaiva imagination based on solid information of a period. In other words, Nagaraj here follows – to use Dilthey's formulation – a hermeneutical procedure of imaginative recreation: i.e. the book is an attempt to understand Allama in relation to Nagaraj's own concerns.[135] A project of historical reconstruction that cannot rely on material

---

[134] See Abhinavagupta, *Para-trisika-Vivarana*, p. 70. For more on it, see *Vaidika-Avaidika*. Also see YouTube, "Bharatiya Tatvika Parampare".

[135] Anderson, *et al.*, *Philosophy and Human Sciences*, pp. 69–70.

evidence may be understood with the help of an observation by Gadamer:

> The past is an active force providing an inexhaustible supply of possibilities and not passive, inert, merely an object of contemplation. Texts, events and so on come to acquire different meanings as they become part of new hermeneutical situations; as the interpreter's horizons change with the understandings which he acquires, so he reconsiders and reviews the texts, etc., and what they mean for him.[136]

The idea is that Nagaraj's reading of Allama comes to us as what Allama means for Nagaraj. Many might object to this as a misreading of Allama. But the solidity of Nagaraj's arguments about Allama comes from his building them over and above how the Kannada imagination of past periods has read Allama. Nagaraj offers a better interpretation of Allama. This method suggests an approach to "knowledge not as a static set of correct propositions, but as a continuing search for better interpretations."[137]

Allamaprabhu mattu Shaiva Pratibhe is a book much admired but infrequently engaged with. Upon its publication it evoked two immediate responses from Kannada critics, appreciation and harsh attack.[138] In H.S. Shivaprakash's assessment, though the purport of the book is suggested and not demonstrated, disjointed insights are scattered like pearls throughout it.[139] Rahamath Tarikere, while praising the work for showing an immense possibility for the study of Kannada texts, accuses Nagaraj of an intellectual showing-off which he believes makes the book unnecessarily dense. He also faults Nagaraj for ignoring how Allama engaged with local traditions such as Arudha and Avadhuta. He is unhappy with Nagaraj for being apolitical and moving away here from his socialist beliefs – those with which he began his critical practice.[140] In his

---

[136] Ibid., p. 73.

[137] Polt, *Heidegger*, p. 41.

[138] For essays and reviews on Nagaraj's *Allamaprabhu mattu Shaiva Pratibhe*, see Byadarahalli, *Anannya Prathibheya*.

[139] Shivaprakash, "Fascination of the Difficult".

[140] Tarikere, "Shaiva Pratibhe mattu".

Avaidikate mattu Kannada Sahitya (2008), Ram.Sha. Lokapur criticises Nagaraj sharply for his reading of Allama on the grounds that Nagaraj forces his own (idiosyncratic) interpretations upon vachanas. He argues that anubhava is more important in Allama than poetic sensibility, thereby denying Nagaraj's claim for Allama as a poet-philosopher. According to Lokapur, Allama comes from Nathapantha and has nothing to do with Kashmir Shaivism or Sanskrit; rather, his worldview is shaped by Prakrit.[141]

Over my own engagement with this book I have come to see some of its limitations. Its stylistic errors and repetitions are a minor flaw as in a posthumously published text these can be dealt with editorially; a more serious problem is that many of Nagaraj's arguments are ad hoc. They are likely to have sounded better phrased if Nagaraj had had the chance to properly prepare the text for publication. However, the book's many merits outweigh these blemishes. It is an ambitious work which offers a bold reading of the texts and traditions which lie behind it, and with which it grapples. Though Nagaraj was not a Sanskritist and his understanding of Indian darshanas, especially rasa theory, was inadequate, he is skilful in his use of English translations to build his arguments. Overall, it can safely be said that no vachanakara has been understood and explored in the ways that Allama has been by Nagaraj. His reading of vachanas may at times appear far-fetched, but it provides deep insights into religion, history, literature, and culture. Nagaraj is not interested in establishing the "Truth" about Allama, knowing that would be a futile exercise; but what he largely proposes about the Allama world has considerable truth value.

Allama after Nagaraj

It has been more than two decades since the publication of Nagaraj's book. Since then the Kannada intellectual and cultural world has continued its engagement with Allama and the vachana tradi-

---

[141] Lokapur, *Avaidika mattu*. For further criticism of this book by Chalapathi and Shashikala, see Byadarahalli, *Anannya Prathibheya*.

tion in various ways. We now have an excellent work on the vachana tradition in Prithvi Datta Chandra Shobhi's doctoral dissertation, "Pre-modern Communities and Modern Histories: Narrating Vīraśaiva and Lingayat Selves", which has "destabilized the core narratives of 'canonical' Vīraśaivism by casting doubt on the historicity of the canonical vacanas."[142] No other Kannada premodern tradition has intrigued contemporary Kannadigas as much as Virashaivism and its figures. Banjagere Jayaprakash's *Anudeva Horaganavanu* created a controversy regarding Basavanna's birth and caste.[143] And, as part of S.N. Balagangadhara's research programme some studies on vachanas provoked a debate between progressive writers and the Balagangadhara research group in *Prajavani*, the leading Kannada daily, during the 2010s.[144]

Allama remains a living presence in the Karnataka cultural and intellectual world. Recently, the Allamaprabhu Peetha Kanthavara (Trust) brought out a huge collection of writings from the premodern period to contemporary times on Allama.[145] There are folk theatre productions on Allama, and a film on his life and times titled *Allama* was made recently.[146] Siddheshwara Swamiji's commentary on Allama's vachanas, two anthologies of criticism on the *Shunyasampadanes*, and Allama and his vachanas have all constituted important works of criticism on Allama.[147] Nagaraj's line of thinking in the present book has, moreover, triggered the imagination of Kannada scholars after him, leading them to engage

[142] Quoted in Ben-Herut, *Śiva's Saints*, p. 9. For more, see Chandra Shobhi, *Pre-modern Communities*.

[143] For a review of the book, see YouTube, "Was Basavanna a Brahmin or a Dalit?"

[144] This debate is available in Vividha Lekhakaru, *Vachana Sahitya Samvada*. Also see Jalki, *Vachanas as Caste Critiques*; Hegde and Shanmukha, eds, *Kottakudareyaneralariyade*.

[145] Hegde, ed., *Allama Adhyana Loka*.

[146] Nagabharana, *Allama*.

[147] Siddheshwara Swamiji, *Allamaprabhudevara Vachana-Nirvachana*; Nugadoni, ed., *Shunyasampadanegalu: Samskrutika*; Nugadoni, ed., *Allamaprabhuvina Vachanagalu: Samskritika*.

with local traditions and mystics differently. Chief among them is Vasudevamurthy who – while examining Allama not only in relation to Indian mystics such as J. Krishnamurti, Sri Ramana Maharshi, Sri Ramakrishna Paramahamsa, and Sri Aurobindo but also Kannada literary figures such as D.R. Bendre (1896–1981) and Madhurachenna (1903–1952) – challenges many of Nagaraj's arguments.[148] Nataraja Budalu, in his *Nagarjuna-Allamaprabhu: Ondu Taulanika Adhyana*, traces the influence of Buddhism on vachanakaras and undertakes a comparative analysis of the Buddhist thinker Nagarjuna and Allama.[149] Budalu's other book, *Pratyekabuddha Allamaprabhu*, contains twelve separate essays on Allama and his vachanas and tries to build an image of Allama as pratyeka Buddha – a "lone Buddha".[150] (Budalu uses the term to present Allama as a disciple without a guru.) Besides these, the post-Nagaraj period has not to my knowledge produced a theoretically ambitious work on vachanakaras comparable to Nagaraj's.

Translating Nagaraj, Translating Allama

Now for the task of the translator. Instead of proposing my theory of translation adopted in this book, I would like to narrate the way this translation progressed – for, as Nietzsche has it, all theory is autobiography (or, more accurately, autobiographical).[151] Before that, a short detour into the history of translating the vachanakaras and Allama is in order.

The translation of vachanas began with European officers in the subcontinent.[152] It continued in works by Indian scholars like Fa. Gu. Halakatti.[153] With these precedents, A.K. Ramanujan's

---

[148] Vasudevamurthy, *Pashanada Hangu.*

[149] Budalu, *Nagarjuna-Allamaprabhu.*

[150] Budalu, *PratyekaBuddha.*

[151] Quoted in Pollock, "Areas, Discipline", p. 914.

[152] For example, Rice, *A History of Kanarese.*

[153] Following Halakatti, we have attempts made by Masti Venkatesh Iyengar: see Basavanna, *Sayings*; S.S. Basavanal and K.R. Srinivasa Iyengar: see

translation of vachanas in *Speaking of Siva* (1973) was a break-through which introduced vachanas to a global audience.[154] Following Ramanujan, many attempts have been made to translate the vachanas.[155] As far as Allama is concerned, there are three exclusive works of translations.[156] More recently, there has been a surge in translating premodern Kannada texts: for example, classics like *Kavirajamarga, Vaddaradhane, Gadayuddha, Harischandra Kavya,* and *Kumaravyasa Bharatha* have been published in English translation. As part of this, two anthologies of medieval Kannada literature include English translations of the vachanas.[157] While these translations have brought literary works in Kannada to English, the present book is the translation of a theoretical and scholarly work. This presents different challenges and makes different demands on the translator. As Nagaraj shows in its first chapter, historians of Indian philosophy get it wrong when they read desi discourse (such as vachanas and Virashaiva compositions) rendered in Sanskrit because the Kannada nuances are lost in translation. He calls this the problem of translating desi. The same observation applies to

---

Basavanna, *Musings*. Then, we have the translation of a *Shunyasampadane*: see Gooluru Siddaveeranna, *Sunyasampadane*.

[154] Ramanujan, *Speaking of Siva*.

[155] For example, see Hill and Prabhu, *Naming the Nameless;* Swamy, ed., *The Sign*; Shivaprakash, *I Keep Vigil of Rudra*; in commemoration of Basava Jayanthi, the Basava Samithi, Bangalore, initiated a Multilingual Vachana Translation Project with the aim of translating vachanas into thirty Indian languages, including English and Urdu, and the anthology published in English translation as part of this initiative includes 218 vachanas by Allama. See Kalburgi, *Vachana*. Recently, the retired professor of English D.A. Shankar has translated an abridged version of *Shoonyasampadane of Shivaganaprasadi Mahadevaiah*. See Shivaganaprasadi, *Shoonyasampadane of Shivaganaprasadi*.

[156] Two anthologies provide the translation of all the available vachanas of Allama. See Allama Prabhu, *Lord of the Cave*; and Allama Prabhu, *Vacanas of Allama Prabhu*. Manu V. Devadevan's excellent translation of Allama's vachanas includes about two-fifty compositions. See Allama Prabhu, *God is Dead*.

[157] Chittampalli and M.G. Hegde, eds, *Kannada Literature*; Ramachandran and Vivek Rai, ed., *Medieval Kannada Literature*.

translating Nagaraj's Kannada work into English. I have tried to address this problem.

I began enthusiastically, without much thought and preparation, being in a hurry to complete the translation of the text because of a deadline by the New India Foundation (NIF)'s translation fellowship. I had previously translated from English into Kannada, strictly following the bilingual critic (Kannada and English) G.S. Amur's conviction that one should translate from other languages into one's own language.[158] However, this conviction weakened as I began to understand the new ecosystem of translation over the recent past. I was impressed by the translation project of the Murty Classical Library of India, especially Vanamala Viswanatha's translation of the premodern Kannada poet Raghavanka's *Harishchandra Kavya*. Above all, the NIF's translation fellowship inspired me to push myself into translating Nagaraj's Allama into English, which is my second language, picked up in an academic milieu after my matriculation. My only preparation for this task was my reading in English as an academic. Teaching translation theory and practice has helped me understand the nuances of translation.[159] This understanding has been shaped by the ideas and reflections of various critics and thinkers, including Kirtinath Kurtkoti, O.L. Nagabhushana Swamy, Sundar Sarukkai, Rita Kothari, Walter Benjamin, Jacques Derrida, Paul Ricoeur, Edith Grossman, and Gayatri Chakravorty Spivak. Though I have not yet entirely digested most of their arguments, their insights are indirectly evident in my translation.

The translation has gone through at least nine rounds, maybe more. In the first round, my concentration was on the Kannada text, getting it right and staying as close to it as possible. At this juncture I wanted to remain unfailingly faithful to the source text, even

---

[158] G.S. Amur argues that the native speaker of the target language is more likely to produce a natural and fluid translation while the second-language speaker's translations come out stiff. Quoted in Bickman, *A Literary Journey*.

[159] At Tumkur University, where I teach now, I offer a course, Translating the Word and the World.

translating the ambiguities in it. The idea was not to leave a single word untranslated. However, I was not happy with the result, and in the second round I realised that translation does not just require mastery over two languages, but also the registers of a domain knowledge.[160] So I tried to familiarise myself with the major registers or discourses that constituted the source text. In this regard I identified three main registers in Nagaraj's book – the register of medieval darshanas, primarily the Virashaiva and vachana idiom, besides other Shaiva and medieval Indian darshanas; the register of social and literary theorisation; and finally, the register of Nagaraj's distinctive writing style.

Then I began to read the vachanas in Kannada sources and English translations, scholarly books on Virashaivism, Kannada literary history, and primers on Indian darshanas. While making myself familiar with these domains of knowledge, I went back and forth making amendments to my translation. As someone who taught literary and social theory, I was at home with the theoretical proclivities of Nagaraj's writing, but his writing style posed a problem: the prose often presented ambiguities and made the meaning of various sentences imprecise or insufficiently clear to me. Translation thus became a kind of puzzle-solving activity and some of the sentences I read repeatedly to reach clarity. To familiarise myself with Nagaraj's style and vocabulary I also read his other works and consulted "Nagaraj experts" and his former students. Rearmed, I went back to my text and improved it – or so I think.

I also sought feedback from my own students and friends. Some of them, whose labour I detail in the acknowledgements, sat with me and read both Kannada and English versions. Group reading and feedback have refined my translation. My reading of Ricoeur's idea of translation as an ethical act of interlinguistic hospitality was a revelation to me. As he puts it, "[T]ranslation sets us not only intellectual work, theoretical or practical, but also an ethical problem.

---

[160] What I mean here is that each knowledge system has its own idiom – what linguists call a "register".

Bringing the reader to the author, bringing the author to the reader, at the risk of serving and of betraying two masters: this is to practice what I like to call *linguistic hospitality*."[161] Though it might sound like a big claim, I understood his notion of translation ethics as taking care of the Other, my reader.[162] While in the early drafts I stayed close to the author, in the later ones I began to shift my focus to the reader. Considering my implied readers as my guests, I concentrated on serving them. I became aware of the problem of what Bakhtin calls "addressivity";[163] Kannada words are addressed to Kannada readers, while my task was to translate them so that they addressed English readers. When the addressivity – the ecosystem of words and readers – changes, the words and their environment and their context need to change as well. Therefore I needed to change the text at several levels, from changing the syntax to inserting additional words and sentences (besides supplying necessary information in additional footnotes to address English readers). Literalism is, in any event, the bane of translation, and the best translators have often pointed out that each language has its own way of saying things, so that what is by broad consensus an admirable idiomatic equivalence must be the translator's aspiration. Apart from trying to reach this virtually impossible ideal, the work demanded independent research on my part, and I have appended (DRN) to the footnotes found in Nagaraj's original, to distinguish mine from his. Beyond that, I developed the confidence to rearrange Nagaraj's paragraphs, or to move around one or two lines within a paragraph, to delete repetitive phrases or sentences.[164]

---

[161] Ricoeur, *On Translation*, p. 23.

[162] The target audience is a problematic issue, as Walter Benjamin discusses in his "Task of a Translator", pp. 70–82. However, I read my translation from the point of view of a non-Kannada reader, even if such a reader is fictitious.

[163] According to Bakhtin, language is dialogic. He believes in language's capacity to model addressivity and dialogue. Even if our utterances are above and out of the context, they address someone; it is difficult to imagine a language without an addressee. For more, see Holquist, *Dialogism*.

[164] Apart from rearranging paragraphs within chapters, I have, in two instances, shifted paragraphs from one chapter to another, after consulting the

It remains for me to mention a couple of other ways in which I have taken a liberty with the source text. Given the assumption that discourse and sentence patterns work differently in different languages, I have tried to look for semblance, changing the patterns of sentences. For example, Kannada syntax will do without a subject, but in translation I have used the first-person pronouns "I" and "we". However, I have always kept discourse, the larger unit beyond the sentence, in mind. The individual words or sentences I use make sense as part of the paragraph, text, and discourse.

Nagaraj is known for using metaphors in critical writings, and I have retained these metaphors in my translation, except when a particular metaphor didn't suit the flow in English translation. Whenever the Kannada metaphors work in English, I have translated them. My choice is clear: I have focused on translating what has seemed apparent to me as the meaning of Nagaraj's text – a text which, though focused on a poetic figure, is itself classifiable as shastra, where meaning must prevail over emotive utterance and effusion. Likewise, in some places, when Nagaraj's manner of expression (dense language and too many ideas packed into a single sentence) came in the way of clear communication, I have intervened in the interest of comprehension and readability.

Coming to the translation of ninety-odd vachanas quoted by Nagaraj in this book, I had a good deal of material to help me. In the beginning, I used already available translations, especially my teacher C.R. Yaravintelimath's.[165] In my later editing rounds, however, I felt the need to retranslate the vachanas myself to suit Nagaraj's interpretation and analysis.

Working on this book has helped me gain a deeper understanding of the worlds I inhabit – of Kannada, the Lingayat way of life, the English-speaking world, and others. It has profoundly affected my reading of Kannada literary and cultural history, especially that relating to vachanas and Virashaivism, besides the fulfilment of

---

manuscript. Thanks to Mrs Girija Nagaraj for giving access to Nagaraj's handwritten manuscript.

[165] Allama Prabhu, *Lord of the Cave*.

engaging with premodern Kannada literary texts. My immersion in this text has changed my sensibility and deepened my understanding of the Lingayat way of life – the work has translated me too. Meanwhile, my wrestling with the English language was frustrating, fun, and revealing at the same time, and made me *dwell* in the language. It has broadened my horizons, resulting in what the Germans call Bildung, which I understand as the growth and formation of the self.[166] I can only hope reading it will be as enjoyable an experience for the reader as making it has been for me.

[166] As Ricoeur observes, what German translators such as Goethe, von Humboldt, Novalis, the Schlegel brothers, Schleiermacher, and Walter Benjamin aspired from their desire to translate was "broadening of the horizon of their own language" with Bildung. See Ricoeur, *On Translation*, p. 21.

1

A Historical Survey of Shaiva Darshanas

SURENDRANATH DASGUPTA is a big name in twentieth-century Indian philosophy. But the remarks of this eminent historian of Indian philosophy on Virashaivism left me greatly perturbed. Over a historical survey of Shaiva darshanas in his *A History of Indian Philosophy*, Dasgupta downplays the overall contribution of Virashaiva darshana.[1] Moreover, his perspective on Basavanna, the leader of the Virashaiva movement, is particularly condescending (not to mention his assessment of Virashaiva thought).[2] He perceives Basavanna, the pioneer of a revolution in the Kannada world, as an ordinary conspirator and rabble-rouser. This kind of misinterpretation is bound to seem troubling. Since Dasgupta's writings on Indian philosophy enjoy worldwide prestige, his remarks could mislead readers to a wholly unjust dismissal of Basavanna as a mere troublemaker. Here is what Dasgupta writes about Basavanna:

[1] Dasgupta, *A History of Indian Philosophy*, vol. 5.

[2] A twelfth-century Kannada vachana poet and statesman, also known as Basaveshwara, Basavarajadevaru, and Sangana Basavanna (among others). He is believed to have led the Lingayata-Virashaiva movement in the city of Kalyana during the reign of King Bijjala of the Kalachuri dynasty. For a primer on Basavanna, see Thipperudraswamy, *Basaveshwara*. For a historical biography of Basavanna, see Desai, *Basavesvara and His Times*.

So far, our examination has not proved very fruitful in discovering the actual contribution to Vīra-śaiva philosophy or thought or even the practice of *ṣaṭ-sthala* or *liṅga-dharaṇa,* made by Basava. He must have imparted a good deal of emotional enthusiasm to inspire the Śaivas of different types who came into contact with him, either through religious fervour or for his financial or another kind of patronage. It seems from the *Basava Purāṇa* that his financial assistance to the devotees of Śiva was of rather indiscriminate character. His money was poured on Śaivas like showers of rain. This probably made him the most powerful patron of the Śaivas of that time, with the choicest of whom he founded a learned assembly where religious problems were discussed in a living manner, and he presided over the meetings.[3]

Why does Dasgupta write so? There is no point in dismissing his interpretation as simple petty prejudice. Instead, if we begin to think a little deeper about it, a great problem in understanding Indian culture and darshanas in the twentieth century seems identifiable. I call this the problem of translating "desi".[4] To explain it in the jargon of contemporary cultural politics in India, the problem arises when a religio-philosophical movement of the many (bahujan) is translated into the language of the elite (mahajan).[5] Several of India's Desi dissenting religious movements, including the twelfth-century Virashaiva movement, happen to have been recorded in the regional languages (bhashas), and, when accessed in Sanskrit translation, are likely to be misunderstood. Before we understand this problem of translation, let me explain my arguments about Desi dissenting traditions in plain language.

---

[3] Dasgupta, *A History of Indian Philosophy,* vol. 5, pp. 45–6.

[4] Desi and Marga are two concepts that scholars use in order to make sense of two traditions, the local and the cosmopolitan. Desi here refers to the local, regional, non-Sanskrit, etc. In a non-essentialist but relativistic way, Nagaraj defines Marga–Desi as a dynamic process in the history of Indian intellectual culture. For more, see YouTube, "D.R. Nagaraj Sandarshana".

[5] "Bahujan" means literally "many people"; here it connotes non-elite, non-Vedic, and non-Sanskrit people. "Mahajan" is literally "great people", here connoting elite, Vedic, and Sanskrit sections of the people.

The Desi dissent against a tradition's originary matrix (mula-matruke) is often launched by well-defined movements or by individual mystics (anubhavis) who speak in the bhashas.[6] Of the former, the Mahimadharma of Odisha and the Kannada Virashaiva movement serve as good examples; and for the latter, Kabir, Saraha-pada, and Allama Prabhu – the centre of discussion in this book.[7] It is important to understand that the tradition is not composed as a binary comprising an originary matrix and its opposite, the dissenting emanation; these movements and individuals represent distinct forms of Desi without being entirely opposed to their originary matrix. Therefore, there is a need for theoretical discussion on the nature of the relationship between the originary matrix and the Desi rebellions emerging against it. To theorise this, I use the Vachana movement as my basis.

We cannot say that Desi movements express themselves entirely differently from the originary matrix. In their use of jargon and philosophical tools, Desi movements share surprising similarities with the originary matrix, although they are essentially different from it. This curious dissent of Desi traditions is unique in the cultural history of India. It is interesting to note that the Desi movements declare themselves to be the true originary matrix, and by doing so try to seek greater validation. They try to gain immediate authenticity by projecting their newness and subversion (vidroha) as manifestations of the originary matrix – which they see as theirs.[8] How-

[6] "Mulamatruke" means the source from which the rebellious branch has emerged. In the religious domain, Virashaivism did not arise suddenly from nowhere, it emerged from the Shaiva tradition, which is its mulamatruke. In ch. 5 Nagaraj uses the word almost as a synonym of the notion of tradition. Generally, contemporary editors of vachanas use mulamatruke to mean the source from which vachanas are used in their versions. Mulamatruke may be translated as "root paradigm", "root matrix", "proto-tradition", and "originary matrix". I have used the last.

[7] Kabir: fifteenth-century mystic poet; Sarahapada: eighth-century Buddhist, one of the founders of Vajrayana Buddhism.

[8] "Vidroha", literally translated as betrayal, an important concept Nagaraj uses in his later phase as a postcolonial critic, involves the idea of "opposing and

ever, over time these dissenting Desi movements are gradually absorbed into the very fabric of the traditional originary matrix which they have tried to subvert and protest against. It wouldn't be wrong to call this phenomenon a fundamental principle following which Indian culture has evolved. The history of the Pancharatra darshana in the Vaishnava tradition attests to this,[9] and we see that Yamunacharya puts forward the same argument in his *Agama Pramanyam*.[10]

The Desi rebellion breaks out from the very womb of the originary matrix – because it perceives from its experience that the originary matrix has become weakened and distorted over a period of time. This is a direct rebellion against the very elders of the originary matrix, and the idea of a mutiny against elders resurfaces time and again in Allama's vachanas. Apparently, the rebellion of this new order replicates the jargon of the originary matrix; however, this is only an outward similarity. Internally there is subversion – a massive transformation is evident deep inside the rebellion. The study of the relationship between outward similarity and internal subversion is one of the many complicated issues of Indian culture. Although there are similarities in the outward idiom of the Virashaiva movement with the rest of the Shaiva sects, the essence of subversion remains outside their ambit.

The history of Indian philosophical and religious revolts is indeed a history of the relationship between the above-mentioned apparent similarities and internal subversions. And the work of prominent acharyas (scholarly gurus) in Indian culture was to try assimilating these subversive endeavours of Desi rebellion into the

---

hiding while being with the other." Nagaraj uses it in the sense of subversion and protest, a sort of hidden resistance and rebellion. See Tharakeshwar, "D.R. Nagaraj mattu Vasahatottara Chintane", pp. 114–30.

[9] Pancharatra darshana was a forerunner of Vaishnavism, the worship of Vishnu. The doctrine was systematised by Shandilya. See Britannica, "Pancharatra". For more, see Schrader, *Introduction to the Pañcaratra*.

[10] Yamunacharya, *Agama Pramanyam*. Yamunacharya is a tenth-century Vaishnava saint from present-day Madurai who inspired Ramanujacharya.

originary matrix.[11] In fact, it is deeply rooted in the minds of such acharyas that the Desi rebellions can and should remain safe within the originary matrix. They seem to believe that the originary matrix will preserve the rebellion like salt preserving fish from rotting. I call this method sankalananusandhana, a word and concept introduced by Acharya Abhinavagupta.[12] In fact, in the history of the Indian darshanas it was Abhinavagupta who perfected the method of sankalananusandhana.

Shaiva tantric modes, which fell outside the orthodox traditions, are some of the most interesting demonstrations of subversion (vidroha) in the history of Indian philosophy.[13] In its social stance, spiritual methods, and modes of expression Shaiva tantrism differs completely from Vedic traditionalism. But in his *Tantraloka*, Abhinavagupta succeeded in making Shaiva tantrism a practice acceptable to the Vedic tradition.[14] However, while accommodating the Desi rebellions and differences, the structure and nature of the originary matrix also undergo a change. My main proposition is therefore that over the course of history the nature of the traditional originary matrix keeps changing. This understanding steers us clear of essentialist and absolutist thinking. Shaiva tantrism, which was the victim of scepticism and epistemic violence – often even physi-

[11] The general meaning of "acharya" in Indian intellectual tradition refers to an expert teacher, a learned pandit. There is a tradition of acharyas in Hinduism. For more, see Joshi and Hegde, *Kumarilabhatta*, pp. 44–5.

[12] Nagaraj uses this term differently in the subsequent chapters. He understands it as a hermeneutic method of weaving the whole–part relationship – in other words, as a method of editing and compiling to arrive at truth. Here what Nagaraj means is the negotiation between the originary matrix and the rebellion. In Abhinavagupta, "sankalana" means effecting a harmonious connection of distinct sounds, and "anusandhana" means blending them in a definite, meaningful whole. See Abhinavagupta, *A Trident of Wisdom*, p. 70. For more on sankalananusandhana by Nagaraj, see *Vaidika-Avaidika Darshana*. Also, YouTube, "Bharatiya Tatvika Parampare".

[13] Shaiva tantric modes are, for example, the Kashmiri Shaiva sects, Kapalikas, Kalamukhas, Nathas, and Siddhas (among others).

[14] Abhinavagupta, *Sri Tantraloka and Other Works*.

cal violence – from the orthodox, came to be accepted as part of the originary matrix, in this case the Vedic tradition, after Acharya Abhinavagupta. Thus, both the originary matrix and the rebellion underwent an intense transformation. In this process, it is hard to say whether the originary matrix grew more sensitive and humane or whether the Desi subversion itself became conservative in order to stabilise itself.

The *Shunyasampadanes*, which were composed during the fifteenth and sixteenth centuries, also adopted the method of negotiation termed sankalananusandhana.[15] They sought to assimilate Allama's subversion, protest, and innovation with the originary Shaiva matrix. It is also worth noting that the twelfth-century Virashaiva movement, which shaped its rebellion against the originary matrix of Shaiva tradition, itself became an originary matrix through the *Shunyasampadanes*. That is to say, by then the Shaiva tradition was transforming itself into a hall of mirrors where the elements in the originary matrix and Desi rebellions were reflected in one another. Since I discuss this amazing process in detail in Chapter 5, I will not probe it here.

Let us return to Dasgupta's problem. The root of his misconception lies in his use of Sanskrit texts as a source to understand the

---

[15] *Shunyasampadanes*: A collection of Virashaiva verses, vachanas, and dialogues. By compiling various vachanas in dialogic form a narrative of sharanas is woven wherein Allama is the protagonist. They are the life narratives of Allama and other sharanas. The literal meaning of "shunyasampadane" is "attaining void". Four versions of the *Shunyasampadanes* are available, composed by Shivaganaprasadi Mahadevaiah, Halegeyarya, Gummalapurada Siddhalingadevara, and Sri Guluru Siddhaveerannodayara. (For the Kannada text, I have retained the spelling "Guluru. Translated into English, it has been spelt "Gooluru". My use of the two spellings thus depends on the text to which I am referring. For details of the texts, see the Bibliography.) These are believed to have been composed between the fifteenth and early sixteenth centuries. Of these, only Sri Guluru Siddhaveerannodayara's, *Sunyasampadane*, vols 1 to 5. For an abridged version of the *Shunyasampadane* in English, see Shivaganaprasadi, *Shoonyasampadane*. For institutionalisation, context, composition, and content of the *Shunyasampadanes*, see Michael, *The Origins of Vīraśaiva Sects*.

nature of the Virashaiva darshana. When a revolution articulated in Kannada is accessed in Sanskrit translation, its meaning alters radically. Darshanic revolutions are often entangled within the idiosyncrasies of a particular language, and Virashaivism's Kannada articulation is a fine example of this. What appears rough, rugged, bitter, and severe in the Kannada of the Virashaiva movement tends to disappear when translated into Sanskrit. This is the risk involved in translating desi, the danger that lies in transforming the bahujan language into that of the mahajan. All this must be understood against the backdrop of an awareness that in Indian culture most rebellions and breakaways aspire to equate themselves with the originary matrix. Which is to say that the ultimate justification of Virashaiva darshana must be seen within the broader Shaiva cultural framework.

Of course, I am deliberately pushing Virashaiva darshana's historical time into a broader theoretical space. Basing myself on historical logic, I am not rejecting the argument that, theoretically, Kannada Virashaiva darshana came out of the womb of the Sanskrit-based darshana prevalent before the twelfth century. I am only stressing the need for attention to a peculiar process of transformation: when a Sanskrit concept from the originary matrix enters the Kannada world it assumes different attributes and tones. For instance, when a Sanskrit concept such as shunya (the void) is translated into Kannada as bayalu (literally, an open space), mere knowledge of Sanskrit will not suffice to understand the transformation.[16] Likewise, this statement holds when a Kannada concept is expressed in Sanskrit. Thus, Dasgupta's case illustrates what happens when one who has read Sanskrit texts on Shaivism tries to understand Kannada's Vachana revolution, i.e. Virashaivism, through the lens of Sanskrit. What is most annoying is Dasgupta's observation that "there is hardly anything of value from the philosophical point of

---

[16] Bayalu: an important concept in the vachanas, especially those by Allama Prabhu, means plain land, an open place, a spaceless place, formlessness, a void (akin to shunya), etc. This term appears in 242 vachanas. See Vachana Sanchaya.

view in Dravidian literature which is unobtainable through Sanskrit."[17]

It is not my intention here to argue that Dasgupta's interpretation is faulty or inadequate. On the contrary, I would like to demonstrate how a linguistic universe embeds a highly complex cultural process. When Dasgupta perceived the Kannada revolution through his Sanskrit lens, the Virashaiva movement appeared inferior and plain, losing its distinctiveness and seeming to be a simple translation of Sanskrit Shaiva philosophy. Such misinterpretation is not limited to Sanskritists lacking knowledge of Kannada; it has surfaced repeatedly even within the Kannada Virashaiva movement. The tendency to view the movement as part of the traditional originary matrix has occurred regularly over the past four hundred years. Of this the Sankalanayuga of Virashaiva literature is early proof.[18]

Let me present my thoughts in the form of maxims on what happens to Kannada Virashaiva philosophy when understood through the Sanskrit Shaiva lens. Here, I proceed not only with Dasgupta's thoughts but also keep in mind the views of another prominent Sanskritist, Pandit Gopinath Kaviraj.[19] (It is important to note, though, that Kaviraj has grasped the philosophy of Virashaivism with greater competence and nuance than Dasgupta.)

1. The Sanskrit Shaiva philosophy perceives Virashaivism as a unified school, erasing significant philosophical differences among Basava, Allama, Siddharama, and Akkamahadevi.[20] Consequently, a great injustice is done to Allama Prabhu. How the broad and abstract principles of darshanas such as Virashaivism undergo subtle transformations within the intellectual forge of a unique thinker such as Allama remains outside

---

[17] Dasgupta, *A History of Indian Philosophy*, vol. 5, p. 149 (DRN).

[18] Nagaraj seems to be referring here to the age of compiling vachanas in *Shunyasampadanes* during the fifteenth and sixteenth centuries of the Vijayanagara Empire.

[19] A twentieth-century Sanskrit scholar, Indologist, and philosopher.

[20] Other saint-poets in the vachana tradition of the twelfth century. For more, see Veerashaiva. Also see Vachana Sanchaya.

such an understanding. When the relationship between the Sanskrit originary matrix and Kannada Desi's unique transformation slips beyond our grasp, twelfth-century Virashaivism loses its significance. Whereas, in fact, the twelfth century should figure as a focal point in the historical analysis of the Virashaiva religion, not just tangentially. But all these nuances disappear when the Virashaiva movement is seen as a unified school.

2. When seen through Sanskrit texts, the structural and creative dynamism of Kannada authors disappears completely. In such cases, only the fixity of philosophical concepts remains, while what is faded out is the surge of philosophical excitement that emerges from the use of poetic ambiguity in vachanakaras like Allama Prabhu. In his vachanas, Allama forges conceptual metaphors (tattva-rupaka) by dissolving the distinction between philosophy and metaphor.[21] However, the historian of Indian philosophy will not be able to grasp the emergence of conceptual metaphors. If we do not notice the process of philosophy undergoing change through a reformulation as poetic composition, then the history of darshana becomes somewhat barren. (I must record here that my belief in the significance of this unique process of transformation has given me, a poetry student, the confidence to write about the poet-philosopher Allama.[22])

Both these points need to be discussed more subtly in the context of the Vachana movement. If analysed against the backdrop of the Sanskrit darshana tradition, Virashaivism appears to be an expression of Shakti Vishishtadvaita.[23] However, it is not apparent that

[21] As Nagaraj further argues, Allama used poetry or the metaphoric mode to do philosophy. Like a philosopher, Allama engages with concepts, but uses metaphors and images to produce conceptual meaning.

[22] The unique process of transformation to which Nagaraj refers is philosophy undergoing change in the course of its reformulation as poetic creation.

[23] Shakti Vishishtadvaita (non-dualism with the distinction of Shakti) is one of the Shaiva doctrines which proposes non-duality in the relationship

all the vachanakaras are in agreement with this school of thought. One can agree that, within the strict terms of philosophical analysis, the Vachana movement may be explained from the framework of Shakti Vishishtadvaita. This might be true in relation to Sanskrit philosophical texts, but when we take vachanas into consideration, this does not hold good.

While writing the history of Indian philosophy in the twentieth century, the idea of a unified Indian darshana has become a key theoretical imperative. Thus, across this century, an attempt to subsume different philosophical voices, segments, and separate existences into one broad unified framework can be noticed in major historical surveys and documentations of these darshanas. Consciously or unconsciously, this theoretical framework, influened by the political consciousness of nationalism, has affected prominent thinkers and historians in their documentation of Indian philosophy. This was not the case in earlier periods. Back then in India, different pressures were at work when compiling darshanas, which happened from the point of view of a particular branch of philosophy.[24] In the twentieth century, however, the decisive pressure on the process of such documentation has been the theoretical framework of nationalism. Consequently, the modern belief has been to perceive all darshanas as "Indian" – a singular grand unity despite their myriad differences. Devoid of a sense of history, this belief has considered a grand unity as more or less a natural state. This is how cultural unification and darshanic unification came to be seen as identical. As a result, darshanic activities in Sanskrit, Prakrit, and the desi languages also came to be understood as all the same. Therefore,

---

between the individual soul and the supreme being (para-Shiva), and shakti is the primordial power of life and expression subsisting in them. The soul derives its existence from the supreme being and ultimately coalesces into him, hence the term Advaya (non-dual). However, the essence of shakti varies between the supreme being and the individual soul. Therefore, the system of philosophy is known as Shakti Vishishtadvaita. See Chakravarti, *Shakti-Vishishtadvaita*, pp. 2–3.

[24] For example, Madhava Acharya's *The Sarva Darsana Samgraha*.

no documentation of darshanas in the twentieth century has bothered to recognise the existence of other voices – those that are different from mahajan discourse.

The major problem with this unifying approach is the creation of larger-than-life personalities within darshanas. Especially in Vedanta philosophy, there developed a tendency to see everything within the framework of a trio of gurus (acharyatraya).[25] For instance, at every hint of Advaya or Advaita, a comparative perspective invoking Shankaracharya began to predominate such studies. This kind of modern reading does great injustice to *sui generis* philosophers like Sarahapada and Allama.[26]

Allama produces his philosophy with the awareness that he is very much part of the tradition and yet distinct from it. He is also different from Shankara, and they part company mainly in two domains. The first has to do with their conceptions of reality and liberation (mukti), and the second is their differences concerning social philosophy. An even more striking difference is the way Allama dramatically engages with the notion of maye (illusion). The manner in which he metaphorises and dramatises everything is worthy of specific discussion.

At this juncture, let me draw your attention to an important aspect. Several Advayavadis (non-dualists) who are different from Shankara are, like Allama, geniuses in their use of metaphors.[27] In particular, the non-Brahmin Advayavadis use metaphorical constructions in their philosophic formulations. Moreover, it must be emphasised that they are all socially progressive. For now, we can

[25] Shankara, Madhva, and Ramanuja – the three prominent acharyas representing the three prominent streams in Indian darshanas: Advaita, Dvaita, and Vishishtadvaita.

[26] Also known as Saraha, Sarahapada is one of the eighty-four Siddhas of the Sahajayana School in Buddhism. See Guenther, ed., *The Royal Song of Saraha*. For a Kannada translation of Sarahapada, see Budalu, *Sarahapada*.

[27] Scholars make a distinction between Advaita and Advaya. Advaita believes in uniting the two parts of chaitanya (spirit), while Advaya believes that there are no two parts – there is no distinction at all. See Tarikere, *Karnataka Gurupantha*, p. 50.

continue this discussion by taking up the examples of Bhima Bhoi of Odisha and Sri Narayana Guru of Kerala.[28]

Bhima Bhoi's *Nirveda Sadhana* is a unique work that explores Nirguna Brahmavada through historical images.[29] For Shankara, history is not a decisive factor in darshana. Therefore, he does not place his philosophical concepts in the process of historical evolution, and there is no construction of a historical personality or figure in any of his works. However, in his commentary on the *Brahma Sutra*,[30] historical personalities do appear – but merely as names representing philosophical positions. On the other hand, non-Brahmin Advayavadis who use the metaphoric mode can craft narratives and create unique characters.

A subtler classification may be attempted between the Advaya-vadis, who are masters of metaphor, and the classical Advaitins: the former can be regarded as Desi-Advayavadis and the latter as Marga-Advaitins. This classification of mine is not just content with suggesting differences in their methods of philosophising. It also sheds light on the close relationship between their methods and the way they deal with power structures in society. The scope of Desi-Advayavadi activity is largely local. Hence, the geo-cultural environment around its proponents provides metaphors for their philosophical poetry. Moreover, their perspective on social norms is more open than that of the conservative sanatanis (Marga-Advaitins). If we are to make a list of Desi-Advayavadis in and around Karnataka, the following names appear: Shishunala Sharif, Kaivara Naraya-

[28] Bhima Bhoi (1850–1895), Odia poet, saint, mystic, and social reformer, was a staunch follower of Mahima dharma. See Mahapatra, *Bhima Bhoi*. Sri Narayana Guru (1856–1928), spiritual leader and social reformer from Kerala, fought against caste practices. See Guru, *The Word of the Guru*.

[29] See Bhima Bhoi, *Nirveda Sadhana*. Brahman (the concept of the Supreme Truth/Ultimate Reality) in Hindusim is described as saguna (iconic) or nirguna (aniconic). The former refers to Brahman as having form and content, which may vary from time to time, and the latter refers to Brahman as having no attributes, beyond time and space.

[30] Sankaracarya, *Brahma Sutra Bhasya*. Also see Radhakrishnan, *The Brahma Sutra*.

nappa, Veerabhramendra, and the avadhutas mentioned in *Kavicharite*.[31] Religious institutions such as the Advayavadi mathas and ashramas that were locally vibrant and active also come within this orbit. And this tradition is comparatively more contemptuous of prevailing power structures. The Marga-Advaitins' philosophy straddles cosmopolitan concerns. However, at the social level they tend to support sanatana conservative values and do not endorse the violation of social values in the religious sphere. Spiritual acceptance among them rests solely on the endorsement of written texts and classical knowledge systems.

Since most Desi-Advayavadis are from non-Brahminical communities, there is a tendency to characterise this school of thought as the non-Brahminical Advayavadi school. However, we must resist this tendency because such a social discourse might fall prey to oversimplification and naive anti-Brahminism. Moreover, this tradition has several rebellious Brahmins, like Govinda Bhatta, the guru of Shishunala Sharif.[32]

Coming back to our discussion of the Desi-Advayavadi method:

[31] Known as a santa (saint), Shishunala Sharif (1819–1889) was a disciple of an unconventional Smartha Brahmin guru, Govinda Bhatta. Sharif was from Shishuvinahala, a village in present-day Haveri District of the Dharwad region in North Karnataka. He is known for his tattva padas (philosophical songs), which are imbued with riddles. As a philosophical songster he is very popular in Kannada folklore. For his life narrative, see Nagabharana, *Santa Shishunala Sharif*.

Kaivara Narayanappa: a bilingual tattvapadakara who wrote philosophical songs both in Kannada and Telugu during the eighteenth century.

Veerabhramendra: a well-known Telugu poet who mainly wrote *kalajnana* (a genre of poem which predicts the future).

Avadhuta: a tradition of renouncers who lead a blissful life, unbothered by the material world. See Shri Purohit, *Avadhoota Gita*. Also see Wadiyar, *Avadhuta*. *Kavicharite*: as the title (literally: "history of poets") suggests, this is a substantial historical account of Kannada writers since the beginning of Kannada literature. See Narasimhacharya, *Karnataka-Kavi*, 3 vols.

[32] Guru Govinda Bhatta (nineteenth century), a Smartha Brahmin teacher, scholar, and worshipper of Goddess Shakti, belonged to a tantric cult. Shishunala Sharif was one of his disciples.

they are storytellers. Bhima Bhoi's *Nirveda Sadhana* is a work that transforms philosophical abstraction into the concreteness of narrative poetry. Bhima Bhoi's social self forms the backdrop of this work. Instead of using logic, *Nirveda Sadhana* employs a new mode of composition — weaving together dramatic events and mythical imagination — to foster nuanced philosophical understanding. More importantly, Bhima Bhoi proposed a new chaturvarna theory quite different from Shankara's. Instead of brahmana, kshatriya, vaishya, and shudra, he formulated a new conception of varna comprising shanti (peace), daya (compassion), kshama (forgiveness), shila (virtuous character), and dharma (ethics). See the following lines from *Nirveda Sadhana:*

> Shanti (peace) to Brahma's left
> Above it daya (compassion)
> At the back kshama (mercy)
> Shila (virtuous character) in Brahma's heart
> Dharma (ethical practice) on Brahma's face
> There is bliss where all these are present
> And that is Brahma's abode
> And the eternal glory of day and night.[33]

There is a more profound and complex background to the metaphoric model of Desi-Advayavadis. When the metaphorical mode appears in place of philosophical abstraction, it becomes coterminous with a historical narrative. For instance, the yogic revolution in *Nirveda Sadhana* becomes a historical and political revolution as

---

[33] The translation of these lines is mine. *Daaru Prathima Na Poojibe* (We shall not worship the wooden image), the original Odia text, was read out in English by Fanindam Deo and translated into Kannada by G. Rajashekhara in Ninasam, Heggodu. See Dube, *et al., Daaru Prathima*, p. 120. The nineteenth-century Mahima Dharma of Odisha, inspired by Bheema Bhoi's *Nirveda Sadhana*, did not believe in idol worship and shunned the worship of Jagannath of the Puri temple. In 1881 the followers of Mahima Dharma set fire to the three idols in the Puri temple. Their clarion call was "We shall not worship the wooden image". This monograph studies the socio-religious shift in Odisha during the nineteenth century.

well. Here, a spiritual experience reveals itself through political and historical images. In other words, the Desi-Advayavadi engagement with metaphor is an engagement with history. Their working with images becomes an attempt to understand worldly relations by liberating themselves from the abstract metaphysical. Here, the fear of losing the density of philosophical abstraction is quite reasonable. Therefore, wherever the metaphorical mode is used instead of the traditional philosophical method, modern historians of philosophy tend to lose interest in it.

The Desi-Advayavadi attempt to capture worldly truth in concrete form through the metaphorical mode, and the method of turning abstract philosophical concepts into images, are dear to their heart. As a result, many of these thinkers are perceived as poets, unworthy of serious philosophical discussion. The fifteenth-century mystic poet Kabir belongs to this tribe. Sri Narayana Guru, one of the chief non-Brahmin Advayavadis, uses the metaphorical mode attentively alongside the traditional philosophical mode: Narayana Guru's composition "Kundalini Pattu" (The Kundalini Snake Song) can be discussed as an illustration of this point.[34]

"Kundalini Pattu", which begins with "Adu pambe nalidadu pambe" (Dance, O snake, watch the frenzied play),[35] uses details from Shiva's puranic personality.[36] The poem progresses by equating the awakening of kundalini in yogashastra with thandava nritya — the dance of Nataraja in purana. Narayana Guru uses a poet's freedom to tackle the problems that arise when yogashastra and puranic narrative modes are integrated. To explain this: in the poem, Shiva's jate (uncombed knots of hair), mrugacharma (the animal skin he wears), the Himalaya (his habitat), and the snake that accompanies him are all real for Narayana Guru's poetic self. But for the Advayavadi philosopher in him, this body itself is unreal. Therefore, in his composition Narayana Guru uses the creative liberty that comes with

[34] For an English translation, see Narayana Guru, "Song of the Kundalini", pp. 69–72.

[35] Ibid., p. 71.

[36] Guru, *Life and Teachings of Narayana Guru* (DRN).

poetry to blend the transactional truth of material reality with that of absolute philosophical truth.

Coming back to Marga-Advaitins, the only poetic mode available to Shankara was stuti kavya (poetic eulogy). Therefore, the power of Shankara's imagination uses the lyrical elegance and melodiousness of language in the poetic mode, but not dramatic and narrative alternatives. By generalising this point, I would like to formulate a proposition. The dominant mode of mahajan marga – the Shankara marga – revolves only around traditional anvikshikiya marga (critical reasoning) and stuti kavya. The statement can be generalised to the extent that even though there is a mutual disagreement about aims and aspirations among darshaniks from the various sects – such as Shankara, Nagarjuna, Acharya Kundakunda, or Ishwara Krishna – there is a surprising similarity in their use of critical reasoning and eulogy.

By contrast, given their organic relationship with the colloquial language, the Desi-Advayavadis' philosophical mode imbibes its cadence and playfulness. In such Desi-Advayavadi cases, the distinctions between philosophy and poetry, between practical and metaphysical truth, dissolve. Likewise, the difference between anvikshikiya and stuti disappears. Since poetic techniques and methods function significantly here, poetry students with the required scholarship can enter this complex world of philosophy without difficulty.

We need to place on record another unique quality of Desi-Advayavadis. For Shankaracharya and others, worldly authority is not a separate philosophical concern. They – and here you may also include Madhusudana Sarasvati – take a conservative stance on caste and the varnashrama system; they often defend caste. In particular, Madhusudana Sarasvati (1540–1640), who wrote *Advaita Siddhi*, shows himself as a fierce defender of the caste system.[37] But from Allama to Bhima Bhoi and Kuvempu, the non-Brahmin Adva-

---

[37] *Advaita Siddhi:* a critique of Vyasatirtha's *Nyayamruta* that criticised the Advaita philosophy. Madhusudana is a prominent name in the great debate between Dvaita and Advaita schools of Vedanta.

yavadis have taken a clear-cut rebellious stance vis-à-vis worldly authority.[38] Bhima Bhoi, for example, dreams of a heaven for Shudras: "The royal umbrella and chowrie of innumerable kings collapse into an earth-chasm."[39] For the philosophers of this group, worldly power is a reality. While taking a philosophical stance, they also examine a social reality that aligns with it. Allama, for example, ridicules elders who serve the gilded treasures of worldly authority as gatekeepers.[40]

In this respect, there is no doubt that Acharya Shankara had severe disagreements with the Mimamsakas.[41] In his bhasya (commentary) on the *Brahma Sutras*, he vehemently condemns their spiritual worldview. In fact, several progressive elements became apparent over the course of his dissent with them, even if, when examined closely, many contradictions emerge in his relationship with the Mimamsakas. When it comes to concrete social issues and values, Shankara embraces positions acceptable to them. He is at home with the beliefs, value systems, and vision of history created by the Brahmin Mimamsakas. Thus, conflict with the Mimamsakas in relation to spiritual issues, and agreement with them in relation to social reality, is a unique feature of Shankara Advaita.

For historians of Indian philosophy, these contradictions and anomalies hardly appear to be a significant problem. Even the surprising discord among Advayavadis themselves has yet to appear as a problem for these scholars. It is unfortunate that the enormous

---

[38] Kuvempu: a major twentieth-century Kannada writer of the Navodaya period, Jnanpith award winner, and an early author from a Shudra community in Karnataka. For a primer on Kuvempu (K.V. Puttappa), see Prabhushankara, *Rastrakavi*. For the Kannada version, see Prabhushankar, *Kuvempu*.

[39] One of the key themes of the Lingayat revolution too was challenging the divinity of kings.

[40] For the full vachana, see vachana no. 1636 in Allama Prabhu, *Lord of the Cave*. About fifty-five vachanas by Allama refer to "elders", such references running to about sixty-eight in number. See Vachana Sanchaya. Chapter 6 of this book includes a section on Allama's critique of the elders.

[41] The followers of Jaimini's *Purva Mimamsa* are called Mimamsakas. Badarayana wrote the *Uttara Mimamsa* and its followers are called vedantins.

gulf between Shankara's revolutionary theories and his conservative position, "apashudradhikarana", in his bhasya on the *Brahma Sutras* has not attracted the attention of our scholars.[42] Among modern philosophers, Swami Vivekananda recognised this contradiction, thanks to his social philosophy. However, even though he noticed minute and palpable disparities in Shankara Advaita philosophy, he neither paid them special attention nor analysed them in depth.

There is another major difficulty for traditional philosophers in understanding the Desi-Advayavadi mode of expression – their translating concepts into metaphors. This may be regarded as an important dimension of the problem of "internal philosophic translation" which I discussed earlier. It should also be observed here that this process – translating concepts into metaphors – happens when Desi-Advayavadis enter into a dialogue with an opponent (purva paksha). In his analysis of the Natha tradition, Hazariprasad Dwivedi explains that this idea of the dialogic form of poetry also applies to Gorakhnath,[43] and to other yogi-poets in the Apabhramsha tradition.[44]

This does not mean that conceptual metaphors are not used in the history of Indian philosophy. When a darshanic tradition at-

[42] Apashudradhikarana involves the exclusion of Shudras from brahmavidya. According to Shankara, Madhva, Vallabh, etc., the Shudra (by caste) is not qualified to undertake brahmavidya. In his commentary on the *Brahma Sutras* (a work ascribed to the sage Badarayana, comprising sutras discussing the nature of the universe and human society), Shankaracharya denies to Shudras the right to study the Vedas (Chapter 1, Section 3, Topic 9, sutras 34 to 38). Topic 9 is titled apashudradhikarana. See Swami Vireswarananda, *Brahma Sutras*, pp. 121–5. Ramanuja is said to have differed in this respect, and famously threw open the doors of knowledge to all castes. See Haq, *The Shudra*.

[43] Gorakhnath: an eleventh-century yogi who belongs to the Natha tradition. He is associated with Hathayoga (strenuous yoga practice). There are Gorakhnath temples, especially in Maharashtra and Odisha. Gorakhnath mandir in Gorakhpur, Uttar Pradesh, and mathas of the Natha tradition at several places in India have kept this tradition alive.

[44] Source not clear in the source text. It might be Dibedi, *Nath-Sampradaya*. However, the source text cites Dwivedi, *Granthavali*, p. 132 (DRN).

tains plurality, a common metaphoric universe naturally emerges. I call this the "primary metaphoric level". Images like the kundalinisarpa (snake) or the hamsa (swan) are of this kind. At this level, a philosopher or yogi-poet does not enjoy much freedom, except the possibility of minor changes.[45] Therefore, we hardly face difficulties when we encounter the primary metaphoric level in poetic compositions by philosophers.

However, we must be highly cautious in relation to the secondary metaphoric level, which I define as the "level of autonomous imagination". At this level, the philosopher achieves the autonomy of the poet by transcending the methods and boundaries of philosophy. Thus, the rich excitement of the poet's imagination prevails over the rigorous and exacting methods of a philosopher. The only rule for this imagination is that there are no natural rules to follow — what Mammata calls niyatikruta niyamarahitya.[46] By becoming a poet, the philosopher brings sacred and mysterious entities to the level of the ordinary.

We may formulate this combination of philosophy and poetry as an issue of denseness-lightness (ghana-laghu). In the rigid path of traditional philosophy, supreme priority is given to ghana, which refers to the dense concepts refined by philosophical rigour. This is one of the reasons why philosophical readings have become a serious business. Laghu here is to be understood as a figurative language of poetic compositions. However, the mutual attraction between ghana and laghu is as seductive as a secret romance. The metaphoric quality of language could be the reason for this. If in language we try to retain pure logic, purging it of images and metaphors, the attempt itself becomes an image or a metaphor; unconsciously, logic becomes an image or metaphor. Nevertheless, philosophy tries to

[45] Nagaraj is probably referring here to the freedom to use and shape new metaphors.

[46] See Mammata, *Kavyaprakasha*, p. 1. In an article on this notion, K.V. Puttappa (i.e. Kuvempu) argues that poetic creations follow certain conventions of the world and at the same time transcend them. See Puttappa, "Kavinirmitiyalli Niyatikruta Niyamarahitya". This notion appears again in ch. 4.

retain its serious and contemplative nature, using laghu as a subordinate-level image or illustration. Thus, a specific relationship between laghu and ghana is formed in Indian philosophical and logical discourses.

In the serious world of Indian darshana and logic, several laghu images float around without significance. However, at times they gain such a dramatic freedom that the wagging tail of laghu begins to shake the animal called ghana. A few laghu metaphors – such as a pot or container, the commoner named Devadatta, and a cow – circulate at different levels in logic and philosophy.[47] We can go on adding laghu images to this list. Although these images – pot / Devadatta / cow – appear as laghu images, they serve the complicated and highly rigorous debates of Indian logic, like foot soldiers fighting the battles of their emperors. Even then, these laghus are usually given a secondary position, and their freedom to achieve diversity of imagery is limited, so that we could call them metaphors without freedom. Some philosophers play around with the idea of Devadatta, discussing among themselves whether he is present inside the house or not without bothering to ask him. But Devadatta listens silently to the cacophony of these logicians. Likewise, the joyous cattle with Krishna, Shiva's vehicle Nandi, and other such entities of the puranic imagination become mute spectators before the web of logic around them. They can't help but carry the weight of rigorous logic.

In other words, metaphors and images in the ghana model cannot escape their profound seriousness. This is the fate of metaphors at the primary level. For example, look at the history of the primary metaphor "giri" (hill or mountain), which Allama also uses. Giri symbolises ghana attributes such as ultimate power and tejolinga

---

[47] In any introductory course on Indian philosophy, these metaphors are unmissable. They create a common vocabulary that all schools of Indian epistemology – be it Nyaya, Mimamsa, Vedanta, or Buddhist logic – employ to put forth their points. In other words, they serve as a common medium through which philosophical battles can be waged. The most famous of these images are of the rope that is mistaken for a snake, and fire rising over a hill.

(luminous linga). This metaphor is truly inflexible. It appears in the teachings of the twentieth-century Advaita-yogi Sri Ramana Maharshi as well – most of his compositions applaud and venerate the Arunachala mountain. By perceiving the concrete hill as an abstract symbol, Ramana's Advaita imagination dissolves the contradictions and binaries of mundane life, such as concrete vs abstract and materialistic vs spiritual. Just as D.R. Bendre evokes an intensely perceptive image of the month of shravana, Ramana turns the temple town Tiruvannamalai into an abstract symbol of his spiritual experience.[48]

However, this does not mean that Ramana always remains in the ghana mode. He also uses laghu to elucidate ghana. To that extent, he adopts the metaphoric method of Desi yogis. His composition "Appalam ittup Paru" (The Song of the Pappadum) testifies to this.[49] Ramana's mother, who knew of his interest in the culinary arts, once asked him to help her prepare pappadum (papad). Instead of helping her, Ramana composed a Tamil poem on the papad – an interesting composition which turns the humble papad into a vehicle of Advaita philosophy. Such compositions are to be seen not only in Kannada but also in other Indian languages. However, they arouse curiosity neither in students of poetry nor philosophy. Since they seem the product of a superficial intelligence, readers lose interest in them. It is here that the distinction between superficial intelligence and dense paradoxical imagination comes to the fore.

This kind of analysis is better carried out using the concepts of poetics rather than the subtle and nuanced tools of philosophy. A figure of speech, the simile, yokes together as similarities two different things. The more elaborate such similarities, the more artificial and clever the similes become. It follows that the limits of similes place constraints on the compositions of a superficial intelligence. It

[48] D.R. Bendre (1896–1981) was a leading twentieth-century Kannada poet of the Navodaya period and recipient of a Jnanpith award. For a primer on Bendre in English, see Amur, *Dattatreya*.

[49] For the context and English translation of the song, see Arunachala Ashrama, "Appalam Ittup Pāru".

is difficult to imagine Shankara analysing Advaita by writing a papad poem in Malayalam. In this respect, Sri Ramana Maharshi's dramatic mischievousness and talent for laghu may be appreciated, but we cannot forget that the figurative power of papad is soft. This is true not only of Ramana's composition but also of a particular model of Bhakti kavya as a whole. Many Bhakti poets bring in laghu phenomena from their work, or from everyday life, to explain ghana. In particular, the twelfth-century vachanakaras, who emerged from the background of the downtrodden, diligently used such devices. To generalise, this type of Bhakti poetry may be called the model of "converting laghu into ghana". Since this process does not go beyond the level of the simile, it is limited.

The above paragraphs are meant to illuminate by contrast the radical, innovative quality of Allama Prabhu's forms of expression. Because his mode of mixing laghu and ghana is unconventional, his compositions attain diversity and complexity. Above all, he exploits an unlimited range of images and metaphors that provide more autonomy to his imagination than the limited freedom of similes. With the unifying imagination of Advayavada, Allama undertakes the process of fusing different states together throughout.

Here, I will focus on the way Allama turns abstract philosophical concepts into metaphors and images. By using innocent images of the natural world in ways that make sense in everyday life, Allama explores philosophical experiences. But time and again the reader experiences these innocent images of the natural world functioning under a different pressure and intensity. The reader realises that Allama is not deploying these images to present everyday experiences, but something beyond. And this leads us to understand his latent techniques of composition. Consider the following vachana:

> If I'm the devotee
> and you the Lord,
> can we see each other as one?
> Can we unite earth and sky?
> Can we play cymbals with the sun and the moon?
> Listen, O Ganga on Shiva's matted hair;

listen, O Gauri on his lap;
can you eat a widow's meal
if Guheshwara-linga dies at my hands?[50] (243)

This entire vachana is imbued with what may be called an unearthly tension. (When Allama confronts tattvas – philosophical principles – he is greatly perturbed.) Two levels of metaphor confront each other in this vachana. Even metaphors of the ordinary domain change their identity, effectiveness, and rhythm when employed in the exploration of an extraordinary experience. Thus, the moon and sun we come across in this vachana are not ordinary. We understand them differently when confronted with the dreadfulness of Ganga and Gauri becoming widows. Here, there is an interface between two worlds, the world of nature (the sun and moon) and the mythical world (Ganga and Gauri).

This vachana is part of Allama's larger conversation with some other figures. In fact, most of his vachanas are the result of multifaceted dialogues with others. Allama constantly engaged with the subtle philosophical debates of the Dakshinapatha and Uttarapatha groups of pan-Indian Shaiva darshana.[51] He was never one to ignore tattvas; believing that wrong tattvas were fatal to spiritual life and he fought intensely against them. Within his expansive vachanas, tattvas are so real that they become more powerful than human beings and, in turn, control them. For Allama, tattvas are not merely human dreams; instead, in his vachanas humans often behave as if they are the nightmares of tattvas. This trait in Allama's

---

[50] The vachanas Nagaraj has quoted in this book are, as he acknowledges, taken from Hiremath and Sunkapur, eds, *Vyomamuruti Allamaprabhudevara Vachanagalu*. After the end of each vachana quoted in this book, the numbers mentioned are as they appear in this edition. See Allama Prabhu, *Vyomamuruti*. The translations are mine, unless otherwise specified. However, Allama's vachanas are available in English translations: see Ramanujan, *Speaking of Siva*; Shivaprakash, *I Keep Vigil*; Allama Prabhu, *God Is Dead*; Allama Prabhu, *Vachanas of Allama Prabhu*; Allama Prabhu, *Lord of the Cave*; Kalburgi, ed., *Vachana*.

[51] Shaiva tantrism was broadly divided into two wings – left (Uttarapatha/Vamapatha) and right (Dakshinapatha).

sensibility contributes greatly to the density of his expression. In his paradoxical mode, the distinctions between active and inactive, concrete and abstract, dream and reality, and thought and image fade away. Likewise, the distinction between visible and invisible. In this respect, with regard to the vachana (243) I am discussing here, Allama is in a dialogue with a particular tradition – a spiritual sadhana marga.

Indeed, Allama's life can be read as a narrative of encounters with others. The *Shunyasampadanes* tell us that Allama had a debate with Gorakhnath.[52] His major philosophical structures emerge from his conversations with Siddharama, Muktayakka, and Gorakhnath.[53] (Or, more appropriately, such a picture appears in narratives which seek to frame Allama's life on particular intellectual and spiritual planes.) Gorakhnath's is a unique case in the world of Advayavada. It is interesting to note that there are stories about him in dialogue with mystics from different ages and places, including Allama. Never mind Gorakhnath as seen in dialogue with Allama – Gorakhnath is even portrayed in conversation with Kabir, who came a couple of centuries after Allama. (Hajari Prasad Dibedi discusses Gorakhnath's conversations with others.[54])

Gorakhnath here is more a symbol than a historical person: he is beyond certitudes of time and place inasmuch as he epitomises a particular yoga tradition. The history of premodern Indian culture is frequently constructed through creatively imagined interactions

[52] See ch. xxi, "Sampadane of Goraksha's Attainment and Everybody's Unitive State", in Gooluru Siddaveeranna, *Sunyasampadane*, vol. 5, pp. 405–502.

[53] Siddharama: a twelfth-century Sharana and vachanakara known as Siddharama of Sonnalige (present-day Solapur in Maharashtra state). His vachanas end with the signature name Kappilasiddha Mallikarjuna. For an analysis of the episode of Siddharama: in *Shunyasampadane*, see ch. 5 of the present book. For English translations of some of his vachanas, see Kalburgi, ed., *Vachana*. Muktayakka: a twelfth-century vachanakarti (woman composer of vachanas) who wrote under the pen name Ajaganna, who was her brother. In ch. 2 of the *Shunyasampadane*, there is an episode in which Allamaprabhu enters into a dialogue with Muktayakka.

[54] Dibedi, *Nath-Sampradaya*. (Hajari Prasad Dibedi is a variant spelling of Hazari Prasad Dwivedi.)

between darshanic traditions and their representatives. This kind of battle over an imaginative interaction seems especially bound to happen when there are outward philosophical similarities between two personalities. Gorakhnath haunted the Shaiva darshanas and religious sects for several centuries, becoming a nightmare and source of unconquerable fear for them. Therefore, a meeting between Gorakhnath and Allama was inevitable in our cultural imagination.

As I said earlier, this is a precept of Shaiva darshana: two leading Shaiva saints of Advayavada had to face off against each other at some point. The philosophies and concepts they propagate bear a love–hate relationship, distinct from them as individual humans. They lock horns in the realm of ideas. In his vachanas, Allama often comes face to face with Gorakhnath's yoga system. To be precise, Allama wrestles intensely with Gorakhnath's Hathayoga. This does not mean that he rejects the system of Hathayoga in its entirety. Nevertheless, all that Allama refutes, he refutes vehemently.

On such occasions, the dramatic playfulness of Allama's philosophical imagination reaches its zenith. In the vachana (243) quoted above, he uses the image of playing cymbals by bringing together the moon and sun. What is the origin of this cosmic image imbued with an unfamiliar intensity? On account of "internal philosophic translation", there are many such puzzling elements in the structure of Allama's vachanas. This particular riddle from the vachana can be cracked with the help of Gorakhnath's "siddha-siddhanta-method".[55]

Ha karaha kathithaha suryashtakarashchandra ucyathe
Suryachandrama samyogat hatayogi nivadyathe . . .

(4) At their centre one should imagine a corpse, which is in effect the seat of the fifteen yoginis. Resting on that there should be a lunar disk, upon that the seed-syllable and upon that a solar disk. (5) The conjunction of these two, lunar disk and solar disk, is the great bliss.

[55] *Siddha-Siddhanta-Paddhati* is a treatise on the philosophy of the body delivered through lessons. See Mallik, *Siddha-Siddhanta-Paddhati*. For the content of Siddha-Siddhanta-Paddhati in English, see ch. 3 in Banerjea, *Philosophy of Gorakhnath*, pp. 29–32.

KALI has become the moon, and the sun has resolved into KALI,
(6) and from this mingling of sun and moon Gauri and her companions
are proclaimed to be.[56]

Allama is always opposed to yoga marga and mythical narratives going hand in hand in spiritual discourse. In a way, *Yogavasishtam* is such a work of harmony.[57] Gorakhnath also represents
this kind of harmony in his discourse. Whatever may be his revolutionary thinking on other matters, he does not have much disagreement with the mythical mode of the Vedic tradition. However, Allama does not always agree with this kind of structure. In addition,
there are intense and elaborate threads of evidence in his compositions about his resistance to employing elements from mythical narratives.

Abandoning the conventional modes, Allama begins his critique
in this vachana (243). Here, Guheshwara is captured in the path
of Hathayoga through a game involving the sun and moon. But
Guheshwara ultimately breathes his last in the hands of Allama,
who does not agree with Hathayoga. Allama believes that the mythical mode is an ally of Hathayoga, and he does not agree with either.
Therefore, in this vachana he plays with them satirically by bringing
in Ganga and Gauri from mythology and making them widows.

Because of this departure from convention, historians of philosophy cannot fully grasp Allama's compositions and he seems alien
to them. Allama believes that the spiritual psychology and mythical
narratives underlying Hathayoga are, in the end, harmful mental
constructions (vikalpas), but difficult to know as such. Given his
deep understanding of the organic relationships across the realms
of spiritual psychology, poetic imagination, and mythical narrative,
Allama rebels against all the philosophical discourses available in
his time and fashions a unique path for himself.

---

[56] Snellgrove, *The Hevajra Tantra*, p. 73 (DRN). Though Nagaraj does not
make it explicit, he seems to imply that the origin of the cosmic image of the sun
and moon might be an intertextual connection between Allama's vachana and
The Hevajra Tantra.

[57] An important text in the Indian spiritual tradition that contains the dia-

To understand this unique path of Allama we need to dive deep into the language he used – Kannada. More importantly, to enter into his spiritual world we must go beyond what he called "kapata Kannada", the deceptive language of his contemporary intellectual practice.[58] We need to believe that a distinct form of poetry can do philosophy in an unusual way. Also, we need to believe that the Advaya imagination does not accept the artificial divide between philosophy and poetry.

It is unfortunate that Allama went unnoticed even by modern Kannada scholars who engaged with the history of Indian philosophy – never mind non-Kannada Indian scholars. Perhaps because his compositions were broadly understood as poetry, Allama became invisible to them, and because those who wrote the history of philosophy with a unidimensional outlook could not fathom the mysterious depths of his vachanas. Even those who thought that multidimensional dialogue is essentially Indian could not notice the uniqueness of Allama's dialogue with others in his vachanas. Expecting the debate between two parties, purvapaksha and its denial, to take place in the received conceptual method, they could not recognise the occurrence of this debate in a different mode.[59] To make sense of Allama's way, we need to take a grand tour of Indian philosophy. Allama himself possessed that disposition. Therefore, on the wings of vachanas, he flies wherever he likes. May Allama bless me, I too want to fly like him a bit.

It becomes quite clear from the vachanas of Allama Prabhu that

____

logue between the sage Vasishta and Sri Rama. For an English translation, see Murthy, *Sri Yogavasishtam*. Nagaraj's point is that this text harmonises mythical narrative and yoga marga.

[58] "Kapata" (deception) is a word Allama uses in his vachanas. See vachana nos 348 and 1377 in Allama Prabhu, *Lord of the Cave*.

[59] Nagaraj's point is this: modern Indian scholars in the field of Indian philosophy have not paid attention to Allama as a philosopher because he did his philosophy through poetry and conducted his debate with purvapaksha through images and metaphors rather than through the language of philosophy – argument, proposition, or logic.

"internal philosophic translation" has its own rules. The main rule is the rule of extreme contrast. That is, when a concept is taken to its ultimate logical conclusion, it dissolves into a metaphor. For example, in the vachana (243) we discussed earlier, Allama takes the ordinary act of musical play – the sun and moon playing cymbals – to its extremity and reaches the point of death. His imagination works as a two-way process: he breaks the seriousness of Hathayoga by turning it into its contrastive image of play; likewise, he takes the notion of the play to its extreme and creates anxiety over the state of death. In so doing he creates a peculiar tension by blending the notion of play with the tragedy of serious Hathayoga.

Thus, one of the cardinal rules of Allama's compositions is to be ever ready for the unexpected in the process of "internal philosophic translation". Traditional philosophers cannot accept this kind of unexpected play or playfulness of metaphor-making. Therefore, what the historian who writes a linear or unidimensional history is expecting is absent here.

II

In this context, we need to develop certain postulations to understand a thousand years of Indian culture beginning from the second century AD. These need to be different from the linear notion of historical understanding we are familiar with today. I will make one such attempt here. The history of Indian culture involves a conflict between binary philosophies waged on an equal footing. I have conceptualised this model of conflict against the backdrop of two particular values – vedapramanya (authority of the Vedas) and varnashrama. Keeping these values at the centre, various binary philosophies comprising protagonist and antagonist emerged. I am not claiming that this is exactly how history played out; instead, I am suggesting that it is possible to reconstruct in our narrative how things might really have been.

The protagonist and the antagonist here are not absolute categories; they are shaped as per individual perceptions. If we begin this narrative with Nagarjuna, he becomes the protagonist, and Acharya Shankara the antagonist. If we begin with Shankara, Sarahapada becomes the antagonist. Such varied forms of intimate enmity have shaped the multidimensional aspects of Indian culture over the centuries. This history can be seen as a narrative of binary consciousness. The problems and hopes of all these protagonists and antagonists are the same. Only the positions they take are different.

There are several methodological and philosophical reasons for characterising such conflict as the clash of binary philosophies. Broadly, this can also be viewed as a conflict between Vedic and Shramanic traditions. Scholars like G.C. Pande have attempted an analysis of the history of Indian culture and philosophy in this framework.[60] However, the most significant limitation of this framework is that it does not grasp the depth of the mutual interactions between the Vedic and Shramana streams. One may study Vedic and Shramana traditions separately, but the method of viewing them as mere binaries falls short of understanding how they tried to appropriate each other.

Though the nature of Brahminism's philosophical and cultural streams has kept changing throughout history, they have kept two aspects intact: ritual power and social power through the caste hierarchy. It may be said that the ultimate aim of Brahminism is to achieve the unity of these powers with a third – spiritual power. This salient feature of traditional Brahminism holds good even today.

The powerhouse of Brahminism was consistent in keeping the gates of its fortress closed. As a result of its concrete power, Brahminism constricted itself (atmasankochikarana).[61] The question of

---

[60] Govind Chandra Pande, an Indian scholar and historian of the Vedic and Buddhist periods. He is the author of *Foundations of Indian Cultures: Two Volumes*. See Pande, *Foundations*. For other works, see Pande, *Studies in the Origins of Buddhism*, and Pande, *Life and Thought of Shankaracharya*.

[61] Nagaraj employs the concepts of self-constriction (atmasankochikarana) and unfoldment (vikasikarana) in order to describe an interesting phenomenon in Indian darshanas. While Brahmanical darshanas sought to restrict the influence of dissident sects and tried to assimilate them under one umbrella, non-

vedapramanya has been the basis of this social constriction. The trinity – vedapramanya, the purity of varnashrama, and the ultimate power of Brahminism – has been transformed into a particular social process. Fierce resistance to this kind of social constriction, particularly to the trinity of Brahminism, came not only from the Shramana tradition but also from within Brahminical traditions.

Fundamentally, this resistance began to be shaped into the question of philosophical liberty and choice. It was therefore possible for Nagarjuna, who was a Brahmin by birth, to launch an attack against the tradition of Vedanta and Brahminism. Philosophical liberty and choice existed to the extent of moving from one religion to another. Therefore, intellectuals and yogis who were born Brahmins could launch a real and fierce fight against Brahminical religion. Therefore, the trinity was not such an impenetrable fortress.

Later, through self-constriction, Brahminism sought to restrict this philosophical liberty and the movement beyond boundaries. This is not to be understood as an abstract question of intellectual history, but as a practical question regarding the relationship of Brahmin intellectuals with material power and the power structure. Brahminism's self-constriction there began its dream of greater worldly power. The desire for Dharmashastra texts and their creation represent this quest for worldly power.

Several philosophical and religious practices which did not agree with vedapramanya began evolving within the Brahminical tradition itself – quite apart from the Shramana tradition. Pancharatra-Vaishnavism and Pashupatha-Shaivism shaped up as sects that ignored vedapramanya and that, at times, rejected it.[62] A complex

---

Vedic darshanas tried to evolve beyond their boundaries by maintaining a cordial relationship with Shramana traditions. Nagaraj recognises the former as an act of self-constriction and the latter as unfoldment in the history of Indian philosophy.

[62] Pancharatra-Vaishnavism and Pashupatha-Shaivism: a type of religious sect with Shiva consciousness that prevailed in premodern Karnataka, alongside Nakulisha, Mahavrati, and Shaiva. See Kalburgi, ""Shashanagallali Basavapurva-Basavottara", pp. 196–202. For the Pancharatra sect, see fn. 9.

line of thought thus began to be formed about the Vedas. There are two dimensions to the Vedas: sthula (macro) and sukshma (micro). The macro dimension involved rituals, including sacrificial methods and manners of yajna-yaga. Yogis did not need it, and they did not care for it either. Among them, the idea that the omkara – the primordial sound of the sacred syllable *Om* – began to take shape as a micro expression of the Vedas.[63]

In the process of its self-constriction, Brahminism viewed the two dimensions of the Vedas, macro and micro, as two faces of the same coin. Though strange, it is true that, in the process of Brahminism's self-constriction, the Advaitin Shankara and the Mimamsakas who espoused staunch Brahminical conservatism were somehow reconciled. Kumarilabhatta and other Mimamsakas could not stand Shankara's philosophy.[64] However, in his commentaries on the Brahma Sutras, Shankara made up for the anger he stoked in them through apashudradhikarana.[65]

The above processes are part of a gigantic effort toward reorganising philosophical and cultural memories. Shankara removed all traces and memories of opposition to the above-mentioned Brahminical trinity, a purging possibly unique in the history of Indian philosophy. Shankara condemned not only the Pancharatras but also other Shaivites because deep within these religious sects there existed greater forces of resistance to the Brahminical trinity. Thus, there are many contradictions between Shankara's philosophical postulates and the religious purge he attempted. The rebelliousness of Advaita was mellowed at the hands of Shankara, and his entire intellectual pursuit intensified the social constriction of Brahminism. Even the Pancharatras, perturbed by these developments, began to interpret atma-sanketa in a new way. The inclination and intellectual focus of Yamunacharya's *Agama Pramanyam* is a prime

[63] Dwivedi, *Granthavali*, p. 144 (DRN).

[64] Kumarilabhatta was an early medieval Indian philosopher of the Mimamsa school of philosophy. See Sharma, *Anthology of Kumarilabhatta's Works*, and McGreal, *Great Thinkers of the Eastern World*.

[65] See fn. 42, above.

example of this process of neo-conservatism. The Shaiva sects, which had earlier ignored vedapramanya, began to display this tendency – neo-conservatism – and the whole of Abhinavagupta's intellectual life stands as testimony to it. Brahmin darshanas began to change by falling victim to the pressures of a new constriction. The thrill and attraction of Abhinavagupta's *Tantraloka* lay in this kind of neo-conservatism. The main characteristic of neo-conservatism is to assimilate the subversive forces operating within the tradition into the register of neo-Brahmanical constriction. This process reached its zenith in Vaishnavism with Yamunacharya, and in the Shaiva tantric sects with Abhinavagupta.

But it was not possible for rebellious sects, which were shaped over centuries, to yield completely to the forces of neo-conservatism. Still, it is true that in the history of philosophy conceptual interpretation can diminish the explosive power of an intellectual stream. This is a regressive form of the "internal philosophical translation" in Indian darshanic and religious traditions. However, the rebellious nature of the Pancharatra sects surfaced again with Ramanuja. Abhinavagupta too, despite his efforts, could not blunt Shaiva tantric forces seeking to challenge the bastion of the Brahmanical trinity. Every Shaiva tantric stream Abhinavagupta sought to harmonise was opposed to the Brahmanical trinity and he was well aware of their explosive power.

To the process of Brahminism's self-constriction and neo-conservatism, two more intellectual experiments were added. First, the generic differences between kavya (poetry) and darshana (philosophy) strengthened; this was not the case in relation to the Vedas and the Upanishads. The second was the emergence of the idea that rasa theory was the only holistic system in aesthetics.[66] Indeed, the gold-

---

[66] Rasa, the most significant concept in Sanskrit literary studies, refers to a certain type of emotion or feeling that works of art evoke in readers or audiences. There are diverse opinions among scholars about the types and combinations of rasas. According to Hiriyanna, "The usual view, however, is that there are eight rasas or nine, with the addition of what is termed santa." See Hiriyanna, "The Number of Rasas", p. 62. The rasa types are: shringara, hasya,

en age of rasa theory and the process of neo-conservatism of Brahmanism went hand in hand; even the idea that Abhinavagupta was the greatest exponent of rasa theory was a part of this grand process.

I do not intend to suggest that these processes were merely battles raging in the abstract intellectual world. I have often wondered if the primordial battles of the intellectual world deployed historical forces as their tools. Human beings are prisoners in the intellectual arena and there is a political dimension to the processes we are discussing here. As Brahminism's self-constriction closed all the doors and windows of its philosophy, it began a determined effort to develop the Dharmashastras. From the eleventh-twelfth centuries to the eighteenth century, the Dharmashastras led a glorified life, revelling in their real and illusionary power.

Sheldon Pollock provides many sources of information that shed light on the political significance of the golden age of the Dharmashastras between the eleventh and twelfth centuries.[67] He says that in the twelfth century Bhatta Lakshmidhara, a minister in the court of King Govindachandra Gahadavalas of Kanauj (*ca.* 1130), compiled numerous Dharmashastras in a fourteen-volume work, *Krtyakalpataru*. These centuries saw a great increase in the imposition of a rigid orthodoxy through religious texts. As a prime example, *Krtyakalpataru* appears to be the final statement on strict conservatism. Why this relentless persistence to establish the legitimacy of the Dharmashastras? Pollock proposes a direct relationship between the mushrooming of these conservative codes and the increase in contact with Central Asia that these centuries had been witnessing.

But what is interesting to note is that, in opposition to Brah-

---

rudra, karuna, bibhatsa, bhayanaka, vira, adbhuta, and shanta. For more, see Pollock, *A Rasa Reader*. As is generally known, bhakti poetry evokes shringara rasa (love, romance, and attraction). Note Nagaraj's frequent references to rasa theory in this book.

[67] Pollock, "Deep Orientalism?"

manism's self-constriction and neo-conservatism, a different kind of "unfoldment" (vikasikarana) began.[68] If Brahmanism retained its persistently hostile relationship with the Shramana traditions, the sects of unfoldment (vikasashila) maintained an intimate and complex relationship with them. Much give and take occurred between Buddhist (one of the Shramana traditions) and Shaiva traditions, leading to an intense struggle against the Brahmanical trinity. If the entire intellectual project of Shankara and Abhinavagupta was an attempt at grand unification, the unfoldment sects sought to dismantle that very attempt.

Philosophically, neo-conservatism was a defender of "forms", whereas the dissident groups – the sects of unfoldment – rejected these forms and spoke only of fundamental truths. Neo-conservatism insisted on respecting all conventional forms. By classifying truth hierarchically at various levels, Shankara paved the way for the introduction of social inequality and discriminatory power into philosophy. I explain all this as part of a grand project because the process of sankocha-vikasa (contraction and unfoldment) took place in a singular intellectual and symbolic order. This process began to take shape in various sects – between which there existed a deep and intimate enmity.

Thus, Acharya Sarahapada appeared as the polar opposite of Acharya Shankara. Both shared a knowledge of Buddhist thought. Which is why orthodox Mimamsakas called Shankara a prachchanna Bauddha (Buddha in disguise). But Shankara received Buddhist thought merely as an intellectual method, purging it of its religious and social aspects. Nevertheless, in the business of philosophy nothing can be received simply as a method as the values internal to the method creep into the receiver's thoughts. Certain concepts of Shankara relating to maya (illusion) and some of his views on language retained the traces of Buddhism. As far as the metaphoricity

---

[68] See ch. 4 in this book for sankocha and vikasa, which are translated as contraction and unfoldment by Jaideva Singh. See Kshemaraja, *Pratyabhijna-hrdayam*. I retain the term unfoldment but not contraction here; I use constriction instead of contraction to mean Brahmanism becoming "narrow".

of language and mental constructedness (vikalpatmakate) are concerned, Shankara could not rid himself of Buddhist scepticism. Moreover, the deep rhythms of Buddhism resonated in his explanation of Brahman; there was much similarity between the Buddhist idea of shunya (the void) and Shankara-Advaita's Brahman, which was not a coincidence. Shankara, too, had followed the intellectual method of "internal philosophical translation", a characteristic feature of binary conflicts. No other intellectual method was available to Shankara at the time. Later Brahmin intellectuals recognised that the Advaita notion of Brahman was not more than a translation of shunya, and Madhvacharya discussed this thoroughly, using it as a prime weapon in debating with Shankara. In the later part of the twentieth century, the philosopher Ramchandra Gandhi categorically states with much excitement that shunya and Brahman are the same. This philosopher was resolute in his wish to unify all the liberatory philosophical sects of Indian culture. So what Madhvacharya saw as a reproach, Ramchandra Gandhi considered sri sathya (ultimate truth).[69] It is not surprising that for Allama, too, shunya and Brahma were the same. Shunya came to him as bayalu.

III

All this invites a deep discussion about how opposing sects appropriated Buddhism. The way Sarahapada internalised Buddhist thought was completely different from Shankara's approach. The former was at home with the Buddhist tantric sect Vajrayana, a by-product of Nagarjuna's Mahayana. We encounter a primordial philosophical battle continuing here. Nagarjuna's philosophical spirit entered Sarahapada and continued its uproar. Through his intellectual concepts Sarahapada reinforced the twin principles of shunyata and karuna (the void and kindness), the fundamental features of Mahayana. He also composed many riddle-like poems: what

[69] Gandhi, *I Am Thou.*

Hindi literary scholars call "ulatbansi" may be called bedagu in Kannada.[70] This poetic form operates on an entirely different plane from rasa theory.

While it may be possible to explain bedagu or ulatbansi within the framework of rasa theory, the effort would seem forced. It is interesting to note that though Sarahapada had a better knowledge of Sanskrit poetry and poetics, he did not attempt that kind of classical poetry. His attempt was to put what was most significant into shorter forms, forsaking the grand narrative form of classicism. Choosing to write in Apabhramsha rather than Sanskrit was also an act of deep cultural politics. Many subtle changes occur when concepts from Sanskrit discourse enter the desi idiom.

We also need to analyse how the interface between Buddhist and Shaiva religious-philosophical streams worked against neo-conservatism. Vaishnava sects could not retain their rebelliousness to the extent that Shaiva philosophical sects did over AD 800 to 1200. This is not to ignore Acharya Ramanuja's reformative attempts. Nevertheless, it is no exaggeration to claim that on account of Brahminism's vociferous self-constriction the Vaishnava Pancharatra sect was subdued over AD 1100 to 1200. Further, Madhvacharya's philosophy strongly advocated the Brahminism's trinity we discussed earlier. The extraordinary rebellious power of Pancharatra was responsible only for the intensification of bhakti. (Hence, there are fundamental differences between Virashaiva bhakti poetry and Vaishnava bhakti literature based on Madhva Siddhanta. And this point makes us recognise that we cannot view the Bhakti movement as homogeneous.)

---

[70] Some vachanas of Allama are in the bedagu mode. A.K. Ramanujan calls bedagu compositions fancy poems. According to Ramanujan, bedagu, especially that of Allama's bedagu vachanas, is more than a riddle. For the nature of Allama's bedagu, see Ramanujan, "Why an Allama *Vachana*", pp. 309–23. According to H.S. Shivaprakash, "A *bedagina* vachana speaks through paradoxes and inversions. It aims to shock the reader out of its conventional way of seeing and feeling. It has also been likened to the tradition of *sandhya bhasa* (twilight language) used in tantric traditions both to communicate and conceal higher truths." See Shivaprakash, "Introduction", p. xixx.

In Vaishnava literature, samsara (worldly life) differs from moksha (liberation). The bhakta (devotee) yearns for Lord Hari to liberate him from the bondage of worldly life. In contrast, the internalisation of Buddhist thought by Shaiva and Siddha sects leads them to acquire their rebellious nature. Brahmanical darshanic sects conceived samsara and moksha as belonging to opposite paths. The process of Brahminical self-constriction made a distinction between vyavaharika satya (worldly transactional truth) and paramarthika satya (divine truth) and placed the things that could not be accepted in the domain of divinity into the domain of the material world. This kind of discrimination between the two domains led to the moral split in Indian sensibility; whatever is done in the material world, following swadharma, came to be regarded as right.

One prominent value the sects of unfoldment internalised from Buddhism was that samsara (worldly life) and nirvana (liberation) were not separate. In this respect, the way Natha-Siddha traditions conceptualised samsara is unique.[71] According to *Hevajra Tantra*, whatever is samsara is itself nirvana:

Evam eva samsaram nirvanam evam evatu/
Samsarahate nanyan nirvanam iti kathyate//
Samsaram rupa shatayaha samsaram veranadayaha/
Samsaram indriyanya eva samsaram dveshakadayaha/

(32) Such as is *samsara*, such is nirvana. There is no nirvana other than *samsara*, we say. (33) *Samsara* consists in form and sound and so on, in feeling, and the other four *skandhas*, in the faculties of sense, in wrath and illusion, and the other three. (34) But all these elements are sunk in nirvana, and it is only from delusion that they appear as *samsara*. The wise man continues in *samsara*, but this *samsara* is recognised as nirvana, for he has brought this about by the process of purification. (35) This nirvana, the thought of Enlightenment, is absolute and relative in form.[72]

---

[71] Natha (literally, "the Lord") and Siddha (literally, realised, perfected one) are Shaiva sects which are recognised under tantrism.

[72] Snellgrove, *The Hevajra Tantra*, p. 104 (DRN).

Several Buddhist intellectuals identify the revolutionary possibilities of Buddhism in dissolving the distinction between samsara and nirvana.[73] This is inherent in Siddha's philosophy, especially in Sarahapada. He argues that this world is a replica of chitta (mind).[74] Marvellously, he uses the image of a "water- wave", taken from Buddhist vijnanavada (doctrine of consciousness).[75] Quiet water is roused into waves by the wind. Likewise, samsara is the wave form of chitta. He also uses the concept of mirror reflection in his philosophy. The mind that sees its own image in the mirror becomes infatuated with itself. This idea of image reflection is a central philosophical metaphor in Kashmiri Shaivism. Thus, according to Sarahapada, the truth of this world is not just external but also internal. This kind of philosophical manoeuvring can be seen in Allama as well.

Let us examine Allama's treatment of samsara and nirvana. In the following vachana, he presents them through the metaphor of the tiger and the deer. Here, he constructs an opposition between the tiger and the deer and then resolves it:

> Witnessing,
>> The safe return of a deer grazing after a tiger,
>> I was awestruck.
> Witnessing,
>> The safe return from a demoness' den after a sound sleep,
>> I was awestruck.
> Witnessing,
>> The safe return from the house of yama (God of death)
>> without dying,
>> I was awestruck, Guheshwara. (27)

What is important is that the philosophy behind bedagu vachanas seeks to destroy the idea of opposites. In this vachana, if the

---

[73] I owe this idea to my friend Rajan Chandi (DRN). This appears only in the manuscript.

[74] Vinod Kumar Gupta (PhD thesis), 128 (DRN). Sources unknown.

[75] Vijnanavada is a school of Budhist thought. Its central doctrine is that only consciousness is real and the external, material world does not actually exist. See Joseph, *et al.*, "Buddhism".

tiger stands for samsara, the deer represents nirvana. We need to understand Allama's philosophical adventure here against a backdrop where several Vedic religious sects have portrayed samsara negatively.[76]

By tearing apart the discriminatory hierarchy of truths, Allama totally changes the way of looking at the world. When we conceive samsara and nirvana as different, we hardly notice the contradictions of the world. Things that appear unrelated become related after the union of samsara and nirvana. Likewise, things apparently oppositional are unified. For a traditionalist, nothing appears intriguing, everything for him is play of fate or God's grace. If at all the devotee is awestruck, it is by virtue of the playful pleasure of God's creation. Thus, for the traditionalist, wonder is another sweet form of God's grace. This is apparent when considering the notion of playfulness in the Srivaishnava philosophical imagination. We may recall the sense of wonder that appears in the poetry of P.T. Narashimhachar – a modern Kannada poet popularly known as Pu.Ti.Na.

The wonder in Allama comes from a different location, not from the excitement of seeing God's playfulness in creation. A believer's simplistic excitement is not at all possible for Allama. His wonder comes from a deep awareness of the contradictions embedded in creation. It is the result of philosophical courage inherited from shunyavada.[77] Just as samsara is attached to nirvana, everything in the universe is interconnected. Therefore, Allama disagrees that liberation from samsara will lead to nirvana. Madhyamika Buddhists, thus, call this interconnectedness of things pratityasamutpada (the relational origination).[78] This idea is the source of the exceptionally

---

[76] The discussion of the two vachanas on the deer and tiger is taken from the manuscript. Since the discussion of these two vachanas appears in ch. 6, it is perhaps left in this chapter in the Kannada version.

[77] This may be Nagarjuna's "The Theory of Void".

[78] While explaining Alfred Korzybski's General Semantics, T.R.S. Sharma compares Korzybski's declaration to look for structures and relations in the world with the Buddhist thinker Nagarjuna's notion of pratityasamutpada. According to Sharma, "Every entity is to be understood in terms of the way it

courageous talent of Allama, one of the most outstanding Shaiva representatives of the mastery of Buddhist thought. Allama does not dissolve the frightening experience of seeing the tiger and deer together into simple spiritual solace. The roots of his artistic theory seem to lie here, as well as the roots of his looking at everything profoundly and intensely. He makes everything seem grand through the magnifying glass of his philosophy. Or we can even say that he does not distinguish between the part and the whole.

Though we can find Buddhist traces in Allama, he is opposed to taking the Buddhist idea of sansara-nirvana (worldly life and renunciation) beyond a point. Just as sansara is not eternal, so Allama considers nirvana an illusion. While criticising the heinous sansara severely, he appears to be influenced by Brahminical sects, but in fact this criticism is the result of his creative imagination which negates the self. While uniting samsara with nirvana, all satisfactory classifications created by traditional thought are dismantled in Allama, and confusion is created, a kind of primordial anarchy. His is a religious consciousness because primordial anarchy does not perturb him, nor does it make him helpless. He views the uproar effected by his philosophical endeavour without fear.

This kind of philosophical courage enables Allama to ridicule the assumption that maya (illusion) is a divine frolic play. But Allama is not one to play around images of destruction only in an external reality – he is always aware of what he has learnt from Buddhist thought, the mind and its endless creation of illusion. Therefore, whatever intense or serious processes he has created are not just an external illusion outside him. The fundamental principle of Allama's philosophy is its awareness of the idea that "since there is no

---

is interwoven with the rest of the universe. And this links with the Buddhist thinker Nagarjuna's notion of *prateetyasamutpada,* the relational origination. We witness at this point how a single term can entail an entire chain, densely woven, of other related terms across different cultures. 'To be is to be related' is another patent phrase with Korzybski." See Sharma, "Can Human Behaviour be Changed?", pp. 7–8. For more on this, see Sharma, *Reading Alfred Korzybski.* Also see Sopa, "The Special Theory of Pratityasamutpada".

'other', the self is an illusion." That is, all chittavilasa (the frolic play of the mind) is created by the false notions inhabiting one's own mind.

IV

Now, it is also important to rethink the notion of "tradition" in ancient Indian culture.[79] In premodern times, responding to internal and external pressures, several sects tried to ascribe specific norms to their originary matrices. There was no question of Brahmin and Shramana traditions following a monolithic originary matrix. But Brahminical sects later tried to create a monolithic tradition on the basis of vedapramanya (the testimony of the Veda) and vedadhikara (the authority of the Veda). This monolithic tradition only created consensus about a particular kind of social power; it could not do much to resolve the intense philosophical and spiritual conflicts within Brahminical traditions, which continued to exist.

Therefore, we can say that the originary matrix here signifies the coexistence of agreements and conflicts. The agreements lie in the distribution of social power based on the Dharmashastras and the rules dividing the varnas. This agreement continued further and strongly after Acharya Shankara. I have therefore called this process the self-constriction of Brahmanism. As the consensus over hierarchical social power intensified, conflicts in other domains began to grow enormous as well.

Though Brahmin and Shramana traditions did not share a common monolithic originary matrix before this phase,[80] they faced a common series of questions and concerns which were:

---

[79] In the source text, this whole section, Section IV, appears at the fag end of the fifth chapter. After looking closely at the manuscript, wherein it appears separately, I have shifted it to its present position because the argument and explanation seem most apt at this point . The reader may be reminded that the Kannada version of this book was published posthumously and its manuscript, which was not greatly organised, had had to be reconstructed for publication.

[80] The phase of self-constriction of Brahminism.

1. The nature of ultimate truth
2. The presence or absence of atman
3. The nature of language and its power
4. The creation of this world and the responsibility for it
5. Spiritual authentication of social hierarchy

These questions and concerns became rallying points for the confrontation between the Brahmin and Shramana sects. Though they opposed each other, their shared questions and concerns meant there were certain similarities in their internal character. The fact is that the exploration of shared questions creates a common philosophical substance even among sects animated by a mutual animus. And it was around these questions that the conflict between Brahmin and Shramana sects reached its zenith. It would not be wrong to call this a kind of intimate enmity which often led Brahmin and Shramana sects to merge with each other on the level of external tools and methods of argument. And their process of merging created amusing upheavals of different kinds. For example, Shramana sects not in agreement with the spiritual authentication of social hierarchy in Brahminical sects accepted, at many later occasions, the practice of varnashrama. Buddhist scepticism about the nature of language entered Brahmanical thought as well. Likewise, Brahmin and Shramana sects began to agree with each other on the nature of Ultimate Truth. However, at different phases of their historical development spiritual leaders emerged in both sects to revitalise the original impetus for the sect. This is how Nagarjuna came to Buddhism and Shankara to Brahminism.

Later, the Vedic sects began to revolve around the monolithic text – the Vedas. Vedic norms separated Brahmin and Shramana sects, creating a wide communication gap. At this stage the notion of the originary matrix gained greater prominence. Further, differences in interpretation of the nature of the originary matrix gave birth to new branches in these two sects. The emergence of the Yapaniya sect in Jainism is the best example of this.[81] Thus, the values of the

---

[81] Along with Digambara and Swetambara, Yapaniya was a third sect (now extinct) in Jainism.

Brahminical religion began to dominate Jainism, which was the mainstream of the Shramana tradition.

This is how intimate enmity comes into being. While staying in contact and arguing with opponents for ages, at some point in time an intellectual numbness creeps into certain sects. This is a state of half-awareness and half-obliviousness where the distinction between one's own viewpoint and the enemy's disappears. It is a dreamy state of the intellectual domain which is also a state of conformity with the enemy. There is enough justification for the argument that even religions require a state of such sleepiness – a state that can often be healthy because minor differences are erased during the interim, like a clearing of consciousness. But then, all of a sudden, the opposing sects once again awake from their sleepy state and shudder as they realise what has happened during their slumber. It is like the potion squeezed into the eyes of the sleeping fairy queen Titania in Shakespeare's *A Midsummer Night's Dream* which causes her to fall in love with a man wearing the head of an ass.

The awakened actors who strive to revitalise religion are stubborn. They believe that their originary matrix has been polluted by the entry of the Other. This attitude could at times prove positive, but at other times it was undoubtedly dangerous. By the tenth century the egalitarianism of the Shramana sects had lost its sheen, especially in Karnataka. The fear of an intersectarian collaborative syncretism having become a reality, tension resulted among these religions. From this point of view, Brahmashiva's *Samayaparikshe* is a unique work.[82] Since Brahmashiva was a believer in the original spirit of religion, he could understand the consequences of syncretism. The deterioration of the originary matrix regarding an individual's social base and spiritual power created anxiety in Brahma-

---

[82] Brahmashiva, the premodern Kannada poet Raghavanka's (thirteenth century) contemporary, "found his faith (Shaivism) less fulfilling, and embraced Jainism. Shortly, thereafter, he wrote the *Samayaparikse*, the first text of its kind from the subcontinent, in which he launched a hardhearted tirade against all major faiths (samaya) of his time, concluding that Jainism was the greatest of all faiths." See Devadevan, *A Prehistory of Hinduism*, p. 34. Also see Shastri and Rao, eds, *Brahmashiva-Vruttavilasa Samputa*.

shiva. He was witness to the self-constriction of Brahminism. The Yapaniya sect in Jainism thus came into being to purify the original spirit in relation to spiritual power. As Brahmanism was swiftly returning to its originary matrix, the Yapaniya sect also attempted to return to its base – the belief in an egalitarian spiritual power which opposed the varna system.

Allama's uniqueness lies here. There is little to suggest that his notion of an originary matrix is based either on historicity or the reinterpretation of elders. In other words, he does not resort to the historical mode at all, and his idea of a tradition or originary matrix is completely individualistic. In him the testimony of the "Self" forms the basis of his tradition. Allama makes fun of the conventional understanding of "tradition" as a union of elders. Note the following vachana:

> Elders in the world,
> who consider themselves great –
> declare, "I am great, You are great."
> What happened to their greatness, their elderliness?
> Guheshwara,
> in true sharana,
> the difference between great and small disappears. (335)

Time and again, Allama makes fun of the idea that elders are the ultimate authorities of tradition, the essence of it. No vachanakara criticises elders as fiercely as Allama. It is in the very nature of tradition's power to classify things hierarchically, as great and small. But Allama does not accept this. In his conception of tradition, there is no room for "tradition". That is, he does not believe in preserving memory. Paradoxically, his entire philosophical adventure engages with the accumulation of memory; his immediate attention is on memories and the nature of the power they seize. It is the nature of philosophical and religious rebellions to organise and reorganise memories of the originary matrix through interpretive traditions of their own choice.

There are several dimensions to Allama's opposition to tradition-bound elders or the notion of tradition in general. His concept of

Guheshwara itself is such that it carries no memories. Nor do memories perturb Guheshwara. "Only Guheshwara linga is firm; the rest are sutakas, tainted [defilements]."[83] In this utterance the attempt is to extend the notion of sutaka, impurity, to more subtle levels. For Allama, all memories are ultimately impure, and the accumulation of memories among elders is also a form of impurity.

Since Allama denies the notion of tradition, he is the only one present in adima shunya, the primordial void. This statement can be interpreted in terms of spirituality too. Being the only one present in the primordial void means being at the final stage of the Advaya. Therefore, there is no fear, doubt, or anxiety in the world of Allama's vachanas. The "angst of pashu, being a humble servant" that Basavanna celebrates in his vachanas is absent in Allama.[84]

That Allama did not accept tradition philosophically does not mean that he did not make use of tradition's idiom. Nor does it mean that Allama's contemporaries agreed with his idea of denying tradition. He used a familiar idiom of the tradition to express a spiritual rebellion that was unfamiliar to the Kannada world of that time.

Allama had conceived his own meaning of guru-linga-jangama-prasada-padodaka, different from the conception of his fellow vachanakaras.[85] Ultimately, Allama rejected the usefulness of these concepts too. Further, his concept of sharana seems to repeat the idea of being alone in mahashunya, the great void. In the following vachana he extends the concept of sharana in this way:

See the age's enthusiasm:
For the five forces, there are five chieftains.

[83] For the complete vachana, see vachana no. 146 in Allama Prabhu, *Lord of the Cave.*

[84] In some of his vachanas, Basavanna addresses himself as pashu, animal (being the Lord's servant), and God as pashupati (the lord of pashu). It is one of the ways in which Basavanna expresses his bhakti sensibility. See Vachana Sanchaya.

[85] In Virashaivism, there is ashtavarana (eight-fold classification) in which guru, linga, and jangama are worshipped through vibhuti, rudraksha, and mantra, the result of which are prasada and padodaka.

Sharana alone knows their ups and downs.
This sharana, being his own self, does not beg of the six
    darshanas,
nor does he require the three darshanas,
nor does he pine for the Vedas, shastras, agamas,
puranas, prosody and lexicons.
For, there is no guru, linga, jangama on the body,
Nor prasada, padodaka in the language.
As these – guru, linga, jangama, prasada, padodaka – have
    become one,
all animals offer their salutations;
all creatures address him with reverence;
all souls pray to him for a dwelling;
all fourteen worlds hail victory
to the feet of Sangana Basavanna, O Guheshwara. (938)

Here, Allama defines sharana with a negative vocabulary – what
he is not; Allama's sharana is not someone who needs the six darshanas, nor is he someone who draws on the Veda, shastra, agama,
purana, prosody, and lexicon.[86] These are all a kind of classical
memory collective. Even though Sanskrit-based Virashaivism tried
to revere all these, its effort could not reconcile with the vachanakaras' Kannada rebellion. This is the first part of Allama's explanation of sharanahood in this vachana.

The second part of the vachana also uses negative vocabulary.
However, all that Allama denies for the sharanahood this time
constitute decisive bulwarks of the Virashaiva tradition. The references to guru, linga, jangama, prasada, and padodaka here are the
very forces that underpin the Sharana tradition. Allama, at the end
of the vachana, says that all these decisive elements dwell in
Sangana Basavanna. Note the first line of the vachana; the "age's
enthusiasm" has witnessed the spiritual festivity surrounding Sangana Basavanna.

It is necessary to raise a new kind of question about a particular

---

[86] The six darshanas being Sankhya, Yoga, Nyaya, Vaisheshika, Mimamsa,
and Vedanta.

stance that Virashaivism took regarding the personality of Allama. Allama's emotional involvement with Basavanna, whose philosophy contrasts with Allama's on several levels, poses a serious problem in understanding the Virashaiva tradition. Because if we go strictly by Allama's line of thinking, Basavanna's philosophy should become an object of his criticism. For example, Basavanna's use of the triad pashu-pasha-pashupati in his vachanas reveals his humility.[87] And here lies also the evolution of his warm and humane sensibility. As far as Basavanna is concerned, the evolution of a religious mindset means the coming together of human dispositions like bewilderment, humility, angst, anxiety, and celebration. It is a condition where separation and union are dovetailed. In Allama there is no room for the humility Basavanna expresses before pashupati. In fact, in Allama's stern view, Akkamahadevi's shringara — the erotic element — and Basavanna's longing for pashupati are really two sides of the same coin. Furthermore, Basavanna's anxious doubts and Akkamahadevi's shringara are the result of a humanising of divinity with which Allama does not agree. The following vachana can be read as Allama's philosophical response to the Basavanna and Akkamahadevi models:

If you believe there is anxious doubt when it is not there,
it haunts you before your eyes as a reality.
If you believe there is a body when it is not there,
that itself comes haunting as maye. (942)

[87] We come across this idea in the Nakulisha Pashupata system, also known as the Lakula Shaiva darshana. The term pashu comes in sixteen vachanas, pasha in seven vachanas, and pashupati in three vachanas by Basavanna. In his vachanas, pashu refers to the image of an animal, signifying a servant (bhakta as serving the Lord); pasha to worldly fetters; and pashupati to the Lord (ruler), the cause of the universe.

2

Allama's World

The Foundations of Shaiva Poetics

I N THIS CHAPTER I would like to explore Allama's vachanas through concepts internal to Shaiva poetics. The chapter is also an attempt to untangle a particular problem that has been bothering me the past few years, and I would like to address it here through Allama. It concerns the importance of interpreting a body of work – created in a specific cultural space and time – using the methods and ways of understanding available in the field to which the body of work belongs. To put it clearly, this involves a process of understanding intellectual decolonisation.[1]

I raise this issue in the context of studying Indian cultural, literary, and historical processes as a whole. For the last hundred years, attempts at studying these processes have been largely shaped by the West, be they Liberal Positivist or Marxist or Subaltern Studies methods. Here, I would like to make a modest attempt to expand the frontiers of native (desivada) critical tools as cosmopolitan methods and place them face to face with other methods. Though it might appear that delving deep into this question while studying Allama's vachanas is not so relevant, discussing some aspects of this

---

[1] While writing this book, Nagaraj was preoccupied with Indian intellectual traditions – as evident from his initiation of the Akshara Chintana Male series (discussed in my Introduction), under which he edited introductory books and translations of Indian thinkers and their texts. In place of Western tools, Nagaraj here is attempting to use Indian tools – available in Shaivism – to interpret and analyse Indian themes and texts.

112

problem is inevitable — because this is a question of the relationship between the works created in a particular culture and the tools we use to analyse them.

We may discuss this as a question of the cultural specificity of the tools and parameters we use in cultural studies and the humanities. I have severe doubts about the universality of study methods. Tools and methods can no doubt be applied universally, but they still retain the traits of their origin and formation. They often transform their object of study in line with their original nature. In fact, this is a discussion regarding the power of tools to perceive and describe their object of study, an important idea that postmodernist and Edward Saidian cultural studies have explored in the last two decades. For example, it is now accepted that the studies and debates about Indian castes and religions in the last 150 years have been mainly shaped by Western intellectual and academic experiences.[2] Some even advance an extreme argument that the notion of caste in India, as understood today, was constructed during the colonial period. The arguments of scholars such as Ronald Inden, Arjun Appadurai, and S.N. Balagangadhara are important in this respect.[3] My answer to their argument is simply this: caste practices and their violent manifestations existed before the advent of colonialism, but colonialism gave them a specific order and structure. Further discussion on this matter is unnecessary here.

Ways of perception and descriptions are not created in a vacuum. What is considered the ultimate form of spirituality by one culture could be perceived by another as vulgar body worship. In some instances, such differences can also appear as internal conflicts within

[2] Quigley, *The Interpretation of Caste*. This is inspired by Hocart's work (DRN). See Hocart, *Caste*.

[3] Inden, *Imagining India*; Appadurai, *Worship and Conflict*. Several studies, especially in Karnataka over the last decade, have dealt with the question of caste. These broadly follow the research programme of S.N. Balagangadhara — the prime exponent of the argument that our present notion of the caste system is a colonial construct. For more, see Balagangadhara, *Heathen*; Jalki, "Vachana Sahityavu Jativyavastheya?"; Jalki, *Vachanas as Caste Critiques*.

a particular culture. This becomes clear while studying Allama's world, and the forthcoming sections discuss this in depth. This abstract discussion may now be turned towards a study of various Shaiva philosophers and poets to understand their uniqueness. In the expanse of the Shaiva imagination, we come across Abhinavagupta, Sekkizhar, Harihara, Dhurjati, Allama, Akkamahadevi, and Basavanna, among others. The following pages aim to fashion the methods that can explain the uniqueness of these thinkers and saints within the scope of Shaiva darshanas.

Perceiving the distinction between Harihara and Allama only as a distinction between Dvaita and Advaya sensibilities limits our understanding.[4] This difference also extends to their narrative technique and metaphor creation, which could be understood by rigorously employing the concepts of Shaiva darshanas. There are three realities in Harihara's narrative world: the consciousness of the bhakta narrator, the bhakta narrative, and Shiva. For Harihara, these three realities are different and unique. The sapience that all the bhaktas in his narrative are greater than him lends a certain humility to his narrative. Furthermore, Shiva is incomparably greater than these bhaktas. The fact that these three realities often appear to converge yet remain distinct establishes Harihara as a unique poet of the Dvaita imagination in Shaivism.

The distinction between Harihara and Sekkizhar becomes significant at this stage.[5] Although these two poets seem to construct the same narrative, they are different in their portrayal of the world and so is the density of their texts. To discuss this point more specifically, we can look at how these two talented poets handle the story of Bedara Kannappa.[6] As noted above, if Harihara is a poet of three re-

---

[4] Harihara (later part of the twelfth century) was a Kannada poet who perfected the genre of poetry called ragale. Known as *Hariharana Ragalegalu*, these compositions narrate the lives of vachanakaras and sixty-three Tamil puratanas. For more, see Ben-Herut, *Siva's Saints*.

[5] Sekkizhar: the twelfth-century author of *Periyapuranam*, a Tamil classic on the Shaiva saints of South India, the sixty-three nayanars. See Sekkizhara, *Periyapuranam*.

[6] Kannappa is one of the sixty-three puratanas whom Shaivas worship.

alities, there is a fourth reality in Sekkizhar – the external world. In the world of Harihara's Kannappa, the external world consisting of jungle, trees, nature, and everyday life is not an intense reality. Only Kannappa is visible to Harihara, besides Shiva. In the intensity of Harihara's bhakti, all other realities become nebulous. For Harihara, Kannappa is just an atma (self/soul) which yearns to unite with Shiva. Harihara does not feel obliged to describe the external world, not even for an aesthetic identification with ornate poetic tradition. As he is not writing within the framework of the epics, which require ashtadashavarnane, he has the freedom to ignore what he does not want in his work.[7] For the poet, the freedom not to see is as important as the freedom to see.

This idea of freedom not to see plays a significant role in discussing the Shaiva imagination. Certain rigid conventions of classical literary culture insisted that some things ought to be included in literary works. The descriptions of eighteen sights, or ashtadashavarnanas, are such pedagogic imperatives for the writer or poet. For the first time in Kannada, the Shaiva imagination – including the vachanakaras and Harihara – spoke about the liberty of not seeing. If Nemichandra sang about poets' freedom to see and imagine whatever they wished, vachanakaras sang about the creativity that proclaimed just the opposite kind of freedom.[8]

For Harihara, only the emotional states of Bedara Kannappa –

As several narratives – such as Harihara's *Kannappana Ragale*, Sekkizhar's *Periyapuranam*, and Shadakshari's *Vrushabendra Vijaya* – reveal, Kannappa was a hunter who offered his eyes to Shiva. As a result of his innocent bhakti, he reached Shiva's sanidhya (abode). The famous Gubbi Veeranna's Kannada theatre repertory in South Karnataka used to enact the bhakti story of Kannappa; later it was made into a Kannada film, *Bedara Kannappa* (1954), in which the role of Kannappa was played by the veteran actor Rajkumar. See Simha, *Bedara Kannappa*.

[7] In the Indian tradition, an epic is supposed to contain ashtadashavarnane (the descriptions of eighteen sights), for example, a city, an ocean, a mountain, a season, moonrise and sunrise, etc.

[8] Nemichandra (later part of the twelfth century), a Jain Kannada poet, is the author of *Leelavati Prabhanda* and *Neminatha Purana*.

as bhakta – are important. But the fourth reality – the external world – vital for Sekkizhar, has made his *Periyapuranam* rich and multidimensional. The aspects of Kannappa's outer world that are inseparable from himself, such as the jungle, flora and fauna, and his clan, all begin to respond in the *Periyapuranam*. This truly expresses the Shaiva philosophy that everything is a manifestation of Shiva. The whole jungle starts humming as though it is another form of Shiva. The description of Kannappa's clan and its tribal life also becomes important in the narrative. Sekkizhar's portrayal of these is so fresh and thick that we begin to see Kannappa's people in the tribal people we come across even today in Tamil Nadu. Since certain aspects of the external world might appear to Harihara as an expression of bhavitana, he does not elevate or consecrate them in his verse.[9] On the other hand, since Sekkizhar's Dvaita imagination reaches the state of Advaya, the external reality appears to him as an expression of Shiva.

Allama is entirely different from both these poets. For his sensibility, only one reality exists. The realities classified as threefold and fourfold in other Shaiva poets are unified in Allama. This is the original nature of the Shaivadvaya imagination. Although Abhinavagupta appears similar in his external organisation of intellectual systems, he differs from Allama. Since I discuss Allama and Abhinavagupta comparatively throughout this book, I will here formulate only one difference between them in the form of a proposition: Allama is an anxious mystic, while Abhinavagupta is a mystic of bliss (ananda). Their fundamental differences in the theory of the body shape them into entirely different philosophers.

Shiva himself is the poet in Allama's Advaya. Or the poet thinks of himself as Shiva. The ultimate state of Advaya is the disappearance of the distinction between the poet and Shiva. In his analysis of *Shvetashvataropanishad*, the Shaiva philosopher Yogaraja explains how the Shaivadvaya imagination shapes its cognition of

---

[9] Bhavitana is the quality of a bhavi, a worldly person not initiated into bhakti; "bhavi" is the opposite of "devotee".

experience.[10] A series of images that we see across Allama's verses can also be found in this work – for example, "seeing without eyes", "hearing without ears", etc.[11] In one of his vachanas, Allama describes the experience like this:

> After seeing those who perish, survive and wander,
> I was longing for
> the ultimate Truth – taintless, unentangled, and formless.
> I was walking without feet, and
> seeing without eyes,
> O Guheshwara. (744)

In another vachana Allama says, "Those who have seen through the sense-eyes, say they [the poet and Shiva] are two" (615).[12] Certainly, Harihara cannot write such lines. The poet who writes this way believes intensely that he is Shiva. Harihara is a poet who sees through sense-eyes. However, when a poet reaches the state of Shiva, the senses lose their sensory qualities. If one were to explain this process using the concept of poetics, this would be an analysis of the poet's creative state of mind as very different from the Dvaita sensibility of Harihara. Here, no difference exists among the states – the poet, Shiva, or the commoner. Yogaraja explains step by step the subtle transformation of senses.[13] At first, the senses engage in their primal tendency to open up to the outer world. Then, this engagement intensifies and reaches a unique state in which the senses are deeply involved with and reflect upon what they perceive. Thus, for example, the ear and the sounds heard are firmly attached to each other. In the third stage, this process becomes more

[10] *Shvetashvataropanishad:* an ancient Sanskrit text that is believed to be one of the *Upanishads* of the *Yajurveda.* Yogaraja: a disciple of Kshemaraja, who was one of the chief disciples of Abhinavagupta in Kashmir Shaivism.

[11] There is also Allama's vachana which talks about "seeing behind the eyes and hearing behind the ears." See vachana no. 829 in Allama Prabhu, *Lord of the Cave.*

[12] For the full vachana, see ch. 3, p. 161.

[13] Yogaraja illustrates this point by quoting the Shaivite *Svetasvataropanisad.* See Dyczkowski, *The Doctrine of Vibration,* pp. 150–1 (DRN).

intense; the differences between the senses and what they perceive dissolve into one another. At this moment, Shiva's radiance glows indivisibly.

This third stage is the initial state in the yogic creativity of Allama, for whom therefore a feeling of wonder does not emerge from seeing the outside world. That is the way of Dvaitis and classical poets. Allama's wonder is the introspective wonder of shivatattva (ultimate principle).[14] At no point in his creative method can Harihara accept this state of Advaya. If this were to happen in Harihara's first stage, there would be nothing further left for him to narrate. He does not even imagine bhaktas in the state of Advaya but only believes that it is the realisation of a higher and ideal state of the narrator's consciousness. For Harihara, Shiva must remain separate from the bhakta.

To use the vocabulary of Shaiva poetics, Allama is a poet of the intense nimilana mode.[15] Here, all differences between the poet and the divine disappear, and the poet reaches a state of union with the divine. Different external realities are consolidated within the poet. All merge into one, creating an astonishing paradox.

In the intellectual state of Advaya, the lines between knowledge and bhakti are blurred. Therefore, it is difficult to call Allama's compositions Bhakti poetry. Harihara, on the other hand, is undoubtedly a Bhakti poet. Similarly, Abhinavagupta's is not a Bhakti sensibility. These distinctions are extremely important. The desire to view the models of Harihara, Allama, and Abhinavagupta, even in the context of other religious worlds, becomes stronger. The feast of comparative data is always enticing to the liquor of the historical method. Or we could say that for the tantra marga called the historical mode, the comparative method is one of the pancha makaras

---

[14] The Ultimate Principle has five aspects — Shiva, Shakti, Sadakhya, Ishwara, and Shuddha Vidya.

[15] Nimilana literally means closing the eyelids. In Kashmir Shaivism a state of absorption with the divine is referred to as nimilanasamadhi. It is one of the meaning-based figures of speech. See Dyczkowski, *Doctrine of Vibration*, pp. 127 and 157.

(five Ms).[16] The "meat" of the comparative method is inevitably a sacred ingredient in the historical recipe.

The essence of Dvaita is that the self and daiva (the divine) are decisively different. In the Dvaita imagination, daiva, appearing in various forms, might trouble, taunt, or please us. This awareness helps the poet create several kinds of narrative contexts. The highest forms of alankara (the figural language) flourish here. But in the ultimate stage the Dvaita mode aspires to the state of Advaya. This kind of aspiration and paradox to reach Advaya are attractively visible in Christianity's pure Dvaita states. As I write these lines, the Christian existential philosopher Kierkegaard tempts me to discuss his work. Given my determination to analyse everything within the framework of Kannada cultural memory, Kierkegaard's thoughts appear to me as a blend of Allama and Harihara. I use Kierkegaard's *Philosophical Fragments* (1963) to explain my claim.

The Christian-Dvaita (Christian dualist) imagination prays by making a narrative of God suffering in agony, bleeding to death, and wandering in bewilderment:

> . . . the God must suffer all things, endure all things, make the experience of all things. He must suffer hunger in the desert, he must thirst in the time of his agony, he must be forsaken in death, absolutely like the humblest – behold the man! His suffering is not that of his death, but this entire life is a story of suffering; and it is love that suffers, the love which gives all is itself in want.[17]

Thus, Kierkegaard narrates the life of Christ with anxiety and sorrow. He can feel sorrow by seeing God as an orphan. Even the stony-hearted will pity the life of Christ. He is God, but He is roaming in this city as an unknown vagabond. Kierkegaard shouts, "Behold where he stands – the God! Where? There; do you not see him?"[18] Even though God is tired, he has no lap to lay his head on. God

[16] In tantric practice, the five M-s / ems are madya (alcohol), mamsa (meat), matsya (fish), mudra (pounded grain), and maithuna (sexual intercourse).

[17] Kierkegaard, "The God as Teacher and Saviour", p. 40 (DRN).

[18] Ibid., p. 39.

is fearful of people being frightened looking at Him. Oddly, He feels anxious over His own strength. Human beings are soft, like blades of grass. God is afraid that the touch of the divine might destroy them. This is God's sorrow. But He loves human beings abundantly. Thus, the life of God is a confluence of abundant love and grief. However, His devotee is also an animal of unprecedented ignorance. Human beings can unleash their beastliness and crucify the divine.

In a critical essay, "The God as Teacher and Savior: An Essay of the Imagination", Kierkegaard tells the stories of God or Christ with the imaginative playfulness of a great storyteller. In one instance, Kierkegaard walks away from the narrative, characterising the narrator of this story as a poet. Kierkegaard says of him, "how could he find it in his heart to play frivolously with the God's sorrow, falsely poetising his love away to poetise his wrath in!"[19] The poet is turning God's anger into poetry!

Though, like Harihara, Kierkegaard narrates Christ or God as a Dvaiti, the idea of Advaya enters the telling. This is something that comparative studies of religions must take note of. Kierkegaard is furious with the poet for describing the story of God as if it is someone else's story and questions the absence of the poet's life narrative in it. With this question, Kierkegaard begins his shift towards Advaya. However, in the later part of the essay he states his doubts about the narrative of Advaya and expresses anxieties. He begins to feel that the poet's singing of the song in which he imagines himself as daiva, i.e. divine, amounts to heresy. But the troubled Kierkegaard oscillates intensely between Dvaita and Advaita states. He concludes the article by proclaiming the Advaya state as a thrilling experience.

In one of his works Kierkegaard calls contemplation on the divine "the absolute paradox".[20] Allama does not see an individual in the divine; instead, he tries to portray it as a complex mystical

---

[19] Ibid., p. 42.
[20] See Kierkegaard, "The God as Teacher and Saviour".

process in a series of paradoxical metaphors. Note the following vachana:

> He, a cripple, journeying at an odd hour,
> dark clouds looming, a leaking roof, the floor being the mattress,
> three clay beads around the neck, stone mortar and waxen
>   pestle behind,
> old rice and a new pot, wet cow-dung cakes being fuel,
> the food cooked in a fireless oven is served
> Guheshwara linga relished it. (1318)

A devotee calling himself lame is a standard trope, for self-deprecation is a fundamental technique in Bhakti poetry. Here, this act of being miserably humble is also the greatest state of spiritual achievement. While Basavanna says, "Cripple me, father",[21] Allama transforms that state of humility into the state of ultimate power. While the Dvaita state continues in Basavanna, in the above vachana the Advaita is visible in Allama's portrayal of the lame person and Guheshwara as one.

This paradoxical sensibility and metaphor formation indicates the lack of a monolithic strain in Shaiva poetics. This kind of metaphor formation is not visible in Abhinavagupta. Although he uses extraordinary situations as metaphors in his philosophical discourse, they are ultimately expressions of rasas. What leads to paradox and anomaly in Allama leads to the union of rasas in Abhinavagupta. For example, if the images of corpses, cremation rites, the cemetery, etc., stand out as intense negatives in Allama, they are positive assertions for Abhinavagupta.

This does not mean that Allama always remains anxious. Had he been so, he would not have been a Shaiva mystic; rather, he would have been a vishada yogi of the Sankhya school.[22] He carefully explores the nuanced state of being which lies between the innocent adoration of Dvaita and the pure pleasures of Advaya. This is one of the significant differences between Abhinavagupta and Allama.

---

[21] See vachana no. 59 in Ramanujan, *Speaking of Siva*.
[22] Vishada is a state of renunciation that sings only of grief.

Certain things are missing in Abhinavagupta's *Tantraloka* since he was trying a grand unification of different Shaiva darshanas. One of the missing elements is this paradoxical state which is explored in Allama. Abhinavagupta adores the body by conceiving it as a perfect state of Shiva. The same picture is possible for Allama too, but in a different way.

In one of the passages in *Tantraloka,* Abhinavagupta describes how all forms of thought burn down to ash in the body and light up the sublime pyre. The bodily state is a state of great bliss.[23] While Abhinavagupta thus adores the material body and captures its abstract foundations, Allama begins his journey from the opposite direction. Their methods differ when they mix the abstract and the concrete. Although Abhinavagupta and Allama appear to meet each other in a broad conceptual framework of philosophy, fundamental differences set them apart. Like Abhinavagupta, Allama is devoted to the notion of Shivananda, the bliss of Shiva. Nevertheless, his perspective about how to reach and capture it is antithetical to the ways of Shaiva tantrism.

How shall I address the glistening light
in the heart-lotus (hritkamala) of timeless sharana?
Water being the pedestal, and solid Brahmanda Shiva's temple,
earth being the seat, and sky the linga,
the seven seas being the five-fold nectar (panchamritha),
    and clouds the pot of holy water,
the rains being a holy bath, and the moon a sandal mark
    on the brow,
stars being holy grains of rice (akshate) and flora holy flowers
Five musical instruments thundered . . .[24] (1358)

The vision and series of metaphors that Allama creates in this vachana come from mainstream Kashmir Shaivism. There are many

[23] Abhinavagupta, *Tantraloka,* pp. 183–5 (DRN).

[24] My translation. For a full translation of the vachana, see vachana no. 762 in Allama Prabhu, *Lord of the Cave*; vachana no. 711 in Allama Prabhu, *Vachanas of Allama Prabhu.*

shreds of evidence showing that this vision in Allama comes from the Spanda branch of Kashmir Shaivism.[25] Kshemaraja, an eleventh-century Shaiva philosopher and disciple of Abhinavagupta, is of the view that the material senses are extensions of vijnanadeha – the body of pure consciousness. Mahapramatru (the supreme Lord) is seated in the heart of this consciousness.[26] Abhinavagupta himself is in full agreement with this philosophical stream. But for him the state of sexual union between Anandabhairava and Anandabhairavi becomes supremely important.[27] This sex-centrism aside, Allama agrees with the rest of this philosophy and extends it in his vachanas.

Both Allama and Abhinavagupta are clear that what they are discussing in their respective works is ahlada – joy. It is the philosophical foundation of Shaivism that Shiva takes essentially the form of joy and bliss (ahladaswarupi and anandaswarupi). Everything in nature is a different manifestation of Shiva's ahlada. The magnificent states of nature are declarations of Shiva's atmananda, the bliss of the self. In the above vachana (1358), Allama denies the necessity of external worship of such a Shiva. He escalates the very idea of Shiva to the grand level by including the earth and sky, seas and clouds and rain, among others, within the ritual of worship. This is how Allama also liberates himself from the conservatism of Virashaivism.

This vachana (1358) also shows how Allama's philosophy and metaphor making are the articulations of a unique Shaiva branch, the Spanda sect. At the same time, it shows indirectly how they differ

---

[25] This is a highly esoteric principle in Kashmir Shaivism. Spanda is described as movementless movement and vibrationless vibration. See Swami Lakshmanjoo, *The Mystery of Vibrationless Vibration*.

[26] Dyczkowski, *The Doctrine of Vibration*, p. 144. For more, see Laksmanjoo, *Vijnana Bhairava*, one of the Agamas' authoritative texts by masters of the Kashmir Shaiva tradition, including Somananda, Abhinavagupta, Kshemaraja, and Jayaratha.

[27] Forms of Shiva and Shakti that combine the qualities of bliss and fearfulness.

from Abhinavagupta's tradition. Though both Allama and Abhi-navagupta agree that shivatattva, the basis of Shaivism, is ananda-swarupi (the state of profound bliss), the way it is expressed in each of them is entirely different. Anadatattva in Allama is not always immediately apparent on the surface. The vision of Advaya union in Allama first finds expression through astonishing metaphors of the external world. For Allama, everything is astonishing and paradoxical. He looks at paradox as a common springboard to astonishment and beauty. In the above-cited vachana (1358), he compares "the glistening light in the heart-lotus [hritkamala]" to the grand images of nature.

For Abhinavagupta corporeal reality is nothing but transcendental reality. The concept of ananda goes hand in hand with bodily pleasure. Interestingly, both ananda and the body are accommodated in the philosophical world of Shaivism. For this reason, definite differences of opinion took shape within Shaiva philosophy. So far as Allama is concerned, he remains a unique pathfinder belonging neither to the left wing nor to the right wing of Shaiva religiosity. His stance toward ceremonial rituals, as suggested in the vachana (1358), testifies to his unique path.

There is a need to discuss in detail where Allama diverges from the left-wing tantrism of Shaiva philosophy. The left-wing Shaiva tantrism, including Kapalika and Kalamukha, places stri Shakti (feminine power) at the centre of their worship. (One of the most important contemporary scholars of Shaivism, Alexis Sanderson of Oxford University, discusses this in greater detail.[28]) In the Uttarapatha (northern path/left wing) of Shaiva tantrism, the spiritual symbolism of the cemetery and the effulgence of female power go hand in hand. Especially from the Bhairavananda stream onward, the emphasis on "female power" steadily intensifies.[29] The philosophy of Uttarapatha appears as nothing but the ultimate victory of feminine power. However, this does not mean that its perspective is

---

[28] Sanderson, *Meaning in Tantric Ritual* (DRN). In the source text Nagaraj refers to the unpublished manuscript of this book and acknowledges his debt to Professor Fred Smith who made it available to him.

[29] Bhairavananda stream: a tantric sect under Kashmir Shaivism.

constantly centred on sexual energy. Concepts such as matrisadbhava, kalasankarshani, and others are completely free of sexuality.[30] It is not true that the philosophy of Uttarapatha endorses at all stages the union of Shiva and Shakti as the ultimate reality. This is clearly visible in the Trika sect.[31] The image of Shakti-tattva is the ultimate truth; a great philosophical shift occurs when Shiva-tattva melts into Shakti-tattva.[32]

The world of Uttarapatha is the world of mantra devates, i.e. deities of incantation. This is a realm in which female power is omnipresent; the number of gods and goddesses increasing a hundred times seems to be the fate of Uttarapatha. Intensely private and secret spaces flourish here. Allama is an opponent of all these spiritual complexities and multiple forms of the gods of mantra. These gods, who are accepted by the philosophy of Uttarapatha as authentic, hold sway over rituals around death and bewitchment, which have worldly influence. So, their worship is more likely to develop into secret societies and eventually become problematic for individuals and society. As the Shaiva philosophy of Uttarapatha thus deteriorated, the Virashaiva movement emerged from its womb.

[30] Matrisadbhava is a Shakta Tantra practice from present-day Kerala which is related to worship of the goddess Bhadrakali. In Kashmir Shaivism, Kali in her highest embodiment is called Kalasankarshini.

[31] In the Trika system of Kashmir Shaivism, three modes characterise goddesses: para, parapara, and apara. According to Yogapedia, this "is the name given in yogic philosophy and Hinduism to a type of energy, or power, which is considered to be the highest form of life force energy. The broader term, shakti, refers to the primordial cosmic energy that fills the universe. In Hinduism, Shakti is specifically the personification of divine feminine creative power." See Yogapedia, "Parashakti".

[32] In Kashmir Shaivism, Parama Shiva is the ideal state of bliss which holds the unmanifested universe just as an idea. Shiva-tattva is the first stage in the manifestation of the universe, where it exists as a "pure light of intelligence" or a "pure I" (chit) without any notion of identity or being. Shakti-tattva is the second element which enters the composition in the manifestation of the universe. It is called a state of profound peace and bliss (ananda). They appear united, a sense of pure intelligence and a feeling of bliss which passes all understanding. See Chatterji, *Kashmir Shaivism*, pp. 22–3.

Allama opposed the worship of mantra devates, but not the practice of gopyayoga.[33] As Virashaivism developed, it gave a special status to Allama's gopyayoga. But here too Allama's stern path became harder and more rigid, and there was no scope for the gods of mantra that he had prohibited. *Paramayoga Mantragopya*, which is said to have been composed by Allama, provides evidence of this.[34]

As this kind of discussion becomes highly technical, there is a danger that the brightness of Allama's talent might fade away amidst classical inquiries. Therefore, it is better to return to the particulars of Allama's world. Furious at the crowd of the gods of mantras, Allama destroys the mystery of Uttarapatha by bringing the gods down to the ordinary. He employs this prominent technique to demolish mysteries in philosophical debates. There is a secret world of the gods of mantra in other systems of Shaivism, including in Abhinavagupta. But Allama exposes them with his intellectual sunlight. Look at the following vachana:

> Maya chased all the gods and
> united them with goddesses.
> O Hara, take a look at this maya.
> O Shiva, witness, it is still there.
> Guheshwara,
> see how billions of pramathas (Shiva's cohorts), ranging from
> those with eyes on the soles of their feet,
> to those with eyes all over their bodies,
> Rudras riding Nandi,
> all guarding the feet of maya! (23)

To understand the philosophical irony in this vachana, one has to look at the throng of goddesses and gods in Uttarapatha. Here is a procession of concept-deities such as Rudrani, Balavikarani, Balapramathini, Bhutadamani, Manonmani, Ishwara, Sadashiva, etc. Critical of these couples, Allama says, "Maya chased all the gods

---

[33] A secret yogic practice in tantrism.

[34] Some scholars do not agree with attributing authorship of this work to Allama. However, it is included in Allama Prabhu, *Vyomamuruti*, pp. 529–32.

and / United them with goddesses." Those who believe in the harmony between Allama and the unified Shaiva philosophy may not agree with my interpretation. And such a unified Shaiva philosophy assumes that its sect is Veda-based. Given his philosophical fierceness, Allama opposes this kind of unanimous approach. In the line "All guarding the feet of maya!" there lies the essence of several complex philosophical arguments. This line indicates that maye (illusion) is not just an extravagance of reality; it can also sneak into spiritual paths. Since Allama takes such a tough stance, he is highly suspicious of certain forms of worship and rituals of adoration that Shaiva philosophy approves.

Shaiva philosophy considers the rituals of adoration as an inevitable phase in the sanctification of the self/soul. The institutional justification of Shaiva philosophy rests on external ritual practices. However, the fundamental philosophy of Allama is antithetical to the conjoint state of ritual practice and institutionalisation of a belief system. Since archane (worship), arpita (offering), achara (conduct), and avadhana (attention) are all expressions of duality or Dvaita, Allama opposes them all. For instance, take a look at the following vachana:

> When two became one, archane (worship) was not needed.
> When two became one, arpita (offering) was not needed.
> When two became one, achara (conduct) was not needed.
> When two became one, avadhana (attention) was not needed.
> When two became one, there was no room for sound.
> Then, is there room for any form, O Guheshwara? (1382)

In what follows I will briefly discuss how the philosophical concept of Shakti is articulated in the Advaya imagination.[35] Especially in Kashmir Shaivism, the notion of Shakti is the elevation of stri-tattva, a female principle. In Advaita, Shiva himself is Shakti. Great importance is attached to Shakti's utterances in Shaivatant-

---

[35] In the source text, this section appears right at the end of the fifth chapter. After referring to the manuscript, wherein it appears separately, it is shifted here as its argument and explanation better suit this chapter.

rism. Parvati, an embodiment of Shakti, asks questions and Shiva answers. In the tantric tradition Shakti worship is a unique path of sadhana – disciplined spiritual practice. But in Allama Shakti is not female.

When Shakti is perceived as a female form, a decisive change occurs in the sensibility. A collective of emotions – affection, love, compassion, friendship, anger – is invoked. In this context we are reminded of different forms of eulogies of devi – the goddess – created by the imagination of Shakti worshippers. Even the Vaishnava imagination adores Lakshmi, the goddess of wealth, by raising her to an extraordinary level. Despite subtle differences, Shaiva and Vaishnava sensibilities achieve commonality, at least in their descriptions of devi.

Even though in her vachanas Akkamahadevi sings of the Shakti principle as if it were her life narrative, the idea that she considers herself Shakti is not conspicuous in her compositions. The Shakti principle is not translated by the vachanakaras into metaphors – not in the way it is translated by other Shaiva saints and poets. The metaphor of "sharana sati, linga pati" (sharana as wife, linga as husband) in the vachanakaras,[36] which defines femininity in relation to linga as husband, differs subtly from the metaphoric translation of the Shakti principle in Shaiva tantrism. There, the Shakti principle makes all of creation resonate with the rhythms of femininity. But in the vachanakaras' articulation of sati-pati there is an element of power relations, put in there either consciously or unconsciously. This issue of Shakti can be considered a fine case study of the philosophical shifts that take place when principles are translated into metaphors.

Allama does not articulate the Shakti principle in the way that Advayavadis such as Abhinavagupta do. In his *Para-trisika-Vivarana* Abhinavagupta explores the theme of dialogue and harmony that takes place between Shiva and Shakti at all levels.[37] He per-

---

[36] Like a wife's devotion to her husband, sharana should be devoted to linga. This is referenced in more than 4000 vachanas. See Vachana Sanchaya.

[37] Abhinavagupta, *Para-trisika-Vivarana*.

ceives kama, a bonding between Shiva and Shakti, as a primordial state of spirituality. Abhinavagupta argues that Shiva and Shakti are two states of the same entity and that it is possible to understand this belief as shringara-based spiritual indulgence. In this process Abhinavagupta deploys his tantric language to give a special meaning to the concept of bindu (the point). Bindu is an extraordinary instrument of the universe called Shakti. In Indian darshanas, especially in tantrism, the concept of bindu has been exploited in various ways. Interestingly, Allama uses this notion the way it is used in Shaiva tantrism. But he removes its spiritual aura and transforms it through his method of internal philosophical translation.[38] Note the following vachana:

Listen, you braggarts,
who claim to have become yogis
by curbing the essence of the food eaten.
You boast of
having conquered maye,
by curbing the impurity of the joined bodies.
How do you know the bindu's secret scheme?
Maye is the mind's impurity.
Bindu is the mind's scheming.
Guheshwara,
what kind of yogis are they,
who know not how to conquer maye
by controlling bindu? (402)

The philosophical concept of Shiva-Shakti in tantrism looks at the copulating condition of "joined bodies" as an instrument of spiritual realisation. By perceiving the bindu as primordial power, Allama, in this vachana (402), seems to interpret the philosophical concept of Shiva-Shakti as having become a victim of bindu's scheming. Here, bindu is at one level semen, whereas at the deeper level

---

[38] Recall ch. 1, where Nagaraj discusses the question of internal philosophical translation in relation to Sanskrit shunya being translated as Kannada bayalu.

it is a scheming or plotting mind. Allama also uses his "anti-bindu" philosophy to deny the frolic play of Shakti. Therefore, in the world of his vachanas he allows no trace of worldly bonding. To raise this discussion to the philosophical level, we can say that Allama cannot freely use the metaphors created by the sphere of Shakti vishishtadvaita. He is not lured into the philosophical merriment that Abhinavagupta can enjoy by doing away with his total commitment to the principle of Advaya. Allama always remains a staunch follower of Advaya.

Through his method of internal philosophical translation, Allama can melt and reconstruct any thought in his bright intellectual furnace. The reconstructed thought naturally becomes dull, as is quite evident from the vachana (402) we have just discussed. The idea of scheming or plotting that we come across in this vachana has permeated throughout Allama's philosophy, directly or indirectly. While stating that bindu is ultimately the mind's scheme, he puts forth a viewpoint closer to Sarahapada's view that realities, including physical ones, are mental constructs. Since this idea of plotting or scheming is extraordinarily useful in intellectual analysis, Allama searches everywhere for the possibility of their existence. The idea that the world is a series of secret plots or schemes has kept Allama perpetually awake.

Abhinavagupta and other Shaiva tantrics dramatise the dialogic interface between Shiva and Shakti at the level of Advaita. Allama too does not accept the idea that Shiva and Shakti are two separate entities. Here is what he says about it.

> When the union of Shiva and Shakti
> has generated body and soul,
> O Chennabasavanna,
> why the need for a separate symbol,
> to understand the Guheshwara-linga?[39] (843)

For his part, Abhinavagupta interprets Shiva as the force of dance and Shakti as the feminine force. For him, everything is natya,

---

[39] For the entire vachana, see vachana no. 1082 in Allama Prabhu, *Vachanas of Allama Prabhu.*

a dramatic art form. Therefore, natya is a metaphor for all art, spirituality, and the pursuit of tantra. Accordingly, Bharatha's *Natyashastra* is a text dear to Abhinavagupta. It is in giving special treatment to the feminine essence called Shakti that Abhinavagupta's literary and spiritual imaginations converge. This view in fact applies to the entire tantric imagination. In Allama's conception of Shiva-Shakti there is no scope for the feminine principle. He gives his own interpretation of the twin concept of Shiva-Shakti in the following vachana:

Tell me, O brothers, how does the union of Shiva and Shakti happen?
Shiva is the dynamic spirit, and Shakti is the consciousness.
O Guheshwara,
a true sharana knows that
the dynamic spirit and the consciousness are one man. (589)

I would like to draw attention to the use of the masculine gender ("one man") in the fifth line. When Shakti (the consciousness) becomes one with Shiva (the dynamic spirit), it becomes a man, not a woman. Allama thus strips the Shakti principle of femininity. What does he aim to achieve by denying femininity to the Shakti principle? He is showing resistance to the way the language of tradition has internalised the Shakti principle. This is because a certain kind of understanding begins to emerge the moment a female is referred to in the languages of tradition. Here the idea of the female exhibits certain essential traits – shringara (eroticism), sammoha (fascination), rati (the Goddess of Love, carnal desire), and pleasure or kama – which begin to emerge in the language. This does not mean that Allama thrusts these qualities on the female principle. On the contrary, attributing these qualities to the female principle is very much part of the tradition. Since this is so in the practice of tradition, Allama is not ready to identify Shakti with femininity. As has already been noticed, Allama keeps himself, as far as possible, away from all manifestations of shringara. If Abhinavagupta takes the dramatic power embedded in the female principle to its apotheosis, Allama explicates its underlying dangers, seemingly without being bothered by it. What is interesting is that the works of Gorakhnath also express ideas quite similar to Allama's stance on this matter. Allama's thought bears witness to the fact that it is possible within the Shakti vishishtadvaita framework to interpret Shakti differently without necessarily ascribing the feminine gender to the principle.

3

—————

Towards a New Poetics

ONE WAY OF ENTERING Allama's poetry is to perceive him as a unique mystic poet of the kind that the Kannada language has never otherwise witnessed. Of late, I have had the strong feeling that this kind of perception is crucial for the literary experience of a linguistic community. This need not be dismissed as a completely self-centred desi argument. Rather, this kind of creative and intellectual self-confidence is a necessary condition for a linguistic community – though not a sufficient condition; we need to explore beyond it. This exploratory condition too is not sufficient in itself. Indeed, it is through the interface between necessary and exploratory conditions that a linguistic community attains its multidimensionality and fecundity.[1]

Certainly, inner satisfaction may be gained by discussing Allama within the self-referential framework of Kannada culture. But this

---

[1] Nagaraj seems to argue that to consider poet-philosophers like Allama as unique to their linguistic cosmos – in this case the Kannada world – is necessary but not sufficient. This is not a "condition for exploration" (anveshaka stiti) either. Yet the interface between the necessary condition and the condition for exploration would be beneficial for linguistic communities like Kannada. We should not restrict Allama to the framework of Kannada culture, as this culture is itself a culmination of several forces. Because Allama's thought and poetry are the result of such a culture, he is capable of transcending the cultural framework. That is, Allama is not merely a vernacular but a cosmopolitan thinker, capable of taking to task theories such as Abhinavagupta's rasa theory, going beyond his Kannada intellectual environment, and engaging with pan-Indian debates.

133

is not sufficient as it abridges our appreciation of Allama. For Kannada culture was historically formed by its encounters with various forces, locations, and situations beyond the Kannada world. So it is not merely an expression of innocent pride when we state that Allama's universe, the product of such a historical process, could resonate well beyond the Kannada world.

Allama's place in the framework of Indian culture stems chiefly from the new poetics he introduced and the literary experiments he made. In the history of Indian literature and mysticism there are indeed mystics as important as Allama, some even greater. But rare are the poets who have explored the relationship between mysticism and poetry as subtly as Allama. To be precise, Allama is considered a dissident figure in the history of Indian literary thought and poetry because of his critique of rasa theory and the manner in which he implanted his philosophical positions into his poetic experiments.

To justify this statement, which could seem an exaggeration, I need to analyse the historical nature of rasa theory and present Allama's thoughts against its backdrop. When so doing, we need to wrestle with the widely held belief that Indian literary thought is nothing but rasa theory. Like spilled ink, this theory has a historical tendency to obliterate the imprint of other philosophical standpoints. However, the grand success of rasa theory is not due just to its internal capacity and potentialities. Ultimately, no intellectual system can emerge victorious simply on account of its innate abilities. Battles and violence in the history of ideas are as terrible as wars. The inner life of ideas reveals cunning schemes and conspiracies unmatched by physical weapons and the human beings behind them. If an intellectual system — a set of ideas — is finally to prevail, it must have a favourable relationship with various outer forces and processes. This was so with the victory of rasa theory.

While discussing how Allama responded to rasa theory, it is essential to examine the formation of literary cultures in medieval India. I will briefly touch upon this complicated and problematic issue before proceeding further. The most crucial event in the development of India's literary cultures was the ascent to power of the Sanskrit cosmopolis. This was arguably the most revolutionary event in medieval Indian culture. The strength of medieval literary cultures lies in the interaction between the Sanskrit cosmopolis and the vernacular. This involved conflict and harmony between Sanskrit and the vernacular languages. The renowned Sanskrit scholar Sheldon Pollock has offered several insights on this from the point of view of global processes.[2]

The relationship between the Sanskrit cosmopolis and the vernacular is that of an intimate enmity. Languages such as Tamil, Kannada, Telugu, and Malayalam refashioned their literary cultures in the face of the Sanskrit model. Here, I am making a distinction between literature and literary culture. Although there is a deep connection between the two, their domains of operation are different. The notion of literature is limited to the inner structure of a literary work. Literary culture is a complex space that includes the work, the text, the author, the milieu of the work's production, the reader, the patronage, the theoretical base, and historical conditions. Literary culture moves heaven and earth to control literature. For, what it designates as "literature" becomes literature. The most important task of literary culture is to provide a definitive place to a literary form by defining it as literature. However, the reader is fortunate in that the definition of literature, going beyond the dictatorship of literary culture, changes with time. What is considered non-literary today may later glorify itself as literature. If Kannada literary theorists of the tenth century had had the power of prophecy, they would not have accepted Allama as a poet. Also, we should take note of the fact that Allama doesn't have such an important place in the literary anthologies that came soon after the twelfth century. Perhaps mystic poetry was not considered literary work. Or perhaps the

---

[2] On the Sanskrit cosmopolis and vernacular literary cultures, see Pollock, *The Language of the Gods*. Nagaraj was also associated with Pollock's project on the exploration of literary cultures in history and contributed a posthumously published article, "Critical Tensions in the History of Kannada Literary Culture", to Pollock's *Literary Cultures in History*.

compilers of those times did not recognise mystic poetry as poetry. Methodologically, a literary culture creates certain types of grand pathways. The compositions that remain off these grand paths, on the periphery, are not considered literature at all.

The above explanation was necessary to describe the impact of a new literary culture introduced by the Sanskrit cosmopolis in premodern India. I have already pointed out that the Dravidian languages reorganised themselves when faced with a rising Sanskrit cosmopolis. This doesn't mean that such reorganisation of vernacular literary cultures did justice to their own enormous internal diversity. (I have discussed the cultural politics of this process elsewhere.[3]) In fact, the folk-desi was left aside in this reorganisation of the literary cultures of deshabhasha – the vernacular languages. That is, cosmopolises were selective in what they defined as desi; they identified the literary cultures of their choice as desi. Contemporary Western literary theory calls this process "literarisation".[4]

This process of literarisation happens with the aid and guidance of literary culture. In this process, activities related to culture-power – such as prosody, and acceptance by literary theory – play an important role. No matter how significant they may be, other works that do not fall under this process of literarisation are not recognised as literature. For instance, the folk narrative *Manteswamy Kavya*, where Allama's personality is equated with that of another mystic, Manteswamy, is also a great work of poetry.[5] However, this work is rarely considered part of the Kannada literary canon. In fact,

[3] See Nagaraj, "Critical Tensions".

[4] Pollock, while making a distinction between "literisation" and "literarisation", explains the former as a breakthrough in writing and the latter as a literary paradigm. See Pollock, *The Language of the Gods*, pp. 4–5, also see ch. 7.

[5] A Kannada oral epic, performed even now by the Nilagara community in South Karnataka. Although there are no historical records, Manteswamy is considered a saint of the Adi Jambava community. Shrines have been built in his memory and there are legends about him. Some readings of this epic argue that Manteswamy, the protagonist, is modelled on Allama Prabhu; others dispute this view. A detailed discussion of this epic is in ch. 5 of the present book.

Pampa and Ranna themselves resort to this variety of correlation in their own works;[6] but when the same technique is used in the folk narrative it seems to have been made impossible to take it seriously – especially if we do not go beyond the artificial distinction between shishta and janapada (literary canon and folklore).[7] Though the composer of *Manteswamy Kavya* is superior to Chamarasa in the ingenuity of his narrative, the depth of his vision, and the intensity of his imagery, this folk narrative does not get the recognition that Chamarasa's *Prabhulingalile* does.[8] *Manteswamy Kavya* has remained a folk narrative, without undergoing the process of literarisation and a recasting of itself in those terms. In this respect modern readers are more fortunate, for they can weigh the unique achievements of these two composers by a comparative examination of on the one hand the "Kalyana Pattanada Salu" (lines on the city of Kalyana) in *Manteswamy Kavya*,[9] and on the other the representation of Kalyana in *Prabhulingalile*, going beyond the directions of literary culture. I have undertaken such a task in this book.

Let us return to a historical survey of the new literary culture that emerged from the interaction between the Sanskrit cosmopolis and the vernaculars. The genesis of the Sanskrit cosmopolis and its rise

[6] The tenth-century poets Pampa, Ranna, and Ponna are known as ratnatrayaru (the three gems of Kannada classical poetry). Pampa, Kannada's adi kavi (the first poet), is known for his epics *Adipurana* and *Vikramarjuna Vijaya*, while Ranna is known for his *Sahasabheema Vijayam*. Pampa, in his *Vikramarjuna Vijaya*, equates the feudatory King Arikesari with Arjuna in the *Mahabharata*, and Ranna equates King Satyashraya with Bhima in the the same epic. Similarly, the folk epic *Manteswamy Kavya* equates Allama with Manteswamy.

[7] Nagaraj maintains that though *Manteswamy Kavya* is deserving of great literary merit, it is not in the canonical Kannada literary tradition considered on par with the works of Pampa, Ranna, or Chamarasa as it has been kept out of the process of literarisation.

[8] Chamarasa was a fifteenth-century Virashaiva poet, the author of *Prabhulingalile*, a poetic recreation of Allama Prabhu's life and thought. For an English translation of *Prabhulingalile*, see Chamarasa, *The Frolic Play of the Lord*. Ch. 5 of the present book discusses *Manteswamy Kavya* and *Prabhulingalile* as life narratives of Allama Prabhu.

[9] This is an important episode in *Manteswamy Kavya*.

to the zenith of its power took place from the fourth to the twelfth centuries AD across Asia. During these centuries the Sanskrit cosmopolis model gained popularity in several national cultures of the subcontinent. During the same period the literary cultures of vernacular languages evolved and a new spirit began to flow into them. Through their interaction with the Sanskrit cosmopolis, Kannada and Telugu refashioned their distinct identities as literary cultures. Although it may be agreed that Tamil had formed its own literary and cultural world much earlier, its literary character became more striking in its interaction with the Sanskrit cosmopolis. During this period the literary cultures of Tamil, Kannada, and Telugu each produced its first treatise on poetics. Dandin, a Sanskrit poetician, provided an important model for Tamil and Kannada poetics. His *Kavyadarsha* became *Tantiyalankaram* in Tamil,[10] and a model for *Kavirajamarga* in Kannada.[11]

Hereafter our discussion of the birth of Vachana literature and Allama's place in it can be continued on the basis of Kannada sources. However, observing developments elsewhere in Asia will give us important comparative insights. For example, in the literary culture of the South East Asian country Java, texts called vavachan were born in a new literary language, called kavi, following the Sanskrit cosmopolis. Scholars believe that vavachan means vachana (speech), and such texts are re-narrations of the *Mahabharata* and

[10] For an English translation, see Belvalkar, *Kavyadarsha of Dandin*. For more on the relationship between *Kavyadarsha* and regional literary traditions, see Monius, "The Many Lives of Dandin". According to David Shulman, "Dandin, a native Tamil speaker, chose to compose his work on poetics in Sanskrit . . . the *Kavyadarsa* became one of India's bestsellers, known throughout Asia and eventually translated/adapted into Tamil (*Tantiyalankaram*, possibly twelfth century)." See Shulman, *Tamil: A Biography*, p. 144.

[11] This is the first available Kannada treatise on Kannada rhetoric, poetics, and grammar. It is believed to be authored by Srivijaya, a poet in the court of Amoghavarsha Nrupatunga (r. 814–878). For an English translation of *Kavirajamarga*, see Srivijaya, *Srivijaya Kavirajamargam*. For more on *Kavirajamarga* and premodern Kannada literary culture, see Pollock, *The Language of the Gods*; Subbanna, "The Kannada Cosmos", pp. 285–98. For the Kannada version of the article, see Subbanna, "Kavirajamargavu Nirmisida Kannada Jagattu".

the *Ramayana*, as in Kannada and Telugu. In other words, when poets like Pampa blossomed in Javanese literary culture on account of the Sanskrit cosmopolis, their works were called vachana. But in the context of Kannada literary culture, vachana compositions are entirely different from the mode of poets like Pampa and Ranna, or utterly their opposite.[12] Such contrasts abound in the literary cultures of South and South East Asia. But that is a different matter.

In establishing its supremacy, the Sanskrit cosmopolis deployed all the schools of poetics, but eventually all these became complementary to rasa theory. The process by which alankara (figures of speech), riti (method and style), and dhvani (suggestiveness) were finally translated into rasa theory has a much deeper significance than we realise. The ultimate victory of rasa theory is that it appropriated opposing or differing philosophical currents, removing their teeth and claws. It would be no exaggeration to say that everything melted into the rasa (fluid) of rasa theory.

Against this backdrop we come across two developments in Kannada literary culture. The first could be called vishva-desi, the cosmopolitan vernacular.[13] This mode of literary imagination interacts with the Sanskrit cosmopolis but retains its desi distinctiveness. Srivijaya, Pampa, Ranna, Ponna, and others belong to this category, which includes Brahmin and Jain poets. This cosmopolitan vernacular model has a deep and intimate relationship with Sanskrit. Literarily and philosophically, these poets constantly converse with texts in the Sanskrit cosmopolis. Regarding the notion of kavya and poetic experiments, these poets do not have any paradigm-shifting conflict with the Sanskrit cosmopolis.

[12] "Vachana is a literary form, a byproduct of the 12th century socio-religious revolution led by Basavanna and other Sharanas. It is at once prose and poetry. It is a short utterance, resembling lyric in many ways, yet different from it, as it is essentially a mystic utterance. It has multiple meanings: word (speech), Agama's statement, the word of Shastra, the word that comes true, word of promise, pledge, doctrine . . ." See Yaravintelimath, *Vachana Lexicon*, pp. 716–19.

[13] Pollock's research programme has developed this notion. See Pollock, "The Cosmopolitan Vernacular"; and Pollock, "Cosmopolitan and Vernacular in History".

The second development may be called pradeshika-desi (regional vernacular), which begins with the twelfth-century Vachana movement.[14] It stands apart in its literary technique, goals, and sources of production. It differs from the cosmopolitan vernacular not just in terms of historical, religious, and spiritual contexts but also in terms of its social value system. In the Kannada sphere, it is a rebellion against traditional social values. As the cosmopolitan vernacular had a cordial relationship with contemporary royal powers and their culture, we cannot expect from them the progressive social values that vachana writers candidly propagated. However, as far as worldview and religious values are concerned, the Jain poets, who are within this cosmopolitan vernacular, offer Shramana perspectives. One can say that the Jain cosmopolitan vernacular is harmonious with Vedic practice in its social values, but conflicting with it in its religious principles. Revolutionary social values apply only to the regional vernacular of the twelfth-century Vachana literature, and these values were by no means universal features.

A revolutionary era began in twelfth-century Kannada literature when the regional vernacular, specifically the Vachana movement, rebelled against the cosmopolitan vernacular. From a literary standpoint, this movement was a revolt against Pampa, Ranna, and the forms and values of the Sanskrit epics. Allama was to ridicule the poets of the cosmopolitan vernacular for their faithfulness to the Sanskrit cosmopolis. According to the cultural consensus framed by the cosmopolitan vernacular and the Sanskrit cosmopolis, creativity evolves only within the framework of a tradition. While the cosmopolitan vernacular respectfully uses the tree as a metaphor for tradition, Allama makes fun of its poets by calling them a "group of parrots".[15] For Allama, the process of re-creating the existing poetic tradition is akin to parroting.

[14] In *The Language of the Gods* Pollock discusses the uniqueness of the Vachana movement — how it was radically different from the idiom of the cosmopolitan vernacular. See Pollock, *The Language of the Gods*, p. 433.

[15] Allama refers to this in two of his vachanas. For full translations of these vachanas, see vachana nos 641 and 965 in Allama Prabhu, *Lord of the Cave*; and vachana nos 641 and 793 in Allama Prabhu, *Vachanas of Allama Prabhu*.

Vachanakaras provided no carefully deliberated philosophical manifesto for the literary protest they initiated. By rejecting the literary forms of the cosmopolitan vernacular, they also abandoned its poetics. Among the vachanakaras it was Allama who, through his poetic experiments, most notably developed a unique counter-poetics to the cosmopolitan vernacular. He stood against the rasa theory which reigned supreme in the cosmopolitan vernacular and the Sanskrit cosmopolis. His interpretation of rasa theory was brilliant, but the manner in which he advanced his interpretation or argument was shaped in an uncommon way. Unlike most others, he did not oppose rasa theory through clear propositions. He engaged with it metaphorically. It is necessary to reconstruct his arguments within his vachanas through the themes that he explored indirectly – in the metaphoric mode.[16] The impetus for Allama's philosophical adventure lies in his search for the right poetic form to capture the divine. He responded to rasa theory from the point of view of a poet. To understand the significance of his endeavour, we need to place Allama alongside prominent thinkers who defined rasa theory. What follows is another round of historical testimonies.

II

Although rasa is believed to be one of the most ancient concepts in Indian culture, Bharatha's *Natyashastra* is accepted as the first source text of rasa theory.[17] Since this treatise, which is in the form of maxims, allowed for multiple interpretations, there later developed an entire industry of arguments and counter-arguments to it. Scholars believe that the *Natyashastra* contains references to and

---

[16] Nagaraj thinks that Allama critiqued the rasa theory not as a philosopher offering maxims or propositions, but through images and metaphors in vachanas. Therefore, it is by reading his vachanas productively that we need to reconstruct how he engaged with rasa theory. Note Nagaraj's hermeneutics of suspicion, the chief method he uses throughout the book, especially when he reads Allama's vachanas.

[17] A treatise on dramatic art in Sanskrit, believed to be composed between the first century BCE and the third century CE.

records on the existence of earlier rasa theory. More importantly, there was a close relationship between rasa theory and kamasu-tras – propositions on the art of sex. This point complements my intellectual project here, for there is a close relationship between Allama's interpretations of rasa theory and kama theory.

At this point, we may state Allama's opposition to rasa theory in the form of a proposition: that for Allama the medium of shringara rasa is not only useless in capturing divine experience but also spiri-tually dangerous.[18] In this context, we may also note that shringara rasa is the primordial – the earliest and most fundamental – con-cept in the history of rasa theory. Though there are references to rasa in the Vedas and Upanishads, it does not appear in them as a theo-retical concept of literature and aesthetics. Furthermore, there is a reference to navarasas (nine rasas), in the fourth chapter of the Bala-kanda in Valmiki's *Ramayana*, but it is believed that the Balakanda is itself a later addition to the epic. According to Nagendra, the term rasa is used in a theoretical sense for the first time in the *Kamasutra*, ascribed to an author named Vatsyayana.[19] There, the word rasa is used in the sense of rati (love-making), kamashakti (libido), etc. The following sentences are very relevant:

> *Rasoratihi pritirbhavo rago vegah samaptiriti rati paryayah*
>   (*Kamasutra* 2.2.65)
> *Shastranam vishayastavadyavanmandarasau naraha*
>   (*Kamasutra* 2.2.32)

Nagendra is of the view that, in Jayamangala's commentary on the *Kamasutra*,[20] the words rasa and bhava are used as substitutes for the rasa of shringara and sthayi-sanchari bhavas, respectively.[21]

---

[18] For rasa theory, see ch. 1, fn. 66.

[19] Nagendra, *Rasa Siddhanta*. Also see Raghavan and Nagendra, *An Intro-duction to Indian Poetics*.

[20] Tripathi, *Kamasutram*.

[21] Sthayi and sanchari bhavas are two types of bhavas (emotive states). The word "bhava" has multiple meanings in Sanskrit, such as state of being, inten-tion, etc. In Indian poetics, bhava refers to an emotive state. The *Natyashastra* and subsequent treatises in Indian poetics recognise two kinds of bhavas based

As far as Allama is concerned, there is an integral relationship between rasa theory and shringara. He calls the rasa theory ogara (cooked rice / meal).[22] Though in Allama the ogara metaphor has other connotations, it takes on a more active role when he uses it in the context of notions like memory and memory reconstruction.

Allama's critique of rasa theory has to be reconstructed on the lines of the sankalananusandhana method. We need to understand that when Allama speaks of ogara, kama, the experience of Guheshwara, memory, language construction, and so on, he is responding to shringara rasa. That is, Allama is not analysing rasa theory at the social level, nor at the level of the thematic or internal structure of a work of art. Instead, he is explaining how fragile the model of shringara rasa is for a poet trying to grasp through it an experience of the divine. In so doing, he proposes revolutionary arguments regarding the method of rasa formation. I ask the reader's sympathy for my thoughts: I do not deploy the empirical and positivist method, I illustrate my argument by reading vachanas in a certain way.[23]

> Taking the fuel of swara (vowel sound / music)
> to a hill's pond, the elders are cooking.
> As the hill does not boil,
> the food cannot be cooked.
> As there is no offering, there is no prasada,
> O Guheshwara. (251)

---

on their origin in an aesthetic experience. Sthayi (stable) bhava refers to primary or durable emotions such as anger, fear, and love. Bharatha lists eight sthayis. The second group is of sanchari or vyabhichari (mobile) bhavas. They are transitory emotions which visit a particular sthayi bhava: for instance, doubt in anger or anxiety in love. Thirty-three sanchari bhavas are listed in the *Natyashastra*. Bharatha states that rasa or aesthetic rapture is created when sthayi and sanchari come together in an apt situation and with proper expression. For more, see Chakrabarti, *The Bloomsbury Research Handbook*.

[22] About twenty-three vachanas of Allama make references to the term ogara.

[23] Nagaraj makes it clear that he has no empirical evidence to prove his argument about Allama's response to rasa theory beyond his interpretation of Allama's vachanas.

This is one of the most mysterious of the Allama vachanas and it has bothered me for several years. After much thought, I feel it is a vachana that truly reveals Allama's poetics. To grasp the philosophical experience of this composition, we must proceed slowly. In Kashmir Shaivism Abhinavagupta interprets swara (vowel sound / musical tone) as Shiva. Shakti is consonant whereas swara is music. (Allama says in another vachana that swara means paratattva, the supreme principle.[24]) In the Chandogya Upanishad we get several insights into the concept of swara. Gods and goddesses try to escape death by first hiding behind prosody.[25] But as prosody too is fragile, they are not safe even there. Finally, they hide behind swara. But what Allama wants to say here is different. His uniqueness lies in using the Vedas, Upanishads, and other bodies of Vedic literature the way he wants them, without hesitation. In the context of this vachana he does the same.

What is Allama up to in this vachana (251)? To put it simply, we can say that he is proposing a new kind of poetics. To be more precise, he is expressing an intense opposition to a particular interpretation of Bharatha's rasa maxim (rasa-bhakti-shringara). This is important in light of the complex discussion about the original nature of rasa. Instead of seeing it as Allama's disagreement with Bharatha, we need to understand it as his disagreement with the way later Indian philosophers, thinkers, and poets used rasa to express their experience of the divine or shunya. To make a comparison with one of his contemporaries, Allama is objecting to Akkamahadevi's poetry.[26] In what follows, I will use Allama's vachanas to explain

---

[24] "Matembudu jyotirlinga, swaravembudu paratattva" (Speech is jyotirlinga, swara [sound/music] is the supreme principle". See vachana no. 1463 in Allama Prabhu, *Lord of the Cave.*

[25] Nagaraj has written an essay on gods hiding behind prosody. See Nagaraj, "Chandassinalli Adagikolluva Devategalu".

[26] A twelfth-century woman-saint and vachanakarti, contemporary of Allama and Basavanna. Her vachanas are addressed to Chennamallikarjuna (a lover-god), which is the ankita (signature name) in her vachanas. Her compositions are generally read as bhakti kavya, evoking shringara rasa.

this. In cases such as this, where there is a complete absence of historical evidence, we must resort to historical reconstruction and the comparative method – sankalananusandhana.

At the centre of Bharatha's interpretation of rasa sutra is the metaphor of ogara (cooked food / meal). Later, the term rasa went beyond this culinary metaphor and evolved as a concept for explaining total literary and aesthetic experience. Here, Allama is talking about the method of turning a particular kind of divine experience into kavya (poetry) by using the same metaphor.

The vachana (251) begins with "the fuel of swara". In Kannada, this reads as swarada hulli. The word "hulli" could mean one of two things: fuel, or horse gram. A favourite practice of Allama is his use of metaphors that unleash multiple meanings. When the vachana refers to "the hill", Allama draws our attention to another central metaphor from the world of his vachanas. In his compositions, "hill" refers to divyanubhava (divine experience). While making use of swara and hill, Allama is making a subtle philosophical distinction. To translate it into the modern idiom, "hill" is the ultimate experience of divinity; "swara" is a tattva (principle). At another level, swara also signifies the musical power of language.

Allama jumps many steps at once. Nothing develops logically in the world of his poetry. Logic chopping is reserved for indolent philosophers. A hill cannot be cooked as food. When he says, "there is no prasada", he is also referencing the quality called prasada in poetry.[27] His argument is that poetry about the ultimate divine experience cannot be composed through the method of rasa production.

In this context, the above vachana (251) provides a sort of bhashya – a commentary on Bhakti poetry. By Allama's time Bhakti poetry had already appeared in Tamil, and anyway Akkamahadevi, a prominent practitioner of bhakti kavya among vachanakaras,

---

[27] According to Bharatha's *Natyashastra*, prasada (perspicuity) is one of the ten qualities of kavya (XVII, 96). Prasada is related to meaning (if swara is related to word) (DRN). See Wisdom Library, "Chapter XVII – Diction of a Play (lakṣaṇa)".

was his contemporary. Later, shringara-centric Bhakti poetry was to flow unabated in Indian languages until the twentieth century. This does not mean that Allama composed this vachana based on poetic experiments that were taking place in his time. Rather, the significance of his imagination lies in the way he grasped various expressive forms of philosophical paths and sensibilities. He is critiquing a mode of thinking about divinity and making it metaphorical. He is also criticising the school of thought which spawned Abhinavagupta.

As evident from his *Abhinavabharati*, Abhinavagupta is a rasa theorist. He speaks of it with enthusiasm, which is appropriate for such a great philosopher from Kashmir. For him, the body is a medium for receiving divya – the divine. The rasa state of the body, the bliss of the divine, and the rasa experience of poetry all belong to the same base. The intense state of sexual intercourse is both the real and symbolic state of all divine experiences. Thus, for Abhinavagupta there is no difference between reality and symbols in poetry. The importance of the rasa experience lies here: rasa emerges when symbol and reality are inextricably mixed. Therefore, the Bhakti poets merged the reality of bodily experience into mystical symbols of the divine. They stitched these together seamlessly. Later, when Madhusudana Sarasvati popularised the theory of bhakti rasayana (alchemy of devotion), Abhinavagupta's triad of rasa-bhakti-shringara continued. Since Allama is analysing this philosophical structure, he can be seen as antithetical not only to his predecessors or elders but also to his contemporaries. Besides, he is also antithetical to poets and philosophers of the future who subsequently practised the triad of rasa–bhakti–shringara. Note his invocation of "the elders" in this vachana (251). Arguably, no one in Kannada literature took elders to task as thoroughly as Allama.[28]

In this vachana (251), there is strong opposition to the way Abhinavagupta developed Bharatha's rasa theory. Although this variety of opposition existed even among the ancients, in the later centu-

---

[28] Ch. 6, in particular, discusses this aspect of his compositions.

ries Abhinavagupta's rasa theory became so widely influential that opposition to it disappeared. What is relevant to us is the claim that rasa emerges as soon as the distinction between reality and symbol disappears. This is the crux of shringara-centric Bhakti poetry. If this is to happen, great faith is required in the capacity of language. This is accomplished by a hearty reception and application of Bhartrihari's theory of language, in which shabda, the sound (meaningful sound, the word), is Brahman. Among all the other levels of the meaning of shabda, the notion of Brahman finally comes and settles there. Consequently, in shringara-centric Bhakti poetry language acquires the qualities of figuration, stylisation, and playfulness. In Akkamahadevi's vachanas, intimacy reveals itself through sound – a figurative quality of language. In her use of every sound (word), she wins our heart. For her there is no difference between shringara (eroticism) and renunciation, and similarly no distinction between symbol and reality. This is also largely true of Vaishnava Bhakti poetry.

But for Allama such fixation with language is not possible. He asserts that language is impure and deadly. For him, reality is distinct from symbol. He does not unpack the divine reality in poetry but only suggests it through symbols. Therefore, he creates paradoxical metaphors. For Allama this is not just a question of poetics, but a high-level philosophical stance as well. We therefore need to approach his symbols mindfully. The spiritual morality deeply rooted in Allama has produced this vachana (251).

Allama is enraged by shringara-centric Bhakti poetry. At one level his anger is directed against the idea that an ecstatic bodily state is the ultimate divine pleasure; this anger is against tantrism. At another level it is directed against the Bhakti model. Allama is opposed to both tantra and bhakti. He is therefore furious at those who employ rhetoric in their poetry to amuse. Adoration of the human body in the name of the divine is unacceptable to him. Tantra is an adoration of the ecstatic state of the body. Bhakti is an adoration of the ecstatic state of the mind, and at one level they both merge. Allama looks at them separately and also together:

Listen, you,
who cannot see beyond
the five senses — sound, touch, form, taste, and smell,
the seven elements and the eight-fold pride,
talk about linga in the vachana.
How do you attain the subtle shivapatha (Shiva's path)
without giving up the desire for samsara (worldly life)?
What use is it if speech (words) alone soaks in Guheshwara,
not the mind? (175)

According to one interpretation, the eight-fold pride comprises prithvi (earth), salila (water), pawaka (fire), pawana (wind), ambara (sky), ravi (sun), shashi (moon), and atma (self). This is discussed in *Karanahasige*.[29] It was believed that anything could be achieved through this eight-fold pride. In the vachana (175) above, there is a hint of why Allama is perturbed. The shringara-centric Bhakti poetry of Akkamahadevi entails a kind of pride. It requires confidence to capture Chennamallikarjuna through the five senses.[30] Akkamahadevi can therefore touch Chennamallikarjuna. She chases him, "going beyond all boundaries and holds his hands."[31] She embraces him against her breasts. In his embrace, she says, her bones will shatter. Only when she is deeply involved in the pride of the five senses will shringara kavya be possible. But Allama identifies a subtle difference between the aestheticism of shringara-bhakti kavya and mystic poetic creation. Even talk about linga can become poetry in bhakti kavya, and sound, touch, forms, and smells become rasa in poetry. There can be no poetry where there is no union with

[29] This is a term used in Virashaiva discourse. It involves explaining in detail the elements, structure, and principles of the physical body. One of the treatises of Chennabasavanna goes by this name.

[30] The Chennamallikarjuna (lit. "lord of white jasmines"), ankita (signature name) of Akkamahadevi, refers to Shiva, Akkamahadevi's lover-god.

[31] Nagaraj is using a line from one of Akkamahadevi's vachanas. It is a famous "Akka Kelavva" vachana (O Sister, listen Sister dear). Pandit Mallikarjun Mansur's rendition of this vachana in Hindustani classical music is a landmark. See YouTube, "Akka Kelavva". For an English translation of this vachana, see Shivaprakash, *I Keep Vigil of Rudra*, p. 153.

Shiva. Simply put, sweat and sperm here are the rasa state of poetry, which is a state of divyanubhava (divine experience).

In the global tradition of mystic poetry, shringara-based bhakti is the most influential mode as well. In this mode, whatever is accessible and available is experienced intensely and turned into poetry. Here, minute objects become the carriers of extensive experiences. The body itself becomes the medium when no abstraction is within reach. This is also the mode of the Song of Solomon in the Bible which describes frenzied abdominal dancing. Therefore, the mind's frenzied state is nothing but the ecstatic state of the senses. Here, the body is understood as the entire universe. Here lies the source of Allama's philosophical perturbation. Our confidence in the five senses makes us look upon language with great respect – that is, it fuels our desire for worldly life. In the philosophical history of Indian languages, speech also signifies samsara (worldly life).[32] Here, soaking your speech (words) to touch the divine becomes important.

Allama appears a sceptic in this vachana (175). Scepticism regarding the spiritual capacity of language is natural to Buddhists. They are the first in the history of Indian philosophy to express philosophical scepticism about language on a grand scale. Acharya Shankara, known as Prachchanna Bauddha, learnt this from the Buddhists. Thereafter, this scepticism about language became internal to all of Indian philosophy. Allama may have gained this from his engagement with the Advaita and Buddhist traditions. In the vachana (175) we are discussing, he is extending his scepticism about language, the scepticism which could occur naturally to the critic of the Navya movement – a literary movement in Kannada from the 1950s to the 1970s: "What use is it if speech (words) alone soaks in Guheshwara, not the mind?"

As far as divine experience is concerned, all statements claiming to search for linganubhava (the experience of linga) are audacious.

---

[32] For example, in Malayalam, the word sansara (worldly life) also means speech (DRN).

Even Basavanna says, "there is no word beyond it."[33] Who will authenticate the world where word or speech does not reach? So, the line between insight and jugglery is rather thin in mystic poetry. All talk of silences beyond the word belong to the material world. The more this kind of ordinary talk gains exceptional power, the brighter the poetry becomes. Here, I assert only that the poetic quality will become brighter, not the experience expressed in poetry. Therefore, searching for talk about linga in poetry is a kind of invocation of black magic. In mystic poetry, therefore, there is a yearning to catch hold of all that is not accessible to word or speech. There is celebration whenever a little has been caught. Allama calls this the "pomp of the word".[34] When he speaks of the vanity of the word or of speech, he also reiterates our inability to foresee.

This is a warning for the moderns, a caution against mistaking poetry for mysticism. It is a matter of drawing attention to the distinction between the map and the territory, or the road sign and the road. Bhakti kavya cannot take birth without "brimming with pride", i.e. the poet's egoism is essential for the production of kavya. But Allama is ruthless and adamant in his criticism. For Bhakti poets, wherever they may happen to feel tired, there is kailasa (heaven). When they cannot see ahead, they glorify the space they are standing in. Even the worldly ones among them think it is from this space that humans touch divinity. Allama is the first Kannada poet to be concerned with methods of grasping the divine. He examines everything in depth and takes matters to their extreme point. Thus, he breaks the pots of speech acts into pieces.

Historically speaking, there is one thing of which we may be certain. Daiva (divinity) is an abstract universal machine. Mimamsakas believed in this idea of the divine as the universal machine,

---

[33] In the source text it is printed as a line from Allama, but it is from one of the vachanas of Basavanna. See vachana no. 527 in *Vachana Sanchaya*. It calls to mind Wittgenstein's statement, "the limits of my language mean the limits of my world."

[34] See vachana no. 609, which says, "Lost in the pomp of word, they can't look behind, nor before . . ." in Allama Prabhu, *Lord of the Cave*.

whereas the Bhakti poets developed the argument that the divine is a personal affair. The formation of ishta-daiva (beloved divine) as a reaction to the universal machine led to an eroticisation of the divine. Allama examines the abstract and concrete dimensions of the relationship between the divine and shringara.

> O irresolute mind,
> you savour the food of grief.
> How strange, you too are bound by maya!
> You can't see the darkness in your eyes.
> The shringara in the light is fumbling,
> Guheshwara! (45)

As mentioned earlier, Allama is extremely ruthless in his criticism of the shringara-based bhakti mode, which he considers as merely a philosophical form. For him this is a sort of base, and he therefore understands the nature of all that flows from it. Here he is criticising the root of the shringara-based bhakti path. Grief and the pangs of separation are indispensable conditions for shringara. Without the backdrop of grief, there can be no picture of unity. Without the fear of separation, there is no festivity of union. Mystic poetry is marked by a peculiar phenomenon; the structure of feelings acquires an exceptional dynamism. That is, grief and celebration, separation and union, remembering and forgetting begin to work as coexisting states. The Bhakti poems of Akkamahadevi, Meera, and the Bengali Vaishnava saints unfold within this structure. Aspects of human love are allegorised in Bhakti poetry. Both the poet's perspective and the reader's reception accept that human love is divine love expressed through allegory. This is a kind of cultural negotiation. In the structure of this negotiation, only when grief becomes food is it digested as rasa in the body of poetry.

Allama is aware of the dangers of this mode. The significant achievement of bhakti kavya is that it humanises the divine experience. God becomes a child, a father, and above all a beloved. In this way, though the divine experience (which is beyond words or speech) was brought down to everyday business — mundane, concrete, and endearing – the adventurousness of human sensibility was dampened. It is true that when God is perceived as a beloved the mind cheers as it witnesses the divine within worldly life. But ultimately this becomes the string of illusion (maye).

This argument when extended becomes a criticism of the puranic imagination of the Bhakti tradition. The puranic tradition is more widespread than the lyrical songs of bhakti. The puranas try to encompass the richness of storytelling beyond the structure of lyrical songs. But Allama is opposed to the purana mode as well. In the above vachana (45), the line "The shringara in light is fumbling . . ." is important. Vedic philosophical traditions had realised that there was no easier way than shringara to grasp the experience of light. Bhakti and tantra, which are generally regarded as different, become the object of Allama's criticism when he mixes light and shringara. Allama thus goes in search of relations hidden deep amidst unrelatedness. Tantra is also a kind of shringara. There were many reasons for considering shringara as a competent mode, and one of them was belief in the body. This philosophical and metaphoric mode can only take birth through devotion to bodily pleasure and energy. If we are hell-bent on searching out the roots of this path, we will find them in the Vedas, or in the original Vedic sensibility.

Allama is intensely sceptical about bodily pleasure as a mode of reaching the divine. At the same time, he does not follow the Shramana tradition's hard ways of disciplining the body. He says, "One should not let a moment pass / That does not gratify the body's wish" (71).[35] This statement seems to be influenced by the Buddhist madhyama marga – the middle path. But considering the body as the only space for all mysteries and richness is altogether different. The finest segments of the Vedas endorse this. No religious literature has adored the body, the flow of semen, and the power of sperm accumulation as fervently as the Vedas. The vagina is also a source of wonder in the Vedas, and Aditi is called

[35] See vachana no. 71 in Allama Prabhu, *Lord of the Cave*; and in Allama Prabhu, *Vachanas of Allama Prabhu*.

ashtayoni (person with eight vaginas).[36] The penis is also a matter of celebration. Alongside, the Vedas endorse and celebrate the worldly institutional responsibilities of the body. The worldly person with desires and attachments is an ideal human being for the Vedic religion. We can observe in the history of Vedic analysis that ideas about the body are eventually transformed into social beliefs.

Allama also agrees that the analysis of the body is at once an analysis of society and an aesthetic theory. However, the conclusions he draws from this conviction are quite the opposite of the views of Vedic religion. When this adoration of the body within Vedic religion was taken further and ended up as tantra, it offered a rather different social vision. Tantric modes focus excessively on the body and its mysteries result in their giving up worldly responsibilities. For the person rapt in the body, worldly life recedes. However, the Shramana tradition opposes the Vedic tradition on different levels. This opposition takes the form of a renunciation that stems from a deep suspicion of the body. Nevertheless, while upholding the life of samsara – of a householder and institutional reality – the Vedic path also accommodates a tantric mode that rejects institutions. Allama is opposed to both the ideas. In this respect, he exhibits the best qualities of the Shramana sensibility. In this too he opposes Abhinavagupta's views.

In many respects, Abhinavagupta is undoubtedly anti-traditional. But it is deeply embedded in his vision of life that the body is a universe of supreme mystery. Therefore, he becomes the father of Shaivatantra. There is a short work called *Dehasta Devata Chakra Stotra* which may or may not have been written by Abhinavagupta but which undoubtedly belongs to Shaiva tantrism.[37] The composer of *Dehasta Devata Chakra Stotra* praises various goddesses and female forces resident in the body. For Abhinavagupta only orgasm truly replicates the highest state of darshana. In other words, for him there is no distinction between these two states. Dehasta

---

[36] In Hinduism, Aditi is an infinite mother of all gods. Ashtayoni also means having eight places of origin.

[37] See Abhinavagupta, "Track 5 Dehasta-devata-cakra Stotra".

chakras (bodily wheels) spin the individual into all types of pleasure. But Allama cannot accept this. He renders Abhinavagupta's or Shaivatantra's chakra (wheel) into Kannada's gali – which also means "wheel". He could have retained the word chakra, but by using the Kannada word gali he expresses his utter bewilderment.

> Look, the legs are wheels [galigalu];
> the body a loaded cart.
> Five men drive it.
> They are not alike.
> If the cart is not driven in tune with its nature,
> the axle will break,
> O Guheshwara! (42)

By expressing doubts and disagreement with the mysterious pleasures of tantraloka in this vachana, Allama shows perplexity instead of deep involvement. We are reminded of the vachana by Basavanna which speaks of the "body as a temple".[38] Even though Basavanna does not agree with the tantric themes of Abhinavagupta and *Dehasta Devata Chakra Stotra*, he finds spiritual peace in making the body a temple. But Allama's vision of the body is more startling, which is why it is capable of grasping a much deeper spiritual truth.

In any case, Allama does not trust the five senses – referred to as five men in the above vachana (42). He cannot quite believe that goddesses and female forces reside in various corners of the senses. In another vachana he talks as an insider to Kashmir Shaivatantra:

> In the anus region lies adhara-chakra,
> earth is its great element.
> Square in shape; the lotus with four petals,
> inscribed are the letters va, sha, sha, sa.
> Its colour golden, its supreme deity Brahma.
> In the phallus region lies swadhishtanachakra, water is its element.
> A lotus with six bow-shaped petals, inscribed are the

---

[38] For the full vachana, see vachana no. 820 in Ramanujan, *Speaking of Siva*.

letters ba, bha, ma, ya, ra, la.
Its colour emerald, its supreme deity Vishnu . . .[39] (188)

Thus, in such cases Allama also speaks the language of the elders. But he is conscious of the fact that accepting the sites of shakti (female forces) is different from receiving them in the form of sexual intercourse. Allama's convictions are distinct and retain their uniqueness because they clash with those of the elders – despite speaking their language. Thus he says, "Why speak of linga experience when you are thirsty with sexual desire?"[40] (230) The wheels in the above vachana (42) do not suit Allama on his divine journey. He turns the philosophical metaphor of chakra into a mundane gali, the wheel of a cart whose axle is sure to break. The cart of shringara should not carry the light: its axle is certain to break. Perhaps for this reason Allama says, "The shringara in the light is fumbling" (vachana no. 45).

> The hill of moonstone is bonded with water.
> The hill of sunstone with fire.
> The hill of the philosopher's stone with elixir.
> By what means is this union achieved?
> Guheshwara knows
> how to prepare food and eat,
> bringing water and fire perfectly together. (252)

This vachana illustrates the clear existence of Allama's poetic imagination. Classical thinkers tend to express a concept in more specific terms. They dare not ruffle too many feathers by oddities in their way of thinking. Equating the divine experience with a hill could turn out to be a philosophical metaphor in their compositions, but this metaphoric relation ought not to change later; if it changes, the accuracy of their logic and reasoning will be impaired.

[39] My translation. For a full translation, see vachana no. 188 in Allama Prabhu, *Lord of the Cave*; and in Allama Prabhu, *Vachanas of Allama Prabhu*.

[40] My translation. For the full vachana, see vachana no. 230 in Allama Prabhu, *Lord of the Cave*.

But Allama is not concerned with this variety of logical accuracy. He therefore calls the hill the moonstone, the sunstone hill the hill of the philosopher's stone. Anaphora is a basic technique not just of bhakti poetry but all kinds of poetry. However, Allama here uses the technique of anaphora in one-half of the composition and changes it in the other half. His meaning is this: the hill – which stands for divyanubhava – cannot be grasped through rasanubhava. Here too he cuts the culinary metaphor with an axe.

Why is Allama so opposed to the culinary metaphor? We cannot answer this only by looking at his vachanas. Like most crucial and critical thinkers who change a paradigm, Allama criticises a habit – of using the culinary metaphor – that the Indian sensibility has cultivated deeply in discussions of aesthetic experience. Perhaps the culinary metaphoric mode is apt for the expression of worldly affairs. Allama does not get into that discussion. From this perspective, he is not curious in the way of ordinary poets. Whatever their concerns, Allama himself thinks deeply only about the breadth of experiences important to him. Behind his analysis of rasa theory lie questions that go well beyond poetics.

Allama outlines a further aspect of this in the following vachana:

> Unimaginable the light in the eyes!
> Indescribable the tune in the ear!
> Incomparable is the taste on the tongue!
> One cannot measure suyidhana, the holy food
> of the inconceivable central nerve sushumna.
> The serene Guheshwara is everywhere,
> in the minutest particles of dust,
> in hardwood and tender grass. (273)

When saying "Unimaginable the light in the eyes!" is Allama suggesting that not all stages of shunyanubhava (experience of the void) should be examined? Although "light" symbolises shunyanubhava in Allama throughout, some who have explored this domain interpret this experience as being literally of light. A great tantric scholar of this century, Gopinath Kaviraj, narrates an interesting story about his Guru Visuddhananda:

One day the teacher, a devotee of the *Devi-Mahatmya*, who was endowed with *surya-vijnana*, the capacity to focus the light of the sun on a particular object and transform it into something else, was out travelling. As evening came, he told his cook, who was travelling with him, that he would be reciting the *Devi-Mahatmya* that night and should not be disturbed. Arising to relieve himself in the middle of the night, the cook forgot this admonition. He inadvertently opened Visuddhananda's door and was blinded by the light, just as the teacher was coming to the end of his recitation. Quickly shutting the door, he apologised the next morning, and was told that it was indeed fortunate that this had happened at the very end of the text. Had it occurred earlier, he would surely have been annihilated by the power that was present.[41]

Relevant here is that shunyanubhava is literally the experience of light. Therefore, Allama receives it as a primary metaphor in this context (vachana no. 273).

Allama's speciality lies in the fact that he uses natural objects – light, dawn, hill, fire, and water – as primary metaphors. He also uses metaphors in a paradoxical mode. The former brings to his vachanas a sense of cosmic wonder. But he also changes the original states of natural objects a bit, and turns them into paradoxical metaphors. Thus we find a fundamental difference between the representation of nature in Akkamahadevi and other Bhakti poets, as against that in Allama. In Akkamahadevi, nature is tinged with a friendly intimacy. The whole earth, sky, stars, and trees are soaked with her love. Her ecstatic love engulfs an entire forest when she says "You are the forest . . ."[42] But when Allama makes use of nature as a basic metaphor, the experience is one of divine awe.

According to the vachana (273) we are discussing, shunyanubhava is accessible to the eye, ear, and tongue. Therefore, when Allama says that it cannot be imagined, he is cautioning against kavi-samaya, the poetic convention readily available to the poet's sensi-

---

[41] This episode is mentioned in Coburn, *Encountering the Goddess*, p. 161 (DRN). Nagaraj has used the 1991 edition (SUNY series in Hindu Studies) published by the State University of New York Press.

[42] For the full vachana, see vachana no. 365 in Vachana Sanchaya. For an English translation, see vachana no. 75 in Ramanujan, *Speaking of Siva*.

bility. Note that in such places Allama uses the language of shastra (propositional knowledge). This leads us to notice a special characteristic of his verses: the fact that he sometimes, like other poets, creates independent metaphors, while at others he uses the language of tantrashastra. In certain places he resorts to the usual tools – images, metaphors, and similes. He undertakes the task that most adventurous poets perform – of creating concrete metaphors from abstraction. For example, note the metaphoric mode in the following vachana:

> Sitting under a rustling tree,
> how can you complain of noise?[43] (89)

This concept of a rustling tree or a noisy tree is as complex as it is exciting. Akkamahadevi expresses a similar idea in a vachana when she says, " Making a home in the middle of the marketplace / why be shy of noise?"[44] But Allama's metaphor is entirely different. One could give many more examples of the way he mixes the concrete and the abstract. In another vachana he says, "Plucking falsehood and worshipping falsehood, they became victims of worry."[45] (214) Elsewhere he uses the phrase "cutting the shadow of water".[46] (111)

However, Allama sometimes begins to doubt this art of metaphor-making. Perhaps he grows anxious at the thought of having become a poet-craftsman. Possibly this anxiety leads him to often eschew the poet's method of metaphor-making and instead resort to technical terms formulated by tantrashastra. Allama's speciality

[43] See vachana no. 89 in Allama Prabhu, *Lord of the Cave*; and in Allama Prabhu, *Vachanas of Allama Prabhu*.

[44] My translation. For the full vachana, see vacahna no. 307 in Vachana Sanchaya. For an English translation, see vachana no. 1209 in Kalburgi, ed., *Vachana: A Collection of Vachanas*.

[45] My translation. For a translation of the full vachana, see vachana no. 214 in Allama Prabhu, *Lord of the Cave*; and in Allama Prabhu, *Vachanas of Allama Prabhu*.

[46] My translation. For a full translation, see vachana no. 111 in Allama Prabhu, *Lord of the Cave*; and in Allama Prabhu, *Vachanas of Allama Prabhu*.

lies in his effortless meandering between poetic metaphor and the technical language of tantrashastra.

The history of medieval Indian poetry shows numerous practitioners of this poetic mode, but not all have had as much expertise and artistic success as Allama. We shall discuss this unique quality in Allama later; here I draw attention to one specific point. This is that Narayana Guru of Kerala also practises Allama's poetic mode but makes use of the concepts of tantrashastra and other philosophies in the shape he finds them – for example, in the poems of his *Kali Natakam* and *Kundalini Pattu*.[47] He begins "Kundalini Pattu", "Adu pambe nalidadu pambe",[48] addressing the kundalini sarpa of Yogashastra as "pambe" – snake. All the mystic poets who engage in the confrontation between tantrashastra and poetry thus bring the mysterious metaphors of tantrism down to worldly reality. Allama, too, in many compositions, addresses kundalini sarpa as ghata sarpa, making it merely a snake. However, beyond a point Narayana Guru gives up the process of sadharinikarana (simplification without dilution) of specialist terminology.[49] Allama too sometimes relents from his adamant stance of poetry being impossible without touching the worldly.

To form the worldly metaphors, the mystic poet must possess the qualities of a devoted homemaker. Everything is important to her; she preserves everything in the hope that they may be of use in the future. Similarly, the poet's concern is to preserve everything, including all that seems small or insignificant. The poet's world has insects, worms, flora, fauna, river, water, wind, disease, army, instruments – literally everything. The poet composing in a tantrashastra–kavya interface tries to express the linguistic register of shastra (trea-

---

[47] *Kali Natakam*: a long poem on the dance of Kali. For an English translation, see SNDP, "Kali Natakam".

[48] For an English translation, see Narayana Guru, "Song of the Kundalini", pp. 69–72.

[49] According to David Shulman, "Kashmiri poeticians, unlike Descartes, insist upon generalization, *sādhāranī-karana* – a movement away from the particular to a nonspecific, almost abstract perception – as the key to all successful imaginative or artistic experience." See Shulman, *More than Real*, p. 71.

tise) by picking up one of the worldly objects mentioned above. However, sometimes he grows tired of it and moves away from the worldly, back to the pure idiom of shastra. This is precisely what happens in Allama's vachanas. While speaking in the language of shastra, Allama questions the foundational position of the poetic mode.

Allama is ever thus: denying the self is his eternal style. His stance is that nothing, including his own way, is absolute and final.

III

Does the fruit taste good if ripened by pressing?
Disaster it is if you desire, fancy and feel.
Look, better it is to die than
Indulge in such feeling, O Guheshwara! (646)

Seeing through the sense-eyes,
they say "they are two."
Going beyond the two,
they say, "they are one."
As there is no desire, no fancy.
As there is no feeling, no desire.
As there is no Guheshwara, there is no bayalu (void). (615)

When the mind becomes linga,
who else is there to worship?
When the will unites with You,
who else is there to desire?
When illusion is dispelled and truth realised,
whom to know and understand,
O Guheshwara? (421)

It wouldn't be wrong to assert that the essence of Allama's poetics lies in these three vachanas. Generally, in Indian poetics the bhashyas (commentaries) are written on poetry that is thought compelling. But Allama does not follow this practice. In this respect he is very modern. He carefully examines even the poetry he does not approve of and ponders over its nature along two main lines of thought. First, he considers the correlation between "desiring, fancying and feeling". In a way, this entails a psychological analysis of the emotions. Second, more profoundly, he clinically examines the frame of mind in which shringara-based Bhakti poetry arises. Here, Allama examines the foundations of poetic creation as an ardent Advaitin. Let us turn to the three vachanas quoted above.

In the line "When the mind becomes linga, / Who else is there to worship?" Allama analyses a particular mindset. Because bhakti poetry is in the end the creation of the Dvaita – the dualist – mind, poetic creation is ultimately a Dvaita creation. Bhakti poetry begins with the premise that the bhakta and the deity he/she adores are different. Akkamahadevi, for example, is distinct from Chennamallikarjuna. Her poetry acquires intensity in the very act of coalescing with him. The origin of such poetry lies in the anguish of separation.

We experience this fully in the compositions of dasa kavya.[50] Here, poetry is being composed in a state of incompleteness. The longing, deficiency, intensity, bewilderment, dissatisfaction, restlessness, despondency, panic, etc., of the Self, are directed towards the Other, the divine. Bhakti poetry is, in the end, a poetry of surrender. The success of Bhakti poetry lies in its attempt at moving towards and uniting with another ultimate reality which is bigger, unique, and perfect. Here, poetry has to be composed by preserving the uniqueness of this union. However, this does not mean that the state of union is permanent. When it ends, agony – an element in Bhakti poetry – ensues because the memory of the blissful union remains. Here the poet needs to beseech the great master, calling him "ayya" – an address of respect – and entreating him by saying, "I am an animal [pashu], you are the master of the animals [pashupati]."[51] Then,

---

[50] Dasa means servant, serving the beloved god. Kannada literary historians designate the fifteenth and sixteenth centuries as the Dasa poetic tradition, with the major practitioners being Vyasaraya, Purandaradasa, and Kanakadasa.

[51] This is one of Basavanna's vachanas. See vachana no. 53 in Vachana Sanchaya.

in search of the deity, the poet has to lose his/her mind.[52] This is the basis of the line "I went mad, I went mad."[53]

Such is the reality of bhakti kavya. The high achievements of Indian Bhakti poetry are the products of the Dvaita sensibility. Vaishnava poetry and the Shaiva Bhakti songs are good examples of this. To simplify the philosophical discussion, we could say that even Advaita consciousness has to capture the experience as Dvaita — at least during the act of creating poetry. Therefore, in Virashaiva Bhakti poetry too we come across this Dvaita consciousness, distinguishing between atma and paramatma.

But Allama does not accept this. His Advaitic consciousness will not compromise, not even in relation to poetry. In Advaita there is no distinction between Self and Other. Anything outside of Advaita consciousness is a pollution of thought. Allama could not have written poetry while harbouring this kind of pollution. While many Advaitins in the history of Indian philosophy had disputes with other philosophical traditions and got into fierce debates, only a few — such as Allama — raised fundamental philosophical questions about the poetic experiment. I say "a few" advisedly, to indicate the limits of my knowledge, for I cannot say with certainty that in this respect there is no one like Allama. Even Shankaracharya does not show the kind of philosophical allegiance that Allama does. For, at least in limited ways, Shankara is able to put aside his Advaita commitment. He can compose bhajans and stotras. More than that, he can produce wonderful aesthetic works such as *Saundarya Lahari*. Deploying the mysterious ways of the tantric tradition and reaching the heights of beauty, he could view the goddess as a reservoir of female beauty, in the way of the Bhakti poets. But Allama cannot. For him a work such as *Saundarya Lahari* is not in the realm of possibility. Composing that kind of work might even have seemed to him like a form of philosophical immorality. Not even the idea of friendship — let alone desire and longing — appears in Allama's vachanas.

---

[52] Das, "The Mad Lover", pp. 149–78 (DRN).
[53] Kannada bhakti song: see YouTube, "Huchu Hidiyitho".

Allama's psychological tools deconstruct all kinds of complex unions. For example, consider the line in the above-quoted vachana (421), "When the mind becomes linga, / Who else is there to worship?" Likewise, Allama may have had reason for contention with the folk song which goes, "Speak, speak linga."[54] This line contains a beauty that arises from the humility of Advaita. But, says Allama, where is the question of humility when linga itself speaks? There is anger in his vachanas; irony and intellectual arrogance too can be found in certain lines. But there is no humility in his emotional dictionary. (There is an important statement in Western philosophy – God should not indulge in theology.) There is no emotion in shunya or linga tattva. God reveals no feeling for canonical philosophy. If at all He cries, rages, loves, and lusts, it is in the puranic imagination and in the fanciful narratives of folklore. Poetry happens when emotion is separated and crystallised. This may be called the womb of emotion. But the state Allama is interpreting is one in which emotion is absent. It is the state of becoming one with the divine. Poetic creation is possible only when we return from that state, only if we descend to a state of illusion. Therefore, poetic creation is just a little "inferior only to the om-sounding conch."[55]

But Allama's consciousness accepts nothing that falls even a bit short, not even if it is poetry about Guheshwara. He considers both poetic experiment and philosophy of this kind as a retreat, as childishness or perversity. Why return to the previous state of illusion after reaching the truth? But poetry is the ultimate beautification of illusion. The bird of the mind regards illusion as real and builds its small nest with the feathers of illusion. If we do not agree that illu-

---

[54] A Kannada folk song: see YouTube, "Mathadu Mathadu Lingave".

[55] This is a line taken from a lyric "Bhavageeta" by D.R. Bendre, the foremost twentieth-century Kannada poet and one of the makers of Kannada Navodaya literary culture. This is a poem about the nature of poetry and articulates his theory of poetry. The first line of this poem is well known to Kannada readers, "Brungada benneri bantu kalpana vilasa" (Riding the back of a bumble bee / Came the glory of imagination). For the Kannada poem, see Bendre, "Bhavageeta", pp. 289–90. For an English translation, see Bendre, "Bhavageeta", pp. 43–4.

sion is also reality of a beautiful kind, there can be no entry into poetry. Therefore, at the most elementary level, poetry needs the quality of childlike innocence. When that innocent belief becomes intense, poetry becomes magical. But such understanding, which uses childlike delusion, has no place in Allama's world. He embodies a stern maturity. Even for pretence or for fun, he cannot become childlike, a naughty lover, or a partner who waits anxiously for her companion.

Allama attacks the joint processes of "desire" and "fancy". One more process – memory – is added, making a triad. The foundation of shringara-based Bhakti poetry is a fervent desire for the divine. Since shringara is the intense expression of a human emotion, that mode prevails. In certain other Virakta (ascetic) sects too, devotion is expressed as a yearning for the beloved. Desire and its possibilities are not restricted to a particular event or situation but pervade the entire personality – of, say, Akkamahadevi or Meera. Such is the sensibility evident in the entire genre of Indian Bhakti poetry.

It is possible to interpret the joint process of desire and fancy as wholehearted love and involvement with the object being written about. This is the reason for the abundance of stotra and stuti (hymns of praise) in Bhakti poetry. Thus, the grand cosmic metaphors when employed with wholehearted love lose their grandeur and become a call to intimacy instead. To put it in the idiom of Western poetics, the sublime becomes familiar, the hard and terrible become soft and mild. For example, the narrative images we come across in "Aladeleya mele malagidavana" (One who rests on the leaf of a banyan tree), "Adisidalu Yashodha" (Yashoda played with Krishna), and "Adalu pogna baro" (Let's go play) are similar to those found in sacred texts such as the Old Testament.[56] The divine here is hard, terrible, and predominantly adventurous. What looks like "holy

---

[56] These are the metaphors and images we come across in Dasa sahitya. The lines here refer to, respectively, the compositions of poets of the Dasa tradition, Purandaradasa and Sripadaraya of the sixteenth century.

terror" in Hebrew Christian religious metaphors becomes a matter of affection in Bhakti poetry. Thus, Allama's logic and criticism can be applied not only to shringara-based Bhakti poetry but to any poetry of affection. That is, Allama raises his voice against the major achievement of Bhakti poetry – i.e. a humanising of the divine.

From this point of view, Allama's position in the history of Kannada literature becomes relevant and important. If we are to call Kannada poetry until the twelfth century "classical", we have to explain its characteristic features. The age of Pampa is – to use a concept from the Old Kannada literature – the Vastuka age, in which there are solid narratives and structures of events in literary works. In terms of types of prosody, it is an age of vritta and kanda.[57] The union of vritta and kanda is the strength of Vastuka poetry. From a thematic perspective, owing to the presence of God, this is religious poetry. To summarise this lengthy discussion, Kannada poetry in the twelfth century turned from vastuka (thematic) to varnaka (descriptive). Or we can say that varnaka became dominant.[58]

The humanising of the divine by the vachanakaras led to the as-

[57] These are Kannada prosodic features. Vritta is derived from classical Sanskrit poetry. It is a verse with a particular number of letters, and there are different kinds of vritta with varying syllables. Kanda is a four-line stanza which follows specific syllabic time lengths (matras) for each line. The first and third lines of kanda have three four-length units (gana) and the second and fourth lines have five four-length units.

[58] Vastuka and Varnaka are two kinds of poetic practices in classical Kannada poetry. According to the *Kannada Kaipidi*, the poetry that follows the poetic and prosodic features of Sanskrit poetic practices is called Vastuka, and poetry that does not follow the model of Sanskrit poetry is called Varnaka. For more, see Puttappa, *Kannada Kaipidi*. For a detailed discussion, see Bhatt, "Vastuka-Varnaka", pp. 308–26. In his translation of Allama Prabhu's vachanas, H.S. Shivaprakash translates Vastuka and Varnaka as objective poetry and subjective poetry. See Shivaprakash, *I Keep Vigil of Rudra*, p. 52. They can also be called thematic poetry (Vastuka) and descriptive poetry (Varnaka). However, Nagaraj is using Vastuka in the sense that poets like Pampa chose themes from epics like the *Mahabharata*, or from the Jain Purana weaving of larger narratives around these, predominantly in the form of vritta and kanda. According to him, the vachanakaras did not follow this tradition.

cendancy of the varnaka imagination in Kannada literature. The Vachana movement achieved in the Kannada context what the Bhagavata imagination did in the context of Vaishnava poetry. The irony here is that Allama thinks there is no scope for humanising the divine in the philosophical womb of the Vachana movement. To be specific, in Kannada it was only Akkamahadevi who took the model of shringara-based Bhakti poetry to its highest level, though this model of humanising the divine can also be seen in Basavanna and other vachanakartis (women vachana poets). But what is important here is that Allama disagrees strongly with this trend. He tries to break the shackles of the "desiring-fancying-feeling" that we come across in Bhakti poets like Akkamahadevi.

In one of the three vachanas (646) we are discussing, Allama gives us a deeper insight when he writes, "Does the fruit taste good if ripened by pressing?"[59] A deeper understanding of Allama is possible if we take note of the similarity between the poetics of Bhakti compositions and the Western romantic theory of poetry. Shringara-based Bhakti poetry achieves its effect through a repetition of emotions. Its fulfilment lies in its depth rather than in breadth. The technique of repetition is the source of strength in Bhakti poetry. Akkamahadevi's vachana, given below, exemplifies this.

Tanu karagadavaralli
majjanavanolleyayya ninu.
Mana karagadavaralli
pushpavanolleyayya ninu.
Haduligaralladavaralli
gandhakshateyanolleyayya ninu.
Arivu kandereyadavaralli
aratiyanolleyayya ninu.
Bhavashuddhavilladavaralli
dhupavanolleyayya ninu.
Parinamigalalladavaralli
naivedyavanolleyayya ninu.
Trikarana shuddhavilladavaralli

[59] This line is a criticism of shringara-based Bhakti poetry.

tambulavanolleyayya ninu.
Hrudayakamala araladavaralli
iralolleyayya ninu.
Ennali enuntendu karasthalavanimbugonde hela
Chennamallikarjunayya.[60]

Ayya,
Where the body is not at work
You wouldn't accept a bath from them;
Where the mind is not kind
You wouldn't accept flowers;
From the ones who are callous
You wouldn't accept fragrant rice;
From the ignorant ones
You wouldn't accept the arati;
Where the feeling is not pure
You wouldn't accept incense;
Where there is no composure
You wouldn't accept the holy food;
Where the body, mind and soul are tainted
You wouldn't accept a betel leaf;
Where the heart is not blossomed
You wouldn't want to stay.
O Chennamallikarjunayya,
You came and nested on my palm.
Tell me,
what did you see in me? (218)

Several kinds of repetitions are apparent here. One is repetition through syllabic rhyme – in Kannada ninu, meaning "you", appears at the end of each line – and another is the repetition of a structure – rejection, and the reason for rejection. With subtle repetitions of the Kannada sound "na" across the entire vachana, the beauty of this composition increases exponentially. Also, by a repetitive emphasis on Chennamallikarjuna's rejections, Akkamahadevi man-

---

[60] See vachana no. 218 in Vachana Sanchaya. The translator has given the phonetic transcription of the Kannada version in order to properly show Nagaraj's phonetic analysis of the vachana.

ages to create a sense of acceptance in the end.[61] She knows Chennamallikarjuna's reasons for the rejections, but she doesn't know his reasons for accepting her. Puzzled by this, she questions Chennamallikarjuna in the last line. Thus, repetition is a successful method in Akkamahadevi's vachanas – and this is exactly what Allama criticises, comparing it to a method of "making fruit ripe by pressing it [repeatedly]."

The idea of ripening fruit by pressing it is not new in classical Kannada poetry. It was used not just in shringara-based Bhakti poetry: examples exist in several such compositions by Pampa. "Alakam mandara shunyam, kadapu makarika patra shunyam"(Her hair suffered for the lack of mandara flowers, / cheeks without fragrant powder) is the best example.[62] This is how Vastuka poetry includes varnaka in its form and achieves its grand expanse. The uniqueness of Allama's poetry lies in denying that the Vastuka technique achieved this grand expanse. Being dense and concise is an important combination for Allama. Whereas the epic poets or Vastuka poets use every opportunity to express a thought over an entire stanza or two, Allama condenses his thoughts into an image within a line. To put it another way, the Vastuka imagination can expand on even the smallest unit. Although Vastuka poetry is controlled by the principle of relevance, its essential nature is to expand. In contrast, Allama's imagination can pack tight even the grandest possibility into its most condensed expression. Since it compresses a large mass into an atom, his poetry has an explosive quality. In this context, we are reminded of Pampa's description in his *Adipurana* of the Sitoda river as an illustration of Vastuka poetry's method of elaborate description:

No stream on this earth can be compared to the Sitoda river, where there live lovely geese, and therefore she is full of a goose tune. She is

---

[61] Note in the vachana Akkamahadevi's Chennamallikarjuna rejection of various things, such as bath, flower, etc.

[62] This is a depiction of Swayamprabhe, an important character in Pampa's *Adipurana*, after she loses her husband.

capable of breaking even the biggest mountains and is intoxicated by butterflies which have swallowed the nectar of cinnamon, mango, and gooseberry flowers that have grown on her banks; she is the one who creates happiness among the people of the country called Videha. (Pampa's *Adipurana*, Chapter 1, stanza 54)[63]

The image of a river that flows leisurely and luxuriously in Pampa's imagination becomes narrow in Allama's. His line "the running river is all legs"[64] is composed as a contrast to the method of making "fruit ripe by pressing it".

Allama's poetics is not text-centric. It is concerned more with the background process in which a text is formed, the mind that creates a certain type of work, and the philosophical framework that shapes such a mind. (It is crucial to note that this analysis of the formation of mind is relevant not only in the context of Kannada poetry but in the history of Indian poetry as a whole.)

Let me explain this further with the help of two concepts – sankocha and vikasa (contraction and unfoldment) – that we come across in Kashmir Shaivism.[65] Sankocha involves ignoring external reality and concentrating on the internal, while vikasa takes into account external reality along with the inner. Allama's is the way of the sankocha mode. Therefore, an image such as "the running river is all legs" becomes a possibility in his eye. But there is also a great poet in Allama: he pays attention to the vikasa mode as well; or we could say he composes poetry in that mode as well. It is important to note that these two concepts mean more than my use of them here would suggest. And we need, beyond this, to elaborate on the idea that Allama is particularly skilful in the sankocha mode. The poet of the vikasa mode, to whichever sect he belongs, gives importance to outer reality and its narration. Kalidasa belongs to this tribe. Although deeply influenced by Shaivism, he is a poet of the vikasa mode. Therefore, he does not create images that reflect reality in the mir-

---

[63] Pampa, *Pampa Mahakavi Virachita Adipuranam*, p. 57.

[64] For the full vachana, see vachana no. 775 in Ramanujan, *Speaking of Siva*.

[65] Singh, "Pratyabhijna Vimarshini", Glossary (DRN). Sources unknown. Also see Kshemaraja, *Pratyabhijnahrdayam*, pp. 86–7.

ror of the internal self. He composes literature within the framework accepted by external reality and lokadharma, the precepts of the world outside. So he can compose plays as well as poetry. But Allama has no patience with this. He draws the entire world into himself, like a tortoise withdrawing into its shell. In the crucible of his imagination the world gets beaten into the shape he sees. It assumes the form he gives it. Hence, his consciousness of having "known within himself / Guheshwaralinga."[66] (784) Common to both Virashaivism and Kashmir Shaivism is the idea that everything is Shiva; everything is Guheshwara linga. But Allama realises this within himself.

The difference between sankocha and vikasa need not be like the difference between Kalidasa and Allama — a difference in language and genre. It may also be a subtle distinction between poets in the same setting. In a way, Akkamahadevi belongs to the path of vikasa, though she wrote in the tight genre of vachanas, which are generally in the sankocha mode. She has the patience for intricate work. The manner in which her images evolve and are interwoven is evidence of this.

Coming back to Kalidasa, the vikasa mode is visible in the way he creates images. Like Allama, he believes in Shaiva philosophical postulates. It is his conviction, too, that this world is full of Shiva's presence. But the way he puts it across is different. The entire philosophy of his *Abhijnana Shakuntala* is believed to be shaped by the notion of pratyabhijnana (re-cognition) of Kashmir Shaivism.[67] Some

---

[66] My translation. For a translation of the full vachana, see vachana no. 1149 in Allama Prabhu, *Lord of the Cave.*

[67] Among the many schools of Kashmir Shaivism, pratyabhijnana (doctrine of recognition) and spanda (doctrine of vibration) are the two which do not extend back directly to agama traditions. Utpaladeva, a tenth-century philosopher, describes pratyabhijnana as the ultimate experience of enlightenment born from the recognition that one's own authentic identity is Shiva Himself. According to him, a soul is bound in this world because he has forgotten his authentic identity. He can achieve liberation by recognising that he is not the slave of creation (pashu), but its master (pati). See Dyczkowski, *The Doctrine of Vibration*, pp. 17–20. For more, see Kshemaraja, *Pratyabhijnahridayam.*

go further and say that the entire play is an allegory of the pratyabhi-jnana theory. To use Allama's terminology, this play is a story of for-getfulness and re-cognition. Dushyanta becomes so oblivious of the past that his union with Shakuntala is broken. Pratyabhijnana (re-cognition) happens through the trace of the ring that he had given Shakuntala. Thus, the play can be read as being about the philoso-phical triad: forgetfulness, trace, and re-cognition. But this does not mean Kalidasa wrote the play to justify a philosophical manifesto. The hallmark of genius is the obliteration of the line separating phi-losophy and experience. There is no separate existence for meta-phor and philosophy. As a story of purely human affairs *Abhijnana Shakuntala* is a successful work at the same time as being a play that evokes pure philosophical excitement. The difference between literature and philosophy lies ultimately in the concrete versus the abstract, as outlined by Lukács. If literature is an expression of the concrete, the foundation of philosophy is abstraction. Thus, all of Kalidasa's philosophical postulates find concrete expression.

We can compare Kalidasa and Allama by considering this poem from *Abhijnana Shakuntala*:

Ya srushtihi srashturadya vahati vidhihutam ya havirya cha hotri I
Ye dve kalam vidhattah shrutivishayaguna ya sthita vyapya vishwam I
Yamahahu sarvabijaprakrutiriti yaya praninaha pranavantaha I
Pratyakshabhihi prapannastanubhiravatu vastabhirashtabhirishaha II

(Invocation from *Abhijnana Shakuntalam*).

(That visible form, viz. water) which (was) the first creation of the Cre-ator; (that, viz. fire) which bears the oblation offered-according-to-rule; and (that visible form, viz. the priest) which (is) the offerer-of-the-obla-tion; (those) two (visible forms, viz. the Sun and Moon) which regulate time; (that, viz. ether) which perpetually pervades all space, having the quality (sound) perceptible by the ear; (that, viz. the earth) which they call the originator of all created-things; (that, viz. the air) by which living beings are furnished with breath – may Isa [the Supreme Lord], endowed with [manifested in] these eight visible forms, preserve you![68]

___

[68] Kalidasa, *Sakuntala*, p.1.

Allama differs in this from Kalidasa. When he finds the world of philosophy problematic, he returns to the play of language. Given the invocation above, we can discuss the differences between Allama and Kalidasa. The philosophy and the linguistic registers in this verse – for example, Shiva's ashtatanu – the eight-fold body – also appear in Allama's compositions. But Kalidasa's method is different. "Ya shrushtihi: srashturadya" refers to the primordial creation of Brahma. According to Vedic mythology, this is "water". But Kalidasa is not explicit on this – just as he is not in reference to anything directly in these lines. For instance, he does not say agni (fire). Instead, he refers to something that carries havirbhaga, the share of oblations offered in the homa ritual.

The renowned Kannada critic Kirtinath Kurtkoti explains the philosophical excitement behind this verse as follows:

> This poem affirms that the relation between God and nature is not just a matter of appearance, but a real one . . . The next step would be the relation between the theory of pratyabhijnana and this poem. Though nature may appear to our eyes as God's body, we cannot experience it immediately. Calling water "water" is one way of understanding it, calling it "the first creation of Brahma" produces a different understanding . . . Just as truth is revealed when one calls it "water", another truth of a similar kind is revealed when one says "water is the first creation of Brahma." It should also be realised that these two are not "different" truths but a single truth revealed in different stages to our understanding. Another question remains. How is this verse related to the theme of the play? . . . Like dhvanyartha (suggested meaning) flashing in the cloud of vachyartha (explicit meaning) in language, the ring of pratyabhijnana rebuilds broken relationships. The process of understanding that occurs in the Invocation unfolds throughout the play.[69]

Kalidasa follows the mode of dissemination – vikasa, prasarana – while Allama moves along the mode of sankocha, or akunchana, the act of contraction. In the following vachana, he describes

____

[69] Kurtkoti, *Uriya Nalige*, pp. 60–1 (DRN). My translation. For an English translation of this book, see Kurtkoti, *Flaming Tongue*.

the tragedy of amnesia whereby there is no possibility of understanding the internal relations constituting Shivaness:

In water, fire was drenched.
In fire, radiance was blazed.
Realise it!
How strange it is, relations are not known.
In light, darkness was hidden
where Guheshwara dwells. (1053)

Look! When remembered without desiring,
an unimagined man arrived.
Look! When remembered without imagining,
an unfelt bliss dawned.
When one understands Guheshwara linga,
there is no "I", and there is no "You"! (444)

As noted earlier, there is in Allama's vachanas an engagement
with several Shaivite streams. He fashions his philosophy by engaging at once with several Kashmir Shaiva and Siddha darshana sects.
The form and structure inherited by other vachanakaras is given
shape by Allama. In the latter vachana (444) quoted above, we get
a clue of the source from which Allama might have adopted the
thoughts for this shringara-based poetic experiment. In this respect, two sutras from *Spandakarika* are very important.

Ayamevodayas tasya dhyayesya dhyayi-cetasi/
Tadatmata-Samapattir icchatah sadhakasya na//6.
Iyamevamrtapraptir ayameva atmano grahah/
Iyam nirvana-diksa ca siva-sadbhavadayini//7.

This only is the manifestation of the object of meditation in the medi-
tator's mind that the aspirant with a resolute will has the realisation of
his identity with that (object of meditation). This alone is the acquisition of ambrosia leading to immortality; this alone is the realisation of
Self: this alone is the initiation of liberation leading to identity with
Siva.[70]

---

[70] Singh, trans., *Spandakarikas,* pp. 121–3 (DRN's edition is 1994).

Kshemaraja gives an interesting insight into the above sutras. The expression "Iha Shivo bhutva Shivam Yajet" means "one should worship Shiva by becoming Shiva". Kshemaraja goes further and interprets "Tadatmata samapattih" as identifying oneself with Shiva, perceiving Shiva as inseparable from the self.[71] Here Advaya reaches its ultimate state of light (i.e. spanda); a state of natural bliss. This interpretation sheds some light on the origin of Allama's antagonistic ideas and imagery. Allama expands what had been a precept in Kashmir Shaivism into a concrete philosophical refutation.

The Trika theory of Kashmir Shaivism has two concepts: atmavyapti and shivavyapti (self and Shiva).[72] If shringara-based Bhakti poetry remains at the level of atmavyapti, Allama progresses to shivavyapti, and from this philosophical position he critiques the position of atmavyapti. Atmavyapti is based on the binary opposition between you and I. That distinction disappears in shivavyapti.

There are many subtleties in the vachana (444) we are now discussing. The most important is the fact that it is expressed from a woman's point of view. We could say that here Allama thinks of himself as a woman. For other Bhakti poets, speaking from a female perspective is not only common but inevitable. In this respect, the notion of sharana sati linga pati (sharana as wife and linga as husband) is quite natural to the philosophy of the Vachana movement. Allama is not one to speak in this idiom. However, in this vachana (444), even though he does not put it directly, the woman's voice can be heard when he says, "Look! When remembered without desiring, / an unimagined man arrived." He also mentions bliss. This is an exciting example of Allama's paradoxical consciousness. In his idea of union there is no sexual desire. In his notion of pleasure

---

[71] Ibid., p.123.

[72] According to Trika Shaivism, on the path to liberation atmavyapti is the initial stage of experiencing "divine grace". It leads an individual to realisation of the self (atma). The second stage is a complete realisation and attainment of the state of "Shiva" and is called "shivavyapti". The distinctions between self and Shiva disappear completely in this stage. See Pandit, *An Introduction to the Philosophy of Trika Shaivism*, p. 187.

there is no feeling – it is unfelt bliss. In his concept of memory there is no imagination. Though he uses material from the intellectual-emotional worlds of other writers, he turns it upside down. Though the techniques of bedagu-vachana (fancy vachana) are at work here, Allama does not, on the surface, use paradoxes to make them conspicuous.

In this vachana (444) Allama uses a philosophical structure for female–male and the notion of pleasure, but presents them as distinct from how they are ordinarily perceived. It is here that a question about Allama's philosophical consistency arises. It is difficult to give a philosophical answer to why Allama uses, at least obliquely, the philosophical structures he rejects elsewhere. A literary explanation may be attempted: Allama too sometimes melts. Although aware of being entirely different from his contemporaries, he tries to interact with them. To convert them through intense dialogue is his philosophical method. He criticises, rebukes, and ridicules those who are not in agreement with him, and can go so far as to create an uproar. He ignores none. The thought that he can disdain those younger and less experienced than himself never crosses his mind. Therefore, even though Allama sometimes appears to embody "spiritual pride",[73] there is also a deep spiritual humility and the notion of equality within him. There is as much power in Allama's appreciation of and deference with his contemporaries as in his criticism and spiritual perturbation. Especially in relation to Basavanna, he becomes emotional and acknowledges Basavanna as greater than him. This is one outstanding feature of his conversation with others.

The vachana (444) we are discussing presents one dimension of Allama's conversation with others. He has to enter the mind of his interlocutors and try to feel like them – at least once. It is like being in a symphony orchestra with the others all playing the same raga. The vachana (89) we discussed earlier may be recalled here as well.

---

[73] Huxley uses this concept while writing about St Francis of Assisi (DRN). See Huxley, *The Perennial Philosophy*, p. 327.

While trying to enter the mind of his contemporary Akkamahadevi when she writes, "Making a home on the mountain / Why
fear the beasts," he transforms it through his metaphoric mode.
His line, "Sitting under a rustling tree, / How can you complain
of noise? . . ." shows a state of mind different from that of Akkamahadevi's – she who would speak of "Making a home on the
mountain."

In this vachana (444) Allama is attempting to make intertextual
connections by engaging indirectly with shringara-based Bhakti
poetry. He tries to enter the state of mind in which Akkamahadevi
speaks of Chennamallikarjuna making love to her. But Allama's paradoxical imagination performs this differently. Thus, even if he says
that he made love, he does not give up his original stand. Such is the
imagination of Allama that it melts everything the way it wants, according to his mould and mood. Although it begins as a vachana of
Dvaita romance, it ends up endorsing the Advaita position. Here
the line "When one understands Guheshwara linga" is important.
Though the experience of pleasure is dominant in others, Allama
perceives the experience as a mode of understanding. Even at the
peak of deep involvement he cannot but experience a surge of understanding. The importance of this vachana is that the surge to
ultimate understanding is not accidental. Allama presents his paradoxical experience step by step in each line, and each dot is connected to the next until there is a final explosion.

IV

Even after singing billions of vachanas,
The mind craved for more.
the mind does not know the ghana (the great absolute)
nor does the ghana know the mind.
Once the mind understands Guheshwara linga,
all songs vanish into one word. (627)

Speech is jyotirlinga (radiant linga)
swara (vowel sound / music) paratattva (supreme principle).
When one's palate and lips

conjoin in the mouth,
what comes out transcends
nada, bindu, and kala (physical, subtle and causal body).
Listen, O fool!
Even though Guheshwara's sharanas speak,
they are not impure. (1234)

In both these vachanas Allama is standing on the shores of poetic renunciation. It is the good fortune of the Kannada language that though Allama has often ventured as far as these shores, he has always returned to poetry. In a vachana (1045) he says, "All master poets. / Perished by angst . . ."[74] Therefore, there is a volcano of angst in the womb of poetic composition. The basis of Allama's poetics is to shed light on the internal relationship between song and longing. The state of longing becomes a state of liberation for those who are satisfied with just their poetic state. From an aesthetic viewpoint, sadness, angst, and regret become material for poetic creation. Allama, however, disagrees with this. For him the mind has to grasp the ghana – the "great absolute" that is profundity – which in turn must grasp the mind. Such understanding is the ultimate state of Advaya. Allama ridicules the poet who does not reach this state despite "singing billions of vachanas". In another vachana he says:

Those who are dipped in poetic fancy
is there a limit? Or limitlessness?
They play the fancy game of composing verses
but fail to understand the mystery of Guheshwara. (497)

Despite being an excellent poet himself, Allama draws our attention to the scepticism that exists in the depths of poetry. Though a touch of scepticism haunts it, poetry keeps searching for divyanubhava (divine experience). As soon as this scepticism about the power of the word or sound disappears, pride in the pomp of the word or sound appears. Allama often cautions us about such pride;

[74] For a full translation, see vachana no. 1068 in Allama Prabhu, *Lord of the Cave*; and vachana no. 1365 in Allama Prabhu, *Vachanas of Allama Prabhu*.

hence the expression "the pomp of the word" forms an important concept in his critical idiom. He addresses the act of forgetting the original purpose and wasting effort in peripheral activities as "Having gone to pluck flowers, / I forgot the basket [of linga]. / Engaged in worshipping, / I forgot the linga."[75] (1161) In many of his vachanas he criticises in various ways the pomp of the word.[76] In his view "the innocent state sans the knowledge of language becomes a great achievement."

What is relevant at this moment is the idea of pride in the pomp of the word, or verbiage. By transposing this idea, we can employ it in the poetics of worldly poetry (laukika kavya: non-mystical poetry). There it becomes the fallacy of hyperbole. But Allama uses this notion in relation to mystic poetry, analysing the situation where speech has grown arrogant and lost its modesty. He expresses this clearly in the following vachana:

> Until feeling is eliminated and desire erased,
> what is great about the union?
> Until the pride in pompous words is shed,
> are words before an object of any use?
> Until the word "Guheshwara" becomes silent
> can anything be achieved
> by toiling for bayalu? (The void). (612)

Though Allama's critique of the word can be useful for an analysis of the world's poetry, it works in the deeper recesses, beyond the reach of worldly thought. Allama speaks of the infertility of the word. In another vachana (625) he says, "The word called Guheshwara became utterly barren."[77] As things wear out with overuse, so do words. They wear out and become barren.

---

[75] For a full translation, see vachana no.1625 in Allama Prabhu, *Lord of the Cave*; and vachana no. 1870 in Allama Prabhu, *Vachanas of Allama Prabhu*.

[76] See vachana nos 701, 264, 291, 406, 491, 564, and 1490 in Allama Prabhu, *Lord of the Cave*.

[77] For the full vachana, see vachana no. 625 in Allama Prabhu, *Lord of the Cave*; and vachana no. 625 in Allama Prabhu, *Vachanas of Allama Prabhu*.

At this point Allama's philosophy of language can be compared with that of other ancient philosophers. A comparative discussion with Bhartrhari and his followers reveals interesting ideas. Bhartrhari is very optimistic about language. Examining his analysis of the levels of language, one may raise objections about the stylistic level – vaikhari – but not about other levels.[78] Spiritualisation of the power of language is a key feature of ancient Vedic thought. Language is considered an organic part of Brahman, and being alive and active with language is nothing but being active in Brahman. The logical end point of this conviction was where grammar began to be perceived as a means for mukti (liberation). The spiritualisation of language obviously involves admiration of the power of poetry. If at all there is scepticism about language, it is not about its primary capacity but about the limitations of the individual imagination in relation to language-use.

At one level Kashmir Shaivism too propagates spiritualising language. Although this school of thought is unconventional and revolutionary in other domains, it remains conservative about human language; it does not doubt the supremacy – Brahmahtva – of language. We can for instance examine this line of thought in Kshemaraja, who says that language is also Shiva's lile (play);[79] hence, there is no reason to suspect it. Shiva shakti (the power of Shiva) is manifest in language, as in other realities. The beauty of meaning in language is also Shiva's grace. This attitude to language is not just true

---

[78] In Bhartrhari's explanation of communication, a linguistic expression resides in the human mind as speech potential (shabdabija) which passes through three stages: pasyanti, madhyama, and vaikhari. Pasyanti is the inarticulate stage which is as non-verbal as it is subtle; madhyama is inner shabda, the being revealed in the mind when manifested by articulated utterance. The final stage, uttered speech, is vaikhari. For more, see Bhartrhari, *The Vakyapadiya*. Abhinavagupta further adds the fourth stage, "paravak": the final stage where shabda resides in the absolute consciousness. See Abhinavagupta, *Para-trisika-Vivarana*, pp. 8–9.

[79] Kshemaraja's Shaiva philosophy of language may be compared with Wittgenstein's notion of "the language game" (DRN). For the discussion of Kshemaraja's philosophy of language, see Harvey, *Mantra*.

in the case of Kshemaraja, but also others. In *Dhvanyaloka Lochana* Abhinavagupta shows no hint of scepticism regarding language either. To classify this attitude to language in a particular framework, its proponents who celebrate language power may be categorised as "celebrators of language". Allama, on the other hand, represents a sceptical strain in relation to language.

We need not conclude from this that Allama developed his linguistic or literary analysis systematically in his vachanas. He formulates an indirect critique. Nowhere does he directly refer to vaikhari (the spoken word of the human being), madhyama (mental speech, verbalised but not spoken), pasyanti (an idea not yet expressed in words), or para (the first stage of sound, where ideas germinate). Without making this kind of classification, Allama looks at language or vak (speech) as a unitary principle and unitary reality. But he brings an enormous quality of theatricality to his compositions that others do not. By calling sound/word the leftover of the ear (vachana no. 564), he leaves no scope for the deification of language. His Guheshwara exists only in the absence of the leftover. While examining the power of words, "celebrationists" eventually reach a crescendo of acceptance. Allama compares this involvement with language to the thoughtlessness of a goat that continues to eat ceaselessly. He possesses the capacity to see the "word" becoming bashful.[80]

Through his method of an indirect critique of language, Allama always teeters at the edge of renouncing poetry. It is natural that poetry should appear unnecessary or even disgusting to one such as Allama who believes silence, or the absence of language, is a state of supreme divinity. However, Allama uses poetry as a means of dialogue with his contemporaries. No matter how concerned he is at the barrenness or exhaustion of the word, he cannot give up poetry. Thus Allama says, "All songs vanish into one word" (627). "One word" here means pranava, the sacred syllable Om. The wave

---

[80] For an example, see vachana no. 264 in Allama Prabhu, *Lord of the Cave*; and in Allama Prabhu, *Vachanas of Allama Prabhu*.

of Allama's sankocha mode rushes towards renouncing the word. His view seems to be that if "all songs vanish into one word", why involve yourself in a futile exercise with words.

Since Allama tries to maintain his uniqueness while working within the vast and multifaceted Shaiva tradition, many arguments and debates resonate even in his saying "all songs vanish into one word". When in the vachana (1234) Allama says "Speech is jyotirlinga (radiant linga)", he is suggesting that pranava itself is linga, the linga of light. The ancients had pondered why one must not call out to "Shiva" directly instead of using pranava. There is an insight about this in Patanjali, who is influenced by Pashupata Shaivism, which may be called "non-theism".[81] According to him, pranava itself has no strength; whatever strength there is exists only in Shiva. Allama says directly and emphatically what Patanjali states mildly. What is forceful about the word pranava? Its importance lies in its meaning, and its meaning is Shiva himself. Note the stance of the following vachana:

Listen, all you wise men, reciting pranava [OM].
Know its meaning.
Does pranava say – "naham" (It's not I)?
Does pranava say – "koham" (Who am I)?
Does pranava say – "soham" (I am He)?
Does pranava say – "chidaham" (I am consciousness)?
It doesn't.
Pranava says "bhargo devasya dhimahi" (may we meet thy
glorious grace).[82]
It says, "savituhu padamangaha syat bhargastu lingameva
chadhimahi padamityesham gayatryam lingasambandhaha"

---

[81] The term non-theism refers to a range of belief systems which are either silent or express scepticism towards the theistic idea of the divine – which believes God to be a person, and accordingly worship. In the context of premodern South Asia, Buddhism, Advaita darshana, and some of the Shaiva sects, including Pashupata, are deemed as non-theistic. See Wainwright, "Nontheistic Conceptions of the Divine", pp. 59–79.

[82] This is a line from the Gayatri Mantra.

(The words "savitur" and "dheemahi" form part of the spell. Maybe
the linga itself is the glorious light.)
The meaning of pranava pervades You,
O Guheshwara! (1158)

There is method in Allama's thought. At one stage he is suspicious of language and says, "all songs vanish into one word". Then
he rejects pranava since it is also at one level a word. And he concludes that the importance of pranava lies in its meaning, which is
Shiva (Guheshwara).

Allama's reflections on the idea of "word" and "pranava" here are
part of the multifaceted debates that have taken place in the history
of Indian spiritual thought. In the backdrop of his reflections there
is a larger debate about the power of word/sound, specifically regarding the meaning of mantras. According to one line of thought,
even if the power of poetry is denied, the power of the mantra may
be accepted. Allama seems to come to this conclusion when he says,
"all songs vanish into one word." However, he does not adhere to
this conclusion entirely. The debate on mantras began with a discussion of Veda mantras. According to traditionalists, mantras have
no meaning. If we consider its meaning, a Veda mantra appears
absurd, says Katya, an ancient.[83] The Vedas are crowded with things
beyond the world's ordinary logic, such as animals with many
heads. By mentioning this, Katya does not deny the Vedas. He asserts that "the strength of the Vedas lies not in the meaning but in
word/sound." Another Mimamsaka, Shabara Swamy, who sees
Katya as his opponent, rejects this argument and argues that the
sounds or mantras in the Vedas are meaningful.[84]

Allama's stance is not in favour of Katya. Since at one level he
speaks in favour of meaning, he may appear to agree with Shabara

---

[83] Nagaraj seems to refer to Katyayana, a Sanskrit grammarian and math-
ematician who is said to have lived during the third century BC.

[84] Shabara Swamy: a scholar who wrote a commentary on *Jaimini Nyaya
(Mimamsa) Sutra*. He is known for reframing the problem of meaning and word
through his method of the structural system of sentences, linguistic analysis,
and philosophy of language. For more, see Sabara, *Sabara-Bhasya*.

Swamy. But there is a wide gap between the arguments of Mimam-sakas like Shabara Swamy and Allama: the threads of the latter's philosophy are woven at a different level.

We may briefly supply its background here. There is a fundamental difference between Vedic mantras and the mantras of the tantric sects. According to the philosophy that lies behind Vedamantras, humans and gods are different. Reciting mantras connects humans with gods, but they do not become one. Humans and gods are merely brought into association through the bond of mantras. The philosophy of tantric mantras is different as it makes no distinction between the human being and the god, subscribing to the ultimate state of Advaya. Allama, who meditates on the non-duality of "You-I", is closer to tantrism. However, in Shaivism tantrism declined on account of going to great extremes. This decline dismayed Allama, who disagreed with the extreme forms while being in agreement with Shaiva tantrism's philosophical positions.

Allama is sceptical about language but uses language, like those he criticises, to grasp Guheshwara. He would not have become a poet without a weakness for metaphors. He opposes the metaphoric mode of desiring–fancying–feeling but tries to see Guheshwara in other modes. In other words, there is a streak of self-denial in Allama, which is why he remains a poet. The following vachana captures this central paradox:

> Keen to witness your radiance [teja],
> I went out.
> It was like a billion suns rising!
> Witnessing a million flashes of lightning (minchina balli),
> I was awestruck.
> O Guheshwara,
> no metaphor can grasp you,
> when you become jyotirlinga (radiant linga). (1179)

Though Allama says at the end, "No metaphor can grasp you", he uses metaphors throughout the vachana (1179). Instead of using the Kannada word belagu (bright morning), he uses teja (radiance). He tries to see the radiance of Guheshwara, which is like "a billion suns rising". The same simile appears in the *Bhagavad Gita*. Though Allama seems to have taken the help of Sanskrit philosophical conventions, he returns to Kannada, where his originality as a poet is evident. Guheshwara's radiance becomes minchina balli (a million flashes of lightning).

Allama's readers are naturally reminded of his view of the word becoming shy, of the word's death, of its rabble-rousing capacity. Seeing multiple flashes of lightning at once is singularly exhausting for the eye. More than that, the word itself becomes exhausted. Thus, there is a unique beauty in the very suffering of the word that tries to grasp gigantic flashes of lightning. The exhaustion of the word becomes poetry.

Thus, a cruel poetic pleasure sets out to capture the divine. The spirit of a Spanish bullfight is very much evident in mystic poetry. Thanks to the pleasure that arises from the suffering endured in the persistent quest to grasp what cannot be grasped, mystic poetry becomes a source of irresistible intoxication for poets. Readers too grow obsessed with such intoxication. In the process, language becomes powerful – its inner layers become active and begin to flow out. The most ordinary words in the language gain the capacity to carry the greatest of thoughts. So Allama, who sets out to be sceptical of words and language, enhances the metaphoric power of the Kannada language. Perhaps it is the basic virtue of language and poetry to extract the life force even from those who, like Allama, oppose it.

The concept of "word defilement" accompanies the idea of "word celebration" in Allama. The "word" dies in the extremities of its pride, and it dies as a result of the rabble it creates. This is word defilement. However, poetry's living quality lies in both word pride and word defilement. Thus, Allama's creativity originates in his scepticism about language. The source of Allama's poetic experiment lies in his understanding that poetry takes birth in a state of disconnectedness. Hence, instead of starting the composition with desire and then passing towards the state of inevitable despair, he begins with a sense of paradox and rupture. Therefore, his compositions are replete with paradoxical images and metaphors.

Let us take a look at the following vachana:

I saw the mind conceive and the hand give birth.
I saw the ear savour the aroma of the camphor.
I saw the nose gulp down the shine of pearls.
I saw the starving eyes devour diamonds (vajra).
O Guheshwara,
I saw the three worlds hide in a sapphire (nila). (101)

Here Allama reinterprets the process of desiring-fancying-feeling through his paradoxical consciousness. While in shringara-based bhakti poetry there is a systematic expression of shringara in the process of union and intercourse before being conceived, in Allama's world all this is turned upside down. Here "the mind conceives, the hand gives birth" and "The ear savours the smell of camphor."[85] Everything becomes absurd. But slowly Allama finds harmony even in this state of chaos, and a system emerges there as well.

Each time Allama speaks of grasping Guheshwara in poetry, he makes use of the image of darkness. In him poetry is not born in a state of union and harmony. His vachana, the image of darkness, and Guheshwara all go in different directions. Poetry thus emerges in an atrocious state of disconnectedness. Whenever an attempt is made to grasp Guheshwara, Allama brings in the notion of darkness and brightness – as in the following vachana:

Darkness on the hand that holds linga,
Darkness on the eyes that see,
Darkness on the mind that remembers.
Darkness on this side
When Guheshwara is on the other side. (219)

As Allama uses darkness and brightness with their direct meaning, with no effort to be skilful, they naturally take on an abstract nature.

Several ways exist for us to understand how Allama's spiritual perturbation is turned into poetry. Allama was confronted with three

[85] In the modernist Kannada poet Gopalakrishna Adiga's *Bhumigeeta* there is an image that reminds us of this (DRN). See Adiga Angala, "Bhoomigeeta".

modes of expression. Or we can say that the medieval Shaiva imagination created three forms of expression: one, the Shaiva-nai-yayikas' mode of logic; two, gitamarga, the mode of song; and three, the pauranic narrative mode. I don't have the expertise to examine the ways in which these paths evolved distinctly, nor is this the right place to do so. It is interesting to note that Allama had before him the path of Shaiva-naiyayikas. Shaivas were the most significant lo-gicians of medieval India. What remains unexamined in contem-porary scholarship is the nature of the relationship between the Shaiva religiosity of these logicians and their logical method. To express which aspect of their Shaiva religiosity did they use their logical method? The problem with present scholarship is that it does not go beyond the primary information that most Naiyayikas were Shaivas.

It is worth noting that Allama rejected all three paths. His is the fourth path, which is impossible to define and explain in a simple formula. But this much is true: there are complex arguments behind his path. We can summarise them as follows.

In his compositions Allama combines Shaiva-naiyayikas' modes of logic and gitamarga. He turns logic into a metaphor by taking it to the extreme. Logic and song lose their individuality and be-come one. At the pan-Indian level too, Allama is prominent among mystics who free gitamarga from shringara and explore other pos-sibilities.

The most important achievement of Allama's poetic composition is the complete rejection of worldly truth as the theme of poetry. Although it appears on the surface that Bhakti poetry achieved the same thing, when we explore the matter in depth we realise that this is not the case. To be sure, Bhakti poetry did not use worldly truth as its theme in the manner of the narrative genres. But it is equally true that it used the theme of love as its primary material. In their poetics of bhakti-love, Narada and Shandilya formulated certain concepts applicable to Bhakti poetry as a whole. These are the emo-tional states where shringara and vatsalya (affection) dominate. These emotional states, which applied equally to Vaishnava and Shaiva

Bhakti poetry, became representative and often allowed themselves to be inflected by certain feelings not in tune with their framework. One cannot make use of any of the concepts of Narada and Shandilya's bhakti mimamsa in analysing Allama's world. His poetic theory and experiments are thus unique in the history of Indian poetics.

4

Allama's Theory of the Body

Lo, when the mouth turns into a vagina and the hand a penis,
the morsels you put into the mouth are semen (seeds).
When such is the basic truth,
O Guheshwara,
why Advaita? (469)

THROUGH THIS VACHANA Allama mounts a direct attack on the foundations of Kashmir Shaivism. More specifically, it is his attack on the Kaula sect.[1] Since Allama works in highly familiar philosophical milieus, he names no one directly within his intense philosophical debates. Here he begins his debate by translating into Kannada the symbols of the traditions he confronts. And when he translates a Sanskrit phrase into Kannada, he often annihilates the aura associated with the words in Sanskrit.[2]

The backdrop of this vachana is Kaula tantrism that Abhinavagupta had put forward once.[3] The above vachana engages with a dis-

---

[1] In Shaivism, there are non-Siddhanta systems which are characterised by an emphasis on the worship of ferocious forms of Shiva, such as Bhairava and Kali. Kapalikas (skull-men) who carried cranium begging bowls practised asceticism in cremation grounds. The Kaula, also known as Kula, tradition developed within the context of Kapalika cremation-asceticism. The term Kula, meaning "family", refers to the families of goddesses (yogini). It is a tantric tradition. See Flood, *An Introduction to Hinduism*, pp. 164–5.

[2] For example, in Kannada the Sanskrit "chakra" and "shunya" become, respectively, "gali" (wheel) and "bayalu" (void).

[3] See Muller-Ortega, *The Triadic Heart of Siva*.

pute regarding the philosophical meaning and spiritual symbolism of intercourse in Kaula tantric lore. According to Kaula tantrism, in the state of pravesha samsparsha (male–female sexual union) the body's anuchakras (lower wheels) are harmonised and a complete experience of Advaya is attained. In his synthetic evaluation, Abhinavagupta describes the process of such spiritual intercourse with great fervour. Here, the ultimate state of intercourse is nothing less than paramashivanubhava – the supreme experience of Shiva. Underlying Allama's satire in the vachana is his deep and comprehensive understanding of this tradition.

To limit our discussion to the above-quoted vachana (469), "mouth" or "mukhyachakra" (the circle of the mouth) is an important tantric term in Abhinavagupta. Gavin D. Flood explains it as follows:

> The supreme abode is equated with union (samghattha), immersion (samāveśa), and supreme joy (parānanda). But more interestingly, Abhinavagupta equates it with the terms "the circle of the mouth" (mukhyacakra) and "the mouth of the *yoginī*" (*yoginīvaktra*), from which flows the spiritual tradition (*sampradāya*) by which one attains (*samprāpyate*) true cognition (*jñāna*). True cognition, explains Jayaratha, is immersion in supreme consciousness (*parasamvitsamāveśa*). The "mouth" or "wheel" is identified with the body of consciousness from which the tradition flows, bringing the cognition of liberation.[4]

The main idea here is that intercourse is identified as a medium of spiritual knowledge. And in this process the vagina of the human yogini is the mouth from which knowledge flows. In his vachana (469) Allama questions the very philosophical framework behind this perception rather than being intolerant of this idea.

This is where the fundamental difference between Allama and Abhinavagupta begins. In his major work *Tantraloka*, Abhinavagupta brought together significant sects of Shaiva tantrism. He illuminated the symbols embedded in the sexual and spiritual modes

---

[4] Flood, *Body and Cosmology in Kashmir Śaivism*, p. 290 (DRN).

of the "Kula process" which comes under the "Trika tradition".[5] The esoteric parts of *Tantraloka* deal with this kind of spiritualisation of sexual intercourse. Using tantra shastra, Abhinavagupta elaborates on the perception that through human intercourse divine power (divyashakti) is attained. Thus, thanks to Abhinavagupta, the Kula tradition gains the support of a broad philosophical framework erected by logic, belief, and rationality.

Allama cannot accept this kind of symbolism in Shaiva tantrism where the mouth represents the vagina. Here, there is an important philosophical conflict regarding the nature of desire itself. The Kula tradition redefines the nature of desire by arguing that it is a path for liberation. It has built its entire ritualistic system on the basis of this argument. Here, desire is not the root cause of sorrow but a facilitator of divine knowledge (divyajnana). But for this desire or sexual intensity should be shaped within a particular ritual framework. Intercourse, especially the stage of ejaculation, the moment of orgasm, is paramashivananda (the ultimate bliss of Shiva). Therefore, the intensity of the human body's animal longing paves the way for experiencing paramashiva. In no other tradition, perhaps, has the spiritualisation of human intercourse been so fervent. In Shaiva tantrism, "the stage of orgasm" is very important as the whole universe loses its separateness and becomes one at the moment of ejaculation. Kalamukha philosophy calls this visarga-prasara (the discharge of semen) – a stage of ubiquitous union. Abhinavagupta endorses this notion and interprets it in the light of Advaita. His view is that during the moment of orgasm both reach the stage of dhruvapada

[5] There are two liturgical systems in the Trika (threefold) tradition (often taken as synonymous with Kashmir Shaivism) – the tantra and kula prakriyas – which regard the body as a means of transformation. "The Tantra system, which is the normative practice of the Trika Śaiva, involves the visualisation of a mandala in the form of Śiva's trident. This trident corresponds to levels of the cosmos and pervades the Trika Śaiva's body. The realisation of one's identity with supreme consciousness is similarly the aim of the second Trika liturgical system, the secret Kula liturgy, which involves love-making between the yogi and yoginī who 'become' Śiva and Śakti." See Flood, *Body and Cosmology in Kashmir Śaivism*, p. 24.

(firm state) in their consciousness. Beyond this "pleasure of inter-touching", they experience aniccha (desirelessness).[6]

It is significant that Abhinavagupta vehemently rejects the philosophical stance of the Virakta and Shramana traditions. The scepticism of Shramana traditions such as Buddhism and Jainism made it difficult to impute spiritual layers to the body. On the other hand, an important basis of a tradition that celebrates desire and devotion — for example, tantrism — is the expansion of the power of sensual bodily perceptions, turning what the body intensely experiences into a spiritual path of added intensification. The moment of orgasm in sexual intercourse becomes a state in which one listens to the words of the cosmos. Abhinavagupta also discusses elsewhere the transcendental words heard during this moment. Intercourse as a notion of yajna also features in the Aitareya Brahmanas.[7] Abhinavagupta adds a level of refinement to this path.

In the background of all these traditions is the idea of romance and intercourse between Shiva and Shakti. In this scheme, all men and women engaged in sexual intercourse are shades of Shiva and Shive (the female form of Shiva). Within the imaginative universe of Kalidasa's *Ritusamhara*, every season is suitable for intercourse, as every aspect of nature stimulates the libido and enhances the ardour of intercourse. The longing for the divine within the body thus flows through sexual desire. The entire universe is a stage for the romantic play of Shiva and Shive. Everything in the universe aspires to the pleasure of touch.

Abhinavagupta brought a touch of sensuality to Advaita. He obliterated the distinction between shringara and vairagya (desire and detachment), considering it artificial. Against this background we also need to understand the difference between Shankaracharya and Abhinavagupta. Except for one or two places in Shan-

---

[6] For visarga-prasara, dhruvapada, and aniccha, see ibid., pp. 283–4.

[7] This work belongs to Shakala shakha, the oldest branch of the *Rigveda*. It is ascribed to Mahidasa Aitareya. For more on the connection between intercourse and ritual in the Aitareya Brahmanas, see Eliade, *Yoga: Immortality and Freedom*, p. 256.

kara, knowledge has no touch of kama, while in Abhinavagupta kama, in a broad sense, is the ultimate knowledge, with the union of Shiva and Shakti as its fundamental metaphor. Abhinavagupta continuously modified the idea of physical experience according to his system of thought.

In the system of gupta (secret) tantrism, "duti", a female messenger, transmits the guru's words.[8] Three levels of philosophical transformation take place here. The vagina of this human messenger becomes the mouth of a yogini. The experience of paramashiva is believed to be attained during orgasm. When the union of bodies achieves the rhythm of equilibrium, Advaya is said to be experienced. Orgasm becomes the path of shivasannidhya (attaining Shiva).

In the vachana we are discussing here (469), Allama is trying to disrupt the method of these intellectual systems. If the tradition of Kaula imagination sees the vagina as a mouth, Allama here literally reverses the roles and makes the mouth a vagina. While the Kaula imagination considers sexual intercourse a solid path to spiritual experience, Allama asks satirically why we shouldn't spiritualise the act of putting morsels into our mouth. While Abhinavagupta, through his unique philosophical imagination, explains the experience of orgasm as a moment of complete spiritual involvement, Allama trivialises the idea. In such places, if Abhinavagupta employs the mode of expanding spiritual symbolism, Allama uses the mode of satirising the spirit. If Abhinavagupta raises vishaya (sensual matter) to the spiritual level of anuchakra (lower wheel) and madhyachakra (central wheel), Allama considers it no more than a sensual matter.[9]

---

[8] Torzsok, "Women in Early Śākta Tantras".

[9] According to Gavin D. Flood, "Abhinavagupta explains this in terms of two kinds of force called 'wheels', the 'central' (*madhyacakra*) and the 'lower' (*anucakra*). The former is a term for the body of consciousness, and the latter for the body of the universe. Indeed, there are several *anucakras* which emerge out from the central *madhyacakra*, conveying the idea of manifestation emerging out from the body of consciousness. In the terminology developed here, the totality of *anucakras* is the totality of shared realities emerging from the essential cosmic body, the *madhyacakra*. The term *anucakra* itself, is akin to *visaya* in referring to the senses and their spheres." See Flood, *Body and Cosmology in Kashmir Saivism*, p. 288.

In the vachana (469) Allama asks: if the ultimate experience of Advaita can be found during orgasm, why is the ordinary act of putting a morsel into one's mouth not a spiritual act?

Consider the following vachana where Allama begins serious confrontations with Abhinavagupta's school of tantrism:

Look,
placing the corpse of pretension
on the spearhead of desire,
how the elders on the earth dissipated.
Guheshwara,
disgusting it is
to see the elders run after desire. (466)

According to some scholars, the chief achievement of Kaula tantrism is the change it brought about in the nature of "desire". In this vachana (466) Allama speaks of the entire community of elders that brought about this change. As in his other vachanas, it is worth understanding this one, too, against the backdrop of Shaiva philosophy as a whole. While discussing such vachanas, we need to keep in mind the historical method of study. If we analyse Shaiva tantric sects using the historical method, it could be argued that the Shaiva tantric traditions had declined on account of the disappearance of the distinction between meaningful tantric rituals and bodily pleasure. From the perspective of the historical method, it was against this decline of tantric sects that Virashaivism took rebellious birth.

However, while studying religious movements, this historical method seems to be of little help — because we are forced to take the information that is currently available to suit the simplified linear model which traces the rise and fall of religious sects. If the Shaiva tantric sects were said to be corrupted by Allama's time, the question would arise whether there had been no such lapses in these sects earlier as well. The limitation of the historical method is that it is incapable of grasping the unfolding and contraction within the philosophical structures of a religious movement or a sect. In other words, the historical method cannot recognise the foetus states in the wombs of original philosophical systems. On the other hand,

Allama's mode may be called tattva-jyotishi (philosophical prediction). What this means is that when Allama adopts a philosophical structure, he can predict its future unfolding from its very nature. In Allama's hands, philosophical systems and metaphors themselves begin predicting their own futures.

Nowhere does Allama use the historical method when he finds fault with the elders in his tradition. He does not criticise the way things are by contrasting them, in a mournful tenor, with the way they ought to be. Instead, he points out that there is a problem in the very direction of the elders' way of life. At one level, this is appropriate because, while discussing religious structures, we cannot trace their "Birth–Rise–Decline" chronologically. Therefore, there is neither temporality nor historicity in the life of religions. If there is anything in them at all, it is space. All who are devoted to religion are unaffected by its "Birth–Rise–Decline" chronology. They remain suspended in this state of belief because religion coexists simultaneously in diverse spaces. This is true even in the case of a religion that may believe in the process of historical continuity. In every religion, there will be periods of rise and fall. A devotee is bound to recognise the indivisible state of these two.

This is the basis of Allama's devotional state. Thus, he never says that the elders have gone astray – as is apparent in the tone of the vachana (466) we are discussing. Instead, through effective metaphors he satirises the way of the elders who have turned the fulfilment of bodily desire into a spiritual path. In the above-quoted vachana (466), the metaphor of "the spearhead of desire" is clear enough at the surface level, while the metaphor of "the corpse of pretension" finds further justification in Allama's vachana corpus. It is customary for him to refer to followers of religious sects with whom he disagrees as impersonators. In this vachana (466) Allama voices his disdain for those who advocate desire as a path of spirituality.

In many such vachanas, Allama presents a theory of the body. In vachana 467 he ridicules imprudent elders who "fill their pots of fog with things of amusement, / With no hesitation they cook the things."[10] It is quite common for vachanakaras to describe the body as a pot. Even Akkamahadevi, foremost representative of the devotional imagination, describes it this way. What the elders describe through the great idiom of spiritual experience, Allama calls the "things of amusement". For him, the body can become a "thing of amusement", wherein lies its greatest attraction.

When we analyse the origins of Virashaivism based on Allama's vachanas, it is difficult to accept that it was only against the decline of tantric sects that Virashaivism took rebellious birth, an approach that the historical method might espouse. Instead Allama's transhistorical mode of philosophical prediction (tattva-jyotishi) helps us understand the origins of Virashaivism. Had Allama followed the historical method of understanding religions in terms of the rise-and-fall binary, he would have tried to purify the fundamental paths of these religions. But both Allama and Basavanna set out to create new paths rather than tread old ones.

I see no one conquering
the vast plantain grove called the body:
The seven seas of samsara surround it.
In the vast forest of bhava (the cycle of birth),
the downpour of the five senses rages.
The ferocious tiger of anger roars.
The rogue elephants of eight-fold pride
are stampeding in the street.
As the rain of embers called lust pours,
no way to step out.
Large snakes of envy are spitting flames.
The child of sin called desire
is wolfing the feast.
The rain-shafts of triple pain
pelt down incessantly.
Hills of excessive pride have slumped across the way.
You cannot look in the dreadful face

[10] For the full vachana, see vachana no. 467 in Allama Prabhu, *Vachanas of Allama Prabhu*.

of the ghosts called the five elements.
The monster maye devours raw flesh.
The wells of sensuality cannot be used.
The creeper of infatuation entangles the feet.
The sharp-edged sword of greed cannot be unsheathed.
Gods, demons, and men,
unable to understand the plantain grove of the body,
have gone insane and run away.
Those who have eyes upon their soles,
those who have eyes all over the body
have lost their heads.
But I have entered this plantain grove,
and have fought my way through,
untouched by thorns.
I understood and conquered this plantain grove,
staying in the ultimate trance called Guheshwara,
I am more tranquil than tranquillity. (1201)

In this vachana Allama continues his theorisation of the body, employing the method of hyperbole and symbolism. Notably, the vachana repeatedly uses the preposition "of" to form metaphors such as "plantain grove of the body", "the seven seas of samsara", and "the vast forest of bhava". Allama expands on the central metaphor of "the vast plantain grove of the body" throughout the composition. As in many of his other vachanas, he tries here to establish an emotional state through various metaphors.

If the "body as a vast plantain grove" is a central symbol, through the method of repeated images he explores how different types of rain affect the vast plantain grove. First, he speaks of "the downpour of the five senses". The five senses are no less than a downpour if the body is a plantain grove. After a point, the plantain grove of the body cannot withstand the heavy downpour of the senses. Allama then goes on to transform this metaphor of rain. Though the nature of the rain changes, the grove is still at risk. In the meantime, this plantain grove has to face the fear of elephants – called ashtamada (eightfold pride) – as well.

As "the downpour of the five senses" continues to intensify, Allama introduces "the rain of embers called lust". By yoking the body to the metaphor of a plantain grove, he confronts the elders of Shaiva tantrism. All such elders have high hopes for kaya (the body), having directed their entire philosophical system towards exploring the mysteries of the body and the nature of energy contained therein. Allama is not in agreement with these elders' optimism about the body's divine power; he indicates the limits of the body by calling it a plantain grove. This is a war being waged against the elders through the use of metaphors. What the elders see as the divine force of the body becomes the object of Allama's critique, which takes shape by pointing out the slow creation of an atmosphere of fear. The rains described in the vachana are dangerous to the plantain grove, i.e. the body; they turn it to ashes. The plantain grove of the body cannot be sustained by waters from the wells of sensuality.

In the latter part of this vachana (1201), Allama speaks with pride of his spiritual attainments. If one accepts the body as a plantain grove, one's relationship with the body changes. Belief in the chakra and anuchakra of happiness within the body disappears. With the help of metaphors from the ordinary world, Allama firmly rejects the experiences that Abhinavagupta has explored with great seriousness. In the following vachana (1200), too, Allama speaks of the experience of entering the plantain grove called the body and roaming around its sense-chambers in search of light:

> One entered the plantain grove called the body,
> went into the cave of life-force,
> and roamed around the sense-chambers in search of light.
> But light dawned on the triple room of the Meru temple
> and Guheshwaralinga assumed a form. (1200)

We can interpret this to mean that the sense organs are only chambers, with no access to the experience of shunya vistara (the horizon of the void). There is no light in these chambers; light is only to be found in another chamber, the Meru temple. Through the metaphor of the absence of light in the sense-chambers, Allama confirms his rejection of tantrism.

Here, Allama creates metaphors to trivialise the body. He is not being completely contemptuous of the body, but is criticising the philosophical process of transforming the body's sensuality into spiritual experience. However, Allama too believes in the body's spiritual receptivity – as he shows elsewhere. His philosophical system also has respect for the nature of energy said to be contained in certain parts of the body. He uses the idiom of kundalini (from tantra yoga) and other concepts with great respect and deep belief. At the same time, by describing the body as a plantain grove and lust as a rain of embers, he maintains the specificity of his paradoxical talent.

We also need to evaluate the poetic nature of this vachana (1201). The vachana becomes significant not because it is a powerful piece of poetry, but because it helps us understand Allama's philosophical roots. The plantain grove of the body and the rain of embers are paradoxical metaphors; the rest are pretty much simple philosophical metaphors. Finally, Allama's main attention is on penetrating and transforming the metaphoric mode of his purvapaksha (philosophical adversaries). This method has worked, to a certain extent, in this vachana. Here, Allama's imagination constructs a broad narrative and leaves it at that.

Coming back to our discussion of Allama's conversation with the elders, we can examine the following vachana:

> When the rainstorm hit Uttarapatha,
> the country was struck by drought!
> All the creatures in the country perished!
> O Guheshwara,
> I search for you in the rudrabhumi (cemetery)
> where they lie charred. (227)

This vachana is significant in so far as Allama's conversations with the elders of the Shaiva tantric sect are concerned. Allama's philosophical uniqueness is fashioned in his intense confrontations with the Uttarapatha sect. Though not considerable in their number, vachanas of this kind are very important for an understanding of the nature of Allama's dialogic mode. Here too Allama speaks in symbols, but always in combination with familiar concepts.

Uttarapatha, quite a familiar term in the Shaiva tantric tradition, also refers to a path in Kaula Shaivism.[11] Another term for this is vamamarga. As mentioned earlier in the analysis, Allama here advances his spiritual views on Kaula Shaivism.[12] However, the problem with this vachana (227) lies in the way he mixes symbolism with realistic and descriptive concepts. We may consider this the unique character of Allama's art. Yet it is not easy to enter the above vachana (227). Allama instructs us to approach it using descriptive concepts from history, but when he expands on these concepts in a symbolic idiom we need to take the help of his philosophical vocabulary to understand the vachana completely. Here it is not difficult to understand the term Uttarapatha. But in order to understand the meaning of "When the rainstorm hit Uttarapatha", we need to make intertextual connections with certain other vachanas of Allama, where, fortunately for us, he makes use of similes and metaphors while explaining his philosophical vocabulary.

In the vachana (1201) we discussed earlier, Allama explicated the metaphor of "rain" as signifying the senses, or lust. While he critiqued the elders directly elsewhere, in the vachana (227) under discussion here his criticism is articulated indirectly, in symbolic lan-

---

[11] In his *Abhinavagupta*, K.C. Pandey, explains how the notions of daksina and vama (uttara) are formed in Shaiva tantrism: "Vama and Daksina margas are so called because they proceeded from the two faces, called Vama and Aghora or Daksina . . . The Daksina patha is so called, because the Agamas, on which it is based, proceeded from the face, called Aghora, which faces the South and the Vama is so called because it recognises the authority of the Saivagamas which emanated from the face, called Vamadeva, which faces the North." See Pandey, *Abhinavagupta*, p. 616 (DRN).

[12] In the "Prathamahnika" of Abhinavagupta's *Tantraloka*, this is mentioned: "since the beginning, *veda* is an excellent *shaiva shastra*. In *shaivism* too, there are *uttarapath and dakshinapath*." See Abhinavagupta, *Tantraloka*, p. 46 (DRN).

guage. After criticising the Kaula Shaiva tradition using the language of historicity and individual metaphors, Allama returns to the use of metaphors in tradition. While a preliminary knowledge about the Shaiva tradition suffices to understand the meaning of Uttarapatha, a problem arises when we encounter the symbol of rudrabhumi (cemetery). To make sense of it, a deep understanding of Shaiva tradition is required. In the entire Shaiva tantra tradition, and especially in Abhinavagupta, the rudrabhumi has a special cosmic significance. The importance given to it symbolises the rebellious nature of Shaiva tantra. Once the traditionalism of Vedic religions became a stagnant system and largely an expression of the traditional grihasthashrama (householder stage), the emergence of Shaiva tantra was a natural outcome as a resistance to that system. Shaiva tantra adored what traditional society was frightened of. The source of fear for people in the establishment was a source of wonder for the Shaiva tantric. What the establishment might try to restrain or limit as pleasurable was an instance of extreme wisdom for the Shaiva tantric. What might appear as bondage for the establishment was seen as a way of liberation for the Shaiva tantric. So a woman who is limited to the role of a housewife within the establishment becomes a messenger of the final path to liberation for the Shaiva tantric. Thus, as the traditional system tries to limit, mediate, and bring everything under control, Shaiva tantra transcends all control by exaggerating everything and shattering boundaries.

We should stay alert not to understand these instances as simple binaries such as authority–resistance, limit–limitlessness, subjugation–freedom, or stability–instability. Such alertness is indispensable while studying the evolution and diversity of the Shaiva imagination, not to mention studying the structure and tradition of Indian culture in general. Shaiva tantrism developed several internal structures as a device to contain its revolutionary nature and manage its explosive power. Although, on the surface, Shaiva tantrism deployed intellectual structures and metaphors that conformed to the Vedic tradition, sometimes it did away with these. Though Abhinavagupta and Goraksha claimed that their methods and world-views were of the traditional Vedic kind and expressed their thoughts in the idiom of universal acceptance, their philosophies were full of ideas that were quite different from the Vedic tradition.

The Shaiva imagination of Abhinavagupta and Goraksha tries to retain its revolutionary nature by combining extremes – limit–limitlessness, tradition–revolution, subjugation–freedom. Allama too inhabits the same imagination. The fact that Advaya Shaivism sees nothing as dualistic seems to be the reason behind its combining of extremes. At times the Advaya Shaiva imagination also esteems what traditional society regards with suspicion, thereby disrupting the system. An excellent example of this process is the symbol of rudrabhumi.

For the traditionalists, rudrabhumi connotes fear, and they are ill at ease with it; in fact, to the traditional Vedic mind, everything related to death is a nightmare. Never mind death – even disease and ill health are causes for fear. Therefore, in Vedic mantras, the yearning to be rid of the fear of death or death itself is a recurring theme. However, there is no fear of the rudrabhumi in Shaiva tantrism; instead the rudrabhumi is viewed as a storehouse of special energy. We need not take into consideration here the connections between tantric rituals, witchcraft, and burial grounds found in the popular imagination. Here, the philosophical and symbolic existence of the burial ground is more important than ritualistic details.

In his *Tantraloka*, Abhinavagupta speaks of the various levels of the symbolism of rudrabhumi. He says, *śūnyarūpe śmaśāne 'smin yoginīsiddhasevite* (29.183; A perfect Yogini enjoys herself in this cemetery which is in the form of the void). And further, *asaṃkhya-citisampūrṇe śmaśāne citibhīṣaṇe* (29.185; She stands adored with all the ashes of innumerable corpses).[13] That is, the source of fear for the traditional mind here takes the form of the perfect Yogini (yogini-siddha sevite). This seems to hint at the revolutionary nature of Advaya Shaivism. Revolutionary philosophical transformation means

---

[13] See Dupuche, *Abhinavagupta: The Kula Ritual*, p. 446.

revitalising what has been disgraced and destroyed, and adoring what has been neglected.

Likewise, the vachana tradition revitalised what had been overlooked in the classical poetic traditions and the imagist method. To be more specific, it brought into focus ordinary details and ordinary lives. This does not mean that depictions of everyday life were utterly absent in Kannada classical poetry; in fact Kannada poetry has never entirely neglected the depiction of everyday life. It has always returned to the details of ordinary life after getting tired of abstract imagery and instances of the kavi-samaya (poetic licence and convention).[14] But the reality of everyday life is only marginal in classical Kannada poetry. So when we find such marginal images in Pampa and Ranna, for example, we are enthused. But it was the vachanakaras who really brought these very marginal concerns to the centre. They raised the narration of ordinary life to the level of great metaphors and made it a vehicle of spiritual meaning. I gave the example of the rudrabhumi here to show that this tendency is found in Abhinavagupta's philosophical activities as well.

By saying in the vachana (227), quoted earlier, "I search for you in the rudrabhumi (cemetery) / Where they lie charred," Allama is suggesting the nature of his relationship and disagreements with Advaya Shaivism. Though he strongly disagrees with the Kaula Shaiva tradition, he has a deep affinity with its mother, the Advaya Shaiva tradition. When he says that he is searching for Guheshwara where charred bodies lie, he is using the word rudrabhumi in the general sense, in line with his use of Uttarapatha. At one level, he speaks the language as it is deployed in common usage, where the meaning is explicit.

In another vachana (418), Allama explores his troubled relationship with the Uttarapatha. Here too he focuses on his disappointment with the way of experience chosen by Uttarapatha in

---

[14] In classical poetry, the description of things contrary to what is known to exist in the world and contrary to shastric knowledge becomes poetic convention, and according to Rajasekhara these descriptions are beneficial to the poet and illuminate the poetic truth. See Rajasekhara, *Kavyamimaṁsa of Rajasekhara.*

the quest for divinity. It is important to note that Allama is disappointed but not perturbed:

> I saw a blazing linga in the temple of wax,
> where there is none to worship God.
> where did the maye (illusion), wrapped around
> the darshanas of the Uttarapatha, go?
> I saw the fire inside the tree, burning the tree itself.
> But the linga called Guheshwara
> stayed there. (418)

The Uttarapatha had revealed its uniqueness by asserting the belief that sexual intercourse could be a path to spiritual attainment. We could even say that it was stubborn about this belief. Allama alludes here and there to the method of such a path, though he does not mention it explicitly. The pursuit of shringara as a spiritual path, he believes, reduces the body to a temple of wax. Although in other places Allama calls the body a temple, while engaging with the Kaula theory of the body he slightly changes his interpretation and calls it a temple of wax. The blazing linga could burn the temple of wax, which cannot withstand fire. For Allama this is a source of paradoxical wonder. According to Allama, the Uttarapatha philosophers believe wax can resist fire, which is the illusion (maye) wrapped around them. "Maye" here signifies darshana, a form of rationality.

The basic strength of Allama's imagination lies in his ability to discern absurdities and paradoxes. What distinguishes him is his ability to make any kind of thought an object of his examination. Elsewhere, he examines his own philosophical approach. It becomes clear to us in the vachana (1073), "What is called thought / is open to doubt, look. / As long as you go on thinking, / how do you know who you are?"[15] Nowhere does he give up his scepticism.

His persistent scepticism has rendered him unique within the Advaya Shaiva tradition. His intellectual austerity and individual uniqueness have pushed him into an inevitable solitude. It has made

---

[15] For the full vachana, see vachana no. 1525 in Allama Prabhu, *Lord of the Cave,* and vachana no. 997 in Allama Prabhu, *Vachanas of Allama Prabhu.*

him say regretfully, "O, look at the elders, who are prey / to the passion of the body, mind and sense" (129).[16] However, Allama is not completely immune to the pressure of cordiality, and therefore he yearns for interaction with the original tradition. He does not speak of it directly but reveals his intimate relationship with the original tradition by using and adapting its metaphors and intellectual structures. In his use of metaphors he is completely absorbed in the tradition, but in his interpretations of them he stands out.

Allama's distinctiveness comes not purely from the pressure of poetic imagination, as it does in Kalidasa. Nor does Allama, like Abhinavagupta, tread the path of philosophical unification. Abhinavagupta examines all the sects of the Advaya–Shaiva tradition, reconciles their common universal aspects, and then initiates the process of unification through which a broad tradition is constituted; indeed, Abhinavagupta achieves this. However, in such a process of unification, the limitations inherent within each sect disappear. Through his sheer capacity for synthesis, Abhinavagupta erases these limitations. He cannot see aporias. But Allama's distinctive imagination holds up a magnifying glass and brings into focus what Abhinavagupta's synthesising outlook overlooks. Though Allama breaks with this kind of unifying model, he desires to be friendly with those traditions which give him a special quality of humility. Several of his vachanas illustrate this. This does not mean that Allama always speaks of Uttarapatha in a regretful and melancholic idiom; in fact, he also uses affectionate metaphors when outlining the weaknesses of such traditions.

> . . . The child of Uttarapatha hidden within the womb of ishanya
>   (north-west)
>   has swallowed sakara sanga while remaining so innocent of the
>   language! . . .[17] (406)

[16] For the full vachana, see vachana no. 129 in Allama Prabhu, *Lord of the Cave*, and in Allama Prabhu, *Vachanas of Allama Prabhu*.

[17] "Sakara sanga": association with the divine form. My translation. For the full vachana, see vachana no. 406 in Allama Prabhu, *Lord of the Cave*; and Allama Prabhu, *Vachanas of Allama Prabhu*.

As one who adores formlessness, Allama laments the fact that Kaula Shaivism's final destination is sakara sanga (association with the divine form). On such occasions, a kind of intellectual compassion overflows within Allama. He humanises the system of Uttarapatha by referring to it as a child. Much as an innocent child swallows virtually anything, the child of Uttarapatha has swallowed the "sakara sanga". Such is its innocence that it cannot even express what is happening to it. For poets like Allama, who are engaged in a more extensive dialogue with philosophical systems, the only way is to speak through metaphors. If Abhinavagupta examines theories and philosophical systems at the level of pure thought, Allama's poetic imagination tries to transform all these into metaphors of the everyday world.

Other seers and poets of Advaya Shaivism do not face the same problems as Allama. For Kalidasa, only the basic intellectual structures of his own traditions are important. His poetic style may be said to resemble pulp growing around the seed of philosophy. Therefore, his poetry can be read and understood without the nuances of Shaiva philosophical discourse. But this is not so in Allama's case. In order to understand his vachanas, one should be familiar with the interfaces and negotiations taking place within the Advaya Shaiva tradition.

Elsewhere, Allama tries to inhabit Abhinavagupta's pure classical mode. Therefore, he maintains both hostile and friendly relationships with tattvas (philosophy). In his vachanas, the experience of wrestling with the essence of tattvas is evident. At the same time, he tries to use the metaphoric mode of poetry. Allama attracts us at first glance because of his unique poetic sensibility. But as we join his trail, he points out that we must also understand his philosophy. We inevitably become partners in his philosophical fight with the elders. However, when Allama poeticises this fight with them, the quality of what Indian aesthetics calls sadharanikarana – simplification without dilution – disappears.

While studying poets like Allama, a concept such as sadharanikarana appears a restriction. In other words, it also seems to acknowledge the limitations of worldly knowledge in understanding

the processes that underpin a certain kind of poetic creation. Allama's
ability to simplify unique, mysterious, and uncommon experiences
testifies to his poetic imagination, but he does not consciously remain
a poet at all times. As he pursues abstract thoughts, his metaphors
act as his hounds, catching a whiff, snatching a bite, and bringing
home what his philosophical consciousness is grasping at. This is
why hunting is such an endearing metaphor in Allama's universe.[18]
While this hunting dog does not capture the prey on every occasion,
in Allama's most successful metaphors the arrow of language strikes
at the heart of what the abstract thought signifies. Notice the metaphor he creates in the following vachana:

> Look, a well of a man's length emerged in the sky!
> An animal that came to drink water
> drowned in the well.
> I took it out with an arrow of flame.
> I saw the animal that died at one shot stepping forward.
> As eyes appeared on the palm,
> the pleasure of union became certain.
> O Guheshwara!
> I realised today the truth of linga being prana (life-breath). (215)

Elsewhere in this book, there is further discussion of the hunting
metaphor across Allama's vachanas. This metaphor is not limited to
spiritual experience but extends to the way he uses language. Sometimes the bow breaks, the arrow does not shoot, and the hunting
fails. There have always been crises in the work of a poet. In such situations, Allama abandons the company of the powerful hound of
metaphorical language and begins to speak directly, using the language of philosophy much like Abhinavagupta.

Allama is aware of the metaphorical power inherent in language;
he is also sceptical of it. When that fails, he does not try to go after
it – that is, he does not make a conscious effort to obtain the meta-

---

[18] For hunting metaphors in Allama, see his vachana nos 557 and 561
(DRN). For English translations of these vachanas, see vachana nos 557 and
561 in Allama Prabhu, *Lord of the Cave*.

phoricity of language. Such an act of consciously working on the poetic language is called kavi-sankalpa (poet's labour). This is quite visible when poets consciously work with prosody and rhythm. As Allama does not engage in this kind of labour, there is no kavi-sankalpa in him, and this also illustrates the difference between kavi-pratibhe (the individual talent of a gifted poet) and kavi-sankalpa (poetic ability obtained with labour – conscious effort and practice). Allama possesses kavi-pratibhe, and therefore does not require kavi-sankalpa. This is a unique expression of the Kannada poetic imagination. When kavi-sankalpa is indivisibly integrated into poetic consciousness, modes such as vastuka, varnaka, and so on appear indispensable. The distinction between the creative need of kavi-pratibhe and the mechanical use of kavi-sankalpa becomes noticeable. Moreover, kavi-sankalpa will be bound to a tradition. Allama accepts this neither in his philosophical world nor in his poetic world. In one of his vachanas he criticises those who can hold forth only on vastuka and varnaka, describing them as "prattling like a flock of parrots".[19]

Because he is not bound by the artificiality of kavi-sankalpa, Allama can, naturally, give up his metaphoric mode. This often happens, especially in the context of his debate with the elders. When he confronts seers or philosophers, he sometimes follows their way. There are enough elders in the tradition of Advaya philosophy with whom Allama can converse and argue. Since Allama in such dialogues appropriates the typical language of a tradition, which is not accessible to the commoner, entry to it becomes limited. Then the sadharanikarana of poetry disappears and the language of philosophical debate takes over.

We will be able to appreciate the beauty of the particular vachana when we make sense of the structure of the idea that Allama is either resisting or transforming. We find clear delineations regarding the internal relationships of Shaivist ideas in the classics of Kashmir

---

[19] For the full vachana, see vachana no. 641 in Allama Prabhu, *Lord of the Cave*. Also see Nagaraja's interview on YouTube, "D.R. Nagaraj Sandarshana".

Shaivism available to us, and there is also the possibility of a broader tradition existing beyond all these. In the following vachana (433), we see Allama elucidating the Shaiva tradition in a philosophical mode, abandoning his metaphoric style:

> The syllable "na" being Nandi,
> "ma" being majestic, "shi" being Rudra,
> "va" being swan, "ya" being awareness,
> "om" being Guru,
> Relation being non-relation, non-relation relation
> When both become one,
> they become Guheshwara linga![20] (433)

It is not the poet's business to construct a symbolic system of meaning by meditating on individual letters. As Kalidasa explains it, the work of a poet begins when word and meaning coexist. However, a tantric philosopher like Abhinavagupta works even with words that are not at the mercy of meaning. This occupies the topmost priority in his way of thinking. He meditates deeply on individual sounds and creates a symbolic system of meanings. This is the case in his *Tantraloka*, and also in *Para-trisika-Vivarana*.

In Abhinavagupta's language there is a technical term for the creation of a symbolic system of meanings with individual sounds, namely sankalananusandhana. He introduces this concept in *Para-trisika-Vivarana*.[21] In a way, this is where the main difference lies between the work of a poet and that of a tantric philosopher. According to Abhinavagupta, Shive or Shakti hears everything. In her capacity to hear, she exercises wonderful freedom. The freedom to make connections among words and sounds that are heard separately by the world is called sankalana, which means "effecting congruous and suitable connexion of distinct sounds". And with the freedom of anusandhana she blends sounds into a definite, meaningful whole.[22]

---

[20] Note the division of the term "Om namah shivaya" in the vachana.

[21] Abhinavagupta, *Para-trisika-Vivarana*, p. 70 (DRN). The translator's edition is 2017, p. 70.

[22] Abhinavagupta, *Para-trisika-Vivarana*, p. 70.

In such cases Abhinavagupta's philosophy reaches the heights of subtle analysis. In this world, several sounds fall on our ears, but we don't hear them because the mundaneness of the world does not have the freedom to hear them. The common mortal does not have the liberty to engage in sankalana – to connect all the sounds of the world. The limits of ordinary mortals lie in the absence of sankalananusandhana. Although sounds enter our ears, they do not enter our minds. Abhinavagupta calls this tatha bhavet (so it happens). But Parashakti (the highest goddess / Shive) has the power to establish this kind of relationship among sounds.[23]

Thus, if the limits of mortality lie in the absence of freedom to engage in sankalananusandhana, the power of Parashakti's imagination lies in transcending this limitation. The poet, however, oscillates between these two. At one level the poet is the prisoner of the unfreedom of mortality to do sankalananusandhana. Hence, at this level he also shares the deafness of the world. But there is also an element of Parashakti's freedom within him which enables him to engage in sankalananusandhana – to some extent. However, he does not have the power of "Parabhattarika" (Supreme Divine Shakti) to hear all the whispers that arise in the world.[24]

A tantric philosopher acquires a portion of Shive's prowess. But the poet doesn't have an entry into the higher echelons of this sankalananusandhana. This notion can be used in making distinctions among poets too. Allama could hear more than his contemporaries and had a greater power with sankalana, which involves compiling and making connections, and anusandhana, which involves blending connections into a meaningful whole. While Basavanna com-

---

[23] In the Trika system of Kashmir Shaivism, there are three modes with the goddesses: Para, Parapara, and Apara. "The Krama reinterprets the three Goddesses of the Trika such that Para is understood to be the knower (*pramatr*); Parapara as the means of knowledge (*pramana*); and Apara as the known (*prameya*)." See Dupuche, *Abhinavagupta: The Kula Ritual*, p. 20.

[24] She is "an expression of the absolutely free manifestation of the bliss of the union of Siva and Sakti denoting the Supreme Brahman", she "is the very power of learning . . . hears everything that is ever uttered in the universe." See Abhinavagupta, *Para-trisika-Vivarana*, pp. 45 and 69.

piles metaphors using the details of social relationships, and Akkamahadevi does so by drawing inspiration from nature, Allama forms
metaphors using the extraordinary relationships that underpin both
social and natural worlds. Equipped with this power of sankalananusandhana, Allama is capable of creating extraordinary bedagu
metaphors derived from ordinary phenomena.

But the sankalananusandhana that takes place in the vachana
(433) we are discussing is of a different kind. All meaning-creations
produced by poets must be realised within the unfreedom of the mortal world. However, Allama rebels against this unfreedom to hear,
which makes him resort to the philosophical mode of tantrism. Abhinavagupta attributes special and mysterious meanings to each letter
of the alphabet. That is, each letter has a mundane meaning and another, a special meaning. But the poet has no fascination with individual letters, he instead works with whole words. A tantric philosopher, however, creates a grand system out of each letter.

Throughout his *Para-trisika-Vivarana*, Abhinavagupta uses
this method. He attributes a divine meaning to each letter of the
alphabet and explains it. For instance, phonemes from /a/ to visarga /
aha / are symbols of Shiva-tattva.[25] The /ka/ and /na/ class of con-
sonants represent the panchabhutas (the five elements − earth,
water, fire, air, and space).[26] Although Abhinavagupta employs these
concepts primarily for his analysis of Advaya, he continues to interpret the distinctiveness of letters throughout the text.

If it is the way of tantric philosophy to begin with the letters of
the alphabet, Allama in his composition (433) quoted above proceeds
by dividing the phrase "namah shivaya" into letters. Although Allama retains the mystery of the tantric method and the eccentricity of
spiritual philology, what he says is compatible with ordinary meaning.
However, Abhinavagupta, based on an important tantric text, *Malini
Vijayottara Tantra*, interprets these letters differently.[27] If /na/ means

---

[25] Glottal fricative.

[26] Abhinavagupta, *Para-trisika-Vivarana*, p. 70 (DRN).

[27] This is a sourcebook on Trika Shastra of Kashmir. See Shastri, ed., *Mālinī-
vijayottaratantra*.

Nandi for Allama, it is Ishvara for Abhinavagupta; likewise, /ma/ is mahat [majestic] for Allama and sabda [word] for Abhinavagupta; / shi/ is Rudra for Allama and sparsha [touch] for Abhinavagupta; /va/ is swan for Allama and niyati for Abhinavagupta; /ya/ is cognition or awareness for Allama and raga for Abhinavagupta.[28] Based on the two tantric traditions called Malini and Matrika, Abhinavagupta also interprets the same letter in two different ways. For example, if / ma/ is "sound" according to the Malini tradition, according to Matrika it is "sparsha" (touch). Interestingly, the phrase "namah shivaya" that Allama interprets is completely consonantal.

This does not mean that Allama does not agree with the rest of the Advaya traditions at any stage of spiritual philology. When he says, "*om* being Guru", he is close to the original tradition, Shaivism. Abhinavagupta clearly says that "the *guru* or spiritual director who inspires this *mantra* to realize should be understood to be Siva Himself." [29] However, Allama's uniqueness lies in his saying that "omkara" itself is Guru. He finally reveals the ultimate Advayavada similar to Abhinavagupta when, at the end of the vachana (433), he says: "Relation being non-relation, non-relation relation / When both become one, / They become Guheshwara linga!" If Abhinavagupta creates a subtle universe of dialogue through the concepts of divya (divine contact), divyadivya sambandha (contact partly divine and partly non-divine), adivya (contact which is not divine), etc., Allama tries to escape from all these ideas.[30] His zeal lies in his effort to do away with complications and achieve simplicity.

Now, let us examine Allama's engagement with Shaiva tantrism through the vachana below.

---

[28] Abhinavagupta, *Para-trisika-Vivarana*, pp. 127–9 (DRN).

[29] Ibid., p. 243 (DRN).

[30] The tantric teachings of Kashmir Shaivism recognise a fivefold contact of master and disciples: *mahān sambandhaḥ* (the great contact), *antarāla samban-dhaḥ* (contact of the master residing in *Sadashiva* and the disciple residing in *Anantabhaṭṭāraka*), *divya sambandhaḥ* (divine contact), *divyadivya sambandha* (contact partly divine and partly non-divine), *adivya sambandhaḥ* (contact which is not divine). See Swami Lakshmanjoo, *Kashmir Shaivism*, pp. 85–6.

Nobody knows
the art of yoga or viyoga (uniting and parting).
It is not yoga
    if you just know the secret of the nine-nerve system.
It is not yoga
    if you think you got into hridaya kamala karnike (lotus-heart)
    after knowing fifty-two letters!
Look, Siddharamayya,
Guheshwaralinga does not stay on shaduchakra (six wheels).
If he is outside, he is actionless.
If he is inside, he is beyond speech and mind! (1183)

The centre of this vachana is the metaphor of hridayakamala – the heart-lotus. Allama speaks of it in other places as well.[31] In another vachana (1485), he asks crudely and directly: "Unless you get rid of the one, / who moves from petal to petal in the heart-lotus, / How can you attain the state of yoga?"[32] This heart-lotus is an important philosophical metaphor in the tradition of Kashmir Shaiva tantrism. While interpreting the ninth poem of *Para-trisika-Vivarana*, Abhinavagupta makes it clear that hridayam (heart) is a form of the vagina.[33] It is the centre of Bhairava, or the shrine of Shiva. Then, in various interpretations, Abhinavagupta uses concepts like "hridayabija" (seed of heart) and "hritkamala" (heart-lotus). In the 35th verse of *Para-trisika-Vivarana*, Abhinavagupta says, "*Hritpadmantargatam dhyayet*".[34] //35// His commentary on this verse follows: "The *yogi* should meditate on *kanda* and *guhya*, i.e. the male *yogi* or *vira* on the female organ (*guhya*) and the female *yogini* or *yogini* on the male organ (*kanda*) as if it were the heart-lotus." Abhinavagupta calls these two organs heart-lotus in a figurative sense because, "like [the] lotus, they are endowed with the characteristic of

---

[31] Nine vachanas of Allama refer to the word "hridayakamala" (heart-lotus). See Vachana Sanchaya.

[32] For the full vachana, see vachana no. 1485 in Allama Prabhu, *Lord of the Cave*.

[33] Abhinavagupta, *Para-trisika-Vivarana*, p. 200 (DRN).

[34] Ibid., p. 262.

contraction and expansion (*sankoca-vikasa*)."[35] Abhinavagupta explains: "In *sushamna*, there is *muladhara chakra*, and . . . finally, there is *mukha-mudra* or *hrit-karnika*. All these together form one *hrt-padma* (heart-lotus). Its centre is the *hrt-karnika*. This is the hrdaya known as amrta-bija."[36] Allama captures this broad interpretation through the metaphor known as hridayakamala karnika.

The allusion to "fifty-two letters" in the above vachana (1183) directly references a particular Shaiva tantra rite. *Para-trisika-Vivarana* is primarily a treatise that meditates on individual letters. The 35th verse of *Para-trisika-Vivarana* says there are fifteen vowels (letters) in the heart-lotus of Shiva.[37] In addition, the notion of six wheels is inherent within it. Here Allama too is speaking of spiritual entanglements which are caught in the form of a vagina.

Allama's dialogue with Shaiva tantrism and other Bhakti traditions is multidimensional. His conversation with those traditions, for example, on the body (which he captures through the metaphor of kadali, i.e. the plantain grove) and shringara is highly complex. He agrees with the union (Advaya) when in the vachana (1196) he says, "shedding the twin sense of you and me, you become yourself."[38] In this vachana he speaks of a plantain grove which cannot be seen, and says, "If you can enter the arena of that grove, you see the glow of bright light." But, as mentioned earlier in this book, Allama believes that by employing shringara in the plantain grove that is the body, it is impossible to attain that ultimate union (Advaya).

The modern sensibility can probably understand Allama's complex notion of kaya – the physical body. There is no room for scepticism about the body in Kashmir Shaivism, especially not in Abhinavagupta's intellectual system of tantric Shaivism. Abhinavagupta does not doubt that the shringara-mediated spiritual journey might be disturbed on account of something going wrong

---

[35] Ibid., p. 263.

[36] Ibid., p. 266.

[37] Ibid., p. 262 (DRN).

[38] For the full vachana, see vachana no. 1313 in Allama Prabhu, *Lord of the Cave.*

with the human body. He is even blind to the fact that, owing to mental or physical crises, orgasm might not be achieved during sexual intercourse. Perhaps premodern times were fortunate in this regard. This good fortune is revealed as a theoretical ideal in Abhinavagupta's writings. Thus, he can be described as a philosopher of bodily prosperity, capable of conveying this through poetic metaphors. His complete involvement is evident in his description of the spiritual journey of intercourse.

Allama is not a philosopher who adores the rich possibilities of the body; rather, he is a poet who doubts them. This does not mean he denies the pleasures associated with the body, but only that he views them at the level of carnal need and desire. He does respect these needs, saying, "One should not let a moment pass / Without gratifying the body's wish."[39] (71) From this perspective, Allama cannot agree with any severe disciplining of the body. Though he believes that the ultimate forces of the body are present in the mind, he knows that the body holds its own unique attractions. But he cannot trust them, and he certainly cannot agree with a system of spiritual liberation based on the forces of the body. His basic position is that kaya (the physical body) is a plantain grove which is impossible to conquer. The human body is like a wild animal. The idea of bending it, moving and transforming it, especially through shringara, seems to him sheer absurdity.

In this respect, Abhinavagupta is an optimist. Thanks to this optimism, a kind of spiritual elegance comes into his thinking and writing. Behind this lies a deep experience of worlds beyond our everyday knowledge. Since he brings an ethereal mystery to the familiar activity of sexual intercourse, his works appeal to modern-day readers. The moderns are indeed devoted to the body. Their secular consciousness, even in search of mystery and the sacred in life, tries to find it within the framework of bodily experiences which can be easily studied. Abhinavagupta explains with complete involvement

---

[39] For the full vachana, see vachana no. 71 in Allama Prabhu, *Lord of the Cave*, and in Allama Prabhu, *Vachanas of Allama Prabhu*.

the kind of meditation yogis and yoginis engage in when they contemplate the genitals – kanda and guhya. Using the notion of another tantric, Bhatta Dhyaneshwar Sharma, Abhinavagupta calls this meditation "shaktyopaya".[40] Images of nature abound here.

Abhinavagupta is aware that all this mastery and achievement can only come with extraordinary training and preparation. He also knows well that the medium which communicates this can be weak. At the end of *Para-trisika-Vivarana* he says he is aware that speech and mind could be handicapped and the entire tantrodyoga – the task of tantra – might be ruined. However, his courage to overcome this setback lends him the power of imagination.

Allama makes poetry from his philosophical debates with the elders. As is evident in many of his vachanas, Allama's self knows that his work is that of a poet too. Such effort is natural for minds engaged with broad philosophical traditions. There are two dimensions to the model of Allama's debate with others. One is of an interaction that takes place within a poetic tradition; the other is of a dialogue that takes place within a philosophical tradition. As far as the interaction in the poetic tradition is concerned, it occurs in its first stage, or primarily within the framework of the Kannada poetic tradition. Some great poets can easily break with their own traditions. They achieve that process of rupture and continuation not with a conscious literary will; rather they create revolutions in poetic forms for larger philosophical reasons. As a result, old poetic forms are shattered. The use of metaphors, modes of expressing feelings, and other features do not become objects of criticism for reasons internal to literature. When various concepts about language, world, and subjectivity come into being, changes take place in poetry. That is, poetry changes because of non-poetic reasons. Such is the change Allama brought into Kannada poetry. This was made possible not by conscious dogmatic literary convictions but by certain philosophical pressures.

---

[40] In Trika philosophy three ways (upayas) of salvation are discussed: the way of Shiva (shambhava-upaya), the way of energy (shakta-upaya), and the individual way (anava-upaya). See Pandit, *An Introduction to the Philosophy of Trika Shaivism*, p. 7.

What interests us most here is the manner in which Allama transforms philosophical debates into poetry. Let us continue this discussion by using two Shaiva tantric concepts we have already discussed; sankocha (contraction) and vikasa (unfoldment). I would like to use them differently here. When Allama confronts the philosophical traditions with which he strongly disagrees, he uses the method of sankocha (contraction). This method is quite popular in Indian logic as well. Allama contracts the entire philosophy and body of works belonging to a tradition. This is the kind of debate he holds with Kashmir Shaivism.

While using contraction (sankocha) in a philosophical debate, the creation of images and metaphors is inevitable. It is a wonder of the poetic process that the tattvas there naturally turn themselves into metaphors and images. It is quite familiar in poetics for the details of everyday life to be crystallised into metaphors. But tattvas also become images and metaphors by befriending and fighting each other in their own world.

A genius such as Abhinavagupta also created metaphors by implementing the process of sankocha and vikasa in his philosophy. The tradition as a whole would create a coherent structure of metaphors. In this context, a philosophical tradition means a certain type of metaphoric structure. Metaphoric structures tend to be more rigidly conservative than the caste system; they acquire a sort of ceremonial power. They gain such considerable position and power of formation that they shape the poet himself. Put another way, poets do not create metaphors; rather, metaphoric structures control and shape poets. How this is possible is an issue not much discussed in literary criticism and theory. It can be explained in a nutshell as follows.

The structure of metaphors involves three components – feeling, linguistic rhythm, and images. Metaphor-making is not, as Indian poetics says, the result of "niyatikruta niyamarahitya" – which means being impervious to the rules of the world. Although it escapes the conventions of the outer world, it is imprisoned by its own internal conventions. From the historical perspective of the classical Kannada poetic tradition, the poet of vastuka is bound to its conventions; likewise, the poet writing in the Dasa tradition of Bhakti movement. This is also true in the case of the modern Kannada poetic tradition.

Thus, due to these internal conventions of metaphor-making, the external matrix of poetry – form and language – gains a particular character which, for example, may be found in poets like Pampa, Ranna, and Rudrabhatta.[41] Poetry acquires a broad macro matrix due to the negotiation between linguistic rhythms and images.[42] This broad macro matrix becomes a poetic tradition. The question of the poet's individual talent also arises here. For the time being, we can say that the uniqueness of the poet lies in how he creates his own subtle micro matrix within the framework of this broad macro matrix. Thus, the question of tradition and experiment is translated into the question of broad and subtle matrices. It is the harmony and conflict between the two that regulate the history of a poetic tradition.

The micro aspect of poetry involves the poet's unique subjective self. Allama's revolution lies in liberating himself and moving away from both the macro and the micro matrices of poetic traditions that existed up to his time. Allama achieves the macro matrix in the company of his contemporary vachanakaras. But he does not give up his freedom with regard to the formation of a unique micro matrix which he achieves through his own way of metaphor-making.

In the formation of his own micro matrix, Allama makes use of the models of sankocha and vikasa, which we discussed earlier. He uses the former while doubting others' thoughts. Being deeply absorbed is the main quality of most Shaiva tantric texts. Allama is not bothered about this deep absorption: he is suspicious of the garrulous rhetoric resulting from it. He is aware that overconfidence

[41] A Kannada poet who lived around the twelfth century and the author of *Jagannatha Vijaya*.

[42] For example, the use of vritta, kandapadya (metrical forms), and prose by poets like Pampa and Ranna gave a particular form to their works in the Champu tradition. In consonance with this, they created images which would give a distinct character to their poetry.

brings these garrulous rhetorical qualities to theories, and he suspects all forms of bombastic rhetoric.

His argument becomes especially colourful when he extols his contemporaries for possessing certain qualities which are opposed to the qualities he is in disagreement with. In such cases, Allama uses both modes – sankocha and vikasa – within the same vachana. Let us take a look at two vachanas:

> I saw the warrior without guts!
> I saw intimacy without youth!
> I saw the valour without arms!
> I saw the sweet smell without flowers!
> Oh, I saw the name Marulushankara
> Dwelling in Guheshwaralinga. (1117)

> Sadyojata is a narrow sage;
> Vamadeva is an impatient sage;
> Aghora is an angry sage;
> Tatpurusha is a transient sage;
> Ishanya is an unbounded sage.
> Look, these are not Chennabasavanna's ways,
> who is an integral sage in Guheshwaralinga,
> I bend before his holy feet. (1131)

Both these vachanas exhibit a definitive model of Allama's philosophical debating, which is the model of turning philosophies into particular personalities and vice versa. Behind these two vachanas is also a certain idea of human existence beyond time and space. To put it briefly, time or historical sense is not a central idea for Allama.[43] We may seem to exaggerate, but we could say that, according to Allama, there is no historical time; there is only a space or spiritual space. Because of this, the transformation of personalities and their philosophies into each other becomes for him an easy task. Though the idea of historical time seems to be embedded in his concept of

---

[43] Unlike Heidegger's time as a horizon of Being (Dasein). For an excellent introduction to Heidegger's thought, see Polt, *Heidegger: An Introduction*, to which I owe my understanding of Heidegger.

elders, they will eventually be associated only with spiritual space – not specific personalities existing in historical time. Thus, because Allama philosophically assumes that all are his contemporaries, he brings people of different ages face to face. The reason for the intensity behind his vachanas is that he presumes everything is contemporary. In him, time periods lose their distinct identities.

In his vachana about Marulushankara, Allama rejects what Shaiva tantras present as the supreme qualities of spiritual leadership in a yogi.[44] Though every utterance of this vachana (1117) has its own history, it is difficult to go to the root of each and comprehend the complete meaning. One has to stop at the general meaning. A yogi in Shaiva tantrism takes birth when bodily tendencies are considered supreme and spiritualised. In Allama the word "gut" has a special symbolic meaning, signifying the quality of being able to see physical desire as a spiritual experience. In Shaiva tantra, intimacy is both the body's energy and a state of mind; the two together constitute a spiritual space. For all these to exist, the youthfulness of the body is a fundamental necessity. There is no path for the tantric-spiritual sect lacking the fire of youthfulness and the power of intercourse. There is a spiritual explosion of tantra in the animal moment of orgasm. Allama says that in Marulushankara there is intimacy without youthfulness, heroism without guts, valour without arms, and sweet scents without flowers. If sparsha (touch) is the foundational concept for Allama's opponents, Allama, in his entire system of metaphors, steers clear of it. While speaking of sweet scents without flowers, Allama is suggesting a state of existence for which the body is not a fundamental necessity. It requires extraordinary spiritual courage to call someone like Marulushankara – a figure who appears in Virashaiva narratives – a dweller in Guheshwara linga. First, Allama describes Marulushankara through the use of negative terminology. When Allama refers to Marulushankara, all the ideal

[44] Marulushankara, also known as Maruladeva (approximately 1160 CE), is the author of *Maruladevara Kanda* and *Maruladevara Vachana*. He is said to have come from Kalinga (in the Afghanistan of today, not the Kalinga of today's region of Odisha) to Kalyana during the twelfth century.

traits of purvapaksha – the philosophical stance he opposes – appear before him. With the help of this contemporary yogi, Allama denies the values of purvapaksha. Here, the distinction between philosophies and personalities disappears.

In the second vachana (1131) quoted above, historical personalities and their philosophies come together in a different way. Since Sadyojata is an important exponent of Dvaita Shaivism, it is appropriate on the part of the Advaitin Allama to interpret him in his own way. On the other hand, Aghora and Ishanya are not only historical personalities but also philosophies. (Ishanya was a yogini of kaya.) It is difficult to say precisely what Allama is talking about here. Yet it is possible to read the aporias in Allama's vachanas productively – thanks to the freedom that the modern reader has. However, such a reading has its own limitations and strengths.

Let us revisit the question of Allama's resistance to the puranic mode. His negation of the puranic mode is mainly the result of his opposition to the narrative imagination of Tamil Shaivism. As has already been observed, Allama does not make any distinction between philosophy and the mode of its expression, treating them as inseparable. He is opposed to the way the *Periyapuranam* valorises stories of Shiva bhakti. As soon as Shiva is humanised, the poet's descriptive and narrative imagination gains unlimited freedom. The boundless experience of human affairs is accessible to the poet, i.e. to his technique of storytelling and the creation of metaphors. Therefore, the puranic mode is simultaneously a philosophical and literary choice.

It is true that the characteristic features unique to the puranic mode hide its relationship with the pure philosophical mode. In general, puranas aspire for harmony by overlooking philosophy's persistent zeal for separation – i.e. making conceptual distinctions. The unique strength of the puranas has always lain in their capacity to incorporate stories and mythemes of various traditions in their fold. Thus, Brahmanic puranas and Shramana puranas, despite their internal differences, share some similarities, which can be explained in terms of three processes: narrativising philosophical concepts;

the mythification of historical elements of religious sects; and the unification of symbolic structures. The ways in which puranic modes go beyond their limited framework to learn and digest other concepts are indeed fascinating.

Above all, puranic models daringly confront contradictions within reality that philosophical modes often cannot manage and explore satisfactorily. Further, the puranas of classical religious sects digest the folk religion, its beliefs and narrative worlds. Likewise, folk puranas assimilate in themselves the motifs and images of the classical religious sects beyond the spiritual authority of the classes which produce them. For instance, the puranas of Sanskrit daivas (gods and goddesses) are transformed and represented differently in the puranas of folk gramadevatas (village deities). In this context, the stories of *Katamaraju* sung by Telugu-language folklorists are worthy of special study.[45] Similarly, the stories of *Kyatarulinga* of the Kadugollas in Karnataka contain an interesting tale of this kind of cultural encounter. (I use the term purana in a definitive sense – as a narrative form of a religious sect's symbols, philosophy, and personalities.) Thus, in the sense of a broad cultural politics, puranas are narratives of the reconciliation between different sects. Given the limitless freedom of the mythical imagination, several unexpected phenomena occur in the unconscious layers of these puranas.

Allama calls the purana "nothing but the conference of rogues".[46] Such anger appears reasonable when we study the Shaiva puranas. Allama, for example, in the following vachana, fiercely satirises the way the path of bhaktas is narrativised in the *Periyapuranam*:

Unlike Siriyala and Changale,
Sangana Basavanna did not sacrifice his child.
Unlike Nambi and Ballala,
he did not indulge in lustful acts.
Unlike Bommayya and Kannappa,

---

[45] I have discussed this elsewhere. See Nagaraj, "Daivasankara", pp. 18–27 (DRN).

[46] For the full vachana, see vachana no. 465 in Allama Prabhu, *Lord of the Cave*; and in Allama Prabhu, *Vachanas of Allama Prabhu*.

he did not inflict violence on other beings.
O Guheshwara,
he is a riddle for your sharanas. (800)

This vachana speaks of conflict between two irreconcilable paths
that claim to be shivapatha – i.e. the path leading to Shiva. Dvaita
Shaivism upholds the shivadhyana (meditation/devotion of Shiva)
and shivakayaka (the deeds of Shiva) of bhaktas (like Siriyala,
Chengale, Nambi, Kannappa) propagated in the *Periyapuranam*
and Harihara's ragales; such a belief draws a line between their devotion to everyday work and the non-violent form of Shiva-tattva.
However, Allama, who is against the puranic and bhakti narratives,
refuses to call the devotion and innocence of bhaktas portrayed in
the Shaiva puranas tapa (penance). When Allama says in the vachana (801), "All sages became the victims / of the samsara called penance . . .", it is a critique of the bhaktas of the *Periyapuranam*.[47] This
line in the vachana (801) is followed by "All those who held on to
Linga / became victims of Linga's samsara / called rewards and status . . ." According to Allama, this type of path is artificial and re-
mote from shivapatha.

The case of Sanskrit puranas such as the *Shri Shiva Rahasya* (The
Secret Teachings of Shiva) and *Linga-Purana* is different.[48] Whatever social power structures Virashaivism generally opposed are
adored in these works as the ultimate truth. In the first place, Allama opposes the very idea of narrativising Shiva by attributing
human qualities and a human personality to him. In the *Shri Shiva
Rahasya*, especially, we come across numerous absurd situations
such as when Vyasamaharishi's tongue falls off as soon as he claims
that Narayana is the greatest God, not Shiva! Brahmin tradition-

---

[47] For the full vachana, see vachana no. 889 in Allama Prabhu, *Lord of the
Cave*, and vachana no. 1272 in Allama Prabhu, *Vachanas of Allama Prabhu*.

[48] *Shri Shiva Rahasya*: an ancillary purana about Shiva. For an English translation see Maharaj Dev, *Shri Shiva Rahasya Linga-Purana:* one of the eighteen
puranas and a text of Shaivism, believed to have been composed approximately
between the fifth and tenth centuries. The author is unknown. For an English
translation, see Shastri, ed., *The Linga-Purana*, I and II.

alism is a massive presence in these works. All that Allama opposes – such as rituals, myths, symbols, or philosophy – flows free of impediment in these works. The inherent nature of reconciliation in the puranas allows them to accept traditionalism in terms of rituals, symbols, and philosophy.

For the puranas, Shiva is a physical reality. He is easily accessible to consciousness and bhakti. Though there is a secret to Shiva beyond this material truth, steps of reality are essentially required to cross over and find it. But for Allama, neither Shiva nor linga is a physical reality. They are not even imaginative realities. In one of his vachanas, Allama reveals his notion of linga in the negative mode.

> Picking a kani (stone) on this creation,
> and placing it on the palm of the eight-fold body,
> they say, "tie it around the neck and worship."
> Born of earth, it became a stone,
> found form in the hands of a mason,
> became an idol in the hands of a Guru.
> How shall I worship such a bastard born for three?
> The one who says he would die if the linga falls down,
> he will go to the arch-hell
> reserved for heinous crimes
> when he dies by weapon, water, in the jungle or sky.
> If the linga on the palm falls down,
> does the linga in the mind fall too?
> Saying this, one should pick the linga
> And offer the sixteen-fold worship.
> Only Chennabasavanna knows the way of
> tying the linga and reaching the linga,
> not the ones who claim of attaining divinity
> by pouring holy water as a habit, O Guheshwara. (1009)

This vachana must be analysed against the backdrop of what Allama elsewhere says "sutaka (defilement) it is, an illusion it is, to utter, 'the linga fell down'." (1004) For Allama, linga is not the truth of the rite, nor is it necessary for the ritual. Puranic modes accept divinity as a physical reality and also present it as an imaginative truth. Besides, they present it as the truth accessible through ritual practice. Because of these three factors, in both traditions – Brahmana and Shramana – listening to a purana also becomes a ritual. Allama, however, has no respect for any part of the trinity (physical reality, imaginative truth, and rituals) which the puranic mode achieves. For him, linga should be in the mind. Therefore, he asks repeatedly, "If the linga on the palm falls down / Does the linga in the mind fall too?"

We need to examine Allama's fascinating comment about the "linga falling down" against the backdrop of the fact that religious warfare and ethnic violence were widespread in ancient India. The puranic modes of religion resorted to bloodshed, believing that the fall of the divine symbols and their destruction were heinous acts. Violence in the name of the divine is one of the characteristic features of Indian history. There is an interesting description of the battle between Jainas and Shaivas in the *Periyapuranam* itself. While narrating the life of the shivabhakta (Shiva's devotee) Thirunavukkarasu, the text describes frenzied violence between the Jainas and Shaivas. "Insane Shramanas" (Jainas) damaged or partially destroyed the temples of northern Thirupulai. Then the Shaiva king, in turn, destroyed a group of Shramana basadis (Jaina shrines). Thousands of Shramana Gurus were also fatally attacked. A jinagraha (Jaina shrine) was turned into a shivalaya (Shiva temple).[49]

In Tamil Shaivism, to which Allama responded, there is adoration of this kind of violence. A shivabhakta resorting to violence in defence of bhakti was considered ganachara in Virashaivism.[50] The modern study of religions calls this "divine violence". Allama analyses the historical roots of violence that are relevant not only to ancient but also to contemporary realities. Here, he examines the tradition of devotees becoming elders by perpetuating religious violence and counter-violence in the name of the ganachara ideal. Such adoration of violence was wholly present in Shaiva memory

---

[49] Kedilaya, trans., *Periyapuranam*, pp. 108 and 111 (DRN).

[50] A devotee's behaviour towards the community as a whole; one of the six acharas (conducts), the others being lingachara, sadachara, shivachara, hanachara, and bruthyachara.

and the puranas that Allama was familiar with. Religion in its institutional form must, at some point or the other, encounter the consciousness of violence. This is an inevitable part of an institutionalised religion maintaining its relationship of conflict and harmony with power structures. Religions may examine violence at the philosophical level but may not be able to avoid it in daily life, even less so in times of dire crises. Thus, when exploring violence in religions there are three spheres: the philosophical, the mundane, and the critical. Religions that prohibit violence at the philosophical and mundane levels generally cannot maintain the same prohibition during crises.

Allama examines the question of violence simultaneously with respect to these three spheres. In his scheme there is no difference among them. More importantly, for him religion means only bayalu – an open space or void – or Guheshwara Himself. There is no historicity for him as far as religion is concerned. To him it seems too artificial for a religion to have a historical existence or memory. From his perspective linga has no form, so there is no spiritual justification for those who resort to violence by thinking that the form of linga has been destroyed.[51] No cataclysm can destroy linga, nor does linga speak. Allama thus cautions us against all those historical distortions in which bayalu became an object of violence in the hands of people. But the narrative model of the puranic mode inevitably grows by considering all these distortions seriously and intensely. The purana has to grow as a story of love and hate; even the act of renunciation grows as intense love. There would be no excitement in the puranic mode if asceticism, too, could not become an intense state of deep love and devotion. Shiva, an object of narrative devotion in the puranic mode, has to possess all the qualities of chaturvarna – the traditional system of four varnas. Allama therefore negates at once all description of Shiva that exists in the Shivapuranas. For him, Guheshwara is neither Ishwara nor Maheshwara.

---

[51] Note the reference to "the linga falling down" in the above-mentioned vachana (1009).

He is not the three-eyed Shiva, who burnt three cities,
not the one who danced, trampling over Andhakasura (a demon),
not the one holding a skull,
not the one wearing a garland of heads,
nor is he the one who roams around mandala (the world).
He is neither Ishwara nor Maheshwara.
The linga called Guheshwara is beyond all this. (999)

By saying that Guheshwara is neither Ishwara nor Maheshwara, Allama leaves no space for mythical description. Rejecting the puranic mode involves renouncing a particular mode of image creation. Various stories told in the puranas and poetic narratives create various figures of speech for Shiva. The nouns pertaining to such narrativisations become signifiers of Shiva. This applies to Shakti as well. It is like describing Chamundi as Mahishasura Mardini – the killer of the demon Mahisha; and Shiva as Gangadhara – he who wears the river Ganga; and Mukkanna – the three-eyed. These kinds of epithets are subtle forms of the puranic mode. And their complex forms unfold in a grand manner. Allama nowhere praises Shiva in the puranic mode, and emphatically states that Shiva is not a puranic figure. He justifies his basic philosophy against the puranic mode when he says that he does not count the mythological aspect of Guheshwara: "My mind blushes to know / that once in the past you burnt the triple town. / It makes me sick to know your pride / of having burnt the God of love and / earned the title – Destroyer of the love-God."[52] (1064)

Allama does not advance for-or-against arguments about Guheshwara on social grounds, he does so at the spiritual level. By refusing to place Guheshwara within history, he makes Guheshwara more relevant to the contemporary reader. Just as a historical method can place spirituality in a particular framework, Allama's method of spirituality can manage history from its own perspective.

Let us continue this discussion in relation to the question of the linga falling down and historicity. Note the following vachana:

---

[52] For the full vachana, see vachana no. 1307 in Allama Prabhu, *Lord of the Cave*, and vachana no. 969 in Allama Prabhu, *Vachanas of Allama Prabhu*.

Does one become a bhakta by tying a linga?
Does one become a traitor if he knocks down the linga?
Is it in one's hand to tie it?
Can it fall when one knocks it down?
Can the world survive if the linga falls down?
Can prana (life-force) last, when pranalinga is lost?
Sutaka (defilement) it is, an illusion it is, to utter,
"the linga fell down."
One should not hear it.
Epochs pass into history, not the linga.
"The linga fell down" are the sinful words of a traitor,
I can't hear it any more, O Guheshwara. (1004)

Here, Allama raises the concept of linga to cosmic heights. The idea that the world does not survive when the linga falls down is fascinating. This world, with everything in it, is Shiva's creation. On the other hand the idea of an epoch is a temporal concept. Therefore, it is the epoch, not Guheshwara, that becomes a thing of the past. Likewise, in another vachana Allama adds another notion: kritya – ritualistic acts.[53] One meaning of kritya is ritualistic practice. At another level it means speech acts related to (narrativising) Guheshwara. Allama is opposed to kritya in both senses. Guheshwara linga is not accessible through ritualistic practices. Likewise, those who believe that Guheshwara can be grafted in history tend to believe in the possibility of demolishing linga. By stating that one who drops his linga is not a traitor, Allama takes a spiritual position regarding an important source of violence in history.

This position of Allama on the falling of the linga is nothing but his perspective on the power structures of medieval times. Philosophical debates in medieval India were transformed decisively because of the compromise they struck with power structures. On this ground, there was no difference between Brahminic and Shramana traditions. The way Allama analyses the notion of sutaka (defilement) explains the indivisible relationship between history and

---

[53] For the full vachana, see vachana no. 1349 in Allama Prabhu, *Vachanas of Allama Pabhu.*

power. History is nothing but the thoughts of elders – whose disposition is to surrender to power and be subservient. Allama enumerates one by one the motifs that give rise to history and power structures. Instead of making a list specifying "this is power, and this is history", he explains all the factors that constitute power according to his spiritual psychology. It is our task to bring them all together and arrive at a conclusion.

In other words, for Allama history itself is sutaka. Several sutakas make a grand sutaka called history. Allama lists them in one of his vachanas: kula sutaka (clan defilement), chala sutaka (defilement of will), tanu sutaka (bodily defilement), mana sutaka (mental defilement), nenahu sutaka (thought defilement), and bhava sutaka (emotional defilement).[54] The union of these sutakas produces history and its continuity. Allama knows well that these sutakas are not just limited to human affairs; the nature of creation itself encompasses defilement. In his philosophy there is no distinction between nature and the human world, or between lifelessness and living. His belief that the primordial upheavals which form the human world are also very much part of nature gives extraordinary power to his metaphors.

> Wildfire burns the forest.
> The water fire burns the sea.
> The fire within burns the body.
> The fire of doomsday burns the whole world.
> The fire of anger in shivasharanas
> burns those who berate them.
> Listen, O Guheshwara,
> I will not burn in the raging fire of your maye (illusion). (1063)

This vachana takes a dramatic turn in the last line. The fire is both a physical and a mental state in Allama's world. He thus finds one rule in the entire universe: a state of confining all in one. In the first six lines, Allama suggests that history and nature are equally in con-

---

[54] See vachana no. 1549 in Allama Prabhu, *Lord of the Cave*, and vachana no. 702 in Allama Prabhu, *Vachanas of Allama Prabhu*.

finement.[55] Nowhere does he weave one metaphor with another through logic. However, he establishes their interrelationship through analogy. Whether it is the "fire of doomsday" or "the fire of anger", it is ultimately bound by one rule – that of burning. But the state of ultimate freedom to escape from such a binding rule of burning is indicated in the last line, "Listen, O Guheshwara, / I will not burn in the raging fire of your maye (illusion)." When history becomes an insurmountable state of rules, Allama repeatedly presents the possibility of transcending it.

[55] Note the fire of anger in shivasharanas (historical entity) and fire in natural entities such as forest, sea, and body.

5

Life Narratives of Allama

Three Models

ALLAMA PRABHU became a subject for diverse narratives among later generations. It is a historical irony that although Allama opposed narrativisation in his philosophy, he himself became an exemplary figure for narratives.[1] He maintained that religion should not be caught up in the playfulness of narratives. And yet a variety of narratives about his own life emerged. He deemed any sign(ifier) or symbol unacceptable, yet in subsequent centuries himself became a sign(ifier) and symbol for diverse religious imaginations.

We need to study the role such narrative models played in the religious imagination of medieval Karnataka. In all religious narratives, such representative models perform the function of recognising and legitimising a particular religious darshana. Religions take the help of these representative models in particular when they try to establish their power in the domain of social existence. It is necessary to identify certain theoretical features of various narrative models constructed by the religious discourses of medieval Karnataka – with a special eye on Allama's life.

The life events of a religious figure like Allama undergo certain remarkable transformations when narrativised. The transformation

[1] For more on how vachanas are not stories and narratives, and how narratives followed the Vachana movement, see Kurtkoti, *Kannada Sahitya Sangati*, pp. xli–xlii and 76–7.

230

is all the more dramatic when details about the religious figure are not available for historical verification. Theoretically, we need to observe that the distinction between history and hagiographic (life)-narrative disappears as the latter is interpreted as history, and even accurate details pertaining to the figure become wholly symbolic. Furthermore, the gap widens between events in the lives of religious figures and the meanings ascribed to them in the narratives. In them, events are turned into motifs, themes, and symbols. As these narrative models evolve historically and religions age, they try to negate their historicity, claiming that their origins lie beyond history. They begin to present human activities as being beyond the human. Especially when there is competition and conflict between different religions in the political and social sphere, every act of self-interpretation becomes abstract.

Against the backdrop of this complex process, it is worth discussing how Allama's life narratives evolved as a representative model after the twelfth century. Since no uniform pattern emerged in the life narratives on Allama, he remained a paradoxical figure even after his death. As stated above, there was a gap between Allama's life events and the meanings attributed to them, and different traditions interpreted them differently. Therefore, in these various narrative models, representations of Allama were widely divergent.

I: Harihara and the Shunyasampadanekaras: Literary and Institutional Models

Allama's life narratives fall into three categories: first, the model of Harihara and Chamarasa;[2] second, the model of the *Shunya-*

---

[2] Harihara (later part of the twelfth century): a medieval Kannada poet who perfected the genre of poetry known as ragale, composed *Hariharana Raga-legalu*, the subject matter of which is the lives of vachanakaras and sixty-three Tamil puratanas (ancients). One of the lives narrated here is Allama's, and is called "Prabhudevare Ragale". For more, see Ben-Herut, *Siva's Saints*. Chamarasa: fifteenth-century Kannada poet who composed *Prabhulingalile*, a life narrative

sampadanes;[3] and third, the folk Shaiva narrative model.[4] Though the versions of the *Shunyasampadanes* vary in terms of their focus and symbolic structures, they are homogeneous. Compared to the *Shunyasampadanes*, the two other narrative models take a different philosophical stance not only about the conception of religion as a whole but also about Virashaivism. Though on the surface these models appear to use the same material, they differ in their essence. They imagine the existential and historical dimensions of religion differently.

Let us consider some fundamental aspects of the *Shunyasampadanes* before undertaking a comparative study of these narratives. I call the *Shunyasampadanes* narratives of institutional imagination. The unique structure of the *Shunyasampadanes*, and the aura and theatricality associated with them, indicate the institutionalisation of the Virashaiva movement at that time. No religious movement survives and grows without becoming institutionalised, without becoming part of the historical process.

The *Shunyasampadanes* played a decisive role in making the Virashaiva movement institutionally strong. A socially revolutionary and explosive movement was turned into a "textual community"

---

of Allama Prabhu. For the English translation, see Chamarasa, *The Frolic Play of the Lord*.

[3] Four versions of the *Shunyasampadane* are available, and are believed to have been composed between the fifteenth and early sixteenth centuries. The composers (shunyasampadanakars) are Shivaganaprasadi Mahadevaiah, Halegeyarya, Gummalapurada Siddhalingadevara, and Guluru Siddhaveerannodayara. Sri Guluru Siddhaveerannodayara's *Shunyasampadane* has been translated into English. See Gooluru Siddaveeranna, *Sunyasampadane*, 5 vols. For an abridged version of *Shunyasampadane* in English translation, see Shivaganaprasadi, *Shoonyasampadane of Shivaganaprasadi*. For more on the *Shunyasampadanes*, see the Translator's Introduction.

[4] This refers to the *Manteswamy Kavya*, a folk epic still being performed in some places of the old Mysore region. Here, Manteswamy, the folk hero who is supposed to have lived in the fifteenth century, is portrayed as an incarnation of Allama Prabhu. For multifaceted documentation, textualisation, and English translation of this epic tradition, see Hiriyanna, ed., *Manteswamy Epic*.

through the *Shunyasampadanes*.[5] Seen through the lenses of such transformative turns, we may discern two great epochs in the history of Virashaivism before the twentieth century: the twelfth-century epoch of the Vachana movement itself, and the period of the fifteenth and sixteenth centuries which may be called the Virashiava Sankalana age (the age of compilation of vachanas), when the *Shunyasampadanes* were produced.[6] We need not imagine a simple and unbroken continuity between these two epochs; in fact, there was no unceasing progression.

In the twelfth century – the first phase – which was the beginning of Virashaivism, a comprehensive narrative like the *Shunyasampadanes* would not have been possible. In this phase there were only metaphors and motifs expressed through vachanas. Though there existed internal differences in its philosophy, a sort of grand unity shaped the movement at this time. What is important is that though there were no shared principles, a common counter-philosophy had held the movement together. It was unified at the level of its agenda. That is, the proponents of Virashaivism were sure about their philosophical stance regarding who they were revolting against. It was a time when some influential sects of the Shaiva religion were decaying. Thus, we could say that the twelfth-century Vachana movement began as an internal reformation and eventually created a new religious way of life. This process of internal purification naturally created certain conceptual images and mystical motifs. For

[5] According to Brian Stock, a textual community is one whose life, thought, sense of identity, and relations with outsiders are organised around an authoritative text. See Stock, *The Implications of Literacy*. We are not sure how vachanas survived in whatever form, oral or documented since the twelfth century. But the *Shunyasampadanes* systematically compiled and edited them for their purposes. Thus, this kind of work turned vachanas into authorised texts of Virashaiva or Lingayat reading and this is how an open Virashaiva/Lingayat way of life became a textual community.

[6] During the twentieth century, Lingayat scholars such as F.G. Halakatti and others compiled and edited vachanas as part of print culture. This may be called the third epoch in the history of Virashaivism. For more, see Boratti, *The Discovery of Vachanas*.

instance, it created a conceptual image of ishtalinga in place of static linga.[7] Thus, the idea of the ishtalinga was born out of Virashaivism's counter-philosophy that summarily rejected the static linga.

In this first phase, twelfth-century Virashaivism was completely open and not a closed system. However, with such openness an institutional religion cannot attain unquestionable social power and influence. Thus, the fifteenth century became an age of sankalananusandhana, i.e. of organising and compiling texts and stories. (I take the concept of sankalananusandhana from Abhinavagupta and use it in a broader sense, that is, in the sense of compiling different parts and creating a whole within the context of a particular darshana.) This process of organising and compiling vachanas during the fifteenth century imparted a definitive institutional strength and socially active role to Virashaivism.

It is important to enumerate the major achievements of this age of sankalananusandhana. We could consider the *Shunyasampadanes* as the essence of all these achievements. I believe that the study of this grand process in the medieval Kannada world throws special light on the historical formation of religions in general. Accordingly, the *Shunyasampadane* texts are a document of the major shifts that Virashaivism underwent, and these texts self-reflectively believed that they were playing a vital role in managing the form and direction of these shifts.

There is an intense desire in the *Shunyasampadanes* to retain the openness of the first phase of Virashaivism. But this desire is con-

[7] Generally, it is known that the Vachana movement replaced temple culture by the concept of ishtalinga, which is placed on the left palm and worshipped by the follower of Virashaivism, often known as lingawanta (wearer of ishtalinga). In Virashaivism, there are three forms of relationship with linga: ishtalinga, pranalinga, and bhavalinga. Ishtalinga denotes linga worn on the body voluntarily to initiate oneself to the lingayat (wearer of linga) way of life. A guru offers the linga to the disciple following certain rituals, such as uttering the panchakshari mantra. If ishtalinga refers to the physical object, pranalinga involves linga becoming one's life-breath, and bhavalinga is the highest form of relationship in which the devotee's mind is one with the idea of linga. For more, see Vidyashankara, ed., *Veerasaiva Paribhashika*, pp. 90–1.

trolled by the will to become institutionally homogeneous and organised. In other words, two different pressures have shaped the *Shunyasampadanes*: at one end Allama appears as a philosophical current flowing without any institutional obligation; at the other end he appears as a force embedded in the institutionalised religious practice – the concrete ritual conduct. Although these two pressures appear to compete equally, it is the latter – the ritual conduct of the religious community – that gains the upper hand in the *Shunyasampadanes*.

There is thus the question of the relationship between the discourse that emerges internally from Allama's vachanas and the homogeneous discourse that the *Shunyasampadanes* create. In fact, a homogeneous discourse does not emerge from Allama's vachanas. What he endorses in one place may well be rejected in another. There is a definitive character to Allama's sensibility, but it is not conducive to the provision of a holistically consistent discourse. The vachanas create a particular kind of philosophical space where anything can happen. But the perspective of the *Shunyasampadanes* does not follow this course. Instead, the *Shunyasampadanes* transform the primordial spiritual "indiscipline" of the vachanas into a disciplined discourse – asocial elements morphing into something socially directed.

Nowhere in his vachanas does Allama mention that he has a historical responsibility to propagate Shivadvaita. But the discourse of the *Shunyasampadanes* imposes this responsibility on Allama, who attained spiritual achievement without bothering about any historical function. In this respect, the act of transforming philosophy into a narrative is a mighty achievement on the part of the *Shunyasampadanes*. However, romantic stories from Allama's mortal life are not only irrelevant but dangerous for the *Shunyasampadanes*.

The differences between literary and spiritual discourse have regulated the *Shunyasampadanes*. Pain, pleasure, and disillusionment with worldly life are themes for a literary narrative like Harihara's "Prabhudevara Ragale" but not significant for a spiritual narrative like the *Shunyasampadane*. Hence, the romantic story of Allama's personal life might seem exciting and significant for a modern poet, but not for the *Shunyasampadanes*. Instead, they – setting aside the story of Allama's worldly life – develop his personality by giving narrative structure to themes and motifs culled from his vachanas. According to the *Shunyasampadanes*, a major motif of Allama's life is the conflict between kamatattva (the erotic principle) and shiva-tattva (the principle of Shiva).[8] But there is no scope for the play of literary imagination in the representation of kamatattva in the *Shunyasampadanes*. There is no place either for a detailed description of Allama's love story, because such descriptions belong to the realm of the literary imagination.[9] The episode of Allama and Kamalate could have been a great romantic story in the hands of the moderns, but in the *Shunyasampadanes* it is narrated simply at the level of an allegory. It is quite evident from the *Shunyasampadanes* that the allegory plays a dominant role in spiritual narratives.

The *Shunyasampadanes* tell an interesting story about a Ganeshwara called Nirmaya coming to the human world as Allama.[10] Significant differences exist between this story and the self-interpretations we come across in Allama's vachanas. Shivaganaprasadi Mahadevaiah, the most influential among the composers of the *Shunyasampadanes*, states: "In the heavenly court of Parameshwara, who is eternal, immaculate and all-illuminating, seated are several rudraganas (the entourage of Shiva). It was a Mahaganeshwara called Nirmaya, the greatest among rudraganas" who would later take birth in Banavasi as Allama.[11] If Allama, being an ardent Shivad-

---

[8] Shiva-tattva, the ultimate principle, involves five aspects: shiva, shakti, sadakhya, Ishwara, and shuddha vidye. See Yaravintelimath, ed., *Vachana Lexicon*, p. 774.

[9] A literary narrative such as Harihara's "Prabhudevara Ragale" describes in detail the romantic love story of Allama and Kamalate.

[10] Nirmaya, which means someone without maya (illusion), one of the five Ganeshwaras in the heavenly court of Parameshwara – the others being Nirbhaya, Akshaya, Omkara, and Urdhvamukha. See Yaravintelimath, ed., *Vachana Lexicon*, p. 440. For the storyline of the *Shunyasampadanes*, see the Translator's Introduction.

[11] Shivaganaprasadi, *Shivaganaprasadi Mahadevayyana*, p. 73.

vaita, sees himself as Guheshwara, for the *Shunyasampadanes*
Nirmaya is neither Parameshwara nor Guheshwara. Allama's distinctive spiritual adventure is premised on the notion of the non-
duality between him and Guheshwara; his self is not other than Guheshwara. Yet somehow the shunyasampadanakaras – the authors
of the *Shunyasampadanes* – find it difficult to accept this ultimate
Advayavadi stance – that "the 'self' itself is Guheshwara." In this respect, Harihara's Dvaita (dualism) sensibility has sneaked into the
Shunyasampadanes. Even after grasping several themes and motifs
in Allama's vachanas at a higher level, the *Shunyasampadanes* do not
take his self-interpretation to its logical end. They begin by narrating Allama's life story within the framework of the mythical narrative, one to which Allama's philosophy doesn't subscribe.

In Shivaganaprasadi Mahadevaiah's *Shunyasampadane,* when
Shiva asks the Ganeshwara called Nirmaya to go to the mortal
world and take birth, Nirmaya is humbled but requests Shiva not to
send him away as it will separate him from Shiva. As against the
spiritual arrogance we come across in Allama's vachanas – such as
"Are you the Lord? / No. I am the Lord" – in Shivaganaprasadi we
have a portrayal of Allama's humility.[12] The following section from
a *Shunyasampadane* shows how Nirmaya, who is supposed to be
born as Allama, is humbled when Shiva says:

> "Since you have fallen for maya, you will take birth in the mortal world
> and indulge in lust offered by rudrakannike, the divine lass." The Gane-
> shwara named Nirmaya pleaded, tears flowing down his eyes: "O, Deva!
> Bereft of your divine company, how will I understand you after taking
> birth in the human world?" Then, Shiva, Sachidanandamurthy, who
> bestows deliverance, narrated: "The mortal world is my mint! Does it
> really matter if you are here or there? It does not make any difference be-
> cause I am the creator of all. Fear not. I will dispel the maya that has em-
> braced you. I myself will come as a pranalinga, dwell in your whole be-
> ing, making you attain nija lingaikya (consubstantial linga) and place

[12] For the full vachana, see vachana no. 558 in Allama Prabhu, *God is Dead.*
Also see vachana no. 558 in Allama Prabhu, *Lord of the Cave*; and in Allama
Prabhu, *Vachanas of Allama Prabhu.*

you in the abode of nirvana. From you, shivachara (the discipline of following Shaiva practices) in the human world will be rejuvenated."[13]

Why does Shivaganaprasadi portray in Allama (Nirmaya) this humility that is completely absent in Allama's own self-reflexive vachanas? This is not an unimportant question. It is difficult to believe that Allama (Nirmaya) cried out in a voice of humility. A possible answer to this question could be the pressure of devotional narratives such as Harihara's Bhakti poetry, which was an influential backdrop to the *Shunyasampadanes*. Though far removed in time from Harihara (later part of the twelfth and early thirteenth centuries), the *Shunyasampadanes* (fifteenth–sixteenth centuries) seem to have accepted his conviction that all sharanas are the expressions of bhakta tattva, the principle of devotion where the devotee or bhakta surrenders himself to God. The objective of the *Shunyasampadanes* is the "rejuvenation of shivachara in the mortal world," and they rope in even Allama in the ambit of their objective by assigning a certain role and duty to him. They transform Allama's stance against the kamatattva, which we come across in his vachanas, into a dynamic pro-Shiva-tattva by giving it a different interpretation.

This does not mean that the *Shunyasampadanes* have completely ignored Allama's self-expression as found in his vachanas. The uniqueness of the *Shunyasampadanes* lies in the fact that they faithfully retain the distinction between their own religious concerns embedded in their narratives and Allama's ideas as expressed in his vachanas.[14] It is also true that the *Shunyasampadanes*, later in their narrative, present before us the self-expressive vachanas of Allama. The story of the aforementioned Nirmaya is an imagined construction, and the shunyasampadanakara is aware that Allama's consciousness does not accept this imagined construction. Therefore,

---

[13] Shivaganaprasadi, *Shivaganaprasadi Mahadevayyana*, p. 2.

[14] The stated purpose of Shivaganaprasadi Mahadevaiah's *Shunyasampadane* is to restore Shivadvaita on earth. For an English translation, see Shivaganaprasadi, *Shoonyasampadane of Shivaganaprasadi*, p. 1.

he says, "He [Allama] was cognising that he was born of the force of adichit (primal consciousness) which existed before all the worlds, including this Brahmanda, were born."[15] In other words, on account of the inner necessity of its spiritual discourse, the narrative consciousness of the *Shunyasampadanes* constructs a story, but Allama's vachana denies it there itself. It is interesting to note that both coexist in the *Shunyasampadanes*. Below is Allama's self-interpretation:

> When there was neither a beginning nor a base,
> When there was neither pride nor prejudice,
> When there was neither form nor formlessness,
> When there was no void (shunya) or non-void (nishunya)
> When all the mobile and the immobile in the cosmos were unformed,
> Guheshwara, your sharana emerged.[16]

It is quite natural for the spiritual storyteller, the shunyasampadanakara, to be impatient with worldly affairs. Therefore, the *Shunyasampadanes* are keen to take Allama to the section on "Guru Darshana-Linga Prapti" – which deals with Allama's initiation to linga by his guru Animisha immediately after the loss of Kamalate.[17] They do not recount in detail the episode of Kamalate and his redemption from the curse.[18] The shunyasampadanakara's liter-

---

[15] Shivaganaprasadi, *Shivaganaprasadi Mahadevayyana*, p. 76.

[16] Ibid., p. 64. The *Shunyasampadanes* allude to and quote the vachanas of the various vachanakaras in their narratives, and Nagaraj at times quotes vachanas from the *Shunyasampadanes*.

[17] According to Nagaraj, if other narratives like Harihara's "Prabhudevara Ragale" take much time to come to this episode, the *Shunyasampadanes* reach it relatively soon, condensing Allama's affair with Kamalate. See ch. 2, "Animishadevaru", in Shivaganaprasadi, *Shoonyasampadane of Shivaganaprasadi*, pp. 8–18. Also see "The First Lesson of Prabhudeva's" in Gooluru Siddaveeranna, *Sunyasampadane*, vol. 1, pp. 82–5.

[18] In Allama's life narratives, when Shiva praises the intense renunciation practised by the Mahaganeshwara called Nirmaya, one of the cohorts in Kailasa, Parvati contests this and pledges that she will make him vulnerable to maya. Accordingly, she bestows stunning beauty on a rudrakannike. On

ary imagination becomes active only when he has to build the narrative, not in the description of erotic episodes. The spiritual imagination cannot narrate the pangs of separation caused by death as effectively as does the literary imagination. Even so, the *Shunyasampadane* does record a vachana with a hidden meaning which could be related to the episode of Allama and Kamalate:

> Ayya, her gaze brought me to the mortal world.
> The taste of mating with her engulfed and plagued me!
> As the roots of her desires extended,
> I saw tripura (three cities) ruined!
> As flame swooped on flame,
> I saw the cold emerging!
> I saw the elder wife losing her earring
> when a musk-deer swallowed a black hunter!
> Emerging triumphant from the poet's battle in the fort of dark night
> I saw the buried treasure, O Gogeshwara.[19]

The *Shunyasampadane* compels us to interpret this vachana in a particular way. The traditional reading understands it as Allama's spiritual dissatisfaction with his days of infatuation. But the paradoxical mode of Allama's vachanas makes room for a different response.

The *Shunyasampadanes* try to evade the details of Allama's worldly life. However, Allama has no regrets about worldly affairs in the mortal world since this world is also Shiva's creation. Even the metaphor in the verse above — "As flame swooped on flame, / I saw the cold emerging!" — could be giving a negative meaning from the viewpoint of the shunyasampadanakara, but it propagates a positive meaning from Allama's perspective. Institutional narratives always

---

seeing her, Nirmaya is attracted to her beauty for a while but soon repents that vulnerable state of attraction. When he goes to Shiva's court, Shiva recognises his state of mind and sends him to the mortal world to be born as Allama and to lead a happy life with the rudrakannike, who is born as Kamalate. After a period of marital life, Kamalate dies of a high fever and Allama (Nirmaya) is redeemed from the curse.

[19] Shivaganaprasadi, *Shivaganaprasadi Mahadevayyana*, p. 9.

look for ways of avoiding embarrassment.[20] That a great mystic like Allama once succumbed to maya – his love affair with Kamalate – became a controversial issue in medieval Karnataka. Accordingly, the Vaishnava acharya Mukunda Peddi, who is believed to have debated with Chamarasa, is said to have criticised Allama's erotic life and his bedagu vachanas. The institutionalised religion of Virashaivism had to respond to the conservative (sanatani) insistence that Viraktas like Allama should not be besmirched by intense love and romance. Therefore, aspects of Allama's romance had to be liberated from their sensory qualities. However, we cannot completely erase traces left by a tradition; they stay alive, so at least a bit of Allama's shrouded personal life is accessible in the Virakta ascetic narratives.[21]

Compared to Shivaganaprasadi's *Shunyasampadane*, Harihara's *Ragale* is closer to the paradigm of literary narratives. The latter is deeply interested in Allama, Kamalate, and their tale of love. While it is important for the spiritual narrator to transform philosophy into a narrative, Harihara deems the stages of infatuation in mortal life to be important as well. Harihara's Allama intensely experiences a life of love and eroticism. It is difficult for the Virakta imagination to describe Allama's erotic life in detail; what it does laboriously, Harihara's imagination does effortlessly. The following is how Harihara describes Allama and Kamalate's shringara (eroticism) as lovemaking begins on the bed:

The desirous who removed the obstacles to sexual ecstasy,
the thrill-seekers who opened their eyes to varieties of pleasure.
How can I capture those harvests of joy?
How can I sketch the pleasures of uniting?
Where magical sensations being stretched to the limits,
unfound amorous joys blossoming in them,
in the embrace of love the two becoming one . . .[22]

---

[20] For the composers of the *Shunyasampadanes*, the love story of Allama and Kamalate seems to be embarrassing.

[21] Chamarasa and shunyasampadanakaras are Viraktas. See fn. 64 below.

[22] Harihara, *Hariharana Ragalegalu*, p. 301.

Only when he says, "In the embrace of love the two becoming one" could Harihara have glimpsed Advaya! What is truly embarrassing for the spiritual narrator actually lies further ahead in Harihara's text. The spiritual narrator might agree to an extent that shringara is a stage that precedes spiritual enlightenment. But in Harihara's "Prabhudevara Ragale", Kamalate, while dying of a high fever, feels she has had enough worldly pleasure and enters devaloka (the world of the gods). In the interim Allama writhes in the pangs of separation, as would an ordinary lover amidst us.

> Allama stood suffering, the turmoil inside,
> remembering the pleasures of lost love,
> when Kamalate enveloped his mind again and again,
> Allama murmured, "O Kamalate, O Kamalate."[23]

Scholars are of the view that the parts where Shivaganaprasadi begins to delineate the spiritual life of Allama come in condensed form in Harihara. Harihara could recognise Allama as an excellent bhakta, but his imagination did not extend to giving Allama's personality a historical role – restoring shivachara (the discipline of following Shaiva practices) on earth. While the institutional notion of "rejuvenating shivachara" was clearly formulated in the *Shunyasampadanes*, Harihara is primarily interested in the transformation of the intense infatuation into asceticism. He does not place much stock in the spiritual or psychological processes behind such transformations. In this respect, Harihara is a poet of dramatic situations. This may be due to the profound influence of the prevailing literary imagination of his time.

Here, we need to note that Harihara has not used Allama's vachanas while reconstructing Allama's life in his narrative. Perhaps this is because it is difficult to fit the expanse of Allama's vachanas within the framework Harihara has chosen for his work. Moreover, Allama's vachanas would have arrested the temporality of the narrative, whereas in Harihara's *Ragale* a speedy narrative is a much

---

[23] Ibid., p. 302.

sought after ideal. Important for Allama is the space of spirituality, while for Harihara it is the temporal dimension of the narrative. Harihara prefers external practice and puja rituals that are not part of Allama's philosophical world. Thus, there is a wide gap between the subtlety of Allama's philosophy and Harihara's imagination. Yet, in his narrative Harihara does not force his Allama to do anything that Allama's vachanas do not espouse, as is evident in the following lines:

> Thus, bathing linga with one's very sight,
> worshipping it with flowery wide-open eyes,
> infusing incense with one's breath-perfume,
> waving the lamp of a devoted mind, prostrating;
> faithfully offering a feast of affection,
> putting forth unwavering, pleasant love,
> feeling all pleasures through the eyes alone,
> feasting sight on all the riches . . .[24]

These lines resonate with the ideas expressed in Allama's vachanas. Only in such situations does Harihara take recourse to Allama's vachanas to reconstruct the personality of his protagonist. Everywhere else he uses Allama's life to propagate his bhakti narrative of Dvaita. But, on the whole, Harihara fits Allama into a particular type of grand Virashaiva discourse that had begun shaping during his time. In such discourses the attention would naturally have been on unification rather than difference. Shivaganaprasadi possibly thought that Harihara's Allama would be useful for this institutional process of unification, and therefore he used the story of Nirmaya.

The narrative transformation of Allama into the character of Nirmaya is not simple. The openness, multiplicity, and paradoxical nature of Allama's vachanas make it impossible to construct a unified narrative about him, but it is made possible through the character of Nirmaya. The process of greater authentication and acceptance than the philosophical truths internal to vachanas has worked in this transformation.

[24] Ibid., p. 304.

Against this backdrop, it is possible to metaphorically grasp the 400-year history of Virashaivism in the following manner. The first phase of the twelfth century was a period of the formation and re-formation of metaphors and motifs in vachana compositions; the second phase was Harihara's time (later twelfth and early thirteenth centuries), when narratives began to be created; and the third phase was the period between 1420 and 1520 when institutional narratives developed. Many scholars believe that all the *Shunyasampadanes* were composed during this third period of a hundred years. Therefore, I have classified this period as an important third phase in the history of Virashaivism. In order to analyse this history properly, the framework of Metaphor–Narrative–Institutional Narrative needs to be elaborated upon, which I endeavour below.

During the twelfth century the Virashaiva rebellion created some philosophical images and metaphors. I argue that even though these rebellious images and metaphors were created from within the womb of Shaiva sects that were still active, these metaphors carried the philosophical elements of non-Shaivite sects. The existence of Buddhist motifs and a Buddhist vocabulary in Allama proves my point. Powerful forces from various social backgrounds began to flow into the lead provided by the rebellious Virashaiva sect: several brooks began to flow into the watercourse of Virashaivism. In this respect, the twelfth-century Virashaiva rebellion was organised around two types of conceptual metaphors; ishtalinga and pranalinga.[25]

The idea or image of ishtalinga signifies the rejection of static temples. Virashaivism came to the fore by rebelling against the temples made by the rich, by declaring that if Shiva resided in the temple he was dispensable.[26] This spiritual adventure was the fundamental source of energy for Virashaivism. As an alternative, it advocated ishtalinga. Thus, we see that the notion of rejection and cre-

---

[25] See fn. 7 above.

[26] "The rich will make temples for Shiva . . ." is a famous vachana of Basavanna. For the full vachana, see vachana no. 820 in Ramanujan, *Speaking of Siva*, p. 70.

ation go hand in hand. The historical reality of medieval Karnataka was that the temple had become the centre of worldly power, giving up its symbolic existence. What becomes quite evident from the study of inscriptions of those times is that the temple in the medieval period was the foundation of royalty and state power. In this context, the Sharana movement chose a tiny but explosive symbol of ishtalinga against a great external structure – the temple. However, it was Allama's conviction that the symbol too had to disappear – one should hold on to the sign but then shed it. He reveals his stance regarding ishtalinga and pranalinga:

Tell me, who knows
the difference between ishtalinga and pranalinga?
The outward appears before the word "inward".
The inward appears before the word "outward" . . .
If one would ever find truth in Guheshwara linga,
one must hold on to the sign (kuruhu),
then shed the sign,
O Siddharamayya! (1145)

In the line "One must hold on to the sign, / Then shed the sign" lies the essence of the Sharana movement and its unity, besides the stamp of Allama's individuality. Virashaivism was institutionally organised through the unification of ishtalinga and pranalinga. However, for Allama even this kind of interdependence is finally unnecessary, as he tells Siddharamayya in the *Shunyasampadanes*. The institutional character of Virashaivism rests on the question of the relationship between kuruhu (sign) and arivu (knowledge/understanding/awareness). In the twelfth century, Virashaivism was quite open regarding this question, but when it came to institutional narratives this was considered an important organisational problem. The later controversy regarding Siddharamayya's lingadikshe (initiation to linga) illustrates this.[27] That which was not an issue during

---

[27] In the *Shunyasampadanes*, giving lingadikshe to Siddharamayya is an exciting episode involving a debate on the notion of linga. When Allama brings

the era of metaphors (twelfth century) became controversial during the era of institutional narratives (the period of the *Shunyasampadanes*). Here, the idea of ishtalinga became a question of identity for the Virashaiva community. It became not only a spiritual marker but also an emblem of one's social identity. Against this backdrop the life and character of Siddharamayya naturally began to gain importance. In light of this, we can understand Chidanandamurthy's insight that until about AD 1400 there was no reference to Siddharamayya's diksha in any Virashaiva text.[28] But when the ishtalinga became an emblem of the Virashaiva community, it could be expected that the initiation (lingadikshe) would become a major issue.

The idea of the "karasthala linga" (linga on the palm) is an important theme for discussion in Shivaganaprasadi's *Shunyasampadane*. Siddharamayya asks "Allama to instruct him in the process of attaining the true linga while holding the ishta linga on one's palm."[29] From the perspective of the story, Allama's response here is unparalleled. He offers a philosophically profound and complex reply, which is the context for the line from the vachana (1145) quoted above, "Tell me, who knows / the difference between ishtalinga and pranalinga?" But the answer we get in this vachana is not of much help to Virashaivism towards becoming an institutional religion. This vachana does not endorse the ultimate necessity of the kuruhu, the sign; instead, it advocates its temporariness. When the shunyasampadanakara cannot find a clear direction from Allama's vachanas, he obtains it by developing his plot in a particular way. Here, Shivaganaprasadi is aware of the fact that making Allama speak too much

---

Siddharamayya to Basavanna at Kalyana, Siddharamayya is not allowed to enter Basavanna's house as he does not wear the linga on his body. Allama argues that wearing the linga is not important – it is the linga in the mind that is important. He says further that a true sharana like Siddharamayya needs no tangible symbol like the linga. Other sharanas such as Chennabasavanna and Molige Maridevaru enter into a debate with Allama on this matter. Finally, all including Allama agree that Siddharamayya should wear the linga.

[28] See Chidanandamurthy, *Shunyasampadaneyannu*.

[29] Shivaganaprasadi, *Shivaganaprasadi Mahadevayyana*, p. 131.

would risk the narrative becoming artificial; he is ethically sensitive to the fact that it would make his narrative untrue.

Certainly, Shivaganaprasadi and other shunyasampadanakaras possess a deep knowledge of Allama's vachanas. They exhibit a sensitive moral awareness when the institutional requirements of their narratives come into conflict with the internal stances of Allama's vachanas. When the vachanas come in the way of developing the personality of the sharana in a particular manner, the freedom of a storyteller comes to the rescue of the shunyasampadanakaras. Even though we may suspect that at times kuta-vachanas might be created, the freedom of the storyteller is important.[30] When the shunyasampadanakara finds it difficult to use a vachana in his support, he deploys the freedom of a storyteller by inventing a plot. For instance, when Siddharamayya asks Allama about the idea of ishtalinga, Allama takes Siddharamayya to Basavanna instead of answering the question through his vachana: "Thus, when Siddharamayya devaru asks about the subtle distinction in ishtalinga, Prabhudevaru says, 'Sangana Basavanna knows this subtle matter. I will take you to him, come'."[31]

At this point in time Siddharamayya's response is strange, which holds up a mirror to the mystery of his personality or the complexity of his past. Here, Siddharamayya is not excited to learn the philosophical aspects of karasthala and ishtalinga, but he is excited to see Basavanna. When Prabhudevaru says, "Come, we should meet Basavarajadevaru," Siddharamayya responds as follows:

Ayya, let the holy karasthala (palm) stay with you.
Ayya, let the holy parasthala (cosmos) stay with you.
Look, I desire neither karasthala nor parasthala.
O Kapilasiddha Mallikarjuna,
I was excited when you said you would show me
the holy feet of Sangana Basavanna, the great one whom you adore.
O my God of gods, save me by doing so.[32]

[30] Kuta-vachana: a kind of planted vachana, interpolated in course of time and attributed to a vachanakara who has not really composed it.

[31] Shivaganaprasadi, *Shivaganaprasadi Mahadevayyana*, p. 132.

[32] Ibid.

This vachana embodies the primary reason behind the unity of the twelfth-century Sharana movement. Even though Siddharamayya initially asks questions about the subtle distinction between karasthala and ishtalinga, he is in fact excited to meet Basavanna and, hence, agrees to go with Allama. Here, Basavanna is representative of a new kind of aspiration for the Virashaiva movement. Therefore, in spite of logical disagreements among the vachanakaras, there was unity on the broader spiritual spectrum in the movement.

Shivaganaprasadi could have made Allama himself speak about karasthala and ishtalinga to Siddharamayya. Instead, in his plot he creates a new form of organisational bond between Allama and Basavanna. Shivaganaprasadi sees to it that the internal logic of his narrative does not negate Allama, while at the same time retaining the ideal of Virashaivism. He desires, as far as possible, to retain in his narrative the plurality of the metaphoric era (the twelfth-century vachana age). He knows the significance of ishtalinga and lingadikshe (initiation to linga). But following Allama's idea of shedding the sign of linga, he does not take the discussion further. In Kalyana, Chennabasavanna criticises Siddharamayya severely for not wearing the ishtalinga. He says, "If there is no linga on the body, how can there be contentment of linga in prana (life)?"[33] Allama's defence here is remarkable:

> What need of a long pole for a person
> who can jump to the sky?
> What need of a boat for a person
> who can cross the ocean?
> What need for limits for a person
> who has transcended all limits?
> O Chennabasavanna,
> Why linga for Siddharamayya,
> the unparalleled knower of the Gogeshwaralinga?[34]

But as Chidanandamurthy rightly points out, even though

---

[33] Ibid., p. 235.
[34] Ibid., p. 236.

Shivaganaprasadi and Chamarasa left the problem of Siddharamayya's initiation (diksha) unresolved, it needed resolution later.[35]
In his *Prabhulingalile*, Chamarasa took the liberty of not giving
lingadikshe to Siddharamayya. But Prabhudeva of Kallumatha,
who doesn't subscribe to this kind of openness and ambiguous
freedom, finally makes Siddharamayya acquire diksha from Chennabasavanna in *Lingaleelavilasacharitra*.[36]

The episode of Siddharamayya's lingadikshe is explored elabo-
rately in the later *Shunyasampadanes*.[37] In the *Shunyasampadane* of
Gummalapurada Siddhalingadevara (sixteenth century), the question of lingadikshe, which becomes an institutional necessity and
discipline, gains prominence.[38] The controversy of Siddharamayya's
diksha becomes more intense here. A long hermeneutical debate
begins, and important sharanas put forward their respective arguments. These arguments bring to light the strength of Virashaivism
as an institution as well as the nature of internal resistance to it.
When Allama defends Siddharamayya by saying, "What need of
a long pole for a person, / who can jump to the sky?" Gummalapurada Siddhalingadevara makes Chennabasavanna respond to
him as follows:

A kite in the sky needs a leading thread,
Though it may be flying high.
One may be a soldier, but he too needs training.
Can a cart move without ground?

[35] See Chidanandamurthy, *Shunyasampadaneyannu*.

[36] A fifteenth-century Virashaiva poet, the author of *Lingaleelavilasacharitra*
and the commentator on *Mantragopya*, the authorship of which is ascribed to
Allama Prabhu, this being highly contestable. Prabhudeva of Kallumatha was
one of the 101 (nurondu) Viraktas of Vijayanagara, a contemporary of Chamarasa – the author of *Prabhulingalile*. See Narasimhacharya, *Karnataka-Kavi*,
vol. 2, pp. 61–3.

[37] These are the *Shunyasampadanes* of Halegeyarya, Gummalapurada Siddhalingadevara, and Guluru Siddhaveerannodayara.

[38] Among the several *Shunyasampadanes*, Nagaraj has so far referred mainly
to Shivaganaprasadi Mahadevayya's *Shunyasampadane*. Now, he begins to
refer to Gummalapura Siddhalingadevaru's *Shunyasampadane*. See Gummalapurada, *Gummalapurada Siddhalingadevara*.

> The body should not be alone, bereft of linga.
> O, Prabhu, can one be alone, bereft of Kudala Chenna Sangama
>   devaru?[39]

The question of wearing the linga signals the institutionalisation of Virashaivism, drawing temporal territories and creating compartments within the guru–linga–jangama relationship. To put it in the contemporary social idiom, Virashaivism tried to define its borders and boundaries during its third phase. In this respect, Chennabasavanna is more orthodox than others. He tells Allama directly, "The company of the people without a bond between the body and linga is a disaster."[40]

From here on, Gummalapurada Siddhalingadevaru's narrative genius takes flight, spreading its wings. Two leaders of his religious memory, Allama and Chennabasavanna, are now on the battleground. This battle is over the identity of another leader, Siddharamayya. Allama can use only his personal experience for his argument, but Chennabasavanna differs. Gummalapurada Siddhalingadevara recreates the tension in the atmosphere beautifully and intensely. "Chennabasavadevaru when repudiating [Allama] Prabhu's reply, looks towards the great forces of innumerable cohorts. At that time, Basavanna, Moligeyamaritande [Moligeya Marayya], Mereminda-deva, Urilinga Peddi, Prasada Bhoganna and all the other important seven hundred and twenty cohort [were] enraged and spoke thus . . ."[41]

The mahaganas (great cohorts), an entourage of Shiva sent to earth as sharanas, are provoked and enraged. There is a new kind of valour in the words that come from these mahaganas. Such a warrior ethos in the sharanas' conversation indicates Virashaivism's growth as social power. Moligeya Marayya supports Chennabasavanna's stance regarding lingadikshe.[42] This is clear when he says,

---

[39] Gummalapurada, *Gummalapurada Siddhalingadevara*, p. 161.

[40] Ibid., p. 162.

[41] Ibid.

[42] Moligeya Marayya: a vachanakara, a contemporary of Basavanna's who composed about 819 vachanas. His name appears below the idols of sharanas in

"Does anyone fear the poisonless snake? Does anyone fear a soldier who roars without a sword?"[43] Here, Moligeya Marayya uses the metaphor of a weapon to describe the linga. The sign of spiritual understanding (linga) is transformed into a weapon of religious battle. In the gathering, the support for Chennabasavanna is unanimous. Interestingly, Ajaganna and Marulushankaradevaru, who would have undoubtedly supported Allama, are absent. Allama becomes a minority! Basavanna too takes a stand against him in this regard:

Unless expressed in action, what use is the awareness inside?
If there is no body, where does vital breath dwell?
If there is no mirror, can a person see his face?
Our Lord Kudalsangama is the God
Who is both form and formless.[44]

Though Basavanna's response here is against Allama, it is quite profound and in tune with his personality. Basavanna cannot see the linga as a metaphorical weapon; instead, by using the word mirror, he transforms the linga into a means of self-criticism and puts forward a philosophical proposition that Allama cannot easily deny. As expected, the other sharana group's stand gains the upper hand over Allama. He clarifies that his way is different, though he is spiritually alone. While Allama does not directly say that one should wear the ishtalinga, he says, "Look, inner awareness does not reach the state of sarvangalinga unless there is an outer action."[45]

Not even Gummalapurada Siddhalingadevara can transform Allama beyond this point. Yet the transformation, even to this ex-

———

the Madhukeshwara temple at Banavasi in Karnataka. See Kalburgi, *Shasanagalalli*, pp. 103–4. He also figures in several Virashaiva narratives, and Honnalli Gauravanka has written a purana verse on him. Various mythical narratives say he was a king in "Kashmira" and later came to the city of Kalyana in search of Basavanna. There is a section on him in one of the *Shunyasampadanes*.

[43] Gummalapurada, *Gummalapurada Siddhalingadevara*, p. 163.

[44] Ibid., p. 170.

[45] Gummalapurada, *Gummalapurada Siddhalingadevara*, p. 183. Sarvangalinga: "Linga in every cell of the body", Yaravintelimath, ed., *Vachana Lexicon*, p. 848.

tent, is revolutionary. Henceforth, Siddharamayya gives up his asht-angayoga (eight-fold yoga: yama, niyama, asana, pranayama, pratyahara, dhyana, dharana, and samadhi) and accepts ishtalinga. In addition, the shunyasampadanakara makes Allama utter words that are not in tune with his usual stance:

> The union with linga is not possible for the scholar who has fallen into the cycle of birth and death caused by worldly desires and deems himself to be Brahman (Bomma); in the same way, if a Vedantin who calls himself Shiva, abandons caste distinctions, whining like a dog, and breaking bread with it, the union with the linga is not possible.[46]

These lines arise as a necessity for the institutionalised religion which was taking shape during the composition of the *Shunyasampadanes*. The scholar deeming himself a Brahman (Bomma) is a direct nod to Shankaracharya's "Aham Brahmasmi" (I am the Brahma).[47] Allama could never say that union with the linga is impossible for one who abandons caste distinctions. His fundamental social understanding is that "caste is a defilement". This was such an important value for Allama that he could never reject it even in his paradoxical moments. These narrative interpretations illustrate that as Virashaivism became institutionally powerful, conservatism gradually entered its self-interpretations.

At the end of the dispute, Siddharamayya is humbled and requests the mahaganas to give him lingadikshe. He implores: "When, O Father, can I have the treasure of triple initiation?"[48] Finally, Allama too asks Chennabasavanna to give lingadiksha to Siddharamayya. He also provides a metaphoric justification by saying, "So what if it is a shining gem? It deserves to be set in gold / . . . Without the proper place, the beauty of a painting is not pleasing to the sight . . ."[49] This appears to be a modern metaphor, which raises doubts about the

---

[46] Ibid.

[47] The phrase is from the *Brahdaranyaka Upanishad*.

[48] Gummalapurada, *Gummalapurada Siddhalingadevara*, p. 186.

[49] Ibid., p. 190.

vachana's historical authenticity. Such vachanas could be later compositions – kuta-vachanas.

Finally, Siddharamayya receives lingadikshe from Chennabasavanna. Shunyasampadanakara Siddhalingadevaru describes this process with great devotion. As an ardent follower of outward practices, the author describes all associated rituals. In this section, the *Shunyasampadane* even functions as a text of diksha. It is quite possible to undertake lingadikshe practices methodically by following this description. This ceremonial procedure begins with the method of sanctifying the earth: "Purifying the floor with six cow products – dung, urine, bile, milk, curd, and ghee – filling pancha mudra (five marks) with sacred rice, placing the pancha kalas (five arts) in the outskirts of that marked place, filling the circles made in the corners of the mudra (mark) with five colours of rice . . ."[50] These ceremonial details include objects that are well recognised in the Vedic stream. Here, Virashaivism has started negotiating with the very worldview it vehemently opposed. In the lives of religions, there is never such a thing as complete enmity. The process of one religion entering another and of them digesting one another was quite common in medieval Karnataka. "Pishta Pashu mimamsa" in Madhva philosophy is one such example.[51] Yashodhara's story of sacrifice is another.[52]

[50] Ibid.

[51] According to Madhva philosophy, the sacrifice has to be symbolic, offering models of animals made of flour (pishta pashu), not real animals. Nagaraj seems to think that this notion of sacrifice is the result of the influence of other religions and sects like Jainism.

[52] This was a Jain mythological narrative famous in Sanskrit and Prakrit, before the Kannada poet Janna (AD 1209) wrote a work called *Yashodhara Charite*. King Yashodhara was depressed as a result of his wife Amrutamati's adultery with an ugly mahout. His mother suggested he perform an animal sacrifice to come out of the depression. Since the king was Jain, he could not resort to violence, so he decided to use a model of a rooster made of flour. Like pishta pashu, the sacrifice involved the symbolic offering of the model of the rooster. For more on this myth, see Janna, *Yashodhara*. Girish Karnad's play *Bali: The Sacrifice* dramatises this myth. See Karnad, *The Dreams*.

What was Allama doing when all these ceremonial processes took place? An event has occurred in the *Shunyasampadanes* – Allama surrendering to the other sharanas – which would not otherwise be possible. It is generally held that the *Shunyasampadanes* are nothing but the celebration of Allama's victory. What *Shankaravijaya* is for Adishankaracharya, the *Shunyasampadanes* are for Allama![53] In all other important debates in the *Shunyasampadanes*, Allama convinces the others of his argument, which begins with Muktayakka and continues down to Gorakhnath.[54] In this respect, Allama is unconquerable. However, in the present case he is mute before this grand ceremony of Siddharamayya's diksha. In this regard Gummalapura Siddhalingadevaru makes a poignant statement: "Thus, Prabhudevaru surrender[s] himself to Basavaganas (elders) . . ."[55] This is a moment of great surrender by Allama. It says something about the historical necessities of the period that even one like Allama had to surrender philosophically.

But it is difficult even for the authors of the *Shunyasampadanes* to control Allama for he is not a puppet in their hands. In the next section we will come across the story of Marulushankaradeva where Allama's spiritual philosophy, which had earlier been submitted to the sharanaganas (a group of sharanas), begins its usual aggressive play.[56] Again, Allama's Advayavada transgresses the religious in-

[53] The life story of Adishankara: see Madhava-Vidyaranya, *Sankara-Dig-Vijaya*.

[54] The *Shunyasampadanes* begin with the Muktayakka episode where Allama Prabhu addresses Muktayakka's grief over the loss of her brother Ajaganna, and shows her the right path. Later in his debate with Gorakhanath, Allama Prabhu shows the limits of vajrakaya (the strength of the body) and convinces Gorakhnath.

[55] Gummalapurada, *Gummalapurada Siddhalingadevara*, p. 190.

[56] In an episode in the *Shunyasampadanes*, Marulushankaradeva is described as a gupta (hidden) ascetic. He stayed in the pit of prasada for twelve years, ignored by all sharanas, including Basavanna. Allama, before entering the mahamane (Basavanna's house), recognises Marulushankaradeva in the prasada pit and reveals his true significance. Once his secret penance is known to the world, Marulushankaradeva vanishes into the void. See Shivaganaprasadi, *Shivaganaprasadi Mahadevayyana*, pp. 176–81.

terpretation that has been accepted thus far by the community of shara-naganas. If community symbols like the linga, and certain bound-aries like rituals, find victory in the case of Siddharama's lingadik-she, an exploration of their limits is to be found in the Marulu-shankaradeva episode. The episode of Siddharamayya's diksha is an institutional necessity. In contrast, the Marulushankaradeva epi-sode symbolises spiritual excellence which cannot and should not be eclipsed by institutional necessity. After Siddharamayya's diksha, as Allama moves forward, Marulushankaradeva emerges from the pit where leftover prasada (holy food) is swept in, "like a shoot appear-ing on a mango tree with the coming of the spring breeze."[57] Here on-wards, the narrative is charged again with intensity. Allama exclaims in excitement:

> O ho! Namahshivaya!
> Is this the tranquil sun, hidden behind the great sky?
> Is this the light of linga's knowledge, burning on its own,
>   untroubled by the ten winds?
> Is this the white sheen of pearl called liberation which
>   came by itself?
> Is this the streaking frame of the one,
> which has shorn all raiments, including rudrakshi (rosary)?
> Or, is this the linga of flame, born from the divine fire,
> amidst vain arguments?
> Nobody knows this sublime emergence!
> Look, Sangana Basavanna,
> a wonder appeared before the eyes of Guheshwara.[58]

This is a victorious moment for Allama. All the great sharanas, in-cluding Basavanna, obey the great utterances of Allama. Here there is neither a question of lingadikshe nor of purity and impurity. Even Chennabasavanna adores Allama, as when he says, "Look at him, he is himself guru-linga-jangama, and he is also nothing."[59] The entire sharanagana surrenders to Allama.

---

[57] Gummalapurada, *Gummalapurada Siddhalingadevara*, p. 231.
[58] Ibid.
[59] Ibid., p. 238.

The importance of the *Shunyasampadanes* lies precisely in this. They are composed with a clear understanding that a religion can contain two necessities in conflict. While it is possible to think of Siddharamayya's episode, and that of Marulushankara, as complementary at some level, there really exists a conflict between them. Both ceremonial practices and the prominent figures – those who have the power to perform them – together make religion grow as a social institution. The difference between the internal spiritual force and external social power of a religion gradually fades away. On the one hand the Virashaivism of the time needed the spirit of Marulushankaradeva along with Allama's discourse to recognise this, and demonstrate it to the world authentically. On the other it also needed a concrete form of signs and rituals, as in the episode of Siddharamayya's lingadikshe. While Marulushankaradeva becomes void and formless in the narrative, others remain alive. The sharanas do not have the choice that Marulushankaradeva has. They are handcuffed to history. Since Virashaivism believes in historicity – considering itself an event in history – there is a social mobility to it in Karnataka which other religions do not have. Allama was aware that historicity is a double-edged sword and opposed it in his vachanas. But it was inevitable for the *Shunyasampadanes* to include this difficult figure, Allama, while constructing its institutional narrative. Though Allama was not wholly palatable to the *Shunyasampadanes*, negotiating with him was indispensable for their plot.

Let us summarise our discussion so far. What was a domain of images, metaphors, and open motifs in the first phase, that is, in the twelfth century, turned into a grand narrative during the resurrection of Virashaivism in the fifteenth- and sixteenth-century period of the *Shunyasampadanes*. Since I have borrowed the notion of "grand narrative" from contemporary Western social thought, I need to explain it. A grand narrative is a unitary discourse constructed by a social group for its self-interpretation. The group uses the grand narrative as both mirror and lamp, to self-reflect and illuminate. In this respect, the twelfth-century vachanas are like root texts, a sort of ur-text. Fixing the boundaries and essence of these root texts is complicated. The root text is borderless, whereas the grand narrative sets the borders in stone. The grand narrative always comes after the root text. Following its own logic, the grand narrative emerges by exploiting the social and religious symbols of root texts. In our context, the *Shunyasampadanes* represent a grand narrative.

Therefore, the *Shunyasampadanes*, which appear on the surface as narratives of Allama's life, cannot be considered only as a creation of the language of religious sensibility. That is, they are not predominantly imaginary narratives. Instead, non-linguistic factors use such grand textual narratives for their expression. Searching for the timeless spiritual meaning of the *Shunyasampadanes* is one mode of inquiry. More useful is an attempt to understand the ways of interaction, the silences, and all the aporias embedded within the text. The *Shunyasampadanes* comprehensively document the interface between historical pressures and non-historical motifs. Under what historical conditions were the *Shunyasampadanes* formed? When we place this textual grand narrative in the context of the historical processes of the period, forces previously invisible begin to appear. It is my proposition that the answer to the above question lies in the relationship Virashaivism shared with the Vijayanagara Empire.

A metaphor deeply rooted in the first phase of twelfth-century Virashaivism was "the dead body of the ruler of the land (king)."[60] As Basavanna's vachana sarcastically says, "When a hunter brings a rabbit he has killed, people crowd around to pay the price and take it, but nobody takes any interest in the king's corpse." Basavanna and the vachanakaras must be granted credit for fearlessly deconstructing the image of the king's corpse.

This notion of the king's corpse startled the religious contemporaries of the vachanakaras. One of the bases of medieval royal power was the literary imagination. Nemichandra, a literary figure of the

---

[60] This is a line from Basavanna's vachana which says that when a king is alive he is powerful but when he dies his body is of no use; people may value the dead body of a rabbit but not that of a king. See vachana no. 362 in Kalburgi, ed., *Vachana*, p. 361.

time, too, could not rid his senses of the whiff of the king's corpse.[61] Though he was in royal employ, he did not – like Pampa and Ranna – equate his patron king with his protagonist. Nemichandra dwelt in the temple of his imagination, leaving aside his indebtedness to the palatial chambers of "history". This is illustrated in his work, *Lilavati*. To elucidate this metaphorical expression: in the twelfth century a relationship of conflict had developed between Virashaivism and royal power, and conditions were created such that this troubled relationship became a core motif in regulating Virashaivism. However, there is no evidence, either in inscriptions or in other documents, about Virashaivism ideologically inspiring royal power until the time of Praudhadevaraya in the fifteenth century.[62]

During the reign of Praudhadevaraya the grandeur of history entered Virashaivism. Havoc was created in the inner world of Virashaivism as it began a new kind of interaction with royal power. This does not imply Virashaivism had never previously exercised control in worldly affairs. In fact, after the thirteenth century Virashaivism began to develop as an alternative power centre. In a broader sense, it is possible to call this power centre jangama shakti: the power of jangamas.

Two philosophical metaphors of this period that witnessed great transformation in their mode of existence were ishtalinga and jangama. As we have seen, ishtalinga was a symbolic system created by Virashaivism. Jangama was a system of social power; in the first phase, that is, the twelfth century, the notion of jangama was an abstract, dynamic principle as well as representing a concrete social individ-

---

[61] A twelfth-century Jaina poet who was at the court of Lakshmanaraja and Veeraballala of the Hoysala dynasty. Nemichandra is the author of *Lilavati* and *Neminatha Purana*.

[62] Praudhadevaraya (1422–1446), also known as Devaraya II, was one of the Vijayanagara emperors. He belonged to the Sangama dynasty. An extensive editing, reorganising, and consolidating of twelfth-century vachanas was done during his reign. For more on Praudhadevaraya, see Paramashivamurthy, "Prasthavane". For more on Kannada literature during Praudhadevaraya's time, see Viraktamath, *Praudhadevarayana Kalada*.

ual. These two basic systems of ishtalinga and jangama witnessed a revolutionary transformation later, in the third phase. If the institution of the temple emerged as the sanatanis' power centre, Virashaivism, during the medieval period in Karnataka, created an individual figure, the sharana, and he is committed to thinking about ishtalinga and acting accordingly. The jangama principle then emerged as a social force defending the spiritual territory of Virashaivism. The jangama principle was nothing but a social face of the spiritual aspiration of Virashaivism.

But over the next three hundred years, the two metaphors ishtalinga and jangama assumed a different form. The jangama principle became an alternative power centre by transforming itself into the religious institution of the matha – the Virashaiva monastery. We need not think that this took place overnight. Inscriptions inform us that, prior to the birth of Virashaivism, ancient Shaiva mathas had already grown powerful via their institutional alliance with royal power. In this respect, there was a power transfer as several Shaiva sects, such as Kalamukha, gradually disappeared into Karnataka's womb of Virashaivism. This was a complex process enabled by the combination of social forces and the victory of Virashaiva darshana.

Gradually, the jangama institution became a centre of symbolic power. This illustrates how symbolic powers, deeply rooted in society, eventually augment themselves by attracting material power. We can observe from inscriptions that, after the fourteenth century, the institution of Virashaiva's jangama grew more and more influential. While Vaishnavism and Jainism grew influential because of their favourable relationship with the Vijayanagara empire, Virashaivism had no such advantage. In fact, for Virashaivism the golden age of Vijayanagara was historically an era of isolation from royal power. It was a testing time for the sect. During the period of the Vijayanagara Empire, even philosophical schools were denied acceptance if they lacked association with royal power. Perhaps never in the history of India had public life been so politicised. This phase of extreme politicisation was a time of crisis for Virashaivism, which had found insight through the metaphor of the "dead body of the king". The uprising – i.e. the twelfth-century Vachana movement – that took place earlier within the framework of religion had released a new social energy among the lower strata of society. Though the narratives with royal-power-centric perspectives did not give importance to Virashaivism, it grew by the day as a special power among the different layers of society. There is no reference to Virashaivism in Madhava Acharya's *Sarva Darsana Samgraha* which is considered by some as an encyclopaedia of Indian darshanas.[63] It illustrates the indifference that royal-power-centric narratives showed towards Virashaivism. This work was composed with the assumption that only thoughts expressed in Sanskrit were worthy of being regarded as authentic philosophy. Only after this phase did Virashaivism begin to penetrate the politicised domains, starting with Praudhadevaraya's reign.

This new negotiation was not easy to achieve. The narrative of nurondu Viraktas – 101 Viraktas – provides important, though metaphorical, information regarding this.[64] It is a record of conflicts in relation to new kinds of symbols. In the narratives a sharana possesses something that the king desires. The king asks for it, and the conflict begins. Finally, the sharana merges with the absolute void. It is important to note that sharana possessions are often symbols of worldly power and royalty – for instance, a horse or a bow. It became inevitable for Virashaivism to come face to face with emblems of royal power, pushing aside the signification of the ishtalinga symbol. The compilation and production of Virashaiva narratives was

---

[63] Madhava Acharya, *The Sarva Darsana Samgraha*.

[64] A group of militant Shaiva ascetics in the city of Vijayanagara who were believed to have been sent from Kailasa to the earth to protect and spread Virashaiva devotion. They collected and edited vachanas during the fifteenth century. Shunyasampadanakaras such as Shivaganaprasadi Mahadevaiah, Gummalapurada Siddhalingadevara, Guluru Siddhaveerannodayara, etc., are Viraktas. Even now, the Virakta monastic order functions through what is known as Virakta mathas. For more, see YouTube, "The Viraktas of Vijayanagara".

the result of this new historical necessity. A new kind of "political will" led to the assembling of all these texts as part of a grand narrative. In my opinion, Virashaivism as it is in the modern era took its actual birth in this historical phase, when it began to organise itself as a particular textual community by producing texts like the *Shunyasampadanes* and other Virashaiva narratives. During this phase the metaphors discussed above – ishtalinga and jangama – were transformed into closed categories. A new kind of cultural adventure of translating Allama into Sanskrit also took place in this context.[65] It was also the time when Allama became the protagonist of the *Shunyasampadanes*.

After Virashaivism was thus transformed into a textual community, the larger part of the creative forces produced by the early phase of Virashaivism were inevitably excluded. Unless limited to certain boundaries, religions do not gain social power. As Virashaivism moved towards the process of becoming a power centre, it pushed the forces it had originally produced towards the margins. So, the time of the *Shunyasampadanes* was at once a phase of abandonment and reception. It received rigid boundaries of symbols and social space. It is like the farmer's belief – that it is impossible to protect a field without fencing.

We still need to get an appropriate answer to whether the nature of the classes which were the backbone of Virashaivism also changed. It is quite possible that there was a shift in the leadership of Virashaivism in the process of reorganisation during the third phase. The life and backbone of the twelfth-century movement were the service-providing castes and artisan clans of Karnataka. The Vachana movement had gained explosive power from these communities that were equally oppressed in villages and towns. However, after the sixteenth century the social base of leadership changed as the merchant class, jangamas, and farmers assumed a strong

---

[65] For example, Maggeya Mayideva (fifteenth century) composed *Prabhugeeta*, a commentary-cum-rendering of the selected Shatsthala Vachanas of Allama Prabhu in Sanskrit. See Maggeya Mayideva, *Prabhugeeta*.

leadership. This kind of negotiation with classes was inevitable for the development of the textual community.

The social power of certain communities that Virashaivism had liberated during its first phase became more widespread with time. Since strict adherence to the varnashrama structure was the basis of the imperial religion during the Vijayanagara empire, the social powers liberated during the twelfth century found the legitimisation they required in Virashaiva narratives. But during the time of the *Shunyasampadanes* it was challenging to accommodate a revolutionary openness of the twelfth century since it had once been embedded in those social powers. Therefore, a counternarrative had to emerge from the opposite direction. It is important to note that this counternarrative, too, chose Allama as the protagonist. If he was a direct protagonist in the *Shunyasampadanes*, he became an indirect protagonist in the counternarrative, in an allegorical mode. That narrative is the folk epic the *Manteswamy Kavya*.[66]

II: The *Manteswamy Kavya*, the Story of a Glowworm: A Folk Narrative Model

Before we proceed further we need to answer the question: What is the relationship between the *Manteswamy Kavya* and Allama?[67] It is quite possible that Manteswamy, the titular protagonist of this mystic folk epic from southern Karnataka, is a historical figure, though the details of his life are not verifiable. What is known as the seat of Manteswamy is even today a popular site in Mandya District near Mysore. Since no authentic information is available, we are not even sure about the century in which he lived; based on literary

---

[66] A Kannada oral epic, even now performed by the Nilagara community of South Karnataka. Although there are no historical records, Manteswamy is considered a saint of the Adi Jambava community. Shrines are built in his memory and there are legends about him. Some readings of this epic argue that Manteswamy, the protagonist, is modelled on Allama Prabhu, while others dispute the idea.

[67] For more, see George, *Allamaprabhu mattu Manteswami*.

intertextuality, we can only say that he lived between the fifteenth and seventeenth centuries.

Since the *Shunyasampadanes* are interrelated with the *Manteswamy Kavya*, I can use the literary intertextuality method. As this subtle embeddedness is not simply a matter of one text reflecting the other, the use of the intertextuality method becomes complicated. Even though Manteswamy is a vague historical figure, the folk epic tells the story of this great master, using the technique of narrative grafting. Here, the narrative grafting involves reconstructing Allama's personality by grafting it onto Manteswamy's life events. The folk poet believes ardently that Manteswamy is none other than Allama. This belief is the basis of the spiritual courage we come across in the Manteswamy story. Since this kavya is part of Kannada folklore, it has naturally been disseminated through numerous texts. Here, I am using Hi. Chi. Boralingaiah's edition, the most comprehensive of the texts.[68] Further, throughout my analysis, I will juxtapose the *Manteswamy Kavya* and the *Shunyasampadanes*. This method of interfacing is not the result of my fetish for comparative study. On the other hand, the internal motif and narrative mode of the *Manteswamy Kavya* nudge me to read it in relation with the *Shunyasampadanes*. In particular, the section "Kalyanapattana" in the *Manteswamy Kavya* can be read as a folk re-rendering of the *Shunyasampadanes*. The *Manteswamy Kavya* is a rebellious Shaiva narrative that emerged from the world discarded by the *Shunyasampadanes*.[69]

[68] Since it is an oral epic that has come down to us from premodern times, its documentation in modern times has taken different forms, each with a specific purpose in mind. For example, Venkatesh Indvadi's edited version is specifically produced as a reading text. See Indvadi, *Manteswamy Kaavya*; Hiriyanna, *Manteswamy Epic Tradition*. However, Nagaraj uses the popular and comprehensive documentation by H.C. Boralingaiah. See Boralingaiah, *Manteswamy*. All textual references are from this edition.

[69] The second section in the *Manteswamy Kavya*, which gives an account of Manteswamy coming to the city of Kalyana, where the sharana movement took place. According to scholars like Boralingaiah, this section can be read as folklore's dialogue with sharana culture, and this section is also a kind of cri-

Right at the beginning, in the section titled "The Creation of the World", we come across a dovetailing of Allama with Manteswamy. Like a refrain, this recurs throughout the epic.

> O Guru, you are too dear,
> to all Siddhas.
> come, O great and infinite one,
> O Manteda Lingayya, come!
> The master who brought to the earth
> such light is
> Jyotirlingappa, luminous one,
> He is Allamaprabhu.
> Mantedalingayya is
> Our chosen light.
> How can I praise the glory of
> Such a master of the world, O Father![70]

We have already seen that in the first phase of Virashaivism, that is, the twelfth century, linga was a conceptual metaphor. We have also seen that this was transformed into a symbol of a particular socio-religious domain during the age of sankalananusandhana – the age of the *Shunyasampadanes*. The *Manteswamy Kavya* too rushes towards primordial moorings. However, it does not adopt the notion of ishtalinga, but rather a conceptual metaphor of jyotir-linga. Here, we need not reiterate the too-well-known idea that Allama was a propagator of jyotirlinga. The *Shunyasampadanes* begin with laurels for Allama: "Holy supreme principle, supreme bliss, supreme light, supreme Ishwara, impenetrable", and other such honorifics. But the *Manteswamy Kavya* begins the story by chanting only the metaphor of light, paranjyoti:

> The light in the beginning,
> The light on the street,
> The light that shines on the palm,

---

tique on the state of affairs in the city of Kalyana after the sharana movement. See Boralingaiah, *Manteswamy*, pp. xv–xvi.

[70] Ibid., p. 7.

The light that burns on the forehand.
O Lord, when placed on the heap of dung,
The paranjyoti (supreme light) that shines without discrimination.
O Master, when placed on the grave of the dead,
The jaganjyoti (light of the world) shining whole.
O Swamy, when placed at where the three roads meet,
The paranjyoti that shines everywhere without discrimination.[71]

There is a lot of difference between saying "light that shines on the palm" and ishtalinga on the palm (karasthala).[72] When the folk poet sings, "The master who brought to the earth / Such light is / Jyotirlingappa, luminous one, / He is Allamaprabhu," Manteswamy is seen as Allama Prabhudevaru who brought paranjyoti, the supreme light, to all without discrimination. From this we see that the revolutionary social stimulus from the original Shaivism is still alive.

As mentioned earlier, engaging in dialogue by turning tattvas into metaphors is an easy task for Allama. This can also be found in the *Manteswamy Kavya*. This paranjyoti-parabrahma, Allama-cum-Manteswamy decides, "I have to create a world."[73]

The section on "world creation" in the *Manteswamy Kavya* is a fascinating spectacle of metaphors and motifs. What Allama or the entire Virashaiva movement received from Kashmira Shaivism was a series of joint metaphors such as light, brightness, flame, etc. In Allama's vachanas we have a multidimensional interpretation of the metaphor of light. If we wish to perceive the oeuvre of Allama with a single metaphor, it would be that of light and flame.

The *Shunyasampadanes* follow the classical model of pauranika kavya, where Shiva himself comes in the form of pranalinga. In this respect, the essential difference between classical sensibility and folk-mystic sensibility is evident throughout the *Manteswamy Kavya*.

---

[71] Ibid.

[72] The religious idiom refers to the palm where the ishtalinga is placed for worship by Virashaivas.

[73] Boralingaiah, *Manteswamy*, p. 11.

That difference lies in raising the details of the mundane world to the level of extraordinary metaphors. Here, Shiva's gana (attendant), Nirmaya, does not come in the form of Allama. Instead, Manteswamy/Allama comes in the form of a glowworm, which is known as a creature of light! What is the nature of this creature?

> Ayya, they called that luminous one
> a glowworm. // suvva ba (O come) Chennabasavanna //
> Ayya, it eludes our sight, eludes our grip
> none has seen it glow at all, // suvva ba (O come),
>   Chennabasavanna //
> O Guru, it is hard to catch it,
> now, if there is no light, this worm escapes sight.
> See here O Guru, since it glows like this
> they call it glowworm // Siddhayya //[74]

> My Guru was dubbed a glowworm.[75]
> They left this glowworm to the mortal world, O enchanter
>   // Siddhayya //[76]

When Manteswamy/Allama arrives as a glowworm in this world, he has no institutional obligations. After being given titles and laurels, Guru makes it clear where he has to go.

> The master, leaving the northern country,
> wearing all these titles and laurels,
> he says where he desires to go
> jaganjyoti (The light of this world),
> paranjyoti (The supreme light),
> patalajyoti (The light of the deep world)
> Allama Prabhu Manteda Lingappa
> said that now I shall go to Kalyana // Siddhayya //[77]

---

[74] Ibid., p. 67.

[75] "Guru" refers to Manteswamy/Allama Prabhu.

[76] "They" signifies Vishnu, Ishwara, and Brahma: see Boralingaiah, *Manteswamy*, pp. 66 and 67.

[77] Ibid., p. 97.

In both the *Manteswamy Kavya* and the *Shunyasampadanes* Guru's journey is towards the city of Kalyana. For Manteswamy/Allama, it is a journey of both self-reflection and examination of the city of Kalyana. The *Manteswamy Kavya* fears that the original vision of Kalyana in the Sharana movement might be diminished. But for the *Shunyasampadanes* this city is a perpetual source of inspiration. In both compositions, the city is a confluence of semi-real and semi-symbolic places. In both we come across many familiar names of sharanas. For the *Manteswamy Kavya*, Kalyana is a city of Hole-yara Honnappa, Madigara Chennaiah, Madiwala Machappa, Kumbara Gundaiah, Ganigara Dasaiah, Kurabara Beerappa, Okka-ligara Muddaiah, Dombara Kyataiah, Turukara Beeraiah, and Ambigara Chaudaiah.[78] Besides, several eccentric mystics belong to this city.

Both good and bad things exist in the city of Kalyana where Mante-swamy/Allama arrives. It seems that hypocrites dominate the city. None of the *Shunyasampadane* texts bothers to undertake a com-prehensive moral analysis of Kalyana. Instead, they exhibit a spiri-tual optimism: there will be no evil and immorality where there are great sharanas like Sangana Basavanna. But like Allama, Manteswa-my/Allama of the folk narrative is sceptical. In Basavanna's court there are diverse varieties of jangamas, including the felonious; the lumpen; those who have forgotten shivajnana (the knowledge of Shiva); those who do not observe customs, not to mention those who have forfeited women and land.

In order to understand for himself the complex truth of Kal-yana, Manteswamy/Allama comes to the place in disguise. The description of Guru's disguise in his visit to Kalyana varies from text to text. In the popular texts, Manteswamy/Allama comes to the city of Kalyana with a toddy pot and a dead she-buffalo calf. This account has ignited an interesting discussion about the caste origins of Manteswamy. Since there is a reference to toddy and a

---

[78] These are the names of sharanas; the first word refers to their occupation and social category/caste, and the second word is a proper name, the name of the individual.

dead calf and Guru's insistence that they should accompany him, one could infer that Manteswamy was a left-untouchable.[79] These two objects grow as symbols of self-respect for Manteswamy. Even in the event that Manteswamy is not a left-untouchable, there are textual traces that testify to his belonging to a lower caste. Though Allama's notion of "caste as defilement" is not entirely absent in the *Shunyasampadanes*, it is certainly relegated to a secondary level. In the *Manteswamy Kavya*, on the other hand, the personality of the Guru responds intensely to the question of social humiliation. The Guru appears as a person not only of low social status but also as suffering from a bodily deformity.

> O Master, he made his leg crooked
> his hand crooked,
> he, the enchanter, took on the disguise of a leper, // Siddhayya //
>
> . . .
>
> o Master,
> with oodles of skin diseases,
> with a plethora of itching diseases,
> O Master, with a lot of pus and blood,
> seven crore worms all over the body,
> he looks up at Kalyana // Siddhayya //[80]

In the *Shunyasampadanes*, too, there is an episode where Allama appears in Basavanna's eyes to have this deformity. The *Shunyasampadanes* and the *Manteswamy Kavya* both describe this incident as an event of self-examination for Basavanna. In Shivaganaprasadi's *Shunyasampadane* Basavarajadevaru, on seeing Prabhudevaru, points to his appearance and addresses Chennabasavanna thus:

> Look at his tangled head, hair unbraided, and staggering walk,
> a lump upon the brow;
> due to his unblinking gaze upon karasthala (image on the palm),
> forgetting the outer world, his eyebrows gashed

---

[79] Nagaraj seems to be using the modern categories of classifying untouchables into "right" and "left". These are problematic categories, and the meaning and symbols associated with left or right vary from one region to another.

[80] Boralingaiah, *Manteswamy*, pp. 101–2.

as if struck hard by something;
With staring eyes and lacerated ears, he is stumbling.
Dripping with blood, slipping in dust and rain,
Scarred back; bruised left and right;
scratched by thorns; armpits cleft;
Spectators watch him dismayed,
in the outskirts of the city.
Dripping with filth,
emaciated with hunger, falling and breaking a knee,
as the blood of a fresh wound flows on his aged feet,
with dislocated joints, wounded in his stumbling,
with shattered toes and crushed hip;
Look, Chennabasavanna!
Behold a sight that is awful to the eyes!
How soiled is Lord Kudalasangama's outward form![81]

Note the surprising similarities between the two narratives. The question of who influenced whom is not relevant to the method of intertextuality. Even if one takes matters to an extreme and argues that the modern bard singing the verses of the *Manteswamy Kavya* possesses the knowledge of the *Shunyasampadanes*, surprise at the similarities between the two texts does not diminish. This is a distinct model of narratives with parallels and connections belonging to a common genealogy.

The city of Kalyana is a symbol. The language of literary criticism or social sciences struggles to answer why Manteswamy/Allama came to this city. Fortunately, I am reminded of a poem by Rilke.[82] (I think it is poetry that captures the most complex relationships. All arts are finally poetry.) In his poem, Rilke writes about the homesickness of the ore. The gold ore has become a coin, and as currency it has to pass through several hands. It has to work in all sorts of places. The ore wants to liberate itself from the coin and the trading cycles of currency. It wants to flow back into the veins of the gaping mountains from where it came. It longs to return to the natural space – sunshine, wind, and riverside.

[81] Shivaganaprasadi, *Shivaganaprasadi Mahadevayyana*, p. 276.
[82] Rilke, "The Sovereigns of the World Are Old".

The original eruption of Virashaivism is the primary inspiration behind the folk-mystic poetry of the *Manteswamy Kavya*. It is natural ore, not a reified coin. However, the *Shunyasampadanes* are like a coin. Without an ore there cannot be a coin. Still, the ore cannot have the value of a coin – the range of its influence, its ability to change the course of history. Rilke writes in awe about the desire of the ore to liberate itself from the turning wheel of currency and flow back into the veins of the gaping mountains of its origins. I felt the same awe when I read and heard the *Manteswamy Kavya*. Going to the city of Kalyana is a journey of self-examination for the personality of Manteswamy/Allama, while also being a journey to examine Kalyana.

Manteswamy/Allama is destined to go to the city of Kalyana. Even though Manteswamy is a recent historical figure, he has to go to the holy city of Kalyana for his rebellion to be recognised. Indeed, Kalyana did not exist after the twelfth century. But it has remained permanently in the cultural memory of the Kannada people.[83] Like ruined cities that come alive only at night, the city of Kalyana calls attention to itself in the glittering night of social unevenness. There is one more reason for Manteswamy to undertake at least an imaginary journey to Kalyana. Any kind of protest, despite being against tradition, nurses a desire to be accepted within the framework of a tradition. The protest that comes from within a traditional framework will cherish a hope of staying alive and growing. While this argument may not be true in the case of political and social rebellions, it is undoubtedly true of religious ones. It may seem ironic for a protest to have to establish a relationship with tradition, but that is the inescapable reality. In this respect, Manteswamy's journey to Kalyana is undertaken to gain recognition from a tradition. Any voice of rebellion within the Kannada linguistic cosmos has to converse with the city of Kalyana. That is the historical ontology of the Kannada language and world. Whether in Karnataka's entire geo-institutional territory or in the cultural mem-

---

[83] Prithvi Datta Chandra Shobhi discusses how over the past eight hundred years the Kannada cultural imagination, including Shaiva poetry and the *Manteswamy Kavya,* has captured this premodern city: Shobhi, "Kalyāṇa is Wrecked".

ories of the Kannada language, there is no place more rebellious than the twelfth-century city of Kalyana. So, from the internal logic of Kannada's cultural imagination, Manteswamy's journey to Kalyana is rather natural and entirely to be expected.

Amidst the darkness of social inequalities, the city of Kalyana shines yet brighter and with greater allure. The folk mysticism in the *Manteswamy Kavya*, too, aspires to create spirituality from the womb of social injustice. This work believes that what happened during the twelfth century was itself such an act of creating spirituality out of the social disparities in Kalyana. But there are major differences between the *Manteswamy Kavya* and the *Shunyasampadanes* in the way they perceive Kalyana. For the *Shunyasampadanes*, Kalyana is immortal, free from all ailments, and never subject to change. This city is a historical form of ishtalinga, a state where the jangama principle operates permanently. It is not a nest of mortals; instead, it is a spiritual ideal with no trace of death and evil. Precisely for this reason, the most important events in the *Shunyasampadanes* take place in the city of Kalyana. The *Shunyasampadanes* desire that the entire world should dwell centrally in this city.

The *Shunyasampadanes* come alive whenever they refer to the city of Kalyana, the abode of all treasures in the mortal world, which mirrors the face of vani (the goddess of knowledge) and is a pot full of all the dharmas, the face of liberation, and the confluence of punya (virtue). Allama himself has praised the city of Kalyana thus:

In the clay lamp called Kalyana, pouring the oil called devotion,
when the light called Basavanna lit the wick of right conduct
the bravery/radiance of Shiva flashes and glows;
the host of sharanaganas were blissful under this light.
Isn't it true that
the place of shivabhaktas is the place of mukti (liberation)?
Isn't it true that
the place of shivabhaktas is a sacred place?
O Siddharamayya,
I am alive, seeing my revered Sangana Basavanna
dwelling in Guheshwaralinga. (823)

There is another patantara (version) of this vachana, in which the word pratapa (bravery) is replaced by prakasha (radiance).[84] There is a conspicuous distinction between the two. Bravery is closer to the warrior domain, and radiance is closer to the domain of spiritual seeking.

The manner in which the *Shunyasampadanes* describe the city of Kalyana signifies the transformation Virashaivism underwent during the fifteenth and sixteenth centuries. Ideally, those who are sinful, irate, inveterate liars, and profane should not visit the city of Kalyana. But the Kalyana of the *Shunyasampadanes* also possesses material wealth beyond this ethical glory. It is a city 12 leagues in size, boasting of 365 gateways which in turn have 365 doors with diamond edges, and 225 gates carved out of stone have 450 doors with golden carvings. There are 285,720 mathas of dasoha (where meals are served). For these mathas of dasoha the most important expanse is Basavarajadeva's courtyard, a palace with a thousand golden pillars and a thousand golden cupolas. There is a pool with the depth of a man's height for washing and worshipping the holy feet of guru-linga-jangama; the paddy field watered by this inexhaustible pool grows 12 kandugas (an old measure of capacity) of rice of the rajashali variety. In the majestic palace is a matha capacious enough for 196,000 devotees. And other innumerable such mathas in the city of Kalyana are as follows: 12,000 mathas observing rigorous religious practices; 72,000 mahamanes (great houses); 10,000 mathas regularly observing day-to-day religious practices; 15,000 mathas which practise the vow of using only spring water; 12,000 mathas which are entirely devoted to religious practices and champion the cause of religion; 1000 mathas of pure prasadis; 32,000 mathas that daily feed 1000 jangamas.[85]

And so the description of the city of Kalyana continues. Mathas

---

[84] Patantara: a different textual version of the same text with slight variations is called patantara. Usually, a letter or a word or a phrase of the text varies from one manuscript to another.

[85] For more such descriptions of the city of Kalyana, see Gooluru Siddaveeranna, *Sunyasampadane*, vol. 2, pp. 79–89.

radiate pomp and power as a meeting place of material wealth and people's power. This represents a social and historical victory of the jangama principle. Unlike accounts of other cities that include descriptions of the king, there is no such description in relation to the city of Kalyana. The mighty lord of horses, elephants, and army regiments, the king of kings Bijjalaraya rules here, but Basavanna leads the kingdom of Bhakti with contentment and joy. It is, in fact, the empire of Basavanna – and this is the unwritten rule of Kalyana. Allama praises Basavarajadevaru's house, standing before its main entrance, a meeting place of material power and spiritual force.

There are several contradictions in Shivaganaprasadi's narrative. Standing before Basavarajadevaru's house, Prabhudevaru and Siddharamayyadevaru come across great lingawantas (sharanas who wear the linga) visiting the house. It is a great union of sharanas; a variety of yogis and bhaktas who can recite and listen to vachana shastras. They undertake the study of Shiva-tattvaa (the principle of Shiva). It is an institutional necessity that vachanas have to become a shastra (organised body of knowledge). In this crowd of sharanas, the folk mystic in the *Manteswamy Kavya* can see hooligans as well as tender jangamas. But the composers of the *Shunyasampadanes* are not such sceptics.

At the entrance to Kalyana is an inscription of Basavanna.[86] Since the power of material force has entered religion, sharana institutions have gained a different kind of dignity. But there is an unconscious doubt in the *Shunyasampadanes* regarding whether Allama's point of view about material things might be different. This does not mean that Shivaganaprasadi is ignorant about the possibility of a fissure between the social power of the mathas and Allama's spiritual darshana. Such contradictions and paradoxes are handled throughout in the *Shunyasampadanes*, which is why they have become really complex, going beyond superficial spiritual coherence. When Allama arrives at Basavanna's mahamane (the great

[86] In the *Shunyasampadanes*, this is said to be an inscription written by Chennabasavanna which describes the glory of the city of Kalyana. See Gooluru Siddaveeranna, *Sunyasampadane*, vol. 2, p. 79.

house of Basavanna) in Kalyana, he witnesses mathas filled with people and an oceanic group of sharanas. The section that describes the scene is as follows:

> And, the golden cupolas of the Shiva temple
> were shining like the bright light of
> Basavanna's devotion and knowledge.
> And, expecting the arrival of guru-linga-jangama
> Basavanna's temple was decorated
> with festoons studded with nine types of gems,
> and a sky-high canopy over it, a carpet spread before,
> Prabhu devaru and Siddharama devaru feasted their eyes
> on this temple, decorated in various ways, looking glorious.[87]

The dilemma for the *Shunyasampadanes* is that Basavanna is as indispensable for religion as Allama. The soul of darshana needs the body of the institution. Only Allama can provide the former if Basavanna and Chennabasavanna can supply the latter. The philosophical imagination behind the *Shunyasampadanes* is aware that this kind of union is inevitable. Gummalapurada Siddhalingadevara's *Shunyasampadane* provides the divine background to justify this kind of institutional will. Compared to Shivaganaprasadi, Gummalapurada Siddhalingadevara's position is conservative. He cannot accept the narrative sensibility of Harihara which is evident in Shivaganaprasadi. The deva–bhritya (lord–servant) relationship between Parashiva and the leaders of the Vachana movement is unacceptable to him. Siddhalingadevaru reveals the unity of Allama–Basavanna–Chennabasavanna in the divine mural as follows:

> Basaveshwara, the *sat* (absolute being) of that untainted supreme
> linga, descended on the earth in the form of Guru for the world's
>   welfare.
> Chennabasavanna, the chit (absolute consciousness) of that
>   untainted supreme linga,
> descended on the earth in the form of linga to sanctify the world.

[87] Shivaganaprasadi, *Shivaganaprasadi Mahadevayyana*, p. 150.

> The blissful jangama of that untainted supreme linga came down
> to the earth as Prabhudeva for the welfare of all
> sharanaganas (cohorts).[88]

Though this notion of the great union is especially expressed by Siddhalingadevaru, Shivaganaprasadi also composes his narrative with the awareness that, at some level, Allama should unite with Basavanna institutionally. But Shivaganaprasadi is well aware that there is a difference between on the one hand how he looks at Kalyana, the mathas, and the grandeur of Basavanna's house, and on the other how Allama looks at them. We are again reminded of Rilke's poem contrasting ore and coin.

In the case of the *Manteswamy Kavya*, doubt and excitement regarding the city of Kalyana have both bothered the folk mystic, who has let the surrounding disorder enter his narrative of the city. Howsoever imaginative a creative work may be, it cannot do away with contemporary pressures. At times, these are like the fingerprints of a potter on the pot, which are invisible but present. For a folk mystic there is always an anxiety about decadence, yet also the hope of excitement. By contrast, the classical narrators of the *Shunyasampadanes* see only the pinnacle of success; their narratives establish the permanent state of excitement and fulfilment pervading Kalyana. Even so, Allama's vachanas are powerful enough to penetrate this veil. Allama does not view Kalyana as a city with the golden cupolas of Shiva's house nor as a city decorated with nine gems. The city of Kalyana is nevertheless a dream place in Allama's imagination. It is a spiritual city beyond the realm of worldly power. The jyotirlinga could never be at the mercy of the golden lamppost on which it generally burns. Allama believes that the jyotirlinga can burn independently without the lamppost, which takes him beyond the boundary of power structures.

In Shivaganaprasadi's *Shunyasampadane*, we come across two descriptions of Basavanna's mahamane: one described in the inscription at the gate and another revealed through Allama's vachana. The

---

[88] Gummalapurada, *Gummalapurada Siddhalingadevara*, p. 2.

former, which is nothing but Shivaganaprasadi's description, differs widely from the latter. This is what makes each of them unique. Allama's description of Basavanna's mahamane is as follows:

Sangana Basavanna brought the primal linga
to the earth and built the great house in this mortal world.
When I went to see that house,
it swallowed me before I could enter it!
It has one pillar and six beams, and thirty-six rafters.
A foundation stone with no support of earth and sky.
It has nine locked doors,
one door spits fire!
A pinnacle of ruby is on top of
a canopy propped on a pillar of pearl.
On the pinnacle's point is the cupola of bright gold,
which is invisible to those who could see,
and visible to those who could not see.
Ten servants move about there,
Two sentinels stand guard by the door;
One maidservant is moving about,
Another ministers to the linga worship.
One fetches ingredients, cleaning them carefully;
another cooks food on a fire without flame;
one serves linga and jangama by ministration and repast.
If one eats food on a five-scooped plate set on a tripod,
then, the pramathaganas (cohorts) have come to take
the remnants of the offerings served to him.
Once they entered the house, they stayed there carefree.
O Siddharamayya,
how happy I am to see the great house of Sangana Basavanna,
Guheshwara's sharana! (1110)

Shivaganaprasadi makes use of this vachana in his narrative by retaining the literal meaning of Allama's symbolic language.[89] He turns the spiritual significations into material ones. The birth of institutional Virashaivism lies in the act of translating the abstract into

---

[89] Shivaganaprasadi, *Shivaganaprasadi Mahadevayyana*, pp. 150–1.

the concrete. The image of dasoha, which is very significant for the folk mystic and the composers of the *Shunyasampadanes*, is entirely abstract in Allama. For the folk mystic, dasoha is a concrete thing – a feast. The activity of dasoha grew into an institution, simultaneously symbolising power and critiquing the prevalent power. In Allama's vachana, two sentinels can be seen gatekeeping, and food is being cooked on a flameless fire.

But in the folk mystic narrative of the *Manteswamy Kavya* these well-built sentinels stop Manteswamy/Allama from entering. As far as dasoha and feasts are concerned, the *Manteswamy Kavya* and the *Shunyasampadanes* are similar. The sentinels allow only those who are neat and in robust health to enter; those who are ill are allowed in later and have to wait their turn at the door. In this folk narrative, Manteswamy/Allama arrives at the city of Kalyana as an ugly and ill person, so the sentinels stop him. The strong sentinels in the *Manteswamy Kavya* are referred to literally as the "ones who hold batons".

In the treatment of Allama's arrival at mahamane and his meeting with Basavanna, there is much similarity between the *Shunyasampadanes*, the classical narratives, and the *Manteswamy Kavya* (the folk one). The chief similarity is in the treatment of the meeting of Allama and Basavanna, which takes place despite difficulty. But there are dramatic differences in their descriptions of the details of this event. In the *Shunyasampadanes*, Basavanna is scared when he finds the true image of Allama in the shivalinga he is worshipping. Further, in Gummalapurada Siddhalingadevara's version, Basavanna notices Siddharamayya not wearing a linga on his body. So, even in the *Shunyasampadanes* there are several hidden aspects to the difficult meeting between Allama and Basavanna.

In the folk narrative, Basavanna comes to know of the arrival of Allama not through his eyes but through his ears. As in Allama's compositions, the bedagu (riddle) mode is employed here. There is a hint of Basavanna taking pride in there being no greater Guru than himself – or at least in the fact that he has never seen one. In the *Manteswamy Kavya*, Basavanna has set up a system that in-

forms him whenever a sharana greater than him arrives at the city
of Kalyana:

> Tie a bell without a tongue
> over the door.
> Keep a kettledrum without a stick
> at the door.
> If sharanas greater than us
> come to our Kalyana,
> there sounds a tongueless bell (Come, O Come).[90]

"A bell without a tongue" and "a drum without a stick" are the
kind of metaphors we come across in Allama's bedagu compositions.
The folk mystic here impersonates Allama's imagination, while the
classical mystic, the shunyasampadanakara, uses Allama's compositions as they are and builds his own story around them. However,
there is a strong possibility that the classical imagination, too, im-
personated Allama's imagination. Classical imagination tries to reconstruct Allama spiritually and aesthetically. We also come across
these spiritual and aesthetic reconstructions in several vachanas
that go in the name of Allama.

It is possible to outline in brief the processes used to incorporate Allama. In such processes, generally the individual imagination – here Allama's – that needs to be emulated and incorporated
is first received as a universal model. This universal model emerges
when we imagine certain essential forms in the individual imagination. Without this essentialisation there is no possibility of creating
a universal model. Cosmic transactions that are beyond the world
are very important to Allama. Therefore, even the mundane in
Allama becomes extraordinarily embellished. Disharmony in harmony, transgression in discipline, unrest in similarity, peace in the
womb of fury, and playfulness in cruelty – all these are features of
Allama's model. Thus, only after reducing Allama's world to this
kind of readymade form is it possible to reconstruct that model. In

---

[90] Boralingaiah, *Manteswamy*, p. 103.

Indian culture, this seems the way in which universal models internalise highly individualistic imaginations like Allama's.

If the folk mystic uses the Allama model to create socio-spiritual forms, then the classical mystic uses it to develop spiritual-aesthetic forms. The consciousness of social inequality is deep in the former, and the yearning for spiritual bliss is dominant in the latter. The Allama model thus proves handy in the search for multiple meanings.

In the *Shunyasampadanes*, Basavanna does not initially go in person to welcome Allama. He sends his attendants, which is surprising but true. A major controversy ensues as Allama refuses to enter Basavanna's house and says, "he is deformed, who, being dull-witted, ignores the jangama / even when he sees him / If the jangama enters his house, / he [the jangama] will not be liberated from the world."[91] To this Basavanna responds, "not coming to the house is a matter of human nature, but not of understanding."[92]

Hereafter, the intertextual relationship between the *Shunyasampadanes* and the *Manteswamy Kavya* grows stronger. However, we witness significant differences between the two in terms of the motifs and metaphors they employ. In the *Shunyasampadanes*, Basavanna asks his attendants to "catch hold of Shiva and bring him." Further, Basavanna orders: "If he does not come, behead him and bring him."[93] It is difficult for the modern ethical sensibility to make sense of this order. When Basavanna says, "Behead Shiva and bring him here," the attendants attack Allama with metal weapons. However, these weapons appear to swing harmlessly in the air. When the metal weapons fail, Basavanna tells his attendants to use a weapon of emotion and thought (bhavashastra). Then Allama says, "Can the formless body be accessible to the saw?"[94] After persuasion from other sharanas, Basavanna goes in person to welcome Allama by spreading carpets, holding a pot and mirror, and tying festoons studded with nine gems. Basavanna offers the ultimate forms of humil-

---

[91] Shivaganaprasadi, *Shivaganaprasadi Mahadevayyana*, p. 152.
[92] Ibid.
[93] Ibid.
[94] Ibid., p. 153.

ity. But to Allama Basavanna still appears egoistic. That Basavanna appears egoistic in Shivaganaprasadi's *Shunyasampadane* is a kind of self-criticism on its part.

Further in the plot, Basavanna realises his fault in not (initially) welcoming Allama in person. Feeling penitent, he humbly urges Allama to enter his house. But Allama's objections do not end. Here, in two important vachanas, Basavanna and Allama confront each other dramatically:

Basavanna:

If asked, I'll offer my body; if asked, I'll offer my mind;
if asked, I will offer my wealth to your sharanas.
O glorious one,
I swear on the feet of your sharanas
I will not allow the feeling of desire to enter my mind.
If I seek anything other than you
in my mind, utterance and body,
Kudala Sangamadeva,
keep me in the terrible world of pain, the cycle of births and deaths.

Allama:

The Meru mountains belong to pramathas (Shiva's consorts).
The silver mountains to the puratanas (ancients).
The fourteen worlds to the linga.
The earth is the creator's mint,
His stamping dye, and his kitchen.
The body, mind, and wealth all belong to Guheshwara.
Then, O Sangana Basavanna, what is yours to offer to become
    a bhakta?[95]

Allama argues logically that there is a kind of spiritual arrogance in Basavanna's conduct. But when we consider Basavanna's vachanas, we find no basis for such an accusation. If we are to be sympathetic to Allama here, we may argue only to the extent that Basavanna's excessive humility could appear egoistic to Allama. Basa-

---

[95] Ibid., pp. 166–7.

vanna's words and his emotional world are comparable to those of St Francis of Assisi, whose manifesto is like Basavanna's – "There is no one lesser than I."[96] Aldous Huxley criticises St Francis of Assisi's stance as "spiritual pride".[97] Interestingly, spiritual arrogance is seen to reveal itself in excessive humility and self-criticism.

In the *Shunyasampadanes,* as noted above, Basavanna, instead of welcoming Allama at his great house, is immersed in linga worship. Allama considers this spiritually misguided, because linga worship is questionable when the jangama, i.e. Allama himself, is the real form of the linga; above all Basavanna's behaviour is inappropriate after his acceptance of jangama as linga. So, clearly, there is a difference between Allama's criticism of Basavanna and Huxley's criticism of St Francis. The composers of the *Shunyasampadanes* have presented the face-off between Allama and Basavanna with a deep philosophical understanding of what underlies it.

The *Manteswamy Kavya* does not attempt this kind of philosophical engagement. A kind of insensitivity might creep into religion if it gains material power and prestige; however, the folk mystic doesn't say that Basavanna exhibits such insensitivity. He situates this episode within the organic relationship of guru–linga–jangama. Classical training is not the means to handle this kind of relationship; instead, the requirement of the moment is sensitivity. The sentinels with batons attack Manteswamy/Allama physically; he argues heatedly with them. They have a valid reason for their attack, being obviously angry because Manteswamy/Allama has spoken disrespectfully of Basavanna when saying, "O, neither is Basavanna great nor are you great to me."[98] As in the *Shunyasampadanes*, Basavanna in the *Manteswamy Kavya* is "worshipping a linga on his palm".[99] When Manteswamy/Allama gets beaten up by a butcher called Sangayya, Basavanna and his wife feel the blows.

---

[96] This is Basavanna's famous vachana. See Pattabhirama Somayaji's English translation, vachana no. 99 in Kalburgi, ed., *Vachana.*

[97] See Huxley, *The Perennial Philosophy,* p. 327.

[98] Boralingaiah, *Manteswamy,* p. 117.

[99] Ibid., p. 118.

According to the folk mystic, they are all interrelated, and smiting one affects all.

> Ayya, when Basavanna Guru
> and Neelamma
> were folding their hands to the Lord,
> Butcher Sangayya
> beat Manteda Lingayya thrice.
> Ayya, two blows fell on Basavanna's neck,
> and one on his better half Neelamma.
> Ayya, Basavanna's master,
> then, the tongueless bell tolled.
> And O Master,
> The kettledrum without a stick sounded ("Come, O come").[100]

The *Manteswamy Kavya* narrates this episode with the great sense of excitement, anxiety, and perturbation that one would expect to experience when reporting such an extraordinary event. Suddenly, the oil lamps in the mahamane go dark, and Basavanna and Neelamma rush out. From this perspective, in the *Manteswamy Kavya* the portrait of Basavanna is beyond any kind of spiritual-ethical fallacy. When his social prestige is at stake, Manteswamy/Allama behaves exactly as an ordinary person would and says angrily, "One must eat like those who eat, receive betel leaf just as others do."[101]

In the *Manteswamy Kavya*, Manteswamy/Allama goes and sits on Haralayya's garbage dump.[102] What Basavanna utters in the *Shunyasampadanes* in the episode of meeting Allama actually happens in the *Manteswamy Kavya*.[103] Though not with malevolence, Basavanna dismembers and beheads Manteswamy/Allama and

---

[100] Ibid., pp. 118–19.

[101] Ibid., p. 123.

[102] Haralaiah: a follower of Basavanna; in this context, it is important to note that he is a cobbler.

[103] In the *Shunyasampadanes*, Basavanna orders his attendants to fetch Allama by force. He says, "If he does not come, behead him and get him."

brings him inside his house. While the attendants in the *Shunya-sampadane* fail to get Allama through metal weapons, in the *Manteswamy Kavya* Basavanna draws out the Guru (Manteswamy/Allama) by using emotion and thought as a weapon. But the body of the Guru does not move as a whole. When pulled by the feet, his feet come off. When dragged by the hands, his hands come off. The head too is detached. Thereafter, wrapping the dismembered body in fine clothes, the husband and wife – Basavanna and Neelamma – carry it on their heads into their mahamane.

A peculiar kind of intertextual transaction exists between the text I am using and other versions of the *Manteswamy Kavya*. The dead she-buffalo calf and the toddy pot associated with Manteswamy are important for the idea of protest in this epic. In the text I am using, a unique cultural revision has taken place, yet the important objects and symbols remain. Just as in the *Book of Knowledge*,[104] where revisions are made in successive versions but the essence is repeated, so also here the fundamental symbols continue to feature in such narratives that are subject to constant re-creation and re-presentation in future versions. Even after many reinterpretations in their different versions, these objects and symbols appear in one form or another in all such narratives. The same process has occurred in the text I am using.

In the current text, when Basavanna drags Manteswamy/Allama, his body parts become flesh. Even the blood takes the form of flesh. The head of the great one on the earth (Manteswamy/Allama), which Neelamma carries, becomes a toddy pot. If the other texts of the *Manteswamy Kavya* make direct reference to the flesh of the dead calf and the toddy pot, the text I am using makes a cultural revision by not referring to them directly, instead transforming the body parts into flesh and the head into a toddy pot. Thus, the extraordinary merit of the present text lies in making use of the fundamental symbols and, at the same time, retaining the spirit of cul-

---

[104] An encyclopaedia for children first published in 1912 and continuously revised for further editions.

tural revision. This double accomplishment is no mean achievement.

At the end of the *Shunyasampadanes*, Allama finally occupies the shunya throne – the seat of the void.[105] Though that episode also appears in the *Manteswamy Kavya*, there are epochal differences between the two texts. In the *Shunyasampadanes*, this episode represents a unity of Allama's and Basavanna's philosophies. This confluence of their thoughts was a dream of Virashaivism and an institutional necessity. After establishing the shunya throne, Basavanna waits for Allama – who has gone on a pilgrimage – to occupy it. The description of Allama's shunya throne is entirely different from the description of Basavanna's great house in Shivaganaprasadi's *Shunyasampadane*, which shows his narrative sensitivity. In the case of Basavanna's great house, the description of material wealth is befitting. However, it would have been absurd if luxury and pomp were brought into the description of Allama's shunya throne.

Using Allama's typical register and at the same time negotiating with it, sharana Hadapada Appanna composes a vachana that describes the shunya throne. By the time we come across Hadapada Appanna's vachana in the *Shunyasampadane*, Shivaganaprasadi has made us aware of the fact that Allama's spiritual play is coming to an end and thus prepares us emotionally for another kind of experience.[106] Allama's throne here is not a fact of history, but is described as follows:

> A pillar of concentrated will;
> which has the aura with several pictures.
> In that aura,
> the garland of five pearls is laid on

[105] According to certain narratives based on vachana discourse, Allama presided over the meetings of the Anubhava Mantapa (the Hall of Experience), established by Basavanna and sharanas in the twelfth century. Here, the seat occupied by Allama Prabhu is referred to as shunya simhasana (seat of the void). There are debates about its existence as a historical fact. However, philosophically what it means is "throne of the highest stage of spiritual attainment". See Yaravintelimath, *Vachana Lexicon*, p. 780.

[106] Hadapada Appanna: one of the prominent sharanas and vachanakaras, known as the right hand of Basavanna; he was a betel-leaf carrier.

the crown called brahmarandra.
Making tunes reverberating in the nine nerves,
pleasing parrots, cuckoos, and bees,
spreading tender mango-sprouts
called eternal peace,
lighting the lamps of sun and moon,
setting a golden cupola of the great knowledge,
over the dome of soham ("It is I" – self-awareness),
my supreme Guru Basavanna built
the shunya throne of void and serenity,
in Lord Basavapriya Kudala Chenna Sangayya.[107]

Allama ascends the trividhagati shunya throne (seat of the void).[108] Symbolically, it is possible to interpret this as acceptance of a different kind of leadership. It is also described through the idiom of bedagu: "It was a wonder for the world, / When the bodiless divine assumed his seat / Upon the bottomless throne of flowers."[109] Sharanas such as Hadapada Appanna, Soddala Bacharasa, and others sing "Namo Namo" (hail to thee) at the holy feet of Prabhudevaru. We also come across the image of "the Lord called the Serene, sitting in the mantapa, kiosk of the formless."[110]

Allama also ascends the throne in the *Manteswamy Kavya*. But that is a seat of flame, and it is not occupied by the undivided body of Manteswamy/Allama. Basavanna and Neelamma place the torso and head on the throne separately, which appears absurd; they call all the flowers of the world for Shiva worship, which makes this poetically the most beautiful section. Reading this reminds me of Harihara's "Pushpa Ragale" and compels me to repeatedly draw comparisons with it. Different varieties of flowers are called for worship. Each one is invited after describing its nature realistically and in detail:

[107] Shivaganaprasadi, *Shivaganaprasadi Mahadevayyana*, p. 271.
[108] According to Joladarasi Doddanagoudaru, thrividhagati involves transcending kriya, jnana, and bhava (action, knowledge, and feeling). See Doddanagoudaru, *Bayala Galikeya*, pp. 771–2.
[109] Shivaganaprasadi, *Shivaganaprasadi Mahadevayyana*, p. 280.
[110] Ibid.

Born in the street, and snatching the ends of saris, O palm, do come for Shiva's worship. Born on the fence and grown on the fence, O smiling tumbe flower, do come for Shiva's worship. You, smiling kengal flower, do come for Shiva's worship. Born on a mountain and grown amidst +rocks, O sunflower, folding your hands to the sun, do come for Shiva's worship. Lotus, O mother, born in water and growing in water, do come for Swamy's worship. O mother, you sevantige flower who menstruates in the evening, becomes pregnant at midnight, and begets a son in the morning, do come for Shiva's worship. O mother, you marigold, who becomes pregnant without a husband, do come for Shiva's worship. O red sampige flower, who grows abundantly in Kagudavadi, O mother, you adore the garments of sages, do come for Shiva's worship. O mother, you jasmine of round variety, and basil of round dome, do come for Swamy's worship.[111]

We rarely find such vivid descriptions of beauty even in canonical poetry. If the fragmented prose of a folk song slowly and lovingly describes the virtues and history of each flower, Harihara's narrative moves such episodes forward with urgency and ecstasy. The classical poet does not enjoy the freedom to describe this kind of beauty with languorous, lingering phrasings. In the case of folk mystic poetry, the elements of varnaka are embedded in vastuka.[112] The eye of a folk poet responds to the uniqueness of each flower: "Marigold is like this! O mother, it wears a yellow turmeric sari with sixty-five folds. The kanagile flower (oleander) too wears with pride a starched sari."[113] There is also mention of the marigold and kanagile being unmarried yet pregnant. However, we do not learn of the mythology of these flowers from this kavya.

Though Neelamma invites all the flowers, some of them do not come. And this suggests that all is not well. In a fascinating section, an angry Neelamma curses them: "Why did not you come, you mad fools."[114] Among several varieties, the palm, yekke (calotropis)

---

[111] Boralingaiah, *Manteswamy*, pp. 137–9.
[112] For more, see fn. 58 in ch. 3.
[113] Boralingaiah, *Manteswamy*, p. 138.
[114] Ibid., pp. 139–40.

and maraganagile (big oleander) flowers did not turn up. Thus, the palm flower is cursed:

> O mother, you palm flower.
> go and grow where the stream flows.
> Grow in the land where there is water.
> let your fragrance spread across three miles.
>
> O, mother, for three miles,
> let your fragrance spread, Oh, palm flower,
> Fall as a donkey's drop.
>
> You as donkey's drop
> fall off, O palm flower,
> go around and wander in the Brahmins' street
>
> You palm flower go and roam
> around the Brahmins' street,
> in the Brahmins' colony.
> let those who wear you get a headache for three days.[115]

Here, it is a curse to wander in the Brahmins' street! This kind of value judgement has certainly emerged from the twelfth-century vachanakaras. Especially in the bedagu vachanas of Madhuvarasa, we come across a revolutionary shift in the representation of social hierarchy.[116] He turns the accepted social values upside down. For example, an untouchable becomes a symbol of virtue and the Brahmin a symbol of vice. This technique of shifting the hierarchy in the vachanas has undoubtedly influenced the folk mystic of the *Manteswamy Kavya*.

It is interesting to note that Neelamma's curse is not uttered in complete antagonism. The aroma of the cursed flower spreads for

---

[115] Ibid., p. 140.

[116] Madhuvarasa, whose signature line is Arkeshwaralinga, is also known as Madhuvayya. He was a Brahmin who held an administrative position in the court of the Kalachuri king Bijjala, and became a sharana under the influence of Basavanna. For how his bedagu vachanas turn social heirarchy upside down, see the beginning of ch. 6 in this book.

three miles, but only those who wear it have to suffer a headache for three days. The lines quoted above, which are in the style of tripadi, become possible only in the hands of a folk mystic poet. Neelamma curses not only the palm flower but also another, the yekke flower, which too has not turned up for worship: "Why did you not come, O graceful lass, / O six-faced chaste woman?"[117] Neelamma curses the six-faced yekke flower "to grow on the dilapidated wall" and "be charmed by sorcery and also to be its victim, but to be absent from Shiva's worship."[118] Finally, Neelamma curses the kanagile flower: "O big kanagile flower, go and deck the head of Mari Goddess's forehead.[119] You bedeck the tambittu arati (lamp),[120] but you are not fit for Shiva worship."[121] Here, the big kanagile is representative of folk deities such as Mari and Masani.

From Allama's point of view, Neelamma's cursing of these flowers has a particular symbolic meaning. The palm, yekke, and kanagile flowers are deployed here as representatives of different socio-religious traditions. Her cursing resonates with Allama's opposition to these religious traditions. Allama is not only opposed to sanatana Brahminism but also to the tantric tradition and folk religion. The opposition more usually expressed through scholarly and classical knowledge systems and the criticism made at social and ethical levels are achieved here by the folk narrative through the metaphoric mode, using the imagery of flowers.

Based on the *Manteswamy Kavya*, we can develop a theory around an important technique in the folk mystic narrative. Before that, it is important to reflect on the nature of classical mystic poetry such as the *Shunyasampadanes*. This poetry generally takes pride in

---

[117] Boralingaiah, *Manteswamy*, pp. 140–1.

[118] Ibid.

[119] In the Indian folk imagination, Mari is the goddess of death and Masani is the goddess of the graveyard. These terms appear in six vachanakaras. See *Vachana Sanchaya*.

[120] Tambittu is a round sweetmeat in which a lamp is lighted and waved (as arati) before the idols of gods and goddesses.

[121] Boralingaiah, *Manteswamy*, p. 142.

the fact that it possesses knowledge systems and worlds of emotion that are not easily accessible to ordinary people. It uses this knowledge with the utmost care and faithfulness. The birth of classical mystic poetry lies in the very gap between ordinary people and their knowledge of the shastras. However, it is not really concerned about this gap, nor does it intend to communicate at the level of commoners. As becomes clear even in the *Shunyasampadanes*, the shastra-like precision in classical mystic poetry lends it a definitive structure. It is not easily possible to change this structure. The use of texts as rituals creates a majestic aura around the classical mystic work. But the *Shunyasampadanes* have come only halfway in attaining this majestic aura because the narratives, at least those of Shivaganaprasadi, are revealed in the form of prasanga.[122] Generally, the open dramatic nature of a prasanga is not in consonance with rituals in classical texts. It is quite possible that the *Shunyasampadanes* became more rigid as the need for an authentic sacred text for its community continued to grow, but this process of becoming rigid is incomplete even now because of several constraints. While explaining the process of nation formation, Benedict Anderson analyses how a community at the stage of its integration searches for a text and authenticates it.[123] Studying the relationship between the Virashaiva community and its sacred texts can provide us with new insights into how sacred texts are created when real and imagined communities come together in the social process.

In contrast to classical mystic poetry, folk mystic narratives function within the scope of the worlds of knowledge and emotion that belong to their specific communities. As far as knowledge is concerned, the folk mystic poet has no desire to exhibit pride in his possession of greater knowledge. Though he is a cut above his community in his breadth of knowledge and understanding of emotion, he wanders within the ordinary circle of his community when

---

[122] The prasanga is an episodic narrative in a larger work. This kind of narrative gives importance to storytelling rather than to the authentic analysis of shastras.

[123] Anderson, *Imagined Communities*.

it comes to communicative technique. The folk mystic poet does not expand his horizons but tries to sound greater depths. And even here, not depths of interpretation but of description. Here, description and darshana merge completely. In this respect, the world of Allama strives to be unique by borrowing from both folk and classical.

In folk mystic poetry, the voice that uses figurative language is dominant. The classical mystic has intellectual training in creating feeling out of logic, metaphor out of philosophy, and a universal community out of an individual. Indeed, one cannot become a classical mystic poet without intellectual training. Many moderns have the misconception that mysticism does not require the acquisition of knowledge. But if we theorise using the example of Allama, mysticism is nothing but acquired knowledge denying itself at its ultimate stage. On the other hand, since the folk mystic follows the mode of conceptual metaphor, he reaches the height of intellectual innocence. Through his intellectually innocent narrative, he speaks to the entire world and creates meaning. As a social being, he observes how objects are placed in reality and the way they function; then he writes their history. It is the practice of the folk mystic to narrate the history of objects by observing their particular functions.

I am not presenting an absolute theory here. Therefore, my observations are not simplifications and generalisations. By taking into account the subtle design of this particular kavya, the *Manteswamy Kavya*, I am putting forward a proposition which, I believe, is applicable to several other folk mystic narratives of this kind – because the folk itself is a creation of a specific universal archetype. In fact, the hallmark of the folk is that it is not an individualistic achievement. The characteristics and methods of folk mystic narratives I am discussing here also apply to *Male Madeshwara Kavya* and Kadugolla's *Junjappana Kavya*.[124]

---

[124] *Male Madeshwara Kavya:* Along with the *Manteswamy Kavya*, this is one of the two most popular oral epics sung and performed by subaltern com-

At the thematic level, the *Manteswamy Kavya* and the *Shunyasampadanes* share a striking similarity after the figure of Allama ascends the shunya throne in the *Shunyasampadanes* or the seat of fire in the *Manteswamy Kavya*. Both narratives handle the theme of sharana or jangama protests at different philosophical, emotional, and metaphoric levels. For both, religious crises are primary concerns. But the destinations of their journeys are different. The *Shunyasampadanes* set out with spiritual satisfaction and optimism, and eventually face the fear of a religious crisis. On the other hand the *Manteswamy Kavya* begins with scepticism and perplexity, and inevitably confronts the crisis. In this respect, the folk narrative is more prepared emotionally and intellectually to face the crisis. While, like Allama, the *Manteswamy Kavya* behaves courageously and paradoxically, the *Shunyasampadanes* reveal above all Basavanna's heart-touching emotion, pain, and sentimentality.

III: The Protest of the Jangamas

As we learn in Shivaganaprasadi's *Shunyasampadane*, 96,000 jangamas were agitated and expressed their rage by beating gongs.[125] This is how he describes the enraged jangamas:

---

munities in the Mysore region of South Karnataka. It narrates the wandering life of Madeshwara, a fifteenth-century saint from a downtrodden community, who founded his own cult. The Kannada word "male" means hill, and today the Male Madeshwara temple is a pilgrim centre located on a hillside of Chamarajanagara District, near Mysore. The performers of this epic are called kamsaleyavaru (those who use big bronze cymbals while singing the epic) or guddaru (children of God). There are various versions of the epic, documented by modern scholars. For an English translation, see Prasad, *Male Madeshwara. Junjappana Kavya:* a folk epic based on the life of Junjappa, who belonged to the community of nomadic herdsmen called kadugollas (cowherds of the forest) and founded a cult of kadugollas, mainly to be found in the Sira, Hiriyuru, and Challakere regions of South Karnataka. For an English translation of excerpts, see Ramachandran, ed., "Junjappa", pp. 83–121.

[125] In this section, Nagaraj is referring to an episode in the *Shunyasampadanes*, where Allama returns to Kalyana after twelve years of wandering. In the

Those with pebbly eyes couldn't stand those with flower-like eyes. Those with bald heads couldn't stand those who wore a bun of hair.[126] But could the group of jangamas who went out remain quiet? They reacted to the scene: "Basavanna made a sorcerer sit [on the shunya throne] / As though he were Prabhu himself / Calling him the pranalinga, / But he never cared to look at us! / What greatness did he find in him? / What vice did he find in us? / He let the bronze go, and clung to mud tiles! / One is worthless, / and Basava, the other, is a renegade. / Both of them do not deserve / The mortal and immortal worlds."[127]

Allama, for the first time, expresses his opinion about the crowd at Kalyana.

This is a mere horde of bodies,
gathered here just for food.
How could they know the truth of linga?
Living for the body and fretting over it,
how could they know the message of God?
They talk like drunken ascetics.
Guheshwara, how could they know your sharana?[128]

From its start, the *Manteswamy Kavya* adopts the same stance as expressed in the above-mentioned lines. But the composers of the *Shunyasampadanes* cannot be as harsh towards the jangamas; nor do they wholly believe that the jangamas are wrong. On the other hand the folk mystic, who is a sceptic from the start, is excited.

It is difficult either for the *Shunyasampadanes*, which believe

---

meanwhile, Basavanna has prepared the shunya throne for him. When Allama returns to Kalyana, he comes in disguise and ascends the shunya throne. Basavanna recognises him and worships at his feet. On the other side, several jangamas are waiting for food in the dasoha mantapa – the hall where holy food is served. These jangamas are enraged at Basavanna; they think that instead of paying attention to them in dasoha, Basavanna is attending a sorcerer (Allama in disguise appears as a sorcerer to others, but not to Basavanna). See "Introduction to the Sampadane of Prabhudeva's Tour and Return", in Gooluru Siddaveeranna, *Shunyasampadane*, vol. 5, pp. 1–5 and pp. 75–103.

[126] Shivaganaprasadi, *Shivaganaprasadi Mahadevayyana*, p. 283.

[127] Ibid.

[128] Ibid.

in the power of symbols for institutionally organising religion, or for Basavanna to accept Allama's opposition to the jangamas. When the jangamas leave Basavanna's premises angrily, Basavanna declares that the parting of the sharanas (jangamas) is no less than the parting of his life. Allama uses all his spiritual logic to console Basavanna. Since the folk mystic does not feel the need to institutionalise religion, he has the imaginative liberty to treat the reaction of jangamas very lightly. So he merely reports the hordes of jangamas – who were waiting for food – leaving the city of Kalyana when they witnessed Basavanna carrying flesh and Neelamma bringing a toddy pot.

In the *Shunyasampadanes*, two kinds of sharana dispersion are at work. First, there is the jangamas protest against Allama ascending the shunya throne. The second comes near the end of the text, when all the sharanas leave Kalyana after its fall. This can be compared with the great expedition we come across in the *Mahabharata*. The first one represents dubious shunya, the second one is a melancholic shunya – a void in history. This episode of historical shunya, a worrying and sorrowful event, is somehow absent from the narrative of the folk mystic. Since the folk mystic places Manteswamy/Allama beyond the domain of history, perhaps he feels no fear about everything that could happen in history disappearing from our memory.

Manteswamy/Allama takes Basavanna to the jangama crowd, saying he will show its true nature. The folk narrative imagination displays its candid interpretation of the soulless samashti (the jangama community). The truth-seeking journey through self-criticism has lent a particular ethical base to this narrative. Manteswamy/Allama shows shunya – the void in the history of the samashti samaya (the community's religious order), to which Basavanna is committed. In the *Shunyasampadanes*, on the other hand, Allama views the rebellion of jangamas as nothing but Shiva's playfulness: "The sport is yours, / The mirth, yours, / The drum and the flute, all yours; to this / I answer neither yes nor no."[129] Further, says Allama, "Does the appetite, even as it leaps upon the earth, consult the living things?"[130]

[129] Ibid., p. 289.
[130] Ibid.

In the *Shunyasampadanes* the false jangamas revolt because their appetite is not satisfied. In the folk narrative Guru (Manteswamy/Allama) himself indulges in sport and playfulness. Like a shaking leaf on a banyan tree, the great Guru comes hobbling in the guise of a 100-year-old jangama to these false jangamas who are addressed by him ironically as satyasaranu matmas – the colloquial form of Mahatma – (truth-seeking great ones).[131] The rebels answer his enquiry about why they left the city of Kalyana: "We should not become those who ignore caste practices."[132]

For those who oppose Basavanna, the question of purity and impurity is the ultimate truth. The varnashrama system of the Vedic religion is organised on the principle of purity–impurity. As the jangamas in the *Manteswamy Kavya* are anxious to learn how to become pure again,[133] Manteswamy/Allama sarcastically replies that they each need to take out their guts and purify them.[134]

The folk narrator here exhibits the height of his talent. Manteswamy/Allama says, "Before taking out the guts and purifying them, take out your linga and drop it in the water."[135] Manteswamy/Allama suggests that by protesting against Basavanna they have proved themselves spiritually unworthy of wearing the linga. Addressing the lingas dropped into the water by the sharanas, he says, "You lingas, go to the whirlpool at Malangi." Following this command, the lingas go into the whirlpool at Malangi, near Talakadu (a town in present-day Mandya District in South Karnataka). Then he addresses the jangamas: "Rip open your chest, take a bath, and purify yourselves." One jangama tears open his chest with his fingers and dies instantly. The rest are rendered fearful: they no longer wish to

---

[131] Boralingaiah, *Manteswamy*, p. 148.

[132] Ibid., p. 150.

[133] In the *Manteswamy Kavya*, the sharanas who are referred to as jangamas in the *Shunyasampadanes* think that they have been polluted by having food served by Basavanna and Neelamma because they had carried flesh and arrack. See ibid., pp. 149–50.

[134] Ibid., p. 151.

[135] Ibid.

disembowel themselves, and so leave the city of Kalyana.[136] Manteswamy/Allama would have been pleased with this dispersal of the crowd. Here his mischief goes beyond the realm of humaneness.

When the sharanas tell Basavanna they no longer want to stay in Kalyana, he listens to them carefully. They say they wish to continue to live as lingawantas – wearers of the linga. Therefore they request that none other than Basavanna retrieve their lingas from the water. Basavanna replies that these lingas will come back at their call, having been dropped in the water by them.[137]

Then, how come lingas in Talakadu
appear in the pond at Kalyana?
They wander about calling,
O linga, come, please come,
and yet they do not appear.
Then, the great one on the earth [Manteswamy/Allama] says,
O sharanas
If standing on this bank you call,
the lingas definitely will not turn up.
If your eyes
can catch hold of them,
O you great sharanas,
you should take out of the water
from this pond in Kalyana and blow it out.
When the entire water is blown out.
you will get the lingas lying here (Come, O Channa).[138]

The folk mystic's narrative proceeds further by amalgamating realistic and symbolic modes. I am reminded of a distinction made between symbol and allegory by Goethe, whose religious consciousness is dense. I am going to use this distinction further in my interpretation of the *Shunyasampadanes* and the *Manteswamy Kavya*. According to Goethe, "Symbolism transforms the pheno-

---

[136] Ibid., pp. 151–2.
[137] Ibid., pp. 155–6.
[138] Ibid., pp. 156–7.

menon into an idea, the idea into an image, in such a way that in
the image the idea still remains unattainable and forever effective,
and, though it is expressed in all languages, yet remains inexpress-
ible." On the other hand, "Allegory transforms the phenomenon
into a concept, the concept into an image; but in such a way that in
the image the concept may ever be preserved, circumscribed and
complete, at hand and expressible."[139] Hence, this concept, being
always subject to a specific interpretation, is accessible to our comprehension.

The *Shunyasampadanes* and the *Manteswamy Kavya* have perfected their forms by evolving in the allegorical and metaphorical
modes, respectively. Since the *Shunyasampadanes* transformed the
phenomenon into a concept and the concept into an image, we certainly require a particular knowledge system in order to understand
that concept. Elements of bedagu and the tantric register are interwoven organically in the structure of the *Shunyasampadanes*. It
would be different if one perceived them merely as a story. But in
that case only the external form of the events would be accessible.
So reading them merely as stories is as limited as reading the Bible
or the Quran as merely factual accounts.

Since the way the concept is developed in the classical knowledge
system is not expected of the folk narrative, it evolves in the composite mode of realistic and symbolic narratives. Here, from the
point of view of the story, it is quite possible to have references to
linga, water, and the search for linga in the narrative. In fact, there
is a thought, an idea behind such references. Here, the idea revolves
around rot in religions and the required purification. This idea
would occur even to those who do not have special classical training.
Further, the folk mystic narrator does not expect to command more
power and esteem than a commoner. Such an expectation would
become, to use Allama's vocabulary, the hubris of knowledge. (This
hubris of knowledge is one among the eight elements in eight-fold
pride.) As the water is emptied in the temple tank, the idea behind

---

[139] Quoted in Luperini, "Symbol and Allegory", pp. 91–2.

this image becomes active and illuminates multiple meanings to the reader. Manteswamy/Allama himself continues the metaphoric utterance and addresses Basavanna:

Basavanna,
for twelve years
this tank putrefied.
Today, after all this
water went out.

Tomorrow, O child
good water will flow here // Come, O Channa //

Oh Basavanna,
good water certainly will flow here.
Ayya, don't worry
In your mind. // Come, O Channa //[140]

The lines above suggest that just as the rotting of religion is quite natural, the will to purify it is inevitable. Since this narrative is developed by making Allama incarnate in Manteswamy, it takes everything towards an extreme. An enchanting narrative has to simultaneously evolve in different directions. The folk mystic narrator cannot merely stop at the episode of sharanas who have dropped lingas into water. He means much more than that.

Again, a commentary on the nature of the linga begins in the metaphoric mode. Is the linga a stone? First, we should examine what Allama himself has to say about this question in his vachanas, and then we may compare it with what is said in the narrative. One of Allama's philosophical concerns is the examination of the notion of the linga.

1. The stone born to the earth, the idol born to a mason
    became linga after uttering a mantra!
    O Guheshwara,
    What shall I call those utter renegades,
    who worship the child born of these three, as linga? (209)

---

[140] Boralingaiah, *Manteswamy*, p. 157.

2. I thought jangama was great.
    He lost greatness by begging for alms.
    I thought linga was great.
    It lost greatness being shaped by a mason. (480)

Overall, the decisive conclusion in Allama's vachanas is that the stone is not the linga. Allama is not swayed by the crowd taking the stone to be the linga. As discussed earlier, this is one of the great debates the *Shunyasampadanes* have explored. However, it was inevitable for the *Shunyasampadanes* to synthesise the two strong arguments.[141] The linga is like a border, a boundary stone separating the composers of the *Shunyasampadanes* into liberals and ardent loyalists.

But the folk mystic is a storyteller, standing in the margins beyond the border. Therefore, his narrative employs irony, inherited from Allama, while describing those hurriedly searching for the linga. These hollow men finally carried away a stone, mistaking it for a linga, after desperately searching for it in the temple tank.

> Ayya, mistaking the stone for linga, they carried it,
> and they left the temple tank. // Come, O Channa //
> Look, great sharanas who found the stone,
> mistook the stone for linga.
> Those who got a stone in the corner went away carrying it,
> thinking it was linga.[142]

The *Manteswamy Kavya* relates that those lingawantas to whose palms their respective caskets of linga would return stayed back in primordial Kalyana. Without rejecting the notion of ishtalinga, the *Manteswamy Kavya* protects its sanctity by placing it in an actual socio-spiritual context. All those sharanas who remained at primordial Kalyana are listed along with their caste denominations. Honnappa of Holeyas (pariahs), Chennaiah of Madigas (pariahs), Machaiah of Madiwalas (washermen), Dasappa of Ganigas (oilmen), Chaudaiah

---

[141] One argument believes in linga as a concrete object and the other (Allama's) does not.

[142] Boralingaiah, *Manteswamy*, p. 159.

of Ambigas (fishermen), Kyatappa of Idigas (toddy makers), Biraiah of Turukara (herdsmen), Appanna of Hadapada (betel-leaf carrier), and Biraiah of Kurabas (shepherds) all continued to stay at Kalyana with Basavanna. They are all Shudras among Shudras.

Receiving the linga in a higher sense is also a theme in the *Shunyasampadanes*. The way sharanas become contented and happy here is quite different from the way they become so in the *Manteswamy Kavya*. But before this contentment, there is intense disputation. Soddala Bacharasa remarks: "Then, is it possible to catch hold of the thing which is lost to the grip?"[143] In the *Shunyasampadanes*, thus, the community of sharanas is not mobilised; instead, a harmony is established. Even though Soddala Bacharasa says, "The broken pearl is no good for currency,"[144] there is finally unity and harmony. It is an unexpected coincidence that Shivaganaprasadi also employs the image of a coin or currency. The ore wants to go back to the mountains.[145] On the other hand, the coin persists in belonging to history. Religion requires limits as well as limitlessness.

IV: The Process of Community Formation

Finally, the interconnections of Allama's vachanas with folk and classical narratives can be discussed in the context of community formation, which is an important theme in the contemporary social sciences.[146] Allama's vachanas do not provide the basis for the formation of a social community. His vachanas can be used as an auxiliary, either as ideals or as metaphors, but not as a fundamental "law".

---

[143] Shivaganaprasadi, *Shivaganaprasadi Mahadevayyana*, p. 307. Soddala Bacharasa: one of the sharanas, whose work was to maintain the accounts of distributing grains in the court of King Bijjala.

[144] Ibid., p. 307.

[145] Note the earlier reference to Rilke's poem on the gold coin.

[146] For the question of how communities are formed in the context of the Virashaiva/Lingayat community, see Shobhi, "Pre-modern Communities and Modern Histories", quoted in Ben-Herut, *Siva's Saints*.

At this stage, the notion of law developed by the influential French thinker Emmanuel Levinas, who thought deeply about religion, is helpful.[147] Without the concept of "law", communities cannot be formed. Especially in Semitic religions, the birth of the shruti (revelation/gospel) simultaneously brings forth the notion of law. This law is a set of rules for the everyday life of a community. In fact, the law is nothing but the rules that bind everyday life with divinity. This kind of law in Hinduism or Vedic religion is understood as the knowledge of shastra. In highly diverse societies, the transgression of laws leads to the creation and establishment of counter-laws. To put it clearly, for the formation of a community in Christianity, Islam, or Judaism the idea of revelation and the idea of the law go hand in hand. From this point of view it is possible for sects of the Vedic religion in India to have the above-mentioned institutional vision. Veda is shruti (what is heard, revelation) and apaurusheya (not created by man), which can be called the "revealed word". The knowledge collective which supports varnashrama gains its legitimacy from the apaurusheya authority of the Vedas. In the case of India, the political commitment and the will to organise, which characterise Christianity, Islam, and Judaism, can be found substantively only in Vedic religions.

In this context, we can say that the fundamental philosophy we come across in Allama's vachanas is the denial of the social community. For him, the notions of spiritual intimacy and mystic associations are endearing. But an extraordinary organising project is required to transform the idea of mystic association into a community that respects and follows the laws which guide its social life. And beyond a point this adventurous project will undoubtedly damage, at least to some extent, the essence of Allama's philosophy.

Even if we consider the historical pressures of the twelfth century, it is impossible to use Allama's vachanas as archives of laws or ordinances. Also, it would be a misadventure to reconstruct Allama as one formulating a proposition of counter-laws against the then pre-

---

[147] See Stone, *Levinas, Ethics and Law.*

vailing laws. In fact, such openness and multiplicity are to be found at the very root of Virashaivism, which may be discerned even today. From this point of view it is possible to see the sentiment about the "community will" only in Chennabasavanna.[148] Basavanna, who stands between the two poles,[149] takes the middle path, while Allama can at most provide the spiritual strength needed for the formation of a religious community. With only spiritual strength as help, it is possible to create individual paths of seeking, not a religion with a vast social base.

The information supplied by the *Shunyasampadanes* to understand the process of community formation and community will, in the context of medieval Karnataka, be useful for understanding by comparison a similar process at the global level. The *Shunyasampadanes* provide the necessary information to study the problems involved in implementing the "community will" in those religions which are not directed by the "revealed word".

Emmanuel Levinas and Paul Ricoeur have discussed the way internal forms of the revealed word of sacred texts shape community formation. They have used the texts of Christianity and Judaism as source materials for their discussions. Though there are limitations to their methods, we can use them comparatively to identify differences in the process of community formation between religions based on the revealed word and those that are not.

In this respect, there are two phases or zones to the internal development of the *Shunyasampadanes*. We can discuss Shivaganaprasadi's *Shunyasampadane* as representative of one phase and Gummalapurada Siddhalingadevara as that of another. In Shivaganaprasadi, we have only the prehistory of the community and its principles. In addition to these we have one more element in Siddha-

---

[148] In Kannada, Nagaraj uses the word kulasankalpa, which is the will to form a community that respects and follows the laws which guide its social life.

[149] On one side there is Chennabasavanna, who is for a law-laden community; on the other is Allama, standing for a mystic association that is not overladen with law.

lingadevara – the manual of rituals and precepts. Siddharamayya's initiation ritual which we discussed earlier can serve as a fine example of this third element of rituals and precepts. Compared to the Old Testament of the Bible, both the phases of the *Shunyasampadanes* fall short of two fundamental aspects: one, apaurusheya shruti (revealed word), and second, the word of the prophet. The problems that occur when these two aspects are absent in the process of community formation have been faced by Virashaivism throughout its existence.

We can briefly discuss a couple of such problems here. The first problem concerns the historical origin of religions. Religions, which believe that their existence is beyond history and depends upon the law-laden ahistorical shruti, consider traditions that have particular historical origins as dissenting branches.[150] We can say that the way in which different branches of Vedic religion have looked upon Virashaivism as a dissenting branch represents nothing but their commentary on the historical origin of dissenting belief systems. Many scholars, notably Chidanandamurthy, who has carried out useful research into Virashaivism, considers Virashaivism as an integral part of Hinduism.[151]

The second problem is the absence of the prophet's word, which raises the question of the inevitable centralisation of religious power. Howsoever sacred the position given to Allama by the *Shunyasampadanes*, the power of prophethood is not assigned to that position. Given the concept of prophethood, there would be no question of challenging it, nor any possibility of the prophet's self-criticism. Thus, two aspects – the revealed word and the prophet's word –

---

[150] What Nagaraj seems to suggest here is that the Vedic traditions, which believe themselves to be beyond history, have considered other traditions that have historical origins, such as Virashaivism, merely as dissenting branches of their own tradition.

[151] M. Chidanandamurthy has often developed this argument in his writings. For example, in 1996 he gave a speech on this issue at the Fourth All India Sharana Sahitya Conference, which is included in his book, *Hindu: Veerashaiva (Lingayat)*. See Chidanandamurthy, *Hindu*.

that characterise the sacred texts are absent in the *Shunyasampa-danes*, and this in fact is responsible for the openness of Virashaivism. Thus, the self-critique of Virashaivism would be possible only from foundational values, not from the point of view of the sacred text. It is important to note the difference between values and sacred texts. In this respect, Gummalapurada Siddhalingadevara's interpretation of the *Shunyasampadane* is worth quoting here:

> This is the philosophy of the supreme guru, supreme Virashaivism.
> This is the firm establisher of Virashaiva practices.
> This is the crown-jewel of the divine Vedanta.
> This is the chief mirror to all shastras.
> This is the teaching of the highest divine experience and
>   supreme knowledge.
> This is the compilation of those who are well versed in religious practice,
> and attained great heights.[152]

The above lines are an intense expression of the will to produce textual communities. But the vachanas on which they are based are themselves detrimental to this kind of will. The more boundaries we create, the more bypasses and shortcuts will appear. Likewise, as limits are imposed to create a textual community, new ways out also are created, and thus the vachanas outgrow the *Shunyasam-padanes*.[153] In this respect, the power of the vachana collective to control the community is enormous. Against this backdrop, it is interesting to note that the folk mystic does not have the will to create a textual community, nor has the will to produce a doctrine or philosophical system. However great the artistic value of the *Man-teswamy Kavya*, it does not birth a textual community.

---

[152] Gummalapurada, *Gummalapurada Siddhalingadevara*, p. 510.

[153] Scholars like Rahamath Tarikere show the gap between the arrangement of vachanas and the flow of narrative in the *Shunyasampadanes*, arguing that the philosophical aspiration of vachanas is different from that of the narrative in the *Shunyasampadanes*. See Tarikere, "*Shunyasampadane* mattu".

6

———

Practical Criticism of Allama's Vachanas

Themes, Images, and Metaphors

I: Caste Defilement

When an upper-caste man goes and builds
his house in the neighbourhood of outcastes,
look, his virtue is not tainted!
When the people of his caste refuse to see his face,
the virtuous outcastes hold his hand.
O Guheshwara!
When it was deemed that he became an outcaste,
the taint of the outcaste disappeared. (50)

THERE ARE RELATIVELY few vachanas in which Allama refers directly to caste. While dealing with social reality in them he, as usual, uses the metaphoric mode instead of critique. Contrastively, Basavanna's vachanas stand out as a model for the mode of critique. The vachana above is one of Allama's rare compositions offering a social critique in the metaphoric mode.[1]

[1] Though Nagaraj here uses the word "pratime" in Kannada, the translation of which is "image", what he means in a broad sense is "metaphor". At times, he uses these two senses of pratime interchangeably. Therefore, I use the term metaphor throughout unless it is clearly used to mean image in the context. This is corroborated when Nagaraj, in his Afterword to *Kathakosha*, says that he uses the term metaphor (rupaka) to mean any literary technique, such as the use of images. See Nagaraj, "Hinnudi", p. 85.

304

The philosophical outlook that lies behind this vachana (50) may be described as a method of "turning reality upside down". This outlook is not unique to Allama, we see it in the bedagu compositions of other vachanakaras as well. The main feature of this format is to reverse the symbolic significance of values widely accepted as normal. For example, the Brahmin who normally symbolises superiority becomes, in bedagu compositions, a symbol of wickedness and sin. In Madhuvarasa's vachana, "People of the village went hunting and killed a haruva (Brahmin)," the haruva being a symbol of negative force.[2] Likewise, holeya (outcaste male) and holati (outcaste female) symbolise positive forces. This kind of metaphoric reversal is distinct from the philosophical ideals of Bhakti kavya. Though Vedic Bhakti sects generally try to reform Brahmanism, they accept its core principles. So the issue of untouchability within the Brahmanical structure continues to exist perennially. These Bhakti streams lay heavy stress on the moral transformation of Brahmanism but do not bother to critique its stand on social realities.

In the first line of the vachana (50) quoted above, Allama neither speaks like a follower of the Bhakti sects nor follows Madhuvarasa's method of completely turning reality upside down. However, the reversal method is visible in the next line when Allama says, "The virtuous outcastes hold his hand." Here, outcastes rather than Brahmans are virtuous.[3] Nevertheless, even in this reversal method there is a risk — the risk of accepting its meaning as the ultimate truth; it might be over-romanticised. It is quite natural for radical composi-

---

[2] Madhuvarasa, whose signature line is Arkeshwaralinga, is also known as Madhuvayya. He was a Brahmin who held an administrative position in the court of the Kalachuri king Bijjala II, and became a sharana under the influence of Basavanna. For the full vachana, see vachana no. 808 in Kalburgi, ed., *Sankeerna Vachana Samputa: Mooru*.

[3] Nagaraj is saying here that some vachanakaras, such as Madhuvarasa, turn social reality upside down in their compositions, reversing the social norms accepted in day-to-day life. Likewise, Allama in this vachana overturns social reality by elevating outcastes. Nagaraj demonstrates Allama's attempt to lay emphasis on the act of compassion by which outcastes are shown to possess virtues attributed more usually to the high-born.

tions like Madhuvarasa's vachanas to romanticise the meaning that traditionalists abhor.

Allama's uniqueness lies in bringing face-to-face the stances of traditionalists with revolutionary romanticism of the Madhuvarasa kind.[4] He is fully aware that an anti-caste spirit is fundamental to the Vachana movement and conveys agreement with it, but he does not romanticise his anti-caste stance; he resists it as much as he resists the stance of the traditionalists. It is true that this kind of romanticisation by way of reversing social values does occur in a few stray bedagu vachanas. But this intellectual format of reversing values finds its fullest articulation in folk Shaiva narratives like the *Manteswamy Kavya*. As discussed in the previous chapter, the toddy pot, dead cattle, etc. are traditionally taboo for the upper castes, and for untouchables the symbols of humiliation. But in one episode in the *Manteswamy Kavya* Basavanna accepts and embraces these symbols. Thus, in transforming a symbol of humiliation into one of self-respect lies the triumph of the rebellious spirit embedded in dissenting texts or traditions like the *Manteswamy Kavya*.

However, beyond a point Allama rejects the format of reversing values. While in Madhuvarasa's scheme an upper-caste individual entering an outcaste neighbourhood means he, the high-born, has gained spiritual mastery, in Allama it is a different thing altogether. He takes a position suggesting that "the taint of the outcaste disappeared." He does not romanticise the positive connotation of being an outcaste either. Without romanticising this idea, Allama asserts that we ought to go beyond the binary of upper caste and outcaste.

II: History as a Prophecy of Creation

Does one become a bhakta by tying a linga?
Does one become a traitor if he knocks down the linga?
Is it in one's hand to tie it?
Can it fall when one knocks it down?

[4] Note the distinction Nagaraj makes in the previous paragraphs between the traditionalists of Bhakti streams and revolutionary radicals like Madhuvarasa who turn social reality upside down. Further, Nagaraj cautions readers about romanticising this reversal, a tendency commonly seen in radicals.

Can the world survive if the linga falls down?
Can prana (life-force) last, when pranalinga is lost?
Sutaka (defilement) it is, an illusion it is, to utter, "the linga fell down."
One should not hear it.
Epochs pass into history, not the linga.
"The linga fell down" are the sinful words of a traitor,
O Guheshwara, I can't hear it any more. (1004)

It is not difficult to analyse this vachana in the context of contemporary Indian history; indeed it would be worthwhile to do so. The spiritual message of this vachana becomes refreshingly relevant against the backdrop of the Babri Masjid/Ramjanmabhumi controversy.[5]

Moreover, this vachana presents an important problem that troubled Allama, and which is still relevant. The falling of a linga is a significant event in many of Allama's vachanas. The above-cited vachana (1004) and others related to it are concerned with the interconnection of spiritual experience, religious symbols, and violence in history. Allama presents a unique philosophy of history which is embedded subtly but widely across the expanse of his vachanas. In simple terms, he does not approve of what is called "history". According to him, history is a truth neither beneficial nor fundamental. Here, linga is a symbol of religious experience and ethnic community. Symbol-centric violence was widespread in medieval India, with brutal conflicts amongst the different religious sects comprising what is now called "Hinduism". Religious disagreements between Jainas and Shaivas led to bloodshed. Shaivas and Vaishnavas slaughtered each other. Narratives of such massacres are amply documented in medieval literature and inscriptions. These violent

[5] A site in Ayodhya, Uttar Pradesh, was claimed as the birthplace of Lord Rama by many Hindu organisations. A masjid had been built on the site during the Mughal era. On 6 December 1992, the Vishwa Hindu Parishad and allied organisations demolished the masjid and placed the idol of Rama within it. After a lengthy judicial battle, on 9 November 2019 the Supreme Court of India ruled in favour of handing over the disputed land to the Hindus. A Rama temple now stands on the site. The falling linga reminds Nagaraj of the falling of the masjid and the aftermath of violence centred on religious symbols.

events are usually related to either the erection or the demolition of
a religious symbol. Some accounts mention Islamic violence too.
In contrast, the Virashaiva literature of Allama's time hardly documents such religious violence.

The semiotics of Allama's Advayavada (non-dualism) rejects the
notion of "history". In this philosophy, the divine symbol does not
exist separately in the universe. When the entire universe is a manifestation of Shiva, the destruction of one of its minuscule symbols
does not demolish its primordial power. According to Allama, wearing a linga – or to put it in institutional terms building a temple –
becomes the root cause of human arrogance. Allama rejects the mu-
tually conflicting categories of devotee and traitor. The term linga is
applicable to the linga in the temple and also to the linga worn on
the body.

The line, "Can the world survive if the linga falls down?" is the
pinnacle of Allama's philosophy. In this context, the linga is viewed
as all of Creation and its fall represents apocalypse. Allama here
objects to acts of violence that stem from the identity politics of
religious symbols. History shows a series of such constructions and
demolitions of religious symbols. In the next line Allama calls this
viewpoint an "illusion". In such compositions Allama presents a philosophy of history that we moderns cannot access or easily comprehend. However, another of his vachanas is somewhat helpful towards an understanding of this enigmatic philosophy.

> Picking a kani (stone) on this creation,
> and placing it on the palm of the eight-fold body,
> they say, "Tie it around the neck and worship."
> Born of earth, it became a stone,
> found form in the hands of a mason,
> became an idol in the hands of a Guru.
> How shall I worship such a bastard born for three?
> The one who says he would die if the linga falls down,
> He will go to the arch-hell
> reserved for heinous crimes
> when he dies by weapon, water, in the jungle or sky.
> If the linga on the palm falls down,

does the linga in the mind fall too?
Saying this, one should pick the linga
and offer the sixteen-fold worship.
Only Chennabasavanna knows the way of
tying the linga and reaching the linga,
not the ones who claim attaining divinity
by pouring holy water as a habit, O Guheshwara. (1009)

(There is, again, a reference to picking a stone from this earth in another vachana: 217.[6])

As I read the vachanas on the theme of the falling linga, I cannot resist making a historical guess. In my reading the subtext of these vachanas appears to be a commentary on a trauma experienced by the twelfth-century Vachana movement. Allama is described as a trikalajnani – aware of past, present, and future – so his imagination has the potential to anticipate the future. The suggestive tone in his vachanas is a result of this potential.[7] There is also a reference to Chennabasavanna in the above-quoted vachana (1009): "Only Chennabasavanna knows the way of / Tying the linga and reaching the linga, / Not the ones who claim attaining divinity / By pouring holy water as a habit, O Guheshwara." These lines arouse curiosity. Likewise, another vachana says, "because the ancients passed away, they too die for nothing. Is dying like that a right thing, O Guheshwara?" (1010).[8] One might strongly suspect that these vachanas refer to specific historical events. Quite obviously we can hypothesise that Basavanna's self-sacrifice and the events around it have cast their shadow on these compositions.[9] Although Allama's vachanas

---

[6] For English translations of this vachana, see vachana no. 217 in Allama Prabhu, *Lord of the Cave*, and Allama Prabhu, *Vachanas of Allama Prabhu*.

[7] What Nagaraj means here is that Allama as a trikalajnani anticipated the tragic end of the twelfth-century Vachana movement in these Vachanas, as a result of which they can be read as a commentary on the tragedy of the movement.

[8] For English translations, see vachana no. 1040 in Allama Prabhu, *Lord of the Cave*, and vachana no. 845 in Allama Prabhu, *Vachanas of Allama Prabhu*.

[9] After the fall of the city of Kalyana, the sharanas scattered and in the historical imagination Basavanna jumped into the river at Kudalasangama.

are abundantly filled with death, violence, hunting, and so on, these experiences do not feature in any specific historical framework. Therefore, the question here is whether Allama continued to live in Kalyana even after the massacre.[10] If not, was there an attempt among the Virashaivas to think about the history of their own community along the lines of Allama's imaginative model? As we do not have information to enable further discussion in the historical mode, we will stop this hypothetical thinking and return to the discussion of Allama's vision of history.

In the context of the above vachana (1009), what does the line "Picking a kani (stone) on this creation" convey?[11] If one were to tease out a single strain from the complex logic of this vachana, one could assert that Allama considers the narrative called history nothing but a prophecy on creation. The idea that creation is a perennial reality and a manifestation of Shiva pervades many of Allama's vachanas. If history is merely a narrative of actions occurring in the course of this creation, it cannot be anything more than a prophecy. Therefore, the knowledge system called history is as absurd as prophesying creation. Its facticity exists only at a symbolic level. It is difficult to interpret Allama's philosophy – which considers both worshipping "the prophecy on creation" (history) and worshipping the linga (a religious symbol made from stone) as one and the same. But let me be pertinacious and even foolhardy in my pertinacity. According to Allama, "linga is not susceptible to action" (1007).[12] But the illusion which believes that linga is susceptible to action – falling – leads to a series of events or actions, such as religious violence. Thus, historical events which are created for religious symbolism are a result of illusions.

---

[10] According to several accounts/chronicles, the Sharana movement in Kalyana was very short-lived. After the massacre in Kalyana, the sharanas left the city and were dispersed.

[11] The word "kani" in Kannada means both a stone and prophesying.

[12] For translations of the full vachana, see vachana no. 1132 in Allama Prabhu, *Lord of the Cave*, and vachana no. 1349 in Allama Prabhu, *Vachanas of Allama Prabhu*.

Often, it is Allama's contemporaries who provide the occasion for his analysis of history. This philosophical debate around the linga, its creation and destruction, begins to levitate in the *Shunya-sampadanes*. As expected, Siddharamayya emerges as a representative of this dreadful enterprise – the business of building and breaking the linga.[13] He begins to appear to Allama as an archetype of building linga and temples which he critiques in the vachanas I have earlier analysed. Allama considers these thoughts and acts of building and breaking forms of human arrogance. In one of his vachanas he mocks Siddharamayya's pride in building temples and asks him to place the linga in his heart, not in a temple.[14] By this assertion Allama unsettles premises, such as the construction of temples, in which Siddharamayya has believed all along. Elsewhere, his advice is straightforward: "O Siddharamayya, / sever the links with past and future, / and bind yourself fast to Guheshwaralinga" (1027).[15] For Allama, history represents a dialogue between past and future. He calls it a prophecy on creation and opposes philosophical approaches that accord it the status of worship. In his vachanas Allama repeatedly mentions the tragedy of religions which are presumed to look beyond history yet come to be trapped within it.

History is the story of both past and future. To put it in Allama's words, it is the story of birth and demise. On several occasions he equates historical creation with external worship in a religion. The following vachana (1157) is an excellent example of Allama's critique on the limitations of history. While history deals with birth and demise, creation lies beyond these. Therefore, the act of worshipping them through history becomes irrelevant:

[13] In the *Shunyasampadane*, Siddharamayya is revered by his people for building temples, lakes, and his devotion to the linga. Allama breaks his pride by showing that the physical linga is insignificant for the path of a true sharana. See Shivaganaprasadi, *Shivaganaprasadi Mahadevayyana*, pp. 104–33.

[14] See vachana no. 1044 in Allama Prabhu, *Lord of the Cave*, and vachana no. 992 in Allama Prabhu, *Vachanas of Allama*.

[15] For translations of the full vachana, see vachana no. 1135 in Allama Prabhu, *Lord of the Cave*, and vachana no. 1213 in Allama Prabhu, *Vachanas of Allama*.

In the mansion of bayalu, open space,
I saw a child that was beyond birth and demise.
When I worshipped it by touching,
the child swallowed me whole.
I could not touch it, nor could I see it,
no bindings for its worship.
Then, Guheshwara is bayalu, open space. (1157)

Here, bayalu, an open space (the void) corresponds to the Advaitin idea of Brahma as well as the Buddhist idea of shunya (the void). Numerous mystic streams were born in medieval India through the intermingling of Vedanti Advaita and Buddhist Mahayana paths. Allama's philosophical world was also shaped by one such confluence. The notion of kaya (the body) in Allama and the kaya of the Mahayanis are related. Thus, in order to point out the various sources from which Allama obtains his philosophical apparatus, one needs a deep understanding of several darshanas and shastras. But Allama builds his own path by assimilating these sources in his own unique way. In this assimilation, how much is the poet's own and how much belongs to the path of the Virashaiva tradition? This is a pressing question.

III: God is Dead

The creator of the worlds, Aja's horns broken.
Descended down to the ground the sun and the moon.
If the dawn stands, dusk creeps in.
The village burnt, leaving silence behind.
What a miracle!
The God is dead, the Goddess ruined,
and I survived, O Guheshwara. (539)

The death of God is an important theme in Allama. Vachanas dealing with this theme are numerically few, but in their exploration of an experience they are unique, especially in Kannada. Not even in the Upanishads is there any scope for exploring this kind of experience.

While speaking of the experience of shunya or bayalu, Allama does not employ the pleasant images that are common in Indian religious cultures. Instead, he creates a violent milieu through his imagery. By describing an ambience of primitive catastrophe, war, hunting, and violence, he suggests a contradictory state of affairs. The vachana (539) we are discussing now operates in paradoxes. The experience of the narrator's life, i.e. his survival, appears only in the final line of this vachana. This is a statement of spiritual awakening. In the rest of the lines there is a portrayal of death, destruction, and upheaval.

This is one particular way in which the paradoxical imagination of Allama works: we witness a philosophical struggle between the signifier and the signified in his compositions which requires a reading different from how we read Bhakti poetry. The way we read philosophical and religious texts plays a prominent role here. An emotionally engrossing reading and listening experience regulates our understanding of Bhakti literature, which leads to rasanubhava — an intense aesthetic experience.

Allama is essentially an opponent of the mythical imagination (pauranika pratibhe). Therefore, he is opposed to the multiplicity of deities in mythical narratives. His belief is that these kinds of religious narratives are spiritually harmful, that they are the paths of human frailty. Allama prefers a courageous and adventurous spiritual path. In his universe there is no scope for the emotional and tender expressions of the kirtana form.[16] In the present vachana (539), divyanubhava — the ultimate divine experience — is revealed through unconventional metaphors and images. The "horn" of Aja — the creator (literally: the unborn) — the moon, the sun are all destroyed, and the village is burnt. Even the god and goddess die. The god in this vachana is an entity lesser than the ultimate manifestation of Guheshwara. The Guheshwara state is an odyssey, a grand journey, a conquest. As Guheshwara progresses, gods and goddesses die, and mythical imaginations crumble. Guheshwara is in this sense a vio-

[16] Other sects of the Bhakti tradition, especially Dasa saints, popularised this form in which they narrated in song the stories of gods, saints, and heroes, covering religious, mythological, and socially relevant themes.

lent entity. "I" will survive only when the horn of Aja, the creator of the worlds, is broken.[17] According to Allama's principle, there is no discrimination between Guheshwara and "I".

In another interesting vachana (541), Allama calls Guheshwara a "talawara", meaning a lower-caste messenger.[18] Following the technique of bedagu vachanas, the revolutionary reversal technique is employed here.[19] Guheshwara is not an emperor or commander; he is neither a Brahmin, nor a brave Kshatriya warrior. Instead, he appears as a talawara, engaged in what was considered an undignified occupation in medieval Indian society. Such philosophical reversals are common in the Natha and Siddha texts,[20] and reach their zenith in the *Caryagiti-kosa*.[21] In these discourses, outcastes in ghettos, untouchable women, and those engaged in "unclean" occupations become new spiritual symbols, shedding their original identity. While elite spiritual narratives use symbols based on the values of the caste system, Natha and Siddha texts offer resistance to these elite symbols by reversing their values.

What is this talawara called Guheshwara capable of? He can handle with ease the various occupations that are natural to the untouchable. He breaks the limbs of water and chops the ears and nose of fire. He beheads the wind and sends the sky to the gallows. Like other reformers of the Bhakti sects, Allama does not emotionally wail about spiritual equality and the violence of varnashrama.

[17] "Horn" here seems to suggest vanity or arrogance.

[18] A talawara is usually a person of lower caste employed in the bureaucracy to look after correspondence and carry messages for official purposes.

[19] The reference is to Madhuvarasa's technique discussed at the beginning of this chapter.

[20] "Natha" and "Siddha" are spiritual traditions in Hinduism. The former, known as Nathapantha, flourished in medieval India. This tradition, believed to be founded by Gorakhnath, worships Shiva. The latter is the older tradition, and the Siddhas – ascetics who have attained perfection – belong to the Diksha parampara, where the guru initiates the disciple into a particular spiritual way of life. For works in Kannada, see Tarikere, *Karnatakada Nathapantha*; Krishnamurthy, *Siddha Saahitya*. For English-language work, see White, *The Alchemical Body*; Bevilacqua and Stuparich, *The Power of Natha*.

[21] Bagchi, ed., *Caryagiti-kosa*.

He equates Guheshwara with talawara, a representative of the social world that elite society views with disdain. Here, slaughter and butchery are not undignified acts. Then, how powerful is this talawara? Let us read the following vachana:

> This robust talawara,
>> breaks the limbs of water,
>> chops the ears and nose of fire,
>> beheads wind, sends the sky to the gallows.
>
> This robust talawara,
>> baffled all three – the king, the chief, and the minister.
>> Closing nine doors with mighty locks,
>> he slayed nine thousand, and yet survived, Guheshwara. (541)

Both these vachanas (539 and 541) engage with issues ranging from transactions of the universe to historical events, and finally conclude with ruminations on the body – the reference to the body as a surviving entity in the former and nine doors symbolising nine exit points of the body in the latter. The talawara is at the lowest rung of the caste order.[22] In the metaphoric idiom of varnashrama, Allama uses the lifeworld of the reigning class and outcastes distinctively. He invites peace, mercy, bliss, etc., through their opposite states. He says, "O brave warriors, look at my hands" (547).[23] In this vachana he describes even the elders in the idiom of the reigning class, adding the reflection that he has gained a special experience and understanding not accessible to the elders.

Let us move to another vachana:

> Great warriors of renown, our brave-hearted elders,
> completely lost their marbles!
> The God died, Brahma bore the corpse, Vishnu held the fire,
> both Gange and Gouri became widows!
> I was amazed, O Guheshwara! (549)

[22] According to the Purusha Sukta from the *Rigveda*, the untouchables emerge from the lowest part (feet) of the God's body, hence talawara represents the lowest rung of the varnashrama system.

[23] For English translations of the full vachana, see vachana no. 547 in Allama Prabhu, *Lord of the Cave*, and in Allama Prabhu, *Vachanas of Allama Prabhu*.

In the declaration "Both Gange and Gauri became widows!" there is also an indirect metaphor suggesting Shiva's death. Allama here makes a dramatic distinction between Guheshwara and Shiva. In his perception, even Shiva is a state of mind that must disappear in his spiritual journey. Gradually, this becomes a lonely journey of enormous peril. Therefore, it is called bayalu, meaning open space or void; it contains nobody, and everything that exists there is singular. This is the unified state of Advaya, where all differences disappear. Therefore, at the root of the metaphor of Gange's and Gauri's widowhood lies a sense of wonder. The death of Shiva, a part of Guheshwara linga, can be found only in Allama. The death of the divine can become a metaphor in Allama's imagination. Though Allama is opposed to the mythological narrative, he can use the mythological material to frame his metaphors:

> I saw the mind conceive and the hand give birth.
> I saw the ear savour the aroma of the camphor.
> I saw the nose gulp down the shine of pearls.
> I saw the starving eyes devour diamonds (vajra).
> O Guheshwara,
> I saw the three worlds hide in a sapphire (nila). (101)

In Allama's best compositions in the paradoxical mode, the debate between philosophical and religious sects is esoteric. Even if they are not fully comprehensible, the modern tendency is to see no hurdle in studying these compositions as kavya. This does a great injustice to Allama. If the intellectually adventurous were to stretch the words vajra and nila that appear in the last two lines of the above-cited vachana (101), they might even reach the Vajrayana of Buddhism and Nilamata of Kashmir Shaivism. I dare not undertake this adventure. It is better to accept the meaning accessible to the commoner within the framework of generalisation without dilution (sadharanikarana).

Being metaphorically adventurous like a poet is dearer to Allama than being conceptually clear like a philosopher. By bringing together objects that do not mingle or match, he presents before us an aesthetic that emerges out of the havoc. Even an ordinary Advaitin knows that Advaya is a state of indivisible unity. But Allama captures the unity that lies in the depths of paradoxes or differences. It is difficult to say whether the vachana (101) above expresses a positive experience or a negative one. Does the line, "I saw the mind conceive and the hand give birth," imply the path of sadhana with ishtalinga on one's hand? Similarly, the word nila (sapphire) in the last line could mean a precious stone that accompanies the diamond mentioned in the previous line, or it could mean maya (illusion). The first line, as well as the entire vachana, is transformed depending on how we interpret the last line. (As I read this poem, I am reminded of similar imagery in Gopal Krishna Adiga, where aural and visual experiences get mixed up.[24])

I was particularly attracted by this composition (101) in which Allama keeps inserting images into one another. At no point does he leave any clue on what they stand for, which might have assisted the reader in interpreting the composition. Such are the challenges that Allama poses to the readers of his poetry. Pre-modern readers must have faced problems similar to those we moderns encounter in accessing Allama's world. It would be difficult for the "common reader" (mukta oduga), who lacks the orientation required to access Allama's world in its entirety.[25] Maybe poetic traditions ultimately reveal all their subtleties only to those initiated in the tradition. However, the best readers are those who are capable of going, at least a little, beyond the schools of traditions in which they are trained. The vachana we are discussing at present makes us rethink the concept of a "reader".

---

[24] A chief exponent of the navya (modernist) movement in Kannada during the twentieth century, known for his imagist poetry. The poem referred to here is one of Adiga's well-known compositions in Kannada, *Bhumigitha* (Song of the Earth). For the full poem in Kannada, see Adiga Angala, "Bhoomigeeta". For an English translation of Adiga's select poems, see Adiga, *Selected Poems*.

[25] By the term open reader (mukta oduga in Kannada) Nagaraj is referring to a common reader without any disciplined training in reading a text in any particular way.

We the moderns have gained unlimited freedom to read anything as literature. The birth of the modern reader lies in the act of transgressing boundaries of conventional textual meanings and metaphors. However, this modern reader is not an odd adventurer born out of nowhere at a recent historical juncture. Such transgressive readers have existed since ancient times. They would cross their traditional boundaries in order to gain knowledge from other streams. Buddhist, Jaina, Shaiva, and Vedic intellectuals constantly interacted with the "other". But such contacts and associations could also create tumult. At times, those who learnt from rival traditions and celebrated their intellectual plunder were eventually traumatised by a sense of guilt and sin. There is one such story about the Vedic traditionalist Kumarilabhatta.[26]

Allama transforms the common reader with no orientation into an exploratory reader. At first, the reader begins to approach Allama for the aesthetic excitement of reading a literary text. This innocent reading will introduce the reader to the power of Allama's world – to an extent. The composition we are discussing now (101) certainly has a secular aesthetic.[27] Most bedagu vachanas are of this kind. The metaphors and images here evoke an enormous sense of wonder, but they also have the characteristic of a puzzle, a riddle. Here, curiosity is roused, leading readers to search for a specific interpretation beyond the aesthetic of metaphors. There is also unde-

[26] Kumarilabhatta was a Vedic darshanika who is believed to have lived somewhere between the sixth and eighth centuries. Some scholars argue that he was a contemporary of Shankaracharya. According to one story, the Buddhist scholar Dharmakirti went as a servant to Kumarila and learnt shastra from him. After being defeated by Dharmakirti in debates, Kumarila was converted to Buddhism. In another story, Kumarila went in disguise as a Buddhist to Nalanda Vishwavidyalaya in order to learn Buddhism, and defeated a Buddhist teacher in debates. Whatever the truth of these stories, the point being made is about darshaniks learning from rival traditions. See Joshi and Siddapur, *Kumarilabhatta*.

[27] Notwithstanding Nagaraj's previous argument about a common reader without any orientation approaching Allama's compositions for the aesthetic excitement they provide, he seems to suggest that this composition certainly yields itself to a common reading or to a secular aesthetic.

niable elegance in Allama's placing of images. None of the pairings – mind–hand, the aroma of camphor–ear, the shine of pearls–nose, and diamond–eyes – can be regarded as anything but luminous. There is nothing to choose between them; all are equally elegant. Owing to the poem's surprising stability via these pairings, common readers become aware of the limits of their own sensibilities. They are then troubled by various questions: is the balance superficial or real? Does this imagery suggest a much deeper philosophical structure? At this point, they are ready to go beyond the boundaries of their limited sensibilities.

Allama does not help the reader in this adventurous journey. He might have other merciful qualities, but he shows neither compassion nor sympathy for common readers. However, unlike other esoteric poets, he does not restrict entry into his world. A conventional reader can even enter Allama's world through another vachanakara. But while all readers are permitted to enter Allama's world in principle, and though a substantial part of it is readily accessible to them, philosophical discontent gradually grows within them.

It is our general expectation that kavya blunts our interest in philosophy, but in fact the experience of reading Allama increases our appetite for philosophy. Allama persuades his readers to believe that his poetry is inextricably intertwined with his philosophy. He gives the impression that without understanding his philosophy it is not possible to appreciate his poetry. However, this is not entirely true, which is a blessing in disguise for readers.

IV: Mysticism in the Company of Samashti[28]

In the lotus called heart, a tiny bee was born.
It flew and swallowed up the whole sky.
In the whirlwind of its clap and fling,
all the three worlds were turned upside down.
When the cage of the five-hued swan was broken,

---

[28] "Samashti" refers to collectivity, community, totality, or the whole.

the bee fell off with broken wings.
Guheshwara,
I saw the dawn of glorious truth dwelling
in the company of your sharanas' mysticism. (95)

It seems astonishing that Allama, who appears to be an ardent follower of vyakti vishishta (individualist practice), would compose this vachana.[29] I make this observation because the notion of samashti samayachara (community discipline) is visible in this vachana.[30] Except for the last two lines, the mystic metaphors in the earlier lines are quite typical of Allama. But in the last two lines of the vachana he rather unexpectedly puts forth an image of "the dawn of glorious truth" in the company of sharana (samashti / community) mysticism, which is the reason for my astonishment.

The lotus heart, a tiny bee, and other familiar images from Allama's world appear in this vachana. The wind from the tiny bee's fluttering wings turns the three worlds upside down. This is inevitable because only then can the experience of "truth's dawn" begin. The metaphors used so far are commonly found in the poetry of seekers.[31] However, the reference to being in the company of sharanas in the following lines offers a new perspective. To continue this debate, it is necessary to invoke the history of that period.

The notion of samashti samayachara (community discipline, accordant rituals, and the practice of faith) is natural to religious movements. (One may raise objections to the use of the term "movement", which belongs to the vocabulary of contemporary history and politics, while explaining the processes and streams of a bygone era.) But samayachara connotes the creation of a new kind of community (samashti). Only a thinker like Allama can conceptualise the practice of faith without a community (samayachara devoid of samashti). Among twentieth-century Indian yogis, Ramana

---

[29] Individualism, individual uniqueness, as against community practice or collectivity.

[30] The discipline of the community, accordant ritual, practice of faith. See Yaravintelimath, *Vachana Lexicon*, p. 835.

[31] Nagaraj seems to be referring particularly to mystics.

Maharshi had a similar approach. Because he followed individual-centric samayachara, he did not bother to respond to the political and social struggles of his time.

Though Allama endorses the company of sharanas, he retains his uniqueness among them. The lines "I saw the dawn of glorious truth dwelling, / In the company of your sharanas' mysticism" carry a deeper meaning altogether, different from the simple concept of a social gathering. Allama does not consider a social gathering as the setting for samayachara. But by referring to the company of Sharana mysticism he participates in the twelfth-century Virashaiva samayachara. Despite presenting spiritual solitude as an ideal state, he yearns for "the company of mystic sharanas". Though spiritual soliloquy is the true method of Allama's articulations, he welcomes dialogue with his contemporaries. This does not mean he completely agrees with their ideal of samashti samayachara. He is always aware that the practice of rituals in quest of a spiritual ideal might lead to another form of sansara (worldly life).

> Those who held on to linga were subject to the sansara
>   of material gains.
> Those who held on to jangama were subject to the sansara of
>   sayujya, oneness with Shiva.[32] (801)

Being aware of the fact that his own ideals and faith can become prisons, Allama recognises the significance of being in the company of Sharana mysticism.

V: The Infant Called Tranquillity

> Milk from Hari's mouth, butter on fire's hand.
> An infant on the hill is crawling over.
> Lo, call him to drink the milk.
> Lo, call him, who is going back,
> mounting the elephant of surapati (Lord of Devas).
> O Guheshwara,

---

[32] For English translations of the full vachana, see vachana no. 889 in Allama Prabhu, *Lord of the Cave*, and no. 1272 in Allama Prabhu, *Vachanas of Allama Prabhu*.

how shall I describe,
the way he stayed gloriously,
with his toe pressed on the head,
on the trident of Shiva's churning rod. (238)

Allama's infant is different from the conception of the infant among poets in the Dasa tradition.[33] During Allama's time, the prevailing medieval Indian Bhakti sensibility perceived Hari (Vishnu, the supreme deity of Vaishnava tradition) as an infant.[34] Milk spilling out of Hari's mouth was considered a symbol of the Bhakti imagination. Allama's imagination draws from the mythological world whenever necessary; like a tiger, he prowls the forests of mythological (pauranik) narratives for sustenance. Allama, as is his usual practice, views nothing from the perspective of absolute logic. His imagination flies from the milk in Hari's mouth to the infant on the hill. Based on textual evidence in other vachanas, we can comprehend the hill (giri) as a divine experience (divyanubhava). The symbolism of the infant on the hill lends an irony to the practice of perceiving Krishna as an infant.

In Allama's vachanas there is no lullaby for the infant, no milk brought by gopikas, and none to offer butter. Perhaps Allama worries that the proliferation of such stories may cause the mind to lose its essential spiritual strength. Though there is butter in his vachana, it lies in the fire's hand. Thus, familiar images – brightness–light–fire – autonomously create for themselves new meanings and significance in Allama's world. Elsewhere, Allama directly mentions feeding butter to the child, but the point he makes here concerns the naming of the divine.

Who fed butter to the infant called tranquillity,
    and gave it a name?
Look how the word is ashamed of itself!
All the mystics, who did not understand Guheshwara,
    were tormented. (264)

---

[33] For example, in the Dasa tradition, kirtanas describe Krishna as an infant.
[34] Nagaraj seems to be referring to the Bhagavata tradition here; later the Dasa tradition too conceived Krishna as an infant.

If the divine has to be seen as an infant, it would be an infant called tranquillity; "Guheshwara linga is tranquil" (120 and 302). History commences by naming this infant, as names are the horses that propel history forward. In naming God, man imputes his polluting presence to the divine. Word or language possesses not just metaphorical power but, in fact, as modern philosophers of language suggest, is fundamentally metaphoric. According to Allama, word or language has an inherent quality of narrativity as well. There is an intrinsic relationship between this feature of narrativity and features of the Buddhist concept of vikalpa.[35] Thus, Allama's spiritual linguistics boasts of an intellectual adventurousness that is not easily attainable by us moderns.

Just as verbs are natural to a language, the units of narrativity these verbs signify are also natural to a language. In fact, every sentence is a narrative. In the womb of a sentence lies a hook that connects to another sentence and continues the narrative. Each language is a womb of infinite sentences and stories. No matter how limited the tools and designs for generating sentences in a language, the sentences and narratives they produce are infinite. For a language, the ability to produce narratives is as innate as the ability to produce songs. Songs are also a form of narrative, because they cannot emerge outside the context of events.

A mystic must have an awareness of the above-mentioned fundamental traits of language. When he says, "Look, the word is ashamed of itself" (264), Allama is taking on the Bhakti tradition.[36] He is referring indirectly to the deva sati (God as husband) sensibilities of the Bhakti sect which "feeds butter to the infant called tran-

---

[35] In the Buddhist tradition, "vikalpa" means the construction of narratives, constructedness.

[36] It is a vachana that shows the futility of naming the nameless infant. It says that the word, indeed language itself, is ashamed of this ritual of giving a name. According to Giraddi Govindaraj, this vachana problematises the limits of human language. He thinks that there is an aporia in the vachana: naming the tranquil, which is like giving form to the formless, is not possible but it is inevitable. Therefore, language which names the nameless belittles itself: "the word is ashamed of itself." For more, see Govindaraj, *Vachana Vinyasa*, pp. 11–12.

quillity and gives him a name" (264).[37] This "shame of the word" torments those mystics who have not understood Guheshwara. The way of sharana sati (sharana as wife to Shiva/linga) is a natural model of sensibility in Bhakti poetry that can view God as the beloved and also as an infant. Such a sensibility derives from "attributes of the body". However, Allama's spiritual path rests on his "suspicion of bodily attributes".

The metaphor of infancy carries multifaceted connotations. In this respect, infancy means something that is beyond good and evil, truth and untruth, existence and non-existence, and love and hate. It is not at all concerned with the web of words; it is a state of being innocent of words. Thus, Allama says elsewhere, "Guheshwara linga, resting in the heart of the hundred-petalled lotus, was innocent of words" (291).

While Allama does use familial metaphors of infantile affection and motherhood, he employs them only as cosmic transactions and negates their human felicity. Composing a lullaby like "tugire Rangana, tugire Krishnana", for example, would be impossible for Allama.[38] Since all human transactions in Allama's world emerge through the cosmic aura, they obtain a quality of sublimity. He extends the metaphor of the infant in another vachana. "For an infant called tranquillity, a cradle called earth, / a mother called nijaikya (one who is one with Reality) feeding the child milk and butter, / And while Vayu (the God of wind) arrived to rock the cradle and sing a lullaby, the sky picked up the child to provide nourishment!" (665) But Allama laments the fact of innocent worldly women not knowing how to ask for this tranquil infant.

[37] Sharana sati, linga pati (like a devoted wife, sharana is devoted to linga and linga is like husband). "Deva sati" means a wife devoted to deva (God). The words "wife" and "husband" are metaphors for the devotee, who sheds his/her ego by surrendering himself/herself; and deva (God) to whom the devotee is wedded. For more, see Yaravintelimath, *Vachana Lexicon*, p. 766. Here, according to Nagaraj, Allama is critiquing the sensibilities of the Bhakti poets.

[38] This is a well-known composition of Purandaradasa, a fifteenth-sixteenth century Bhakti saint in the Dasa tradition. This composition is a lullaby to Ranga and Krishna (both forms of Lord Vishnu).

Here we witness Allama's tendency for self-denial. Emergent in him is the awareness that a certain kind of poetic felicity has crept into the depiction of cosmic familial ambience. When felicity, melody, and affection surface in a composition, Allama grows vigilant. At times the poet's habit of metaphor-making besieges even the stern Allama. But the moment he realises that his compositions have created an emotional ambience of which he philosophically does not approve, he negates it in another vachana. Accordingly, he creates a contrast to the portrayal of a tranquil infant being fed milk and butter, sung a lullaby, and rocked to sleep. Allama destroys this emotional ambience in the following vachana:

> O orphan infant,
> being self-begotten and growing up on your own!
> You are content with your own joy.
> You are shining on your own,
> impregnable to invaders!
> Your story is natural to you, Guheshwara! (765)

The experience of tranquillity means nothing but liberation from human emotions. Not taking pride in the body is essential to Shiva-tattva, the principle of Shiva. In the previous vachana (665), a mother called nijaikya (being one with Reality) was present. Rejecting all of this, Allama now reiterates the ancient Upanishadic truth that an infant called tranquillity is born and grows up on its own. Perhaps Allama was troubled by the suspicion that he had been responsible for another narrative by naming the infant and assigning it a sansara (worldly life).[39] When named, a form naturally emerges. It is Allama's logic that if form emerges the remaining characteristic features come into being on their own. Allama's question is – "Form is perishable, how can one worship it?" (770)

When the human imagination enters the domain of language, certain routine practices emerge, bearing characteristic features. This is a problem that troubles Allama deeply. When the form comes into being, it inevitably gains attributes like mobility, existence,

---

[39] For example, in the above-quoted vachana, 665.

vulnerability, success, and so on. Stories of the divine then begin. In Allama's view, when the narrative process thus becomes predominant, a human keeps seeing only himself in the narrative.

Employing the metaphor of an infant, Allama demonstrates a variety of playful indulgences. By bringing up lullabies, deploying the act of naming, referring to breast-feeding and other such contextual acts in various dramatic situations, he reveals his paradoxical consciousness. In an earlier vachana (264), we have come across an "infant called tranquillity", and in the following vachana tranquillity becomes a mother:

> As the wind slept, the sky sang a lullaby.
> As bayalu (open space) was tired, tranquillity breast-fed.
> The sky disappeared, the lullaby stopped,
> Guheshwara is there, as if he is not. (668)

If in the above vachana bayalu becomes an infant, in the following vachana (670) the infant feeds from the breast, becomes content, and asks for its name. Allama, who played with the worldly metaphor of an infant in earlier vachanas, now makes a sudden leap into the world of colours. A certain kind of intertextuality continues here as well. But leaving behind the Bhakti tradition, he transitions into Kashmir Shaivism in the following vachana:

> Sucking the mother's breast and being content,
> the infant asked for its name.
> Ayya, what can I compare it to!
> When the garments of lighter colours
> swallowed the black pupil in the eye,
> who will not fall for the illusion of colours?
> As the complex of colours
> swallowed varied colours,
> the birth of words
> swallowed Guheshwara's existence. (670)

There is in Shaiva tantrism a unique philosophy of colours. A particular section in the first chapter of the *Tantraloka* assists us in interpreting the above vachana. Jayaratha, in his commentary, carries out a colour analysis of hrudaya (heart) and Shiva-tattva in an interesting way.[40] The metaphor of hritkamala (heart-lotus) is repeatedly used in Allama, and this is in accordance with its usage in Kashmir Shaivism. This notion of hrudaya (heart) is itself a mystery. It is a symbol of Shaiva's linga, the driving force in all expressions of the world and also a destroyer of everything. It is Krishna varna, dark in colour, which Jayaratha interprets as its ability to engulf all – like the darkness of night.[41]

In the above vachana it is clear that Allama is interacting with the interpretive tradition of Abhinavagupta–Jayaratha. Allama here cautions against the danger of garments of lighter colour swallowing the black pupil in the eye. Although in the glossary of bedagu compositions within the volume I am using,[42] the term "dark" has negative connotations of obliterative darkness, ignorance, and blemish, I feel the interpretation attributed to Kashmir Shaivism is more relevant here. Despite knowing that it is not possible to capture it in a metaphor, Allama is making an attempt to explore a state of dark night wherein the black pupil is swallowed by garments of lighter colour. Finally, he cautions us about the birth of words, etymology – the philological analysis of language. Allama states that philology can subsume Guheshwara's position, and in this context etymology would be a dry exercise in spiritual logic or intellect. The vachanas we have discussed in this section demonstrate that in Allama's universe babysitting is not just child's play.

VI: The Wounded Sun

Death is an important theme for Allama. He does not see it as an inevitable phase in human affairs but as an event with a special significance in the entirety of creation. His analysis of death is essentially an analysis of death as a metaphor.

[40] Abhinavagupta, *Tantraloka*.

[41] Ibid., vol. 1, p. 40 (DRN).

[42] "Bedagina Padagala Arthakosha" (Glossary of Bedagu Vachanas), in Allama Prabhu, *Vyomamuruti*, pp. 651–96.

Look,
>   As the incessant rain from the dark clouds
>   poured down, the whole earth was drowned.
Look,
>   As several suns rose in the eye of the darkest night,
>   the right path was lost.
>   Unless killed with a fatal wound,
>   several suns will not die, Guheshwara! (340)

Allama offers no straightforward introduction enabling us to understand this vachana, nor does the conventional method of interpreting bedagu compositions help us much. Therefore, we must make an attempt to understand what this vachana might be saying by bringing together the intertextual method and, to a great extent, the method of philosophical speculation. The description of a downpour signifies a state of spiritual experience. Here, "several suns rising in the eye of the darkest night" is not exactly a positive image that we might associate with romantic nature poetry. If the experience of one sun is for good, the rise of several suns destroys one's sense of direction. The whole earth is drowned in the downpour from dark clouds. Among Buddhists and Kashmir Shaivas the earth represents a state of spiritual pilgrimage. Buddhists, in particular, wrote many commentaries evoking myriad earths.

The background to the present vachana is a belief that twelve suns will together shine during pralaya, the cataclysm.[43] Allama was aware of this. He speaks of the killing of suns. Though a staunch advocate of non-violence, he does not hesitate to use violence in his metaphoric world, making symbols of the most creative acts. It is impossible for Allama's imagination to ignore violence when it is one

---

[43] According to the Merriam-Webster dictionary, in Hindu philosophy pralaya is a period of dissolution or destruction of the manifested universe at the end of a kalpa (a cycle of the cosmos) — the end of the world. Several texts in Indian tradition refer to pralaya, a period of complete destruction of the manifested universe. The *Vishnu Purana* speaks of three kinds of pralaya: naimittika pralaya (occasional), prakritika pralaya (material), and atyantika pralaya (final). See Klostermaier, *A Survey of Hinduism*, p. 496.

of the fundamental realities of creation. On many occasions he also shows violence as an intense form of the mind.

As is the case in many of Allama's vachanas, there is a state of paradox here as well. Absolute binaries like good–evil and existence–non-existence have no place in Allama's vision of life. The birth of Allama's imagination lies in a space where these binaries are intertwined. Even here, there is a dialectical relationship between the aesthetics of metaphors and their philosophical morality. Though the image of several suns rising is exciting, Allama shatters the state of aesthetic involvement in such a sight. Irrespective of his spiritual-ethical stance about a certain condition of reality, he thoroughly exploits the possibilities of metaphor-making opened up by that condition. In this respect, he is a complete poet. The task of a poet is to create metaphors using any sort of material. Allama produces beautiful metaphors out of death, pain, agony, panic, frustration, and other such heart-wrenching situations. Indeed, a poet is fated to create beautiful metaphors. Thus, despite all his mockery of the transactions of a poet, Allama is, like a poet, committed to the creation of imagery. Using all his resources, he creates a world of metaphors and then comments on it with the same intensity. He empowers both metaphor and the ethical commentary that follows evenly.

In his method of creating metaphors and then commenting on them, Allama is closer to the Buddhists. It is even possible to say he has learnt it from them. Buddhists do not believe that a mode of expression is spiritually true and useful just because it is beautiful and attractive. When the dual traits of language – lyricism and narrative – are combined with a particular sensibility, aesthetically attractive expressions are bound to emerge. According to the Buddhists, this happens in Brahmanic or Vedic religious literature. The Vedas and Upanishads abound in such aesthetically attractive expressions of spiritual ideas. But Buddhists consider this aesthetic addiction dangerous. They call it a fixation on spiritual adoration. The mind is capable of portraying anything beautifully. But to appraise its consequences and value objectively, a different kind of capacity is required. Allama is in agreement with this line of thinking.

However, this does not mean that Allama gives boundless freedom to his imagination while creating metaphors. His poetic imagination is brought to express itself in a controlled manner through yogic discipline. Without chasing grand narratives, he very cautiously uses the technique of creating a compact dramatic situation. He knows that a particular kind of aesthetics emerges when vikalpas (mental constructions) are mixed. From the perspective of poetic experience, the cosmic metaphor of "several suns rising" holds tremendous potential. But Allama does not get infatuated by it, nor does he chase after it in a frenzy. The zeal for aesthetic creation takes other poets to the heights of imagination and emotion. Allama is sceptical of this sort of literary zeal. So, right after the exciting portrayal of multiple suns, he points towards "losing the right path" and cautions the reader about the ethics of such an experience. The sun might be a symbol of everything benevolent in the ordinary world. But this is not true of several suns – so far as this vachana goes. Whatever the extent of the dialectic ambience created by the grand density of metaphors, Allama quietly suggests parameters for evaluating the situation. In his world, the death of suns is inevitable. The path does not become clear unless the several suns die. In the spiritual battle that Allama suggests, the suns have to be mortally wounded and killed.

We are again reminded of Kashmir Shaivism's analysis of colours, where spiritual secrecy is symbolised by dark colours. While certain religious sects, especially those based on the Vedas, worship Surya (the sun god), the Shaiva imagination accords special status to dark colours. A sense of direction over the dark night must be preserved by wounding and killing the sun. In another vachana (439), which will be discussed in the next section, Allama presents before us a different facet of daybreak (dawn) in the narrative on the sun. Though the utmost importance is given to light and dawn in Shaivism, Allama presents an experience that differs from that of the mainstream. While Shaiva darshana can be seen entirely as an adulation of light, we find some vachanas of Allama that deviate from this. The following vachana can be understood as the non-dualistic expression of Advaya, which ultimately considers the duality of night–day as artificial.

VII: The Dead Hen Crowing

I saw a dead hen rise and crow.
I heard the thick mango tree speak.
I saw the dark night becoming a bright day.
I saw people rise at dawn, and lose their way.
I do not understand what it is all, Guheshwara! (439)

The hen came to be an important symbol, used not only by vachanakaras but also in the Kannada mystic tradition that followed. In one of Shishunala Sharif's later-nineteenth-century compositions, "a hen swallows a monkey".[44] However, in their compositions mystical symbols have only one meaning, and we can easily grasp the entire meaning of the composition if we get to the bottom of the bedagu (symbols). But Allama's bedagu compositions are not so easy to comprehend. The conventional bedagu has a singular meaning, or, even if it contains multiple meanings, these remain largely complementary. But this is not so in Allama, for two reasons. First, he has a way of creating chaos by destabilising the definitive meaning behind his bedagu at any point. Second, he can perplex the conventional reader by using metaphors formulated paradoxically. For example, let us consider the metaphoric use of the concept of kadali (literally: a plantain grove). Before proceeding further, one must clarify that bedagu is a conceptual metaphor.[45] Kadali is used paradoxically in Allama, as a fragile body on the one hand, and as a spiritual space on the other. However, Allama retains the body as a stable meaning for kadali. That is to say, for other commentators bedagu unites the connotative and denotative meanings of a metaphor, but Allama might respect only the consistency of denotative meaning — at most.

[44] See ch. 1, fn. 31.

[45] Recall A.K. Ramanujan's definition of bedagu in relation to Allama discussed, in ch. 1, fn. 70.

Another unique feature in Allama's use of bedagu is the ambiguous ambience he suggests. While for others bedagu ceases to be bedagu when the symbolic meaning becomes neutral, for Allama it doesn't. My assertion will be clear when we observe how the metaphorical meaning of bedagu has become neutral in the line, "I saw a dead hen rise and crow." According to the conventional interpretation, one can grasp the dead hen that rises and crows as a metaphor for the positive experience of an awakening of self-understanding. However, in the lines that follow Allama goes on to destabilise this definitive meaning. Even if we consider that the "speaking mango tree, and darkness changing to daylight" are open to a conventional interpretation, the line "I saw people rise at dawn, and lose their way" suspends all previous interpretations. The first four lines describe experiences of "seeing" or "hearing", but the last line states that the entire series of experiences has not been understood. If we are to accept the conventional bedagu meaning of the hen, by the end of the composition a positive understanding must be revealed and there should be no scope for any ambiguity – which is not so here. In the vachana discussed at the start of the previous section, we have seen how Allama uses the metaphor of the sun negatively. One might therefore suspect that the term "dawn" is used in a similar manner. The creation of catastrophic chaos by destabilising conventions and traditions is a model favoured by Allama.

VIII: Pussy Cat, Pussy Cat

Look,
>   When given a stylus,
>   maye (illusion) wrote laguna (auspicious time) and viguna
>   (inauspicious time).
Look,
>   If a waxen doll is draped in flame,
>   the flame adorned it beautifully.
Look Guheshwara,
>   The parrot playing in the sky
>   swallowed the cat in the cage,
>   and left Rambha's arms! (36)

There are plenty of animals and birds in Allama's universe. He adds a few unique traits to their characteristic features. He plays with them with love and perplexity. As we comprehend the general meanings of a cat, a horse, a parrot, etc., they arrest us with distinct meanings in Allama's vachanas. All of a sudden his cat becomes a stranger staring at us. Only such unusual animals can survive in Allama's unnatural ecosystem. It is easy to understand mystic compositions created in the traditional bedagu mode. They are difficult to follow until we enter into their world and become acquainted with their unusual nature. But Allama's bedagu compositions are not in this mould. While composing his bedagu vachanas he experiments like a poet. He needs both the resources of the bedagu tradition and poetic experiment. Therefore, his reader becomes a sort of Duryodhana who enters the palace built by Maya.[46] The reader, like Duryodhana, lifts a leg to step over a waterless space thinking it contains water. Then, when the reader stumbles into the water assuming it is dry land, Allama laughs and claps – like Draupadi mocking Duryodhana. When we step into Allama's world expecting tradition, there is experimentation. Where we think we see Allama's individual talent, we encounter the whirlpool of tradition. Even Allama's cat is of this kind. At times it scares us in the dark, at other times it becomes a wild cat. On one occasion it brims with affectionate arrogance, on another it becomes food for a parrot.

Allama begins the above-cited vachana (36) with a reference to marriage.[47] In other compositions he is more interested in marriage processions than marriage rituals. Here, without any background or foreground, he brings up marriage and directly proceeds to describe the bride – the waxen doll. Out of courtesy, he does not initially call the woman by her name. With admiration, nay sar-

---

[46] In the Sabha Parva of the *Mahabharata,* a gifted architect named Maya builds a majestic palace for the Pandavas in their new capital, Indraprastha. When invited during the time of the rajasuya yagna, Duryodhana enters the palace and is mesmerised by it. He mistakes the floor for water, painting for real things, and makes himself a laughing stock.

[47] Nagaraj interprets "auspicious" and "inauspicious" as referencing marriage, an auspicious occasion.

casm, he calls her "waxen doll". For Allama the body is either a plantain grove or a waxen doll. It cannot withstand the attack of an elephant called liberation. The waxen doll cannot bear the flame of self-understanding. If Kashmir Shaivism celebrates the sources of power in the body without egotism, Allama stays away from it all, deeming them burdensome.

In the present vachana (36), however, Allama does not exhibit a negligent attitude toward the body as such. Nor does he highlight the unique beauty that exists in fatal circumstances. The flame that drapes the bride signifies self-understanding. (Here, it is possible to have several spiritual interpretations.) The melting of the waxen doll too becomes a beautiful scene. Allama's attention is directed towards the delightful flame rather than towards the piteous event of melting wax. Anyway, the wax must melt while the flame highlights its beauty.

It is quite strange to find a cat in a cage shown as a companion to a woman likened to a waxen doll. All at once we are made to face the cat and the parrot, and observe the shift that has taken place in Allama's world. Customarily, the parrot would be in a cage and the cat would have the freedom to jump around. But the cat here is locked up in a cage. According to the conventional interpretation, the parrot is a life force, a symbol of paramahamsa – the Supreme Swan, signifying ultimate purity – while the cat is a symbol of worldly desires. Allama presents us with a scene, in all its complexity, of the liberation of the parrot called paramahamsa from the company of the waxen doll called Rambha, a beautiful young woman. The poet's stance seems to be that though liberation is not an easy business, it is possible. It is true that the parrot also has to embrace Rambha. In the day-to-day world these are miracles, but for Allama miracles are mundane realities. When he composes verses using birds and beasts, he erases the distinction between miracles and common occurrences.

The cat, which is important as an animal protagonist in Allama's imaginative theatre, is not limited to the role of villain. Allama creates nothing as an embodiment of unchanging essence. In this respect he is like God; monotony is unknown to his creations. He imparts to every creation unexpected twists and turns. Monotony is a boring moment of creation, or a moment of sound sleep. Though this kind of leisure is necessary, it is momentary. Allama too awakens and abruptly changes the roles of his characters. Accordingly, in the following vachana, the cat plays a role that reverses the previous ones:

> A cat was born in the dawn of mystic experience.
> On that cat's head was born a mountain.
> On the top of that mountain were born two gems.
> When one went in search of them,
> the gems caught hold of him.
> One gem caught hold of his body,
> the other, his life-breath.
> O Chennabasavanna,
> I hail "namo namo" to Guheshwara's sharana,
> Siddharamayya,
> who embodies the glow of these gems. (1191)

Allama is here simultaneously using two different forms of expression – symbolic language and historical narrative. In the narrative of the *Shunyasampadanes* this vachana can be read as Allama's assessment of Siddharamayya's personality in his own philosophical register. Here, Allama is reflecting on his relationship with Siddharamayya. The cat, the mountain, and the gems we come across here can be interpreted in both general and particular terms, as Allama carefully explains the development of Siddharamayya's personality and its limits.

While speaking of personalities, especially historical ones, Allama generally does not employ the method of psychoanalysis. It is the method of modern novelists to compose plots by interweaving the psyche of an individual with the social realities of life. To an extent, this is also the method of the ancient Indian epics and puranas. The model of psychoanalysis reveals itself richly in the structure of narrative work. One of the main reasons Allama does not use this model is that the poetic structure of vachanas has certain limitations. The model of psychoanalysis works better when it is possible to document minute but significant details in narratives such as novels and epics. Psychology picks up naturally floating details in the stream of autobiography and makes use of them as special clues and means of interpretation. For example, in Freud's psychoanalysis these minor details hold up a mirror to a larger turmoil. The coming together of these large narratives and small details creates the field for a study of Freudian concepts such as condensation and overdetermination. Allama does not use the model of psychoanalytical exploration to evaluate the personality of Siddharamayya in detail, for he is constrained by the structure of the vachana.

More than this, there exists a solid reason for Allama's avoidance of this model; his basic scepticism of psychological analysis. In the Indian knowledge traditions, the school of spiritual psychology is very appealing. Buddhists in particular took its study to the level of special expertise. (We are reminded of Western scholars calling the Buddhist thinker Vasubandhu a Buddhist psychologist.[48]) Though Allama learnt several things from the Buddhists, he did not take to their psychological analysis. We can briefly summarise his objections to the entire model of psychological analysis as follows: in psychological analysis, the affairs of the mind are the objects of study and the mind itself is the method. Then, it is difficult to distinguish between the two – the object of study and the method of study – and determine which one studies the other. To put it in Allama's words, it is difficult to believe "the instrument [way] of remembering [mind]."[49] Or, it is difficult to make a definitive distinction between the view and the viewed.

---

[48] Vasubandhu (fourth to fifth century) is a Buddhist philosopher and a logician. His masterwork of Abhidharma thought, *Abhidharmakośabhāṣya* (the *Commentary on the Treasury of the Abhidharma*) is to this day the primary resource for knowledge of "Śrāvaka" or non-Mahayana philosophy among Tibetan and East Asian Buddhist schools. For more, see Stanford Encyclopedia of Philosophy, "Vasubandhu".

[49] For the full vachana in English translations, see vachana no. 824 in Allama Prabhu, *Lord of the Cave*, and no. 858 in Allama Prabhu, *Vachanas of Allama Prabhu*.

So, instead, Allama uses the symbolic mode for his analysis of historical characters. In the present vachana (1191), not all the symbols are signifiers of final spiritual achievement. Here, Allama seems to suggest that Siddharamayya is a seeker travelling through different stages of achievement. Maybe the cat in the first line of the vachana is Siddharamayya?

In between, the cat goes missing. When we go in search of it, we find the following vachana in which Allama speaks of a cat on which six hills are born.

> On a flower is born a hillock,
> on a cat are born six hills!
> Those who dwell on the hill
> have searched for a stone,
> but none could find it.
> The mountain is one,
> but has a hundred and forty-eight lakh faces.
> Look, O Guheshwara,
> I dwell in one face! (767)

Here, it is possible to interpret the flower as a life force upon which lies a hillock of egotism or arrogance. The cat refers to worldly desires. The six hills on it refer to arishadvarga, i.e. (the six-fold enemy: – kama (lust), krodha (anger), lobha (greed), mada (arrogance/pride), moha (infatuation), and matsarya (jealousy/envy). For those who are on the hill, the linga becomes a mere stone. It is tragic that they cannot even see it. Traditional commentaries seem to be right when they say that Allama makes a distinction between hill and mountain. The mountain exists beyond the hills. Those who are standing on the hill can see the mountain's innumerable faces. There, Guheshwara resides only in one of those faces. Thus, this vachana portrays a picture of great anxiety, dilemma, despair, and confusion. Allama situates the hills of abstract concepts around the symbol of a concrete animal – here a cat. Where there is a cat, there must be a mouse running around. In an interesting vachana (1214), Allama once again knocks down the possibility of reading along the expected lines:

The mouse scurrying in the attic,
hid in the eyes of the cat,
which was waiting to pounce on it.
Both the mouse and eyes of the cat
could not see Guheshwaralinga. (1214)

Traditional commentators interpret Allama's mouse as wisdom (viveka). In which case, what about the cat? The same interpretation says that the cat is a symbol of intense concentration. Another meaning attributed to the cat is that it represents the perfect knowledge that can see even at night. But the cat here cannot see Guheshwaralinga. It is quite clear that Allama's creative model of paradox is at work here, and in full measure.

IX: Struggle and Friendship
with Deluge

I do not know how many deluges happened in the past,
and how many will happen in the future.
If one does not understand oneself, isn't that a deluge?
If one's own vachana (promise/speech) turns against him,
isn't that a deluge?
O Guheshwara,
are there such deluges in you? (655)

There are instances of deluge (pralaya) in Allama's world. They are not different from deluges described in cultural and religious memories of this world. To a large extent the deluge here, as elsewhere, represents total destruction and complete disarray. However, Allama gives distinctive philosophical underpinnings to the theme of deluge — as he does with other fundamental themes. In the present vachana, Allama is exploring the futility of historical memory.

The notion of history is not just limited to human affairs. Human epochs, the beginning and end of human phases, do not constitute all of history. The tendency of historical knowledge is to attach pastness, presentness, and futurity to creation — the universe or the earth. As observed earlier, Allama opposes all forms of memory, particularly historical memory. He detests the supreme importance attached to chroniclings of the external, believing that internal happenings are of greater significance. It is impossible to understand the memory of human history, let alone the memory of creation.

In spite of this, the change and uproar of creation are at the centre of Allama's consciousness. He is against using the historical method to understand the soul (atma), and spirituality (adyatma), but is not blind to the events that happen in the process of creation. In the following vachana he reveals his perspective on this:

When epochs after epochs die,
universes after universes perish,
who understands what linga is?
Shiva Shiva!
They are all deceived illusionists,
What do they understand of what God is?
Shiva Shiva!
Your sharana knows the fire
that hides itself in the hay, Guheshwara! (653)

In the process of creation, historical epochs take birth and pass away. Whole universes and galaxies disappear and become extinct. They are the waves that rise and fall in the ocean called linga. Allama is not perturbed by these extinctions and destructions: he experiences them intensely. One who is frightened by this continual process of creation cannot understand the nature of linga.

In this respect, Allama's imagination becomes important in the history of Kannada cultural sensibility. Of course, knowledge of astronomy in medieval India was limited relative to modern astronomy. Certainly, in Allama's time there were not as many details available about the mechanics of creation as are available to the moderns through the physical sciences. Ironically, while the modern mind has more detailed knowledge, its holistic vision is less sharp. Modern Kannadigas have more information about the birth and death of planets and stars and primordial uproars in the universe.

But as information pours in, holistic understanding is lost. The sensibility of Allama's time shows us all knowledge within a religious and spiritual idiom. The notion of the universe here is born out of spiritual wonder rather than compiled from empirical detail. The notion of the epoch, too, is different. It is a phase that involves the entire universe, including human affairs. A deluge characterises the end of an epoch. The deluge is nothing but a play of creation beyond the ethical and unethical concerns of the human world.

In Allama, the notion of the deluge does not produce fear. The spiritual optimism that there lies a calm and quiet sea of linga behind the roaring waves of the deluge gives Allama the courage to document it. There is no detailed description of the deluge that appears in his vachanas. He does not use similes or metaphors to describe it. The deluge does not create a sense of fear in Allama, in fact "the fire that hides itself in the hay" creates a sense of spiritual wonder in him. From his perspective the sharana's view of human and non-human affairs in creation is quite different. His sharana is neither attracted to the external affairs of the world nor afraid of them. Unlike a modern physicist, he is not determined to gain a deeper knowledge of all these. For him, to keep an inventory of deluges would be a futile exercise.

From Allama's perspective, the absence of self-understanding is like a deluge. He focuses his attention on an individual's internal state, where the lack of self-understanding is like the deluge that brings about the extinction of universes. Thus, the deluge within Allama is fundamentally an inner experience. He also compares the interior life of an individual with the state of Guheshwara. If we analyse the above vachana (653) against the backdrop of Advaya philosophy, he seems to foresee a transformation in a sharana's personality; that is, the sharana becoming one with Guheshwaralinga. As long as there is duality, there is a fear of the deluge, the fear that "the fire burns the hay". When a sharana reaches the state of Guheshwara, he does not fear the deluge.

As has already been observed, Allama rejects what he elsewhere accepts. If in the above vachana (653) he is spiritually optimistic about the sharana becoming one with Guheshwaralinga, in the following vachana (1030) he gives up his spiritual optimism. Here, Allama's sharana makes a distinction between the world and the linga:

> Ayya, can there be iron jewels for the statue of alchemy?
> If the world is in linga, and linga in the world,
> why did deluges take place in the past?
> Then, what about the deluges of the future?
> The world is what it is, and linga is what it is.
> Your sharana knows the difference between the two,
> O Guheshwara! (1030)

In this vachana Allama roams around exploring the world of varying sensibilities. This is a sceptical world of Dvaitins. Allama himself has clarified in other vachanas that the notion of "linga in the world" is the stance of Advayavada. However, in this vachana he ends by stating that only a sharana knows the difference between the two – the world and linga, a stance which seems close to Dvaitin sensibility.

This kind of vachana testifies to Allama's self-examination and tests the spiritual training of the reader. One of Allama's primary concerns is to wipe out the paradoxical relationship between the simple binaries of yes and no. An intense exposition of any ready-made model might result in naive devotion, which Allama opposes. In his view, an individual has to reach a state of devotion through hard work. One of the fundamental lessons of Allama's world is that there is a thin line between blindness and insight. For this reason, self-denial in Allama is not just employed for creating unexpected metaphors. It is an inevitable dimension of spiritual awakening; a life-saving practice, keeping us from drowsiness in the presence of perilous icebergs.

In Allama's world there are these experiences of multiple worlds and epochs. He can include others' perspectives too. Therefore he can move across several worlds – such as "the wonders of creation," "fatal paradoxes of human history", "the world of animals and birds", "others' structure of feelings", "the religious sensibility of the other" – and all these worlds leave their imprint on his vachanas. His ventures into these unfamiliar worlds of experience, the touch of their scents and shadows, make Allama a unique poet. In this regard, he is a poet of great adventure.

Even conventional poets move across other worlds. Conventional poetic modes have certain structural requirements that direct poets towards various realities. In this process, poetic descriptions come to their help. The richness and breadth of their descriptive worlds may not touch or disturb a conventional poet. If they approach the other worlds for their structural necessities, Allama enters them for his philosophical needs. This is the main difference between a mystic poet and a conventional poet. The question of Creation and the different stages of its evolution act as external pressures to a conventional poet. Often, these are pressures of narrative context, or the inevitable practices of their religious world that they need to follow in order to complete their narratives. Though the world, objects, and concepts that appear in the works of a conventional poet are also very much present in Allama, they live in a state of density, a state of flux. In him, the experiences of deluge and primordial creation are also in a state of density and flux.

Deluges are transgressive. The borders that were accepted until the coming of the deluge are now dissolved into one state and then the transformation starts. At some point in time, an idea comes to mind – that the deluge is an inevitable and creative act even in spiritual life. Symbolically important imaginaries (vikalpas) and metaphors will be wiped out in the deluge. The one who bears the weight of this knowledge is wise and enlightened (jnani). Whereas others lay stress on the state of ignorance (ajnana), Allama focuses on the burden of knowledge. While the jnani derives pleasure from the state of knowledge, Allama pays attention to the responsibility and the divine suffering that come with knowledge. Therefore, the notion of the deluge in Allama represents a painful experience brought by knowledge. It is easy to carry the darkness of ignorance, but facing the light of knowledge is a great adventure. In the following vachana Allama expresses the understanding that the deluge brings with it the destruction of all that is adored:

> Kailasa [heaven] is a silver hill.
> The one who dwells there is Rudra.
> O Guheshwara, your sharana knows
> that both the silver hill and Rudra
> can be destroyed in the deluge. (1049)

As usual, the technique of turning a negative image into a positive one is at work here. As has already been observed, in conventional interpretations the hill is a symbol of egotism. Allama here is talking about illusions that are created at the lower level of spiritual evolution. In this context, Rudra is different from Guheshwara, and there need not be any relationship between them. But Dvaitin narrators treat Kailasa, a silver hill, Rudra, and Guheshwara at the same level. Subtle philosophical distinctions do not help the devotional narrative to evolve easily. It is difficult for Allama's sharana to be humble and emotional like Bhakti poets. For others, the silver hill and Rudra might be sacred. But Allama knows that they are also subject to destruction by the deluge. In his view, Kailasa is the body of Shivasharanas which is also subject to destruction.

Circumstances which might raise emotions in Bhakti poets bring only courage to Allama. Situations which could be reasons for empathy elsewhere are for him spaces where ruthlessness takes birth. Death and deluge do not produce grief in him, nor do birth and beginnings bring joy. His imagination is active beyond simple sentimentality. Likewise, his exploration of the deluge does not aim to scare the frightened mortal soul. He does not employ the threat of the deluge in order to encourage humility in humans before the enormity of creation. This is reserved for nature-worshipping romantics. In Allama the deluge happens in order to awaken Shiva consciousness in the seeker. Thanks to the uniqueness of Allama's world, the metaphor of extinction awakens the spirit of adventure. When such consciousness is awakened, even the deluge loses its typical character and becomes humble. It makes friends with the sharana. Thus, Allama's world plays with the deluge.

X: Unkind Towards Dogs

See, how the dogs wrangle
over the lying corpse of samsara!
See, how the corpse cackles as the dogs wrangle!
Look, the linga called Guheshwara is not there. (46)

Allama is extremely unkind to dogs. Often, dogs roam around in Allama's world, but, beaten by the stick of irony, they run away. Even then they stick around, whining. Though Allama is indifferent to dogs, they are fascinated by him. Dogs are attracted to adventurers and travellers. Only a dog followed Dharmaraya up the Himalaya in the *Mahabharata*. But Allama does not remember the dog affectionately during his vital moments. (If we look for writers who are sympathetic to dogs, we are reminded of Kuvempu and Tejaswi in Kannada, and among westerners Guy de Maupassant and Anton Chekov.[50]) Allama is also indifferent to cows. Somehow this stern yogi disparages the animals which are loyal to humans, perhaps because they are the animals attached to samsara. Humans are not the only species yoked to samsara – so are cows and dogs.

Like a mischievous boy, Allama even chases a cow and jabs it with a stick. He says, "swallowing a ruby, a cow got brahmeti [delusion]" (54).[51] Later, he asks: "How can you probe or grasp it [a cow]?" (54). Finally, feeling pity, he requests Guheshwara "to be kind" (54). We must leave the story of oxen, buffaloes, and cows for discussion elsewhere. For now, the issue is the dog seen in the vachana above.

The animal found most prominently in samsara heyasthala – the

[50] K.P. Purnachandra Tejaswi (1938–2007), Kuvempu's son, an iconoclastic modernist Kannada writer.

[51] Another meaning of "brahmeti" is the crime of killing a Brahmin. For English translations of the full vachana, see vachana no. 54 in Allama Prabhu, *Lord of the Cave*, and in Allama Prabhu, *Vachanas of Allama*.

contemptible space called samsara (the world) – is the dog.[52] In the present vachana, dogs come to tear down and eat the corpse of samsara. Perhaps they are wild dogs. Some scholars rightly point out that Allama uses the dog to represent the five senses. In his metaphorical mode Allama goes off into extremes and disseminates new ideas. On many occasions he uses soft metaphors for the senses. He calls the body a banana plant – yet he can be enraged in the next moment. His eyes can redden with anger quicker than excited dasas are moved to tears in their Bhakti poetry. When Allama's eyes go red his metaphors become deviant and special meanings begin to emerge. It is appropriate to call the senses dogs that brawl over the corpse of samsara. Is there any feeling of concurrence or unity among them? No.

There is always an unusual trace of mirth that Allama's perturbed mind creates. The line in the vachana (46), "the corpse cackles as the dogs wrangle!" illustrates this. The dogs are incapable of tearing the corpse completely and eating it; instead they fight. Even the corpse comes alive and laughs at the situation. At times like this Allama's sarcastic humour goes and sits in the front yard of absurdity. At other times he creates a series of complex metaphors, like wheels within wheels. But in instances like the present one he creates only an effective visual, the corpse and the wrangling dogs. He recreates this image with the eye of a painter. As in trataka yoga, his philosophical mind here is fixed on the image.[53]

[52] In Virashaiva darshana the word "sthala" refers to a stage in spiritual ascent (elsewhere it also connotes parashiva, or the ultimate reality). Six prominent sthalas or stages in the spiritual journey of a sharana described in the Virashaiva literature are: bhakta, maheshwara, prasadi, pranalingi, sharana, and aikya. However, prior to the bhakta sthala, there is another set of sthalas: pindasthala (embryo stage), samsaraheyasthala (disgust towards the material world), mayavilasavidambanasthala (shunning the temptation of maya-illusion). In the Vachana tradition, vachanas are often organised on the basis of the sthalas discussed here. See Yaravintelimath, "Introduction", in Allama Prabhu, *Lord of the Cave*, pp. 110–21.

[53] A yogic posture in which the practitioner tries to perfect the power of concentration by fixing attention on an object or a symbol.

Unlike their behaviour in the mundane world, dogs in Allama's world do not remind us of a human habitus. For Allama the barking of dogs does not signify the dwelling place of humans; he portrays instead an uncommon picture – of dogs feasting on a corpse. Likewise, the barking of a dog suggests a ruined location. In Allama's world where there are corpses there are dogs:

> Ayya,
> As the carcass of an elephant lay,
> I saw a monkey come and caress it.
> I saw a harlot in the woods,
> calling men and luring them for her profit.
> I saw dogs wrangle in a deserted village.
> Tell me Guheshwara,
> what kind of puzzle is this? (49)

It is in this kind of situation that Allama's mode appears rather extreme. Here we have the carcass of an elephant being caressed by a monkey, and dogs wrangling in a deserted village. According to the bedagu lexicon in *Allamana Vachana Chandrike*, the elephant suggests a body full of egotism, and the monkey here refers to the mind.[54] To make the atmosphere a bit grimmer, there is a harlot in the woods. As in other bedagu vachanas of Allama, creative ambiguity here permeates the entire structure of the vachana (49). Following the meaning given in the lexicon of bedagu in *Allamana Vachana Chandrike*, it is possible to turn the whole text towards a positive meaning of spirituality. If we take the elephant as egotism, the dead elephant could have an opposite meaning. Likewise, the monkey could mean a reasoning mind. Even if we understand the metaphor of the prostitute negatively, the ambiguity continues to exist.

Here, the presence of the dog determines the meaning. Nowhere in his compositions does Allama free the dog from sin and make it clearly a dog of light. (The twentieth-century poet D.R. Bendre did

---

[54] The bedagu lexicon Nagaraj refers to appears at the end of *Allamana Vachana Chandrike: A Complete Version of Vachanas and Songs of Allamaprabhu*. See Allama Prabhu, *Allamana Vachana Chandrike*, pp. 360–1.

this, as we may recall from his poem titled "Kalpavruksha Vrun-davanangalali": "Light-dog is coming, smelling the body."[55]) In Allama the dog is not liberated, which stabilises the meaning of this vachana. The dog's presence makes us conclude that the composition is all about an egoistic body and filthy business.

In another vachana Allama gives purposeless importance to the dog. After a rare controversial statement about a great sentence of Indian philosophy – tattvamasi: You are that – Allama refers to a dog. So the dog is rewarded for having faithfully followed Allama and has unexpectedly got a place in his work, at least as witness and metaphor. As I mischievously set out to look for vachanas in which dogs roam, I found quite unexpectedly the following vachana, for which I am indebted to the dog.[56] We may safely assume that the Kannada mind has not hitherto mused on dogs and discussed their presence in Allama.

> The world, unaware that it is pure and eternal
> chanting "tatvamasi" dubiously, died a dog's death.
> When they stuck to reading what the dead have written,
> without achieving self-understanding,
> how is liberation achieved, Guheshwara? (648)

This important vachana appears in more than one textual version. Here, my concentration is on the opposition Allama has mounted against the great pronouncement "tattvamasi" (You are that).[57] But in another textual version, "tattvamasi" is replaced by the statement "The Veda is a burden."[58] This sentence too could be authenticated if deemed suspect as there are several sarcastic statements aimed at the Vedas in Allama's verses. It is appropriate on the part of the

---

[55] For the full poem, see Bendre "Kalpavruksha", pp. 12–14.

[56] Sixteen of the Allama vachanas refer to dogs.

[57] This is a well-known statement in the *Upanishads*. M. Prabhakar Joshi and M.A. Hegde show how scholarly skills enable different interpretations of tattvamasi. See Joshi and Hegde, *Bharatiya Tatvashastra*, p. 149.

[58] See Allama Prabhu, *Vyomamuruti*, p. 232.

editors of the first version to conclude that here Allama has probably launched an attack on the statement "tattvamasi", which occupies a prominent place in Indian philosophy. This is because Allama generally takes on prominent philosophical ideas in his vachanas. This textual version is closer to Allama's imagination.

No other formulations in Indian philosophy have received greater attention than the two statements, "aham Brahmasmi" (I am Brahma) and "tattvamasi" (You are that). Modern scholars have written extensively about both. Even Babasaheb Ambedkar, who fiercely and relentlessly criticised several propositions and statements of the Hindu religion, wrote with love and respect of "tattvamasi". In a short note he lamented the fact that Indian culture, which was founded on statements like tattvamasi – a great statement that embraces equality – degenerated into a system of caste discrimination.[59]

I wonder why Allama belched fire against this statement? Was his sensibility forged by spurious logic? Is he a prophet of the neti – "not this" – argument that pounces upon all established propositions?[60] Therefore, is he using the sword of satire? Like the Buddhists, Allama creates his metaphors by using certain techniques of situationism and spurious logic. This is how bedagu vachanas are composed. The fundamental rule of the bedagu model is to materialise what is impossible and that which is antithetical to the ethics of the world. The impossible is possible there; the tendencies that are antithetical to the ethics of the world shine there. But Allama does not use the similes and metaphors of bedagu to contest the great sentence tattvamasi. To evoke a feeling of disgust, he could perhaps have used the familiar metaphor of the dog. That is a different mat-

[59] See Ambedkar, "Riddle Number 22", pp. 281–7.

[60] "Neti neti" (not this, not this) is the phrase the sage Yajnavalkya utters when asked about the true nature of the self. The expression which seeks to describe atma or Brahman through negation is discussed by many Indian darshaniks, including Shankaracharya. Here, Nagaraj wonders whether Allama has an intellectual trait of negating all philosophical statements. For more on negation in Indian darshanas, see Coward, "A Hindu Response to Derrida's", pp. 201–5.

ter. What is important here is that Allama is not getting into an indirect argument, as would a poet. Instead, like a philosopher, he is using reasoning and logic. He is satirising the way the elders lived.

Did Allama recognise in the sentence tattvamasi a degree of condescension toward the Other, or a subtle egotism and air of superiority? There are philosophers who interpret aham brahmasmi and tattvamasi as two faces of the same coin. Allama is austere. Since he does not accept the temporary separateness implied by tat (that is), this contention might have come up. The distinction between self and other is not acceptable to Allama. The dissolving of the distinction between "I" and "Guheshwara" is for him an ultimate spiritual ideal. The concept of tat (that is) is only external. Allama satirises the world that considers this external entity as everything, saying it will die a dog's death. The unwanted dog that followed him is punished! The tinge of Dvaitism in the statement tattvamasi may have made Allama criticise it. There is no discussion of this statement elsewhere, though in another vachana (652) Allama simply states that the statement tattvamasi turned into a falsehood.[61]

Though treated unkindly in Allama's world, the dog became a pretext for a great debate. Now, how can we ignore the frog?

XI: The Story of the Frog

Slicing water's shadow, swallowing Mount Meru,
tying the mouth of Goddess Sharade,
the flowing water swallowed the harvest of dark clouds;
the path swallowed death and kept laughing.
When the husband mounted the back of his lady,
the pitchers broke into pieces
while fetching water from the river.
When a thorn in the bush was chasing and clobbering warriors,
A loose braided maid united with a gorava (begging monk).
A jackal swallowed the elephant,

---

[61] For full translations of the vachana, see vachana no. 652 in Allama Prabhu, *Lord of the Cave*, and Allama Prabhu, *Vachanas of Allama Prabhu*.

a water snake swallowed the sea,
a sitting infant swallowed many people;
as a mother-in-law, mating with the son-in-law,
gave birth to a monkey,
that swallowed the snake-charmer nearby.
When a frog, crushed and swallowed a serpent,
white and red marks appeared on its neck.
Guheshwara's sharana,
became calm and carefree,
like the light of camphor before the eyes. (111)

This is one of Allama's most beautiful and complex bedagu vachanas. In it the frog cannot be ignored as trivia because it is finally the frog that determines the meaning in this text. This frog carries the truth of the Upanishads. We have already observed that there are often two paradoxically opposite meanings of the same word and metaphor in the bedagu vachanas of Allama. This makes our reading of Allama fascinating as well as problematic.

Why does Allama think in terms of paradoxes? What truth is he trying to put forward through paradoxical metaphors? In order to get answers to these questions we need to distance ourselves from Allama. Kierkegaard suggests a reason why philosophers think in terms of paradoxes. He says the philosopher tries to reach through paradoxes a realm beyond all thought.[62] Paradoxes are the final stage of intellectual pursuit. What lies beyond paradoxes is the silent zone. In paradoxes the intellect frantically arrives at, and finally becomes the victim of, the tiger called silence. As far as Allama is concerned, this is the truth. Through paradoxes Allama takes us to the limits of thought. Beyond this, whatever it may be, is an interaction with great silence, an engagement with wonder.

Even so, the bedagu vachanas are home to a weird kind of beauty. If poetry is the business of the vakrakavi – the poet who deals with indirectness – the composing of bedagus is the most profitable

---

[62] "The paradox is the source of the thinker's passion, and the thinker without a paradox is like a lover without feeling . . . The supreme paradox of all thought is the attempt to discover something that thought cannot think." See Kierkegaard, "The Absolute Paradox", p. 46.

venture in that business. Allama does not push bedagu vachanas into the abyss of the completely mysterious and unknown world. His world is half-dark half-bright, where the ordinary world and extra-ordinary experiences remain distinct even after mingling with each other. Shadows, colours, and shades are half-known and half-un-known. Since Allama's vachanas half-drown us in and half-lift us up from the colours of the mundane world, they attract both material-ists and mystics. The materialist reader gets excitement from the ambiguous beauty of the metaphors. For the mystic reader, they test his own knowledge of yogashastra. Though he may have learnt how to attribute meanings to the symbols in traditional texts, it is like learning to swim by reading books. On the other hand, going deeper into Allama's waters, the waves of bedagu rise up and make even the mystic reader panic. Initially then, Allama's world chal-lenges readers, and then slowly develops an intimacy with them.

In the present vachana (111), there are metaphors and objects with opposite meanings. One meaning of water refers to a fickle mind. Another meaning refers to meditative bliss. There are two dimen-sions to Sharade (the Goddess of Learning): vagvrutti, which is the business of speech or rhetoric, and brahmavidya, divine knowledge or higher learning. The symbol of the elephant has two sides to it, pride which is slightly negative and a sense of completeness which is more positive. Thus, paradoxical or opposite meanings pull the met-aphors that control the structure of this composition. The voice of narration here is also important. Only at the end does Allama adopt the stance of adoration, justification, and clear interpretation; while describing the preceding events he remains unaffected. This feeling of calm even while witnessing the strangest of transactions permeates the vachana.

Now we may attempt a specific understanding of the vachana (111): let us assume that the water, at the start, signifies a fickle mind. We can then consider the meaning of Sharade as vagvrutti – speech or rhetoric – which connotes that speech is egoistic about its ca-pacity to capture anything. That is the attitude of Sharade. "Water's shadow" indicates maye, illusion, the fickle mind. Is "slicing the wa-ter's shadow" fruitful? It is possible only for a mystic like Allama.

The metaphor of flowing water in the third line finds a meaning which is the opposite of blissful water. "The harvest of dark clouds" signifies the body's self-delusion. Here ends one event in the poem's narrative, with other eventful stories still in the offing. This initial segment of the text is open to multiple readings. If we interpret "water's shadow" in the first line as blissful water, and the "flowing water" in the fourth line as the fickle mind, the meaning of the first segment in the vachana is turned completely upside down. Fortunately, that is a headache for the mystic reader. In such instances Allama occasionally separates the mystic reader from the materialist reader.

In the first event of the narrative there is a goddess called Sharade, and the second story begins with a lady. If in the former we see the motif of "path swallowing death", in the latter we see the image of "a loose braided maid uniting with a begging monk", which is the opposite of death. In the entire vachana, the water's flow is incessant. The expanse of water thus spreads across the structure of the poem as "mind", "body's water", "death", or "copulation". To get back to the second story, there is a picture of the husband mounting the back of his lady where the back signifies the enlightened behaviour of a sharana, while the husband signifies the guru. In the second story, just when we feel everything is going well, there emerges the image of "a thorn in the bush chasing and clobbering warriors." "A thorn in the bush" indicates the jeopardy of worldliness and the "warrior" stands for a steadfast sharana. In this image there appears a mood of despair and friction. But in the next line "a loose braided maid unites with a begging monk." The story of Ganga and Shiva here is translated into the maid and the beggar monk. While a Dvaitin poet would have preferred to eulogise this kind of situation, Allama consciously avoids doing so. Hence he ends the second story with the metaphor of copulation.

In the third story it is animals that play a prominent role. Here, water assumes the form of a sea. But even here two interpretations are possible. The jackal – a translation of the Kannada word ballu – also connotes the shivoham (I am Shiva) sound. If we accept the meaning of jackal as the sound of shivoham and the elephant as a symbol of the ego, a different kind of narrative emerges. And, if we take a "sense of completeness" as another bedagu meaning for an elephant, the story of a monkey swallowing a snake-charmer begets an opposite meaning. This composition illustrates how the structure of a bedagu vachana depends upon striking a balance between multiple and paradoxical meanings. If we proceed down the path of spiritual interpretation, the jackal (ballu) is nothing but the sound of shivoham. Again, an infant monkey becomes active and gulps down the snake-charmer.

In Allama's bedagu vachanas ordinary animals and birds organise and construct the central meaning. To reiterate, the entire meaning of the present vachana is dependent on the frog. It plays a prominent role in the bedagu, making it a simple spiritual comment by dispelling its ambiguity. In the earlier lines the metaphors of morally heinous sexual relations have created a tumultuous situation: as the mother-in-law copulates with the son-in-law and gives birth to a monkey. Then the frog appears, gulping down the serpent. In Indian poetics this is a metaphor that goes against the conventions of the world. According to one commentary, the frog carries the connotations of peace and tranquillity, while the serpent stands for evil. White and red marks begin to appear around the frog's neck. This suggests the diminishing of sathvika and rajasa (virtuous and pleasure seeking) qualities. Only at the end of the third story does Guheshwara's sharana become calm and carefree. The light of camphor before the eyes begins to burn at the end of three complicated and unusual stories. It is the frog that is responsible for this auspicious ending. So it is impossible to ignore the frog in Allama's world.

XII: Elders are the Gatekeepers of Lakshmi

Donning the garb of vibhuti (sacred ash) and rudrakshi
     (sacred beads),
well versed in the Vedas, shastras, puranas, and agamas,
and merely observing the daily rituals,

these elders, like earthen dolls,
wait on the doors of the master,
Who offers them food, cloth, and wealth.
If you ask the reason, it is said,
    "Vedavriddha vayovriddhaha shastravriddha bahushrutaha|
    ityete dhanavriddhasya dvaretishthati kinkaraha"||

"Elders versed in Veda, agama, and shastra / are servants, waiting
    at the door of him, / who is elderly in respect of wealth."
So all the elders became attendants at Lakshmi's
    (goddess of wealth) door, Guheshwara! (1005)

Allama, who is regarded as an elder not only in the Virashaiva
tradition but also in the Shaiva–Siddha tradition, is extremely impatient with the elders.[63] It should be stated that in this respect Allama is different from other spiritual leaders. As discussed earlier in
this book, most rebellions broke out in the domain of Indian philosophy and spirituality alongside an adoration of the elders. When
writers invoke the elders at every opportunity, it leaves room for
the suspicion that they are in fact conspiring against the elders. In a
lighter vein, one may observe that across Indian history there have
been cases where the elders have been lovingly overturned in the
tenor of adoration.

First, a clarification. Allama addresses prominent figures in his
own tradition and other sibling traditions as elders. From many
angles, he appears to be a highly individualistic mind in Kannada culture, so it is true that he cannot be discussed in relation to tradition.
But each time he gets into a debate, he engages with the prominent
propositions of Shaiva traditions. His affection and conflicts lie in
the same realm too. Though he brings in an understanding of other
knowledge traditions and sects, the historical and theoretical context
of his creativity is situated within the Shaivism of medieval Karnataka and India.

Thus, even in the context of the present vachana (1005), it is

---

[63] There are about fifty-five vachanas of Allama which refer to the term
"elders" (hiriyaru) about sixty-eight times. See Vachana Sanchaya.

the elders of Shaivism that Allama severely satirises. Elsewhere, he critically examines the philosophical positions of Shaiva elders and then puts forward his own alternatives. But in this vachana he mocks at the institutional and power relations of elders. Here he critiques the relationship that the major forms of Shaivism of the time had with power structures and kingship. True, there is no direct reference to a ruler or temporal power, but it was customary in medieval Karnataka to refer to the king or kingship through the literary trope of Lakshmi – deployed also by Pampa and Ranna. With kingship being the subject of adoration, eulogising Lakshmi symbolically is common in Kannada literary culture. For example, there is praise of Lakshmi in the first stanza of each canto in Ranna's *Sahasabheema Vijayam* (The Triumph of Adventurous Bheema).[64] The method of Basavanna as social critic is to directly address the king as king, and he ridicules "the ruler of the land" in plain words. But the bent of Allama's imagination works as usual by choosing a conceptual metaphor.

Contemporary research into the nature of kingship or royal power provides support to my argument that Lakshmi is an image of this power. It is evident from this research that royal power created and enhanced its charisma through charity and gift-giving. Charisma is the basis of power. And the charisma of any material or worldly power in medieval Karnataka would have rested on charity, endowments, and gifts. In particular, charity to religious institutions was the basis of worldly power. There are several inscriptions in Balligavi from Allama's time which support this argument.[65] These inscriptions are particularly related to the Kalamukhas and provide indirect reasons for the moral outrage that Allama might have felt.[66] It was not merely royal power that practised charity and

---

[64] This is also known as *Rannana Gadayuddha*. See Ranna, *Gadayuddham*.

[65] Balligavi: the birthplace of Allama, now in Shikaripur taluka of Shimoga District in central Karnataka.

[66] Kalamukhas are one of the four prominent Shaiva sects from premodern India. Based upon the inscriptions and the works of Yamunacharya and Ramanujacharya, it can be said that they were more influential in South India,

endowment; the practice was deeply rooted in all sections of society. It was considered essential for maintaining the charisma of power, for the cleansing of social stigma, and for the practice of spiritual renunciation.

It is quite possible to interpret this vachana (1005) as embodying Allama's derision for royal power. During Allama's time the dominant sects and institutions of Shaivism were subdued by royalty and lost their explosive nature. The charity and endowments that the mathas and Shaiva temples attracted were impossibly large. Royal power sought to enhance its aura through huge donations. An inscription of Allama's time dated to 1124 narrates to great effect the story of a heroic philanthropist, Bommagavunda.[67] We are given to understand that his desire to donate and offer an endowment to the Brahmeshwara temple of Abbaluru was stronger than his desire to unite with his beloved. He is said to have mounted his horse and declared that he would donate as much land as the galloping horse covered. He then offered worship at the holy feet of the Kalamukha Guru Jnanashakti and made good on his promise. Another inscription, from 1149, tells the story of a great donation to the Kedareshwara temple which is likely to have created a sensation in Balligavi back then. A feudatory ruler under the Chalukya King Jagadekamalla worshipped at the holy feet of Gautama Panditadeva, a disciple of Vidyabharana-Pandita, and donated a whole village to the Kedareshwara temple.[68]

---

especially in the Mysore region, during the tenth to thirteenth centuries and patronised by royalty in many places. See Lorenzen, *The Kapalikas and Kalamukhas*, pp. 3–4, 97.

[67] Hultzsch, ed., *Epigraphia Indica*, vol. 5, p. 233.

[68] "It records the grant of the village Kundur in Kodanad-30, of the Santaligi 1000 and 2 *mattars* of wet land, to Gautama-Pandita, a disciple of Vidyabharana-Pandita for the offerings of god Kedareshvara, for the repairs of the temple for the food of the ascetic and for education at the temple in the presence of Kedareshwara at Balligavi as *sarvanamasya* along with *tribhogabhygantaa-siddhi* by the Santara King Jagadevarasa who is stated to be ruling from Setu together with his Kumara (son?) Bammarasa, at the request of Bammarasa. It further refers to the grant of the villages Abbasa and Hosavalli in Kodenada Kampana, Govin-

There is a subtle irony in these inscriptions. Though they record that it was a matter of great gratification on the part of royal power to donate and worship at the holy feet of religious power, only one face of the connection between them is revealed here. It was characteristic of medieval Karnataka that institutions such as aramane (palace) and gurumane (the house of Guru) and devalaya (temple) had an ideologically interdependent relationship. If the royal power bowed symbolically before religious institutions, in fact it was the elders of these religious institutions that beseeched patronage from royal power. This was a common phenomenon in medieval polities of the region.

The king's beneficence was the sweet dream of the intellectual classes. However, when the relationship turned bitter, the dream became a nightmare. Royal patronage to the intellectual classes of medieval times was at once life-saving and life-threatening. In order to understand the problematic relationship of Shaiva intellectuals with royal patronage, we can examine the life and writings of Kannada poets like Harihara and Raghavanka and the Telugu poet Dhurjati. Dhurjati's *Kalahstishwara Shatakam* is the touching commentary of a Shaiva poet reflecting on the wickedness and disgraceful behaviour of the royal court.[69] In it the choice is finally between the generosity of the royal court and Shiva's compassion: the former provides material pleasure but not self-esteem. The self-respect lies in taking refuge in Shiva, though this may mean a half-filled belly. It is a choice between the lingatattva (the principle of linga) and royal patronage; the former facilitates limitless freedom and the latter material benefits with its concomitant, humiliation. It seems that the latter was essential if the religion was to grow institutionally. Allama chose the limitless freedom of lingatattva.

It is against this background that we have to read the present vachana (1005). Who is Allama satirising in the first two lines of the vachana? Since there is no empirical evidence regarding this, it is safe

---

danahalli in Muduvalala-Kampana with free of all imposts to the same god . . ." See "Inscription no. 215", in Rice, ed., *Epigraphia Carnatica*, p. 235.

[69] Heifetz and Narayana Rao, eds, *For the Lord of the Animals.*

to state that he is targeting a type – the model of religious gurus. One such model emerges from Balligavi itself; an inscription of 1192 records the Hoysala King Viraballala II donating lands to the Dakshina Kedareshwara temple of the Kalamukha sect. The rajaguru Vamashaktideva was the most prestigious pontiff of the Kalamukhas. In the inscription this guru is applauded as being well-versed in vedanta, siddhanta, agama, the six types of logic, grammar, theology, and all other disciplines.[70] In inscriptions of the previous century, we come across similar descriptions of Shaiva elders. It is my guess that Allama would have been enraged by such descriptions. It is interesting to note that the description of elders we come across in Allama's vachana is, incidentally, similar to the description of Shaiva gurus in these inscriptions.

Hermeneutically speaking, the lines "So all the elders became attendants / at Lakshmi's (goddess of wealth) door, Guheshwara!" assume a special meaning. It is not simply the elders beseeching royal power that Allama finds worthy of condemnation. It is also possible to read in these lines his opinion that the elders of religious institutions became the guardians of royal aura and charisma. Allama becomes important in this context because he stands spiritually and ideologically apart from the triad of aramane–gurumane–gudi. Allama does not belong to any religious institution, such as a matha (Virashaiva monastery). He is the type of person who asks "Why matha, and why mountain?" He criticises the elders because religion gradually loses its transparency and spiritual power when it joins hands with Lakshmi (the goddess here signifying royal power). In

[70] "It states that Viraballala's *mahapradhana, sarvvadhikari, mahapasayita* Ereyanna son of Maramayya and Nagaladevi, made a grant of cash income from Chiyana-Saliyur in the Muddha-Kundani-Vritti in the Santalige-nad belonging to his chieftaincy with free of all imposts and further records that first 18 *gadyanas* payable to the treasury (*poththada-modala gadyana*) as *sarvanamasya* to *rajaguru* Vamashaktideva, a disciple of Gautama-muni, for the worship of god Dakshina Kedareshvara of Balipura (Balligave) and for the offerings, perpetual lamp, *chaitra-pavitra* etc., and for the temple repairs and food for the ascetics with the permission of the king." See Hultzsch, ed., *Epigraphia Indica*, vol. 5, pp. 225–6.

Allama's idiom the idea of elders is a symbol of institutionalised religion. These elders, he believes, represent a rotten state where religion, losing its purity, becomes another spritually barren institution. Allama complains of this to Guheshwara himself.

He is aware of the fact that when Guheshwara is institutionalised as a temple, he too is chained to this vicious circle. Precisely for this reason, Allama is against making a temple for Guheshwara. The moment Guheshwara is seen in the form of a stone idol, the provisions and practices of the concrete historical world come into play. Allama fears the forces that might imprison Guheshwara himself. These forces may operate in different forms – such as religious practices, with undue importance given to elders, rituals, etc. The most important insight Allama shares is about the danger of binding Guheshwara down to worldly life (samsara). Take a look at the following vachana:

> The wearers of linga embraced the worldly life of linga.
> The worshippers of jangama embraced the worldly life of sayujya
>   (union with god).
> Those who have bonds with prasada and padodaka embraced
>   the worldly life of prasada.
> I bend before Chennabasavanna,
> who is free from every kind of worldliness,
> and dwell in Guheshwaralinga.[71] (1296)

The objects and institutions mentioned in this composition are essential to the institutional form of a religion. Externally, the linga, jangama, prasada, and padodaka mentioned in the vachana are the authentic emblems of Virashaivism. Thus, Allama is speaking of how these external symbols push the inner self of Virashaivism into the captivity of samsara. Samsara is a state of imprisonment. If linga is a symbol, Guheshwara is the essence. Allama is cautioning against the state in which only symbols shine by imprisoning the inner self. In the Virashaiva tradition, it was Allama who thought

---

[71] For the full vachana, see vachana no. 1283 in Allama Prabhu, *Lord of the Cave*, and no. 1062 in Allama Prabhu, *Vachanas of Allama*.

deeply about the incompatible relationship between the internal self
and external symbols.

This is also true in the case of elders who became a part of external
forces. Allama is always bothered by the thought of elders – as the
instruments of external forces – destroying the truth of the internal
self. It is against this background that we must understand Allama's
scepticism of elders and their tradition. But this does not mean that
Allama is antagonistic towards the entire notion of elders or tradition. It is simply that rather than admiring elders of the past, he ap-
preciates the real seekers of the present. From this perspective there is
no other mystic in Kannada culture who adores the present as much
as Allama. The fear that all memories become stale and poisonous
makes Allama especially sensitive to concrete experiences in the
present. Excitement over things in the present is all-important.

> Could you not recognise the linga,
> dwelling in your front yard?
> O Sangana Basavanna,
> behold Marulushankaralinga,
> who is the divine companion, formless, immaculate Brahman
> dwelling in the prasada pit, in the company of
> Guheshwaralinga. (1118)

Where are the elders whom Allama has accused earlier? Where is
Marulushankaralinga, who in the form of linga stands in the front
yard? The former elders are ostensibly after clothes, gold, and lavish
feasts, while Marulushankaradeva resembles Shiva coming to ask
for alms. When Shiva begs for alms there is the possibility that even
jangamas will not recognise him. (There is a flash of this motif in
H.S. Shivaprakash's powerful poem on "Marulashankaralinga".[72])
In this respect Allama is posing a question to Sangana Basavanna
himself. Gaudily attired elders are visibly prominent here, but the
pure spirit of Brahman in the form of Marulushankaradeva is buried
in the prasada pit!

We need to carefully analyse this metaphor of the prasada pit.

[72] Shivaprakash, "Marula Shankaradeva", pp. 25–6.

Prasada is an important concept in Virashaiva philosophy as well as a metaphor for Basavanna's food charity (annadasoha). When these two become a matter of ritual, there is always the danger of them becoming a pit or well, signifying the danger of falling. When the philosophy of food charity (prasadatattva) becomes static, there is the danger that its practitioner will not be able to recognise the religiosity of the other. When the spirit of prasada is institutionalised as daily charity (dasoha), the vanity of being a philanthropist might make one see as beggars all who approach for alms. Thus, Marulushankara is lying in the pit of prasada. Spiritual whimsicality, a trait in Allama, is also plentiful in Marulushankara. He can slip easily into the pit of prasada. He might go unnoticed even by Basavanna, who is now in the company of material power. In the earlier vachana about the elders and in the present vachana about Marulushankaradeva, Allama is offering us two alternative models. Ultimately, Allama's choice is Marulushankara. The elders are gatekeepers, and Marulushankaradeva too stands at the door of the front yard; yet there is such a difference between the two!

XIII: They Drank the Blood of Perverted Spiritualism

The thieves in the forest keep searching for
the swamy clad in deer skin (kadavasana).
Their torch flames died out, they cannot see.
The gluttonous elders, who do not understand their own selves,
drinking lavishly the lips of women,
are now begging for the wine of gods.
Look Guheshwara,
a learned Brahmin (haruva),
holding in his hand a severed head,
drank the blood of perverted spiritualism! (33)

In medieval literature there are ample satires of this kind. Such religious satires were generally expressed in plays. Farce and bhana (one-act monologues in the Sanskrit tradition) were congenial to this kind of satire. There are significant differences between the religious satire at work in these farces and the kind that we come across in this particular vachana. Before discussing these differences, it is necessary to describe religious satire as implicit in farces.

In the genre of farce, religious satire is mainly expressed in the form of social mockery. Rather than religious or philosophical positions, the social conduct of leaders from other religions was made the object of severe mockery. In this respect a bhana by Shyamilaka, who is said to have been Kalidasa's contemporary, and the play *Mattavilasa Prahasana* (Farce on a Drunken Brawl), which belongs to the time of the Cholas (seventh century), can be seen as representative texts.[73]

In the *Mattavilasa Prahasana* the followers of Shramana sects are the main object of criticism. This work is a testimony to the intense conflict between Buddhists and Brahmins. The unconventional lifestyle of Shramana followers is lampooned, presented as grotesque and twisted. Here, sanyasis of the opponent sect drink toddy and dally with prostitutes, indulging in activities considered disgusting by the standards of householderly duty (grihasthadharma). The religious symbols of Shramanas are also satirised within this text. In the bhana of Shyamilaka, a Buddhist bachelor is the protagonist. He has sex with a prostitute even as he eulogises renunciation (vairagya) and freedom from all passions. In this text certain philosophical concepts of Buddhism are positioned for perverse entertainment. The prostitute Radha is described as writhing in the pangs of separation, yearning for this Buddhist "bachelor". The dialogues in this section are, in particular, fertile ground for satire. If he is really committed to Buddhism, he should show loving kindness (maitri);[74] he should make love to her. And if he is not a staunch follower of Buddhism, what is the point in troubling oneself to be a sanyasi? Is it not better to revel in romance with a lady longing for love?

---

[73] *Mattavilasa Prahasana:* One of the two great one-act plays written by the Pallava King Mahendravarman I (571–630 CE).

[74] Gopal Guru and Sundar Sarukkai discuss the idea of maitri in relation to B.R. Ambedkar and Buddhism. See Guru and Sarukkai, *Experience, Caste.*

In these satirical works, adversarial characters are tortured by the distortion of philosophical concepts at the level of food, drink, and sex. But what is important here is ridicule of the social self from the perspective of an opposing religion. This perspective in farces and bhanas is that of traditional Vedic and Brahmanical religions. Their criticism emerges on account of a total social acceptance of all ashramas, and intolerance with those who oppose them. A social critique of religion is the focal point here.

However, the satirical element in Allama and Sarahapada comes from a philosophical ground and is based on values that may be called socially progressive. In the present vachana (33), Allama is expressing his strong opposition to sorcerous elders. According to the bedagu lexicon, the forest is bhavaranya — the forest of worldly life.[75] While kadavasana literally means the skin of a deer, in the bedagu lexicon it stands for fake skin and falsity.[76]

In this vachana (33), three types of seekers are subjected to criticism. All of them are sorcerers of different kinds. Those who appear in the first three lines are solitary seekers. Strictly speaking, they cannot be called sorcerers. In this context we are reminded of the categorisation of two types of Buddhist monks. The categorisation of Buddhist monks into village-dwelling monks and forest-dwelling monks can be broadly applied to the sects of Hinduism as well. The solitary seekers in Allama's vachana are of the second type — forest-dwelling sanyasis. These are depicted seeking what is, essentially, falsity — and in the dark to boot. Even the torch-flame held in the hand has died out. It is dark everywhere. Without stating the matter specifically, Allama achieves his goal by creating a metaphoric environment. What happens through characterisation in farces happens in Allama through metaphors.

It then immediately occurs to us that the second type of seekers are tantrics. Allama has used the term gluttonous (anna-pana) to represent the four elements in the pancha "ma" karas (five Ms) of

---

[75] "Bedagina Padakosha", in Allama Prabhu, *Allamana Vachana Chandrike*, p. 364.

[76] Ibid., p. 361.

vamachara: madya (alcohol), mamsa (meat), matsya (fish), mudra (pound grain).[77] By stripping them of their symbolic meaning, he presents them in the form of their fundamental physicality, mixing up several concepts without distinguishing between them. What we need to notice here is that, according to some scholars, Ramanujacharya too did the same while discussing Shaiva tantras in philosophical terms in his *Sri Bhashya*.[78] With respect to Allama there is at least some small justification for this kind of method. He is not writing an elaborate philosophical commentary or a logical treatise. The metaphoric method is his chief mode.

What Allama calls "lips of women" (adharapana) is a female in the form of the Shakti that we encounter in tantrism.[79] She is called mahamudre, or duti (a messenger). But so far as Allama is concerned, "Drinking lavishly the lips of women" (adharapana) is merely a sensual experience, it cannot be a divine one. He rejects the very argument that sensory passion can include a spiritual touch. He dissects each of the five Ms. Is it possible to call the intoxication of alcohol divine excitement? In Allama's view there is an organic relationship between goals and means, even in the spiritual realm. It is precisely for this reason that Virashaivism emerged in revolt against Shaivism. At this level, Allama too is a willing participant within the general Virashaiva uprising.

The third model is a terrible one. There is a vivid picture of the violent achievement of a learned Brahmin (haruva). It is quite common for sorcerers to boast about their Brahmanical background. In Abhinavagupta's thought there is appreciative reference to the social prestige of Brahmanism. They who claim the Brahmanical religion as their lineage share the opinion that they have taken to this path owing to the superiority of their knowledge of tantrism. The imagery that Allama provides in the vachana is not stated explicitly, it is mysterious. The lines "A learned Brahmin (haruva), / Holding in his hand a severed head, / Drank the blood of perverted spiritualism!" represents the practice of smashana sadhane, i.e. penance in

---

[77] The fifth M is maithuna (sexual intercourse).

[78] A commentary on Sri Badarayana's Vedanta or Brahma Sutra.

[79] The act of pressing one's lips on the lips of another person.

the graveyard, and narabali sadhane, meaning human sacrifice, in the quest for Shiva (shiva sadhane). Without bothering to elaborate on these aspects in his vachana, Allama says that what such seekers (sadhakas) drink is not human blood but the blood of perverted spiritualism. He is not criticising these practices, however, on the basis of the moral sentimentality of the conduct of family life (grihasthadharma). Nor is he afraid of darkness, graveyards, severed heads, or the drinking of blood in tantrism. He criticises them on account of spiritual disgust. For Allama, nothing is more disgusting than spiritual perversion, whether in the form of shringara or smashana sadhane. In his world there is no compassion.

XIV: Anti-Veda Stance

The Vedas are mere texts for reading.
The shastras are mere market tales.
The puranas are a mere rogues' conference.
Logic is a mere fight of rams.
Bhakti (devotion) is a mere profitable exhibition.
Transcending all these,
Guheshwaralinga is the Great Absolute. (465)

The above vachana, obviously, targets Vedic culture. In ancient India it was difficult to be revered as a mystic after criticising the Vedas. But Allama enjoys that kind of rare reverence. The present vachana reveals not only his unique spiritual poetics but also one of the most prominent debates of Indian darshana as a whole. One of the perpetual debates in Indian darshana stems from the conflicting stances regarding the role of the Vedas and their veracity. As suggested by its name, Vedic religion believes that the Vedas are the ultimate spiritual power. But there are different readings regarding the power of meaning in the Vedas. Here, I am using the term "reading" in the sense of the hermeneutics used in Western philosophy; reading as meaning-making.

By the twelfth century the Vedas were already established as primary texts of traditional Brahmanism. What the Vedas originally communicate, and what meaning, motif, and values they profess were all dependent on hermeneutic interpretations of them. Traditionalist Vedic interpretations proposed three types of "truths" and "values". One, the Vedas are apaurusheya and epistemologically unquestionable.[80] Two, they are the basis of the social system and the source of traditionalist power. Three, they are the authorities on spirituality and the basis for theism. Proponents of the Vedas, as well as their opponents, looked upon the Vedas as the basis for the organisation and concentration of traditional power. Gradually, the stance that the Vedas were ahistorical expressions of Brahma gained credence. But Allama vehemently rejected these three traditionalist propositions.

It is possible to say that his reading of the Vedas is literal. He feels an intense spiritual dissatisfaction with the crowded presence of gods in the Vedas. It was common in Allama's time for various gods, several types of miracles, and mysterious rituals to derive their power and aura from the Vedas themselves. In Indian darshana – apart from the Shramana sects – even the other traditions, which could be called their rivals, sought the help of the Vedas for their justification. As a result, the growth of hermeneutics of the Vedas reached such a stage that the original nature of the Vedas became obscure. The law of hermeneutics works so: its original object of interpretation must become hazy. Interpretations clash with each other and proliferate themselves like Raktabijasura's offspring.[81] The main success of Allama's spiritual life lies in the fact that he was not caught up in the wilderness of hermeneutics. In the traditional Vedic world, even the dissidents gained power by resorting to the Vedas. From this point of view, hermeneutic interpretation is like vatapigarbha.[82] Dissidents wander perpetually in the intestines of the Vedas.

---

[80] Beyond human power, in the sense that they are not human creations.

[81] In Hindu mythology, Raktabija is an asura (demon), who gains a boon from Lord Shiva, which ensures that, whenever a drop of the demon's blood falls on the ground, more raktabijas emerge from the spot. Nagaraj is using this as a metaphor.

[82] In Hindu mythology, Ilvala and Vatapi are demons who invite travellers to a feast. Ilvala cooks Vatapi's body and feeds it to the guest. After the meal, Ilvala calls, "Vatapi, come out!" Then Vatapi bursts out from the stomach of the

Being aware of this danger, Allama refused to enter the Vedic world. By calling the Vedas mere texts for reading, he becomes relevant even to our time. He is diminishing their spiritual and mystical dimensions by suggesting that the Vedas are merely to be read and interpreted. This is not something that is acceptable to other Shaiva sects. This stance is also largely unique to Allama.

There is something else we need to pay attention to in the present vachana (465).[83] Allama is here creating a familial structure for the Vedas by reconfiguring the five branches of knowledge – Veda-Shastra-Purana-Tarka-Bhakti – as members of the same family. It is easy to understand his opposition to the first four branches. But, what about bhakti? According to Allama, bhakti too is an integral part of a tradition that he does not agree with, and he opposes it at different levels. But by placing bhakti in a particular configuration, he has made definite his opposition to it.

Allama believes that, essentially, bhakti is a manifesto of duality. The idea of it emerges by making a distinction between the self and the divine. It emerges out of the pangs of the divisible condition. Therefore, "dasaham" (I am a servant of God) is the refrain in the Bhakti sect. Allama belongs to the Soham sect (I am God). Therefore, for Guheshwara the act of adoring oneself is absurd. However, regarding Allama's take on bhakti here, it is difficult to say whether he is satirising the rituals of worship or the psychological transactions of the Bhakti sensibility.

> If a crow flying to Mount Meru
> does not change to a golden hue,
> isn't a grassy mound better than the mountain?
> O god,
> even after worshipping you,
> if one is still restless,
> isn't the earlier state better than adoring You?

---

guest, thus killing them. Here, vatapigarbha does not refer to Vatapi's stomach, but the stomach of the ill-fated guest from which Vatapi emerges.

[83] For a different interpretation of this vachana, see Akshara, *Shankara Vihara*, pp. 40–3.

O Guheshwara,
if death befalls after worshipping You,
isn't the god of death better than you? (66)

Kierkegaard says "faith is restless".[84] But Allama asks "Why be restless in religion?" Even so his stance in this vachana is a bit surprising as he explores the goals and anxieties of restlessness in religion. We are perturbed by Allama looking down upon restlessness here.

One aspect of the difference between Allama and the Dvaita sensibility surfaces here. Kierkegaard, St Augustine, and Basavanna speak of their own restlessness. Their expressions of anxiety or states of anxiousness have a sense of urgency precisely because of this personal restlessness. There is no autobiographical tinge in Allama's restlessness. Nor is there a reason to think that he is here referring to himself. Exploring the restlessness of the self is very important in religious poetry. It is deeply rooted in literary thought that religious poetry provides a portrait of the evolution of the self.

XV: Tiger and Deer as a Pair

A tiger-headed deer, or
a deer-headed tiger!
The two merge in the middle!
It is neither a tiger nor a deer.
Look,
it came near and chewed the cud.
Look Guheshwara,
If a headless body feasted on dry leaves,
the leaves vanished! (39)

As Umberto Eco has observed, animals in medieval Europe revealed much without being aware of it.[85] In Allama's world there are

[84] According to Kierkegaard, "Faith expressly signifies the deep, strong, blessed restlessness that drives the believer so that he cannot settle down at rest in this world." See Kierkegaard, *Provocations*, pp. 273–4.

[85] Eco, *The Name of the Rose*.

plenty of animals and birds, and they converse too. But, according to him, they speak consciously. In ancient Europe Epicureans and Stoics expressed varying views on animals and animal language. Somewhat similar debates about animals and birds took place among vachana writers. Intellectuals who lived in such close proximity to animals as vachanakaras are rare, and among them Allama stands out. The dog is prominent in Aristotle and Augustine, but in Allama, as noticed earlier, it is not treated with much respect. For the ancient Greeks the howling of a dog presents a great philosophical problem, but for Allama it is a matter of irritation.

It is the company of wild animals that Allama finds more interesting. This does not mean that he wants to view them as potential pets. He is not one who wishes to play the snake-charmer with defanged snakes. No tamed or domesticated animal appeals to Allama. Here too we are reminded of animals pacing around at night in medieval Europe. European cities were alive at night with wailing patients and barking street dogs — not to mention with the occasional appearance of chickens, parrots, and pigeons. But there were no cats at all; perhaps they were busy playing with dreadful witches.

Likewise, Allama does not believe in cats. Some say the cat is untrustworthy. All the same, such animals loiter around Allama — tigers and deer often roam around in his world. He is neither afraid of the tiger nor fond of the deer. He does not seem to like either. Over his period the forests in the malnadu were dense and wild animals were never distant. Had Allama ventured out even a little, vast forestlands teeming with wild animals would have become apparent. There were times when Allama sat in a cave for penance and glimpsed the approach of wild animals.

Two animals that disturbed Allama's penance were the tiger and the deer. The deer represents the doe of maye (illusion), and there is a commentary that interprets the tiger's face as a representation of the five senses. Unlike the poet Blake, Allama does not view the tiger in a positive light. While exploring the relationship between the tiger and the deer, he exhibits most elegantly his natural gift for "paradoxical consciousness". It is true that the deer is beautiful. Until a particular stage in spiritual development, the deer represents a form of the five senses. According to another commentary, the doe characterises the quality of being unsteady, of a vain illusion. The tiger symbolises a variety of bodily pleasures and the luxuries of life. The five senses are thus at once the deer and the tiger. The body, like a tiger, reaches the zenith of pleasure in sexual intercourse but suffers disease a hundred times more. Here such a body is represented by Allama's powerful imagery of the union of tiger and deer: a "tiger-headed deer" or a "deer-headed tiger". Collectively this constitutes Allama's powerful commentary on the body.

With regard to attraction and repulsion in relation to the body, Allama differs greatly from other mystics of the Virakta sect. A majority of Viraktas fear the body. Given their theoretical stance, they do not stand face-to-face with the experience of the body. If the bodily experience were wholly constituted of pain and agony, there would be no intense attraction between man and woman. Allama therefore, doesn't reject the idea that the body takes humans to the zenith of pleasure – as spiritualists usually do. Instead, he produces tattva, a theory, out of the experience of the body by exploring the integral relationship that the body has with happiness and agony. His view is that the one cannot exist without the other.

Within the primordial field of Allama's theorisation there is a prominent place for the body. If we can believe certain stories about Allama's life before he became an ascetic, the doe of the five senses was once everything in life to him. It is difficult to believe that this earlier memory of the body completely disappeared during his ascetic days. In Allama the experiences of past, present, and future continuously examine and edit each other, changing each other's shades. In other words it is on the basis of his theory of the body that Allama formulates his other principles. Since the immediacy of bodily experience is extended to other philosophical domains, they also become dense.

Allama shows no aversion for the body; rather, he is wonderstruck by it. This wonder is not the result of his appreciation, nor does it end in appreciation. It is because he is fully aware of the possibilities of the body that he is awed by it. Allama is filled with wonder at the power of the body to unshackle itself from consciousness and behave independently. In him, the theory of the body is a theory of wonder.

> Witnessing,
>   The safe return of a deer grazing after a tiger,
>   I was awestruck.
> Witnessing,
>   The safe return from a demoness' den after a sound sleep,
>   I was awestruck.
> Witnessing,
>   The safe return from the house of yama (God of death)
>   without dying,
>   I was awestruck, Guheshwara. (27)

Other Viraktas would totally reject the idea of a deer's safe return grazing after a tiger. Since Allama is thinking in metaphors, he does not care for such simplistic rejections. Instead of accepting common principles, he examines them with the help of metaphors. His metaphors overturn natural laws.

What is remarkable about Allama is that he not only thinks metaphorically but also meditates on the nature of metaphors. It is quite common for saint poets to think metaphorically. However, beyond a point they cannot use metaphors: instead, metaphors control them. This is precisely the case with Kannada Dasa literature, where the logic of a metaphor's particular context constrains the Dasa poet.

At this point it is appropriate to compare Allama and Kanakadasa.[86] Kanakadasa's theory of the body is very simplistic. When composing a song or kirtana he resorts to a simple spiritual rejection of the body. He translates the body as social life. A characteristic

---

[86] A warrior turned saint-philosopher, Kanakadasa (sixteenth century) belonged to the Haridasa tradition. Known for his major works *Ramadhanyacharita* and *Mohanatarangini*, he also composed kirtanas which are often sung in Carnatic music performances.

feature of the entire Dasa tradition, including the works of Kanaka-dasa, is that it does not look at the body as an asocial site of primor-dial pain and pleasure. If we were to begin with the assumption that the body is meaningless in our spiritual journey, the depth and wonderment Allama offers would not be possible for us.

The Dasa imagination sets itself apart, particularly when it comes to mythical narratives. The mythical narratives about Krishna are characterised by adoration of the body. Adoration of the body is fine for Krishna, but not so much for ordinary mortals. If we look at descriptions that use intense shringara in Kanakadasa's *Mohana-tarangini*, the free-flowing style of the composition and the plea-sure of sexual intercourse are one and the same. In both, there is sweetness and delight. The body here is a site of special experience: everything is acceptable. The description of shringara is so explicit that one wonders if it was Kanakadasa, who devoted himself to the virakta mode, who wrote it. Kissing the sensitive parts and genitals is just one example of this openness. A justification would be pos-sible here: since he wrote *Mohanatarangini* as a kavya, the norms of poetic convention might have compelled him to include explicit descriptions of shringara.

Unlike Kanakadasa, Allama does not naively express a feeling of involvement, but rather retains the feeling of wonder. He does not directly say that going to the den of a demoness to sleep is an illusion, but proceeds to accept the fact that there is pleasure even in illusion and that illusion is also a kind of reality. Since Allama accepts the illusory reality in all seriousness and then breaks it, the distinction between reality and illusion collapses in his vachanas. The meta-phors of animals and birds are the dominant medium in driving home the distinction between reality and illusion.

Yogashastra (postures in yoga) believes that the state of nature – animals and birds – resides in the body. This is the organising prin-ciple behind yogasanas. According to yogashastra it is dangerous to let animals and birds be present in the body as they are; they need to be explicitly named in asanas. When asanas are named, a unique relationship is established between consciousness and the body's innate nature – the presence of animals and birds. Shalabhasana, mayurasana, kukkutasana, bakasana, parvatasana – all these are manifestations of nature in the human body. Practising these bodily postures is a way of awakening the state of animality and thus controlling it. This is the concept operating behind the yogic act of vyaghra vishwasa – the act of awakening and controlling the body's beastly states.

Perhaps Allama received this idiom from the conventional yogic imagination with full awareness and discriminatory consciousness. Thus, the animal images in Allama are nothing but images of the body. Elephant, cat, tiger, monkey, and snake – all are present in the human body. The human body is a forest, and the fickle-minded doe enters this forest. A particular sense of beauty is then evoked and the enchanting dance of maye (illusion) begins. Maye in Allama is not an external principle, it is a reality that is perpetually and permanently active within. As the fickle doe wakes up and begins to run, the tiger of time in the body of the forest begins to chase it. These two are inseparable states of the body. If there is no deer, there is no tiger. If the movement of human muscle is the movement of a doe, it is also the movement of a tiger (death). Sexual intercourse is the pre-state of death. In the body the creative act of a dove (intercourse) and the fatal blow of time-tiger (death) are interrelated.

In Allama's imagination there is an image of kadali – a plantain grove – that represents the body. When he tries to think allegorically, this kind of conceptual metaphor comes into being. When such metaphors are used repeatedly, monotony results. Perhaps in order to negotiate with the tradition of bedagu-allegory, Allama resorts at times to such monotonous metaphors. But amidst such monotony, when Allama inserts dynamic and explosive metaphors the environment is revitalised.

The creative paradox in the joint image of tiger and deer has come from one who understands the body very well. There is one type of mystic who knows what is happening to their consciousness and who records it with minute observation. Allama is such a mystic; he explores what is happening to the body and what pressure it can build up on consciousness through the collection of memory. If the tiger–deer attraction were to be understood merely as a symbol of hunter–hunted, Allama would seem wholly pessimistic. At times, this attitude of fatalism causes dejection in Sankhya philosophers. Uchchedavadis argue that it is impossible for any hunter to enter the forest of the body.[87] Allama would never entertain such ideas because for him no state is permanent. Everything merges into the other and keeps changing. Tiger becomes deer, deer becomes tiger, and both sport in the forest called body. It is the intensity of this sport that invites the hunter. It is not only the tiger that kills the deer; the deer perishes in many other ways too. In the following vachana, Allama describes such a state:

When an arrow with a red feather was shot
at the deer standing on a rock,
it hit the target without missing.
In one shot the deer fell down !
The string was snapped and the bow broken.
O Guheshwara,
where did the deer vanish? (557)

There is a commentary on this vachana: when the hunter called Sharana kills the deer of illusion, shooting the arrow of good knowledge with the bow of loyalty by pulling the string of will, the illusory deer dies at once.

[87] A sect which does not believe in the afterlife.

7

Kings, Commoners, and Mystics

Understanding Premodern
Kannada Literary Culture Through
Allama's World

Words spoken on Vastuka, Varnaka, and Tristhana
speak of what is in this world.
Who knows what is beyond this world?
They can't know the real.
How can they, who prattle like a flock of parrots,
know You, Guheshwara?[1] (641)

I N THE PRESENT chapter I aim to critically survey premodern Kannada literature through Allama's perspective. I believe it will be an intellectually stimulating adventure to identify the thematic preoccupations of premodern Kannada literature and analyse them in light of the values embedded in Allama's vachanas. Another objective of this chapter is to understand how Allama's interior world – the Virashaiva imagination and its institutional forms –

---

[1] Vastuka (objective poetry) and Varnaka (subjective poetry) are two forms of composing poetry in classical Kannada literature. For more, see ch. 3. In his *Allamaprabhudevara Vachana-Nirvachana*, Sri Siddheshwara Swamiji interprets them as forms of mantra, and Tristhana refers to the three stages of uttering these mantras – udatta, anudatta, and swarita. See Siddheshwara, *Allamaprabhudevara*, p. 992.

have received and transformed Allama in their framework, and how all these posed challenges to Kannada literary culture.

There is a negotiation between the major themes of premodern Kannada literature and Allama's world. In one way or another, they converse and provoke each other. The above-quoted vachana (641) illustrates that Allama was conscious of working within a literary tradition in a particular historical context. One of his prime philosophical concerns was the relationship between experience and expression. In particular, the challenge of capturing divyanubhava (divine experience) in language always troubled Allama. Since he is acutely aware of these philosophical problems of poetic expression, he may be considered a poet. He is a poet who is self-consciously sensitive about the craft of poetry. For this reason he continues to appeal to us moderns.

Several themes Allama has explored in his vachanas reflect the problems of premodern Kannada literature. I do not use the empiricist method of writing literary history to justify this claim. Instead, I attempt to unravel specific structures by placing the prominent themes of Allama's world face-to-face with Kannada literary culture. The characteristic of a great poet is that through the binoculars of his images and themes we can see the entire world, not just the world of literary culture. One of the themes of premodern Kannada literary culture was the relationship between the "scribing and erasing" process. I have borrowed this concept from one of Allama's vachanas, quoted below. Literary culture is entirely a world of scribing and erasing practices, and Allama interprets this in the context of the expression of divyanubhava:

> After practising the letters of the alphabet,
> why this exercise of scribing and erasing?
> As they have not understood the form and the formless,
> Guheshwara is tranquil,
> in the beginning, in the middle, and the above. (642)

The first line of the vachana seems to question the ability of writing (scribing) to record the divine experience. This scepticism on writing (scribing) could be extended to writing practice in literary culture. Thus, extending the concepts that emerge in the religious domain to other broader contexts is not something new in the intellectual history of the world. For example, the concept of "alienation", predominantly developed by Marxist theory, also has religious roots. But that is a different matter.

Historians of premodern Kannada literary culture have to work with several constraints. They need to keep in mind the invisible ones while writing about the works and writers present and visible before them. Even today, numerous manuscripts remain unread and uncompiled. This yet-to-be-discovered world of texts poses a great challenge in painting a holistic picture of our literary culture. That is, it is difficult to theorise with full confidence about texts that are known, unknown, or lost.

The historian of Kannada literature has to work like Penelope in Greek mythology. Several authors and works might disappear from sight during their historical odysseys but might return at any time. And those who return may come in disguise, just as Penelope's husband Odysseus appeared to her as an old beggar returning from the Trojan War after two decades. I raise this issue not just in the context of unknown authors who have disappeared, but also about chandorupa (forms of prosody) which too disappear or come in disguise. Elsewhere I have discussed this as a problem of chadmavesha (disguise) and chatrapatitva (total power) in prosody.[2] The Russian thinker Mikhail Bakhtin formulated the concept of "chronotope",[3] which can philosophically be considered a "historicist knot". In literary culture, forms of prosody present this kind of historicist knot. At times, they appear openly in their original form and attire, and on other occasions they appear in disguise. Sometimes, Penelope can recognise them, and sometimes she cannot. The history of local

[2] In an essay on the oral tradition and modern poetry, Nagaraj says that in *Chandyogya* a commentary begins with an interesting reference to devates (goddesses) hiding behind prosody because of the fear of death. See Nagaraj, "Chandassinalli Adagikolluva Devategalu", pp. 211–19.

[3] Bakhtin, "Forms of Time", pp. 84–258.

prosody and songs in Kannada provides ample evidence for my argument.

What controls the design and relationship between "disguise" (chadmavesha) and "total power" (chatrapatitva) in prosody? In my view, it is the process of scribing and erasing in a literary culture. In a broader sense, it lies in power relations – the relationship between culture (literary production) and sociopolitical forces. Here, literature cannot be limited to the naive and romantic view that it is a fundamental human disposition. At a particular point in history, literature is transformed into literary culture. According to the available sources, by the time of *Kavirajamarga* Kannada literary culture was already a constituent part of the larger domain of royal power; engagement with kingly powers had become an inevitable attribute of literary culture. But this does not mean that literary culture always maintained a consciously cordial relationship with royal power. Both harmony and conflict existed between them. To an extent, this fact helps us reconstruct the complexity of the environment.

In its interaction with royal power, literary culture implements the practice of scribing and erasing with great deliberation. In this context, it becomes a question of literally scribing practice. Literisation (scribing) and literarisation begin to work together as collaborative processes.[4] Thus, the idea that kavya (poetry) is not just a folk song but a refined literary activity of the learned becomes deeply rooted in literary culture.

When scribing in a literary culture was recognised as a sophisticated, expressive form of literary talent, kavya or kate (poetry or narrative) would have lost their natural quality and entered the domain of history. The folk song entering history as kavya is not a unidimensional and straightforward phenomenon. In the context of Kannada up to the twelfth century, literarisation grew as a prominent tool for enhancing the charisma of royal power. I do not intend

---

[4] "Literisation" refers to the birth of writing practice and "literarisation" refers to recognising particular forms of expression as literature. For more on these concepts and processes in premodern India, see Pollock, *The Language of the Gods*, pp. 4–5 and 23–6.

to criticise the early Kannada writers who were part of this literarisation process from the standpoint of democratic and socialist values. Instead, I aim to explain the historical context in which the birth of the "scribing" process in literary culture became possible. Instead of looking at literature merely as an individual's imaginative venture, my method is to analyse it at the level of the institutions and material practices of reading and writing. When we understand literary culture as concrete social practices and institutions, we will be able to recognise a new kind of literary imagination at work. Despite my many doubts, I am trying to use the current methods of the materialist theory of literature. Mine is a misadventure – situating philosophical criticism within the framework of materialist theory.

This is the right place to analyse in detail the vachana that forms the epigraph to the present chapter. Here, I try to extend the internal logic of Allama's vachana. When a folk song becomes kavya in literary culture, it undergoes a total transformation. Literature is constituted as a tradition. There would be no continuity in literary culture if this transformation had not happened in premodern times. In the Kannada context the literary tradition fashioned itself as Vastuka–Varnaka. But these are all the worries of worldly literary culture. The doubts Allama raises about language are deadly to those literary cultures.

When Allama asks "what is in this world / [. . .] what is beyond this world?" in the vachana (641) above, he speaks of the borders and limits of worldly literary cultures. If a literary culture conceives method or tradition as the fundamental state of creativity, a flock of poets will reproduce just what the tradition has taught. Allama calls them "a flock of parrots". This is true both in terms of the methods of handling themes and the ways of description in literature. Allama's extreme criticism of the parroting of tradition is revolutionary. However, nothing new can emerge in literary traditions without such severe criticism or even rejection. Without attacks of this nature, literary traditions will not sprout branches.

As this vachana (641) illustrates, the sole aim of Allama's literary endeavour is to understand Guheshwara. Literary traditions, for all their overconfidence, are ill suited to capture divyanubhava. Mystics usually acquire all they need from literary cultures and then transcend them. For Allama, the undertaking of such a literary experiment arises above all from spiritual necessity.

Regarding the other vachana quoted above (642), what does Allama represent in the context of literary culture's complex practices – scribing and erasing, and appearance and disappearance? When a literary culture undertakes the task of enhancing the power of royalty, it inevitably becomes secular. To a certain point, secular literary cultures may tolerate religious imaginations institutionally. However, mystic poetry rejects secular literary culture at its very birth. Negotiating with the power structure is inevitable for a literary culture associated with royal power. Allama thus appears in the Kannada world as a representative of the mystic literary imagination, which is kept outside the orbit of premodern secular literary cultures. Again, I am not defining mystic literary imagination merely at the level of internal metaphors and forms of expression. I explain it while keeping in mind the physical environment of mystic literary creation and its power relations. Allama is a supreme representative of the creative mind outside of what we call Kannada's authentic literary culture.

II

We need to discuss in greater detail the formation of canonical literary culture in premodern Kannada. The first characteristic feature of a canonical literary culture is the cordial relationship between its self-awareness as a tradition and political power. *Kavirajamarga* is the first text in this canonical literary culture of Kannada. I considered describing this text as a manifesto but decided not to. While a manifesto tries to hide certain things within its body, *Kavirajamarga* is a remarkably mature and complex work; it is an open text that presents, at least obliquely, the problems it is facing and the conflicts it is encountering.

As discussed in Chapter 3, *Kavirajamarga* explains the interaction between Sanskrit cosmopolitanism and regional vernacularism. This work is witness to how Kannada, leaving aside its differences and diversities, fashioned itself as a literary culture. In providing a record of this very important process, *Kavirajamarga* holds a globally unique place amongst works of poetics. And historically it ranks among the earliest works of literary thought in the world.[5]

The importance of this text lies in the way it redefines the vernacular. The Kannada vernacular contains such diversity that even the thousand-hooded Vasuki, the snake god, would be wearied by it. According to *Kavirajamarga*, such diversity is not desirable in a canonical literary culture.

There is also the question of the many ways in which the concept of "desi" can be defined. The idea that Desi and Marga are entirely different is deeply embedded in *Kavirajamarga*. In this context there are two dimensions to Desi: one is an everyday colloquialism, and the other is the rhythmic polyphony that comes from it. Likewise, there are two dimensions to Marga. Marga is a method of engaging with and receiving from the cosmopolitan that is outside the framework of the original language. Here, Marga means a cultured literary sensibility, which, in the context of Kannada, is the result of Kannada's relationship with Sanskrit and Prakrit traditions. Another dimension of Marga is the result of expertise in the literary culture that is internal to Kannada literature. That is, Marga is the mode of sensibility developed by interacting with great Kannada poets like Pampa, Ranna, and Kumaravyasa, even without deeply interacting with Sanskrit and Prakrit cosmopolitanism.[6] While Marga connotes the self-awareness of a literary tradition, Desi implies a state of complete involvement with the self.

The notions of Marga–Desi, which otherwise help us understand the Kannada literary tradition, become mute in the case of Allama. Is Allama Margi? Or Desi? The answer is paradoxical: Allama is both, and, at the same time, neither. When we describe Allama as

[5] For more, see ch. 9, "Creating a Regional World: The Case of Kannada", in Pollock, *The Language of the Gods*, p. 330. Also see Subbanna, "The Kannada Cosmos".

[6] Kumaravyasa: an early-fifteenth-century Kannada epic poet who wrote *Karnata Bharata Kathamanjari*.

Margi we refer to his refined sensibility. But we cannot find in him the cultural prestige and honoured discipleship of literary tradition that generally accompanies Marga. Allama won't spare even giant philosophers, let alone ordinary poets. He engages continuously with perceptions and methods of interpretation outside the Kannada language. In this respect he upgrades Kannada to Marga through the lens of philosophy. He was the first to undertake large-scale philosophical activity in Kannada. Many had done this in Sanskrit, Prakrit, and Pali. But Allama initiated philosophical creativity in Kannada, which even Pampa and Ranna could not do – not that they aspired to, as they were poets on one level and mythologists on the other. Allama's importance lies elsewhere. He is both philosopher and poet – the first philosopher of Kannada to use the resources of a poet for thinking. In this respect Allama transformed Kannada into a fresh Marga.

For a linguistic community to become a comprehensive Marga tradition it must include literature, philosophy, and the knowledge traditions we call social sciences today. Historically speaking, we don't find philosophers in Kannada before Allama. However, there is a tradition comprising Pampa, Ranna, Shivakotyacharya, and Srivijaya that has used the Kannada language sensitively.[7]

Philosophically speaking, Allama is sceptical about the concept of a guru. However, yielding to contemporary pressures of Virashaivism, he seems to have consented to the idea of guru, and recognised its limited necessity. However, Marga involves a respectful relationship with a guru or leader in literary or knowledge traditions. In this regard, Marga is a mode of deflating the ego of personal talent. On the grand path of tradition, individual talent is a small cart. Allama is entirely against such a conception of Marga. Thus, there is hardly any mention of other poets in those of his vachanas hitherto

---

[7] Shivakotyacharya: the author of *Vaddaradhane*. This is the earliest extant prose work available in Kannada, written during the tenth century. There are two English translations of this text; see Shivakotyacharya, *Adoration of the Ancients*; and Shivakotyacharya, *Veneration to the Elders*; Srivijaya: the author of *Kavirajamarga*.

available. However, there are occasional reflections on poetic practice and a general community of poets.

Then comes the question of whether Allama is Desi. If we consider Desi's deep involvement in language, he is not Desi. A Desi poet cannot write lines such as "language is life-threatening" (1017).[8] The idea that "speech is defilement" (1234) does not occur to the Desi mind.[9] In fact, neither Marga nor Desi would agree that speech is a kind of defilement. Especially in the case of Desi, its immense power springs from its complete devotion to language. On the other hand the idea of Desi as a form of intensely organised colloquialism is entirely applicable to Allama. He purifies colloquialism and uses it in its intense form. Likewise, Desi understood as a form of prosody can also be seen in Allama. In this respect, I entirely endorse the view that Allama composed songs, too. It wouldn't be wrong to say that there is a spirit of songs transpiring within the very womb of Allama's vachanas. Consider the following song:

> Part black, part white
> O eagle.
> Two birds have built their nests on one tug.
> Look, if one gets down, another does not.
> Four heads, legs twelve,
> six wings and feathers three hundred and sixty.
> Only our Guheshwara understands this,
> not the inert mortals. (Hadu, song 26)

Although the distinction between Marga and Desi may be valid elsewhere, it completely collapses here. The two birds mentioned in the above poem are the pair familiar to us from the Upanishads. At the same time, this composition can be sung to the accompaniment of an ekatari (a folk musical instrument). The composition incorporates within its structure exclamations natural in singing.

---

[8] See vachana no. 1237 in Allama Prabhu, *Lord of the Cave*, and no. 723 in Allama Prabhu, *Vachanas of Allama Prabhu*.

[9] See vachana no. 1463 in Allama Prabhu, *Lord of the Cave*, and no. 951 in Allama Prabhu, *Vachanas of Allama Prabhu*.

This model of song-vachana may be found in other Indian mystic traditions of which *Doha Kosha* and *Caryagiti-kosa* provide excellent examples.[10] The supreme achievement of mystic poetic traditions was the dissolving of the distinction between Marga and Desi. Although these traditions carry Desi elements of folk songs in their compositions, traits of Marga such as interaction with other traditions and intellectual density are present in them. Some of Allama's vachanas can also be read as him entering into a philosophical dialogue with Shankara. Thus, Allama dissolves the Marga–Desi distinctions that literary culture so carefully tries to maintain.

[10] Both are works of Buddhist philosopher Sarahapada.

Select Bibliography

Primary Sources: Kannada

Allama's Vachanas

Allama Prabhu, *Allamaprabhudevara Vachana Samputa*, ed. B.V. Mallapur (Bangalore: Kannada Pustaka Pradhikara, 2001).

Allama Prabhu, *Vyomamuruti Allamaprabhudevara Vachanagalu*, ed. R.C. Hiremath and M.S. Sunkapur (Dharwad: Kannada Adhyayana Peetha, Karnatak University, 1976).

Allama Prabhu, *Allamana Vachanagalu*, ed. Jeevan M. (Dharwad: Samaja Pustakalaya, 1960).

Allama Prabhu, *Allamana Vachana Chandrike: Prabhudevara Vachanagalu-Swaravachanagalu*, ed. L. Basavaraju (Bellary: Lohiya Prakashana, 1960).

Immadi Shivabasavaswamigalu, *Allamaprabhudevara Teekina Vachanagalu* (Mysore: J.S.S. Grantha Male, 2014).

Other Vachana Anthologies

Kalburgi, M.M., ed., *Sankeerna Vachana Samputa: Mooru* (Bangalore: Kannada Pustaka Pradhikara, 2001).

Vachana Sanchaya, https://vachana.sanchaya.net/.

The Shunyasampadanes

Guluru Siddhaveerannodayara, *Prabhudevara Shunyasampadane*, ed. M.M. Kalburgi and Veeranna Rajur (Gadag: Lingayata Adhyayana Samsthe, 2016).

Gummalapurada Siddhalingadevara, *Gummalapurada Siddhalingadevara Shunyasampadane*, ed. K. Ravindranath and Prakash Girimallanavar (Sonduru: Prabhudevara Janakalyana Samsthe, 2021).

Halegeyarya, *Halegeyaryana Shunyasampadane*, ed. S. Vidyashankara and G.S. Siddhalingaiah (Bengaluru: N. Nagaratna, 2008).

Shivaganaprasadi Mahadevayya, *Shivaganaprasadi Mahadevayyana Prabhudevara Shunyasampadane*, ed. L. Basavaraju (Bengaluru: Sapna Book House, 2017).

Harihara's Ragalegalu

Harihara, *Hariharana Ragalegalu*, ed. M.M. Kalburgi (Bengaluru: Department of Kannada and Culture, 2011).

Chamarasa's Prabhulingalile

Chamarasa, *Chamarasana Prabhulingalile* (Original with Prose Rendering by S. Vidyashankar; Bangalore: Kannada Sahitya Parishattu, 2018).

The Manteswamy Kavya

Boralingaiah, H.C., compiled and ed., *Manteswamy* (Hampi: Prasaranga, Kannada University, 1997).

Indvadi, Venkatesh, ed., *Manteswamy Kavya: Odu Pathya* (Hampi: Prasaranga, Kannada University, 2012).

Other Primary Sources: Kannada

Adiga Angala, "Bhoomigeeta", https://adiga.sanchaya.net/bhoomigeeta-text/, accessed on 14 December 2024.

Anupama, H.S., *Belaginolagu Mahadeviyakka* (Gadag: Ladayi Prakashana, 2022).

Bendre, D.R., "Bhavageeta", in *Ambikatanayadattara Samagra Kavya, Audumbaragathe*, vol. 3, ed. Vaman Bendre (Hubballi: Varakavi Dr D.R. Bendre Samshodhana Samsthe, 2003).

Bendre, D.R., "Kalpavruksha Vrundavanangalali", in *Hadu Padu* (Galagali: Sahitya Mandira, 1946).

Janna, *Yashodhara Charite* (Bengaluru: Department of Kannada and Culture, 2011).

Kedilaya, Shankara, trans., *Periyapuranam* (Madurai: Madurai University, 1980).

Maggeya Mayideva, *Prabhugeeta*, ed. C. Mahadevappa (Bangalore: Sharada Nivasa Bengaluru Samshodhanakoti, 2002).

Nagabharana, T.S., *Allama* (2017).

Nagabharana, T.S., *Santa Shishunala Sharif* (1990).

Pampa, *Pampa Mahakavi Virachita Adipuranam* (Original Text with Prose Rendering in Kannada by K.L. Narasimhashastry; Bengaluru: Kannada Sahitya Parishattu, 2016).

Shastri, T.V. Venkatachala, and K. Raghavendra Rao, ed., *Brahmashiva-Vruttavilasa Samputa: Samaya Parikshe, Dharma Parikshe* (Hampi: Kannada University, 2009).

Shivaprakash, H.S., "Marula Shankaradeva", in *Male Bidda Neladalli* (Bangalore: Kannada Sangha, Christ College, 1983).

Secondary Sources: Kannada

Akshara, K.V., *Shankara Vihara: Adhunikanobbana Advaita Yatre* (Heggodu: Akshara Prakashana, 2019).

Amur, G.S., "D.R. Nagarajara Vimarshe: Marx–Allamara Mela", in *Belakina Bele*, ed. M.G. Hegde (Bengaluru: Vasantha Prakashana, 2017).

Ashadevi, M.S., *Belakiginta Bellage* (New Delhi: Sahitya Akademi, 2016).

Ashadevi, M.S., "Bauddhika Nekara", in M.S. Ashadevi, ed., *D.R. Nagaraj Avara Belebaluva Barahagalu* (Bengaluru: Vasantha Prakashana, 2015).

Ashok, T.P., "D.R. Nagaraj: Kelavu Nenapugalu", in Shivaraja Byadarahalli, ed., *Ananya Pratibheya Pari* (Bengaluru: Ki.Ram. Prakashana, 2021).

Bannanje, Veena, *Akkamahadeviya Dvaita* (Bangalore: Kannada Sahitya Parishattu, 2007).

Bhatta, Kadengodlu Shankara, "Vastuka-Varnaka", in A.V. Navada, ed., *Kadengodlu Shankara Bhatta Vachike* (Bangalore: Karnataka Sahitya Academy, 1995).

Bhoosnurmath, S.S., *Śūnyasaṁpādaneya Parāmarśe* (Bangalore: Kannada and Culture Department, 1982).

Boratti, Vijayakumar M., *Hiriyara Hiritana Hindenayitu: Kannada Sahitya, Vasahatushahi mattu Samudayagalu* (Hampi: Prasaranga, Kannada University, 2011).

Boratti, Vijayakumar M., "Adhunika Itihasakke Allamaprabhuvina Pravesha", in Amaresh Nugadoni, ed., *Allamaprabhuvina Vachanagalu: Samskrutika Mukhamukhi* (Hampi: Prasaranga, Kannada University, 2010).

Boratti, Vijayakumar M., "Praprathama Vachana Prakatane: Paurastya-vada mattu Kelavondu Prashnegalu", *Lokajnana*, vol. 2, pp. 40–50.

Budalu, Nataraja, *Pratyekabuddha Allamaprabhu* (Channapattana: Pallava Prakashana, 2017).

Budalu, Nataraja, *Sarahapada* (Bengaluru: Godhuli Prakashana, 2016).

Budalu, Nataraja, *Nagarjuna-Allamaprabhu* (Bengaluru: Godhuli Prakashana, 2010).

Byadarahalli, Shivaraja, ed., *Ananya Pratibheya Pari* (Bengaluru: Ki.Ram. Prakashana, 2021).

Chakravarthy, Manu N., "Amruta mattu Garudada Punarmudranakke Prastavane", in D.R. Nagaraj, *Amruta mattu Garuda* (Heggodu: Akshara Prakashana, 2009).

Chidanandamurthy, M., *Shunyasampadaneyannu Kuritu* (Bengaluru: Priyadarshani Prakashana, 2020).

Chidanandamurthy, M., *Hindu: Virashaiva (Lingayata)* (Bangalore: Priyadarshini Prakashana, 2014).

Diwakara, Ranganatha, *Vachanashastrarahasyavu* (Bengaluru: Kannada Sahitya Parishattu, 2013).

Doddanagoudaru, Joladarashi, *Bayala Galikeya Belagu: Guluru Siddha-veerannodayara Prabhudevara Shunyasampadaneya Vyakhyana* (Bellary: Ramesh Prakatana Mandira, 1985).

Dube, Saurabh, *et al.*, *Daaru Prathima Na Poojibe*, trans. G.G. Rajashekhara (Heggodu: Akshara Prakashana, 1993).

George, Daisi Jasmin, *Allamaprabhu mattu Manteswamy: Ondu Taulanika Adhyayana* (Siriganda, 2019).

Govindaraj, Giraddi, *Vachana Vinyasa* (Dharwad: Manohara Grantha Mala, 2018).

Gundur, N.S., "Nagarikate Nirupakana Chintanegalu", *Prajavani*, 4 December 2022.

Hegde, G.M., ed., *Allama Adhyayana Loka* (Kanthavara: Allamaprabhu Peetha Kanthavara, 2023).

Hegde, Rajaram, and Shanmukha A. ed., *Kottakudureyaneralariyade: Vachanagala Adhyayanadalli Adhunikara Purvagrahagalu mattu Avugalache* (Sirsi: Nilume Prakashana, 2015).

Hiremath, B.K., *Kannada Hastapratigalu: Ondu Adhyayana* (Jambagi: Virashaiva Adhyayana Vedike, 1992).

Hiremath, R.C., *Mahaayatre* (Hampi: Prasaranga, Kannada University, 1997).

Honnusiddartha, C.B., ed., *Samagra Kannada Sahitya Charitre*, vol. 1 (Bangalore: Centre for Kannada Studies, Bangalore University, 2014).

Huliyar, Nataraj, *D.R. Nagaraj* (New Delhi: Sahitya Akademi, 2022).

Huliyar, Nataraj, *Inti Namaskaragalu: P. Lankesh hagu D.R. Nagaraj kurita Srujanashila Kathanaka* (Channapattana: Pallava Prakashana, 2014).

Imrapur, Shanta, *Akkamahadevi: Jeevana, Sahitya, Vyaktitva-Prabhava Mudre* (Hubli: Moorusaviramath, 2001).

Jalki, Dunkin, "Vachana Sahityavu Jativyavastheya Viruddha Matanaduttadeye?", *Chintana Bayalu*, vol. 1, no. 3, pp. 25–44.

Joshi, M. Prabhakara, and M.A. Hegde Siddapura, *Kumarilabhatta* (Heggodu: Akshara Prakashana, 2011).

Joshi, M. Prabhakara, and M.A. Hegde, *Bharatiya Tatvashastra Pravesha* (Heggodu: Akshara Prakashana, 2008).

Kalburgi, M.M., "Allamaprabhuvina Janmagrama mattu Charitreya Belavanigeya Ritigalu", *Marga*, vol. 2 (Bengaluru: Sapna Book House, 2019).

Kalburgi, M.M., "Shasanagalalli Basavapurva-Basavottara Kalada Shaivaswarupa", *Marga*, vol. 4 (Bengaluru: Sapna Book House, 2019).

Kalburgi, M.M., *Shasanagalalli Shivasharanaru* (Bengaluru: Kannada Sahitya Parishattu, 2014).

Kalburgi, M.M., *Vachana Sahitya Prakataneya Itihasa* (Gadag: Virashaiva Adhyayana Samsthe, 1990).

Kalgudi, Basavaraj, "Shunyasampadanegalu: Oduvudu Hege? Kaliyuvudu Enu?", in Amaresh Nugadoni, ed., *Shunyasampadanegalu: Samskrutika Mukhamukhi* (Hampi: Prasaranga, Kannada University, 2018).

Kalgudi, Basavaraj, *Anubhava Samskrutika Samasye mattu Hudukata* (Chitradurga: Sri Murugharajendra Granthamaale, 1988).

Karnad, Girish, "Lekhakana Nudi", in *Taledanda* (Dharwad: Manohara Grantha Mala, 2015).

Krishnamurthy, Agrahara, "Matige Avakashavideyendare", in D.R. Nagaraj, *Samskruti Kathana*, ed. Agrahara Krishnamurthy (Bengaluru: Department of Kannada and Culture, 2006).

Krishnamurthy, M.S., *Siddha Saahitya* (Hampi: Prasaranga, Kannada University, 2010).

Kurtkoti, Kirtinath, "Prastavane", in *Nuru Mara Nuru Swara* (Dharwad: Kurtkoti Memorial Trust, 2015).

Kurtkoti, Kirtinath, "Purana, Itihasa mattu Kadambari", in *Nuru Mara Nuru Swara* (Dharwad: Kurtkoti Memorial Trust, 2015).

Kurtkoti, Kirtinath, "Chamarasana Prabhulingalile", in *Kannada Sahitya Sangati* (Dharwad: Kurtkoti Memorial Trust, 2008).

Kurtkoti, Kirtinath, "Shunyasampadane", in *Kannada Sahitya Sangati* (Dharwad: Kurtkoti Memorial Trust, 2008).

Kurtkoti, Kirtinath, ed., *Hejjenu: Professor G.B. Sajjan Abhinandana Grantha* (Dharwad: Prof. G.B. Sajjan Abhinandana Samiti, 2002).

Kurtkoti, Kirtinath, *Da.Ra. Bendre* (Bangalore: Prasaranga, Bangalore University, 2000).

Kurtkoti, Kirtinath, "Itihasada Artha", in *Uriya Nalage* (Bengaluru: Kannada Sahitya Parishattu, 1993).

Kurtkoti, Kirtinath, "Itihasada Atikramana", in *Uriya Nalage* (Bengaluru: Kannada Sahitya Parishattu, 1993).

Kurtkoti, Kirtinath, "Itihasada Berugalu", in *Uriya Nalage* (Bengaluru: Kannada Sahitya Parishattu, 1993).

Kurtkoti, Kirtinath, "Itihasada Bhaya", in *Samskruti Spandana* (Dharwad: Manohara Grantha Mala, 1989).

Lokapur, R.S., *Avaidikate mattu Kannada Sahitya* (Belgaum: Nishant Prakashana, 2008).

Malwad, S.S., "Basavannana Kala, Jeevana, Vyaktitva", in C.B. Honnusiddartha, ed., *Samagra Kannada Sahitya Charitre*, vol. 3, pt I (Bangalore: Centre for Kannada Studies, Bangalore University, 2014).

Mugali, R.S., *Kannada Sahitya Charitre* (Mysore: Geetha Book House, 1953).

Nagaraj, D.R., *Vasanta Smriti* (Bengaluru: Sirivana Prakashana, 2015).

Nagaraj, D.R., "Chandassinalli Adagikolluva Devategalu", in *Sahitya Kathana* (Heggodu: Akshara Prakashana, 2006).

Nagaraj, D.R., "Kannadada Kirtige Abhinandane", in *Sahitya Kathana* (Heggodu: Akshara Prakashana, 2006).

Nagaraj, D.R., "Munnudi: Hale Vikalpagalinda Bidugadeya Ase", in *Sahitya Kathana* (Heggodu: Akshara Prakashana, 2006).

Nagaraj, D.R., *Allamaprabhu mattu Shaiva Pratibhe* (Heggodu: Akshara Prakashana, 1999).

Nagaraj, D.R., "Daivasankara", *Ninasam Matukate*, vol. 37, pp. 18–27.

Nagaraj, D.R., "Akshara Chintana", in *Kathakosha* (Translation of 11th Century Jaina Stories from Sanskrit), trans. D.A. Shankar (Heggodu: Akshara Prakashana, 1993).

Nagaraj, D.R., "Hinnudi: Jaina Katha Swarupa", in *Kathakosha* (Translation of 11th Century Jaina Stories from Sanskrit), trans. D.A. Shankar (Heggodu: Akshara Prakashana, 1993).

Nandimath, S.C., *Karnataka Dharmagalu* (Bangalore: Directorate of Kannada and Culture, 1983).

Narasimhacharya, R., *Karnataka-Kavi-Charite*, vol. 1 (Bangalore: Bangalore Press, 1924).

Narasimhacharya, R., *Karnataka-Kavi-Charite*, vol. 2 (Bangalore: City Press, 1919).

Narasimhacharya, R., *Karnataka-Kavi-Charite*, vol. 3 (Bangalore: S.L.N. Press, 1929).

Narayana, P.V., *Vachana Sahitya: Ondu Samskrutika Adhyayana* (Chitradurga: Shri Murugharajendra Granthamaale, 1983).

Nugadoni, Amaresh, ed., *Allamaprabhuvina Vachanagalu: Samskrutika Mukhamukhi* (Hampi: Prasaranga, Kannada University, 2010).

Nugadoni, Amaresh, ed., *Shunyasampadanegalu: Samskrutika Mukhamukhi* (Hampi: Prasaranga, Kannada University, 2018).

Paramashivamurthy, D.V., "Prastavane", in D.V. Paramashivamurthy, ed., *Lakkanna Dandesha mattu Shivatattva Chintamani* (Tumkur: G.S.S. Trust, 2022).

Prabhushankara, *Kuvempu* (Mysore: Institute of Kannada Studies, University of Mysore, 1986).

Puttappa, K.V., "Kavinirmitiyalli Niyatikruta Niyamarahitya", in *Raso Vai Saha, Kuvempu Samgra Gadya*, vol. 1 (Kuppali: Rashtrakavi Kuvempu Pratishthana, 2017).

Puttappa, K.V., ed., *Kannada Kaipidi* (Mysore: Prasaranga, University of Mysore, 2013).

Raghavendra Rao, H.S., *Shatamanada Sahitya Vimarshe* (Bangalore: Karnataka Sahitya Academy, 2022).

Rajur, Veeranna, "Prastavane", in Veeranna Rajur, ed., *Parvatesha Prabhuvina Sangatya* (Mysore: Prasaranga, Mysore Vishwavidyanilaya, 2021).

Rajur, Veeranna, *Vachana Samshodhane* (Bangalore: Kannada Sahitya Parishattu, 2004).

Rama Rao, R.S., "Upodghata", in *Raghavanka Virachita Siddharama Charitra* (Bangalore: Kannada Sahitya Parishattu, 2012).

Rao, L.S. Sheshagiri, *Adhunika Kannada Sahitya Nadedu Banda Dari* (Bangalore: Ankita Pustaka, 2022).

Rao, L.S. Sheshagiri, *Hosagannada Sahitya Charitre* (Bangalore: Sapna Book House, 2020).

Settar, S., "Bharatiya Hinneleyalli Karnatakada Dharmika Samajika Jivana", in C.B. Honnusiddartha, ed., *Samagra Kannada Sahitya*

Charitre, vol. 3, pt I (Bangalore: Centre for Kannada Studies, Bangalore University, 2014).

Shetty, Nithyananda B., *Marganveshane* (Tumakuru: Besuge Publication, 2021).

Shivanna, S., *Virashaiva Hastaprati Pushpikegalu* (Gadag: Virashaiva Adhyayana Samsthe, 1994).

Shivaprakash, H.S., "Manteswamy Parampare Srujanasheela Anusandhana", in Venkatesh Indvadi, ed., *Manteswamy Kavya: Aksharalokada Anusandhana* (Hampi: Prasaranga, Kannada University, 2022).

Siddalingaiah, "Udghatana Bashana", in Venkatesh Indvadi, ed., *Manteswamy Kavya: Aksharalokada Anusandhana* (Hampi: Prasaranga, Kannada University, 2022).

Siddeshwar Swamiji, *Allamaprabhudevara Vachana-Nirvachana* (Mysuru: J.S.S. Granthamale, 2017).

Simha, H.L.N., *Bedara Kannappa* (1954).

Subbanna, K.V., "Kavirajamargavu Nirmisida Kannada Jagattu", in T.P. Ashoka, ed., *Are Shatamanada Ale Barahagalu* (Heggodu: Akshara Prakashana, 2011).

Swamy, O.L. Nagabhushana, *Vachana Prashnottara* (Mysore: Chintana Chittara, 2021).

Swamy, O.L. Nagabhushana, "Shunyasampadanegalu: Rachana Vinyasa", in Amaresh Nugadoni, ed., *Shunyasampadanegalu: Samskrutika Mukhamukhi* (Hampi: Prasaranga, Kannada University, 2018).

Tarikere, Rahamath, "Shaiva Pratibhe mattu Darshanika Hodedata", in Venkatesh Indvadi, ed., *D.R. Nagaraj Avara Samagra Sahitya Chintane* (Hampi: Prasaranga, Kannada University, 2022).

Tarikere, Rahamath, *Karnataka Gurupantha* (Hampi: Prasaranga, Kannada University, 2020).

Tarikere, Rahamath, "Shunyasampadane mattu Democracy", in Amaresh Nugadoni, ed., *Shunyasampadanegalu: Samskrutika Mukhamukhi* (Hampi: Prasaranga, Kannada University, 2018).

Tarikere, Rahamath, *Karnatakada Nathapantha* (Bangalore: Abhinava Prakashana, 2013).

Tharakeshwar, V.B., "D.R. Nagaraj mattu Vasahatottara Chintane", in Venkatesh Indvadi, ed., *D.R. Nagaraj Avara Samagra Sahitya Chintane* (Hampi: Prasaranga, Kannada University, 2022).

Thipperudraswamy, H., *Shunyasampadane: Vivaranatmaka Parichaya* (Mysore: D.V.K. Murthy Prakashana, 2016).

Thipperudraswamy, H., *Vachanagalalli Virashaivadharma* (Mysore: D.V.K. Murthy Prakashana, 1969).

Uttangi, Chennappa, *Anubhava Mantapada Aitihasikate* (Dharwad: Muraghamath, 1976).

Vaidika-Avaidika Darshana: Prachina Bharatiya Vagvadagalu (Bengaluru: Ruthumana, 2020).

Vasudevamurthy, T.N., *Pashanada Hangu: Allamana Darshanika Mimamseya Adhyayana* (Bangalore: Kannada Pustaka Pradhikara, 2011).

Veerashaiva, https://www.virashaiva.com/vachanas/, accessed on 10 December 2024.

Venkannaiah, T.S., "Bijjalanu Jainane?", in H.S. Venkatesh Murthy, ed., *T.S. Venkannaiah Samagra Sahitya Samputa* (Bengaluru: Kannada Pustaka Pradhikara, 2019).

Vidyashankara, S., ed., *Virashaiva Paribhashika Padakosha* (Bangalore: Basava Samithi, 2000).

Viraktamath, Shivanand, *Praudhadevarayana Kalada Kannada Sahitya* (Dharwad: Karnatak University, 1978).

Vividha Lekhakaru, *Vachana Sahitya Samvada* (Bangalore: Prajavani Prakashana, 2014).

Vrushabhendraswamy, S.M., *Kannada Sahityadalli Allamaprabhudeva* (Bangalore: Priyadarshini Prakashana, 2014).

Yeresime Channappa, ed., *Dasoha Siri* (Tumkur: Haleya Vidyarthi Sangha, 1997).

YouTube, "Akka Kelavva", https://www.youtube.com/watch?v=Z0HBUgPP_LA, accessed on 11 December 2024.

YouTube, "Bharatiya Tatvika Parampare: Viadika-Avaidika Darshana, Bhaga 02", https://www.youtube.com/watch?v=ZLX4aToCLAo, accessed on 10 December 2024.

YouTube, "D.R. Nagaraj Sandarshana: Desi-Marga", https://www.youtube.com/watch?v=ZB2EWZOfF2M, accessed on 9 March 2024.

YouTube, "Huchu Hidiyitho", https://www.youtube.com/watch?v=fbpOB95jkWU, accessed on 13 December 2024.

YouTube, "Mathadu Mathadu Lingave", https://www.youtube.com/watch?v=VxCl9ep9nJQ, accessed on 14 November 2024.

YouTube, "M.M. Kalburgiyavaru-Lingayata Veerashaiva Bere Bere", https://www.youtube.com/watch?v=i4kDoTTCkYQ, accessed on 14 December 2024.

YouTube, "Was Basavanna a Brahmin or a Dalit?", https://www.youtube. com/watch?v=f_8oq3-SUuQ, accessed on 12 December 2024.

Other South Asian Languages

Primary Sources

Bhima Bhoi, *Nirveda Sadhana* (Oriya; Cuttack: Dharma Grantha Store, 1955).

Chamarasa, *Prabhulingalile* (Tamil), ed. Ramaswamy Pulavar (Chennai: Shaiva Siddhanta Nurapadippugal Kalagam, 1974).

Chamarasa, *Leela Vishwambara Lile* (Marathi), ed. Shankar Dhondo Sardal (Belgaum: Akhila Bharata Veerashaiva Sangha, 1964).

Chamarasa, *Prabhulingalile* (Telugu), ed. Shiva Sri Bandaru Timmaiahgaru (Kakinada: Chukkakoti Veerabhadravalli Prakashana, 1963).

Chamarasa, *Prabhulingalile* (Sanskrit), ed. Vedamurthy Mannor (Bombay: Nirnay Sagar Mudranalaya, 1825).

Secondary Sources

Dibedi, Hajari Prasad, *Nath-Sampraday* (Hindi; Allahabad: Hindustani Academy, 1950).

Dwivedi, Hazari Prasad, *Granthavali* (Hindi), vol. 6 (New Delhi: Rajkamal Prakashan, 1981).

Mallik, Kalyani, *Siddha-Siddhanta-Paddhati and Other Works of the Natha Yogis* (Sanskrit; Poona: Poona Oriental Book House, 1954).

Primary Sources: English Translations

Allama's Vachanas

Allama Prabhu, *God is Dead, There is no God: The Vachanas of Allama Prabhu*, trans. Manu V. Devadevan (New Delhi: Speaking Tiger, 2019).

Allama Prabhu, *Vachanas of Allama Prabhu*, trans. Armando Menezes, S.M. Angadi, and N.G. Mahadevappa, ed. N.G. Mahadevappa (Dharwad: Karnatak University, 2019).

Allama Prabhu, *Lord of the Cave*, trans. C.R. Yaravintelimath (Bangalore: Basava Samithi, 2016).

Allama Prabhu, *Thus Sang the Veerashaiva Mystics, 1: Allamaprabhudevara*

Vachana, trans. S. Ananthanarayana (Hubli: Moorusaviramath, 1988).

Other Vachana Anthologies: English

Basavanna, *Musings of Basava*, trans. S.S. Basavanal and K.R. Srinivas Iyengar (Mangalore: Basel Mission Press, 1940).

Basavanna, *Sayings of Basavanna*, trans. Masti Venkatesh Iyengar (Gadag: Virashaiva Taruna Sangha, 1935).

Kalburgi, M.M., ed., *Vachana: A Collection of Vachanas by Shiva Sharanas*, trans. and ed. O.L. Nagabhushana Swamy (Bangalore: Basava Samithi, 2019).

Hill, Rowena, and Prabhu Shankara, *Naming the Nameless: 101 Vachanas* (Mysore: Nivedita Prakashana, 1983).

Ramanujan, A.K., *Speaking of Śiva* (New Delhi: Penguin, 2014).

Shivaprakash, H.S., *I Keep Vigil of Rudra: The Vachanas* (New Delhi: Penguin Random House, 2010).

Swamy, O.L. Nagabhushana, ed., *The Sign: Vachanas of the 12th Century* (Hampi: Prasaranga, Kannada University, 2007).

The Shunyasampadanes

Gooluru Siddaveeranna Wodeyar, *Sunyasampadane*, trans. S.C. Nandimath, L.M.A. Menezes, and R.C. Hiremath, vol. 1 (Mysore: J.S.S. Granthamale, 2007).

Gooluru Siddaveeranna Wodeyar, *Sunyasampadane*, trans. S.S. Bhoosnurmath and Armando Menezes, vol. 2 (Mysore: J.S.S. Granthamale, 2007).

Gooluru Siddaveeranna Wodeyar, *Sunyasampadane*, trans. S.S. Bhoosnurmath and Armando Menezes, vol. 3 (Mysore: J.S.S. Granthamale, 2007).

Gooluru Siddaveeranna Wodeyar, *Sunyasampadane*, trans. S.S. Bhoosnurmath and Armando Menezes, vol. 4 (Mysore: J.S.S. Granthamale, 2007).

Gooluru Siddaveeranna Wodeyar, *Sunyasampadane*, trans. M.S. Sunkapur and Armando Menezes, vol. 5 (Mysore: J.S.S. Granthamale, 2007).

Shivaganaprasadi Mahadevaiah, *Shoonyasampadane of Shivaganaprasadi Mahadevaiah*, trans. D.A. Shankar (Mysore: J.S.S. Granthamale, 2023).

Chamarasa's Prabhulingalile

Chamarasa, *The Frolic Play of the Lord (Prabhulinga Lile)*, trans. B.S. Naikar (Bangalore: Basava Samithi, 2023).

Chamarasa, "Selections from Prabhulingaleele", in Ravichandra P. Chittampalli and M.G. Hegde, ed. and trans., *Kannada Literature From the Eleventh Century through the Nineteenth Century: A Reader* (New Delhi: Sahitya Akademi, 2021).

The Manteswamy Kavya

Hiriyanna, Ambalike, ed., *Manteswamy Epic Tradition of South Karnataka*, trans. N.T. Bhat (Gotagodi, Shiggavi: Karnataka Jaanapada University, 2014).

Other Primary Sources: English

Adiga, Gopal Krishna, *Selected Poems of Gopal Krishna Adiga*, trans. Sumatheendra Nadig (New Delhi: Sahity Akademi, 2005).

Arunachala Ashrama, "Appalam ittup Pāru: Song of the Pappadum", http://archive.arunachala.org/docs/collected-worm/appalam-ittup-paru/, accessed on 30 November 2024.

Bendre, D.R., "Bhavageeta", in *The Spider and the Web*, trans. G.S. Amur (Bengaluru: Ruvari, Abhinava Imprint, 2012).

Das, Sisir Kumar, "The Mad Lover", *Indian Literature*, vol. 47, no. 3, pp. 149–78.

Eco, Umberto, *The Name of the Rose*, trans. William Weaver (San Deigo: A Warner's Communication Company, 1980).

Kālidāsa, *Śakuntalā: A Sanskrit Drama in Seven Acts,* trans. Monier Williams (Oxford: Clarendon Press, 1876).

Karnad, Girish, *The Dreams of Tipu Sultan* and *Bali: The Sacrifice* (New Delhi: Oxford University Press, 2003).

Karnad, Girish, *Talé-daṇḍa* (New Delhi: Ravi Dayal, 1993).

Maharaj Dev, Shri Soma-Natha, *Shri Shiva Rahasya: The Secret Teaching of Shiva* (The Yoga Order International, 2006).

Narayana Guru, "Song of the Kundalini: Kundalinipattu", in *A Cry in the Wilderness: The Works of Narayana Guru*, trans. Vinaya Chaitanya (Gurugram: Harper Collins, 2022).

Prasad, Keshavan, *Male Madeshwara: A Kannada Oral Epic*, trans. C.N. Ramachandran and L.N. Bhat (New Delhi: Sahitya Akademi, 2000).

Ramachandran, C.N., and Padma Sharma, trans., "Manteswamy", in C.N. Ramachandran, ed., *Strings and Cymbals: Selections from Kannada Oral Epics* (Hampi: Prasaranga, Kannada University, 2007).

Ramachandran, C.N., and Padma Sharma, trans., "Junjappa", in C.N. Ramachandran, ed., *Strings and Cymbals: Selections from Kannada Oral Epics* (Hampi: Prasaranga, Kannada University, 2007).

Ramachandran, C.N., and Vivek Rai, ed., *Medieval Kannada Literature: A Reader* (Hampi: Prasaranga, Kannada University, 2022).

Ranna, *Gadāyuddham: The Duel of the Maces*, trans. R.V.S. Sundaram, and Ammel Sharon, ed. Akkamahadevi (New York: Routledge, 2021).

Rilke, Rainer Maria, "The sovereigns of the world are old", http://www.aquestionofexistence.com/Aquestionofexistence/Rilke.html, accessed on 15 November 2024.

Sekkizhaar, *Periyapuranam*, trans. G. Vanmikanathan (Chennai: Ramakrishna Math, 1985).

Shastri, J.L., ed., *The Linga-Purana I and II* (New Delhi: Motilal Banarsidass Publishers, 1990).

Shivakotyacharya, *Adoration of the Ancients: Tales from Vaddaradhane*, trans. H.S. Komalesh and Ravichandra P. Chittampalli, ed. R.L. Anantharamaiah (New Delhi: Sahitya Akademi, 2022).

Shivakotyacharya, *Veneration to the Elders: Śivakóṭyācārya's Vaḍḍārādhane*, trans. R.V.S. Sundaram, *et al.*, ed. D.A. Shankar (New Delhi: Manohar, 2020).

Siddalingaiah, *A Word with You, World*, trans. S.R. Ramakrishna (New Delhi: Navayana, 2019).

Secondary Sources: English

Abhinavagupta, "Track 5 Dehasta-devata-cakra Stotra hymns by Abhinavagupta", https://www.abhinavagupta.org/hymns/track-5-dehasta-devata-cakra-strotra/, accessed on 10 December 2024.

Abhinavagupta, *Parā-trīśikā-Vivaraṇa of Abhinavagupta: The Secret of Tantric Mysticism*, trans. Jaideva Singh (Delhi: Motilal Banarsidass Publishers, 2017).

Abhinavagupta, *Sri Tantraloka and Other Works*, trans. Satya Prakash Singh and Swami Maheshvarananda (New Delhi: Standard Publishers, 2015).

Abhinavagupta, *Tantraloka* (Varanasi: Sampurnananda Sanskrit University, 1992).

Abhinavagupta, *A Trident of Wisdom: Translation of Parātrīśikā-Vivaraṇa*, trans. Jaideva Singh (Delhi: Motilal Banarsidass Publishers, 1988).

Abhinavagupta, *The Tantraloka of Abhinavagupta with Commentary by Rajanaka Jayaratha*, vol. 1, ed. Mukund Ram Shastri (Allahabad: The Indian Press, 1918)

Alper, Harvey P., *Mantra* (New York: State University of New York Press, 1988).

Ambedkar, B.R., "Riddle Number 22: Brahma is not Dharma. What Good is Brahma?", in *Riddles in Hinduism: An Exposition to Enlighten Masses. Dr. Babasaheb B.R. Ambedkar: Writings and Speeches*, vol. 4, ed. Vasant Moon (New Delhi: Dr. Ambedkar Foundation, 2014).

Amur, G.S., *Dattatreya Ramachandra Bendre* (New Delhi: Sahitya Akademi, 1994).

Anderson, Benedict, *Imagined Communities: Reflections on the Origin and Spread of Nationalism* (London: Verso, 2006).

Anderson, R.J., *et al.*, *Philosophy and Human Sciences* (London: Routledge, 1988).

Appadurai, Arjun, *Worship and Conflict Under Colonial Rule: A South Indian Case* (Cambridge: Cambridge University Press, 1981).

Bagchi, Prabodha Chandra, ed., *Caryāgīti-kosa of Buddhist Siddha* (Santiniketan: Visva-Bharati Publishing Department, 1956)

Bakhtin, Mikhail, "Forms of Time and the Chronotope in the Novel", trans. Caryl Emerson and Michael Holquist, ed. Michael Holquist, *The Dialogic Imagination: Four Essays* (Austin: University of Texas Press, 1981).

Balagangadhara, S.N., *The Heathen in His Blindness* (New Delhi: Manohar, 2013).

Banerjea, Akshaya Kumar, *Philosophy of Gorakhnath with Goraksha-Vacana-Sangraha* (Gorakhpur: Mahant Dig Vijai Nath Trust, Gorakhnath Temple, 1983).

Belsey, Catherine, "Attention to Language: An Interview with Catherine Belsey", *Limina: A Journal of Historical and Cultural Studies*, vol. 13, no. 1, pp. 1–9.

Belvalkar, S.K., *Kāvyādarśa of Dandin* (Poona: The Oriental Book-Supplying Agency, 1924).

Ben-Herut, Gil, *Śiva's Saints: The Origins of Devotion in Kannada according to Harihara's Ragalegalu* (New York: Oxford University Press, 2018).

Benjamin, Walter, "The Task of the Translator", trans. Harry Zorn, ed. Hannah Arendt, in *Illuminations* (London: The Bodley Head, 2015).

Bevilacqua, Daniela, and Eloisa Stuparich, ed., *The Power of Nāth Yogīs: Yogic Charisma, Political Influence and Social Authority* (Amsterdam: Amsterdam University Press, 2022).

Bhartrhari, *The Vakyapadiya: Critical Text of Cantos I and II*, trans. & notes K. Raghavan Pillai (New Delhi: Motilal Banarsidass Publishers, 1971).

Bickman, Jed, *A Literary Journey: Encountering Writers Workshop* (Calcutta: Writers Workshop, 2009).

Boratti, Vijayakumar M., *The Discovery of Vachanas: Halakatti and the Medieval Kannada Literature in Colonial Karnataka* (Hampi: Prasaranga, Kannada University, 2012).

Britannica, "Pancharatra", https://www.britannica.com/topic/Pancharatra, accessed on 12 January 2025.

Chakrabarti, Arindam, ed., *The Bloomsbury Research Handbook of Indian Aesthetics and the Philosophy of Art* (London: Bloomsbury Publishing, 2016).

Chakrabarty, Dipesh, "The Muddle of Modernity", *The American Historical Review*, vol. 116, no. 3, pp. 663–75.

Chakravarti, R., *Shakti-Vishistadvaita or the Philosophical Aspect of Virasaivism* (Mysore: Sri Kashinatha Granthamala, 1938).

Chandra Shobhi, Prithvi Datta, "Introduction, Garuda in Search of Nectar: On the Narrative Imagination of D.R. Nagaraj", in D.R. Nagaraj, *Listening to the Loom: Essays on Literature, Politics and Violence*, ed. Prithvi Datta Chandra Shobhi (Ranikhet: Permanent Black, 2012).

Chandra Shobhi, Prithvi Datta, "Introduction", in D.R. Nagaraj, *The Flaming Feet and Other Essays: The Dalit Movement in India*, ed. Prithvi Datta Chandra Shobhi (Ranikhet: Permanent Black, 2010).

Chandra Shobhi, Prithvi Datta, "Pre-modern Communities and Modern Histories: Narrating Vīraśaiva and Lingayat Selves" (PhD thesis, University of Chicago, 2005).

Chandra Shobhi, Prithvi Datta, "Kalyaṇa is Wrecked: The Remaking of a Medieval Capital in Popular Imagination", *South Asian Studies*, vol. 32, no. 1, pp. 90–8.

Chatterji, J.C., *Kashmir Shaivism* (New York: State University of New York Press, 1986).

Coburn, Thomas B., *Encountering the Goddess: A Translation of the Devī-Māhātmya and a Study of Its Interpretation* (New Delhi: Sri Satguru Publications, 1992).

Coward, Herold, "A Hindu Response to Derrida's View of Negative Theology", in Herold Coward, and Toby Foshay, ed., *Derrida and Negative Theology* (Albany: State University of New York Press, 1992).

Dasgupta, Surendranath, *A History of Indian Philosophy*, vol. 5 (London: Oxford University Press, 1962).

Desai, P.B., *Basavesvara and His Times* (Dharwar: Kannada Research Institute, Karnatak University, 1968).

Devadevan, Manu V., "Introduction: Allama Prabhu, the Saint Who Made Sacrilege Worthy of Veneration", in Allama Prabhu, *God is Dead, There Is No God: The Vachanas of Allama Prabhu* (New Delhi: Speaking Tiger, 2019).

Devadevan, Manu V., *A Prehistory of Hinduism* (Warsaw/Berlin: De Gruyter, 2016).

Dupuche, John R., *Abhinavagupta: The Kula Ritual, as Elaborated in Chapter 29 of the Tantrāloka* (New Delhi: Motilal Banarsidass Publishers, 2003).

Dyczkowski, Mark S.G., *The Doctrine of Vibration: An Analysis of the Doctrines and Practices of Kashmir Shaivism* (New Delhi: Motilal Banarsidass Publishers, 1989).

Eliade, Mircea, *Yoga: Immortality and Freedom*, trans. Willard R. Trask (New York: Routledge and Kegan Paul, 1958).

Farquhar, J.N., *An Outline of the Religious Literature of India* (London: Oxford University Press, 1920).

Flood, Gavin D., *An Introduction to Hinduism* (Cambridge: Cambridge University Press, 1996).

Flood, Gavin D., *Body and Cosmology in Kashmir Śaivism* (San Francisco: Mellen University Press, 1993).

Foucault, Michel, "What Is An Author?", in Paul Rabinow, ed., *The Foucault Reader* (New York: Penguin Books, 1991).

Gadamer, Hans-Georg, *Truth and Method* (London: Continuum, 2006).

Gandhi, Ramachandra, *I Am Thou: Meditation on the Truth of India* (Pune: Indian Philosophical Quarterly Publication, 1984).

Ganeri, Jonardon, "Contextualism in the Study of Indian Intellectual Cultures", *Journal of Indian Philosophy*, vol. 36, no. 5–6, pp. 551–62.

Gowda, Chandan, "D.R. Nagaraj: The Wonder of Retrieval", in *Another India: Events, Memories, People* (New Delhi: Simon and Schuster India, 2023).

Guenther, Herbert V., ed., *The Royal Song of Saraha: A Study in the His-*

tory of Buddhist Thought (Seattle: University of Washington Press, 1969).

Guha, Ramachandra, "Contending Visions: How D.R. Nagaraj Reconciled Gandhi with Ambedkar", https://www.telegraphindia.com/opinion/contending-visions-how-d-r-nagaraj-reconciled-gandhi-with-ambedkar/cid/443778, accessed on 15 November 2024.

Guha, Ramachandra, "The Rise and Fall of the Bilingual Intellectual", *The Economic and Political Weekly*, vol. 44, no. 33, pp. 36–42.

Guru, Gopal, and Sundar Sarukkai, *Experience, Caste, and the Everyday Social* (New Delhi: Oxford University Press, 2019).

Guru, Nataraj, *The Word of the Guru: The Life and Teachings of Guru Narayana* (New Delhi: D.K. Printworld, 2008).

Guru, Nataraj, *Life and Teachings of Narayana Guru* (Varkala: Gurukula Publishing House, 1990).

Haq, Jalalul, *The Shudra: A Philosophical Narrative of Indian Superhumanism* (New Delhi: Navayana, 2022).

Heifetz, Hank, and Velcheru Narayana Rao, trans. and ed., *For the Lord of the Animals – Poems from the Telugu: The Kalastisvara Satakamu of Dhurjati* (Berkeley: University of California Press, 1987).

Hiremath, R.C., "Sri Basavesvara: A Biography", in Channappa Yeresime, ed., *Dasoha Siri* (Tumkur: Haleya Vidyarthi Sangha, 1997).

Hiriyanna, M., "The Number of Rasas", in *Art Experience* (Mysore: Kavyalaya Publishers, 1954).

Hiriyanna, M., "What to Expect of Poetry?", in *Art Experience* (Mysore: Kavyalaya Publishers, 1954).

Hirsch, E.D., "Meaning and Significance Reinterpreted", *Critical Inquiry*, vol. 2, pp. 202–25.

Hocart, A.M., *Caste: A Comparative Study* (London: Methuen, 1938).

Holquist, Michael, *Dialogism* (London: Routledge, 2002).

Hultzsch, E., ed., *Epigraphia Indica*, vol. 5 (Ootacamund: The Government Epigraphist for India, 1960).

Huxley, Aldous, *The Perennial Philosophy* (London: Chatto & Windus, 1947).

Inden, Ronald, *Imagining India* (Bloomington: Indiana University Press, 2000).

Internet Encyclopedia of Philosophy, "Kashmiri Shaiva Philosophy", https://iep.utm.edu/kashmiri/#H1, accessed on 5 January 2025.

Ishwaran, K., *Speaking of Basava: Lingayat Religion and Culture in South Asia* (London: Routledge, 1992).

Jalki, Dankin, "Vachanas as Caste Critiques: Orientalist Expressions of Native Experience" (PhD thesis, Centre for the Study of Culture and Society/Manipal University, 2009).

Joseph, M., *et al.*, "Buddhism", https://www.britannica.com/topic/Buddhism, accessed on 17 January 2025.

Kierkegaard, Søren, *Provocations: Spiritual Writings of Kierkegaard*, compiled and ed. Charles E. More (Farmington: The Bruderhof Foundation, Inc., 2002).

Kierkegaard, Søren, "The Absolute Paradox: A Metaphysical Crotchet", in *Philosophical Fragments Or A Fragment of Philosophy*, original trans. & introd. David Swenson, new intro. & commentary by Niels Thulstrup (Princeton: Princeton University Press, 1962).

Kierkegaard, Søren, "The God as Teacher and Saviour: An Essay of the Imagination", in *Philosophical Fragments or A Fragment of Philosophy*, original trans. & introd. David Swenson, new intro. & commentary by Niels Thulstrup (Princeton: Princeton University Press, 1962).

Klostermaier, Klaus K., *A Survey of Hinduism* (Albany: State University of New York Press, 2007).

Kshemaraja, *Pratyabhijnahrdayam: The Secret of Self-Recognition*, trans. and notes by Jaidev Singh (New Delhi: Motilal Banarsidass Publishers, 2006).

Kurtkoti, Kirtinath, *Courtesy of Criticism: Selected Essays of Kirtinath Kurtkoti*, trans. and ed. Kamalakar Bhat (Gurugram: Penguin Random House India, 2024).

Kurtkoti, Kirtinath, *Flaming Tongue*, trans. Krishna Murthy Chandar (New Delhi: Sahitya Akademi, 2009).

Lorenzen, David, *The Kapalikas and Kalamukhas: Two Lost Shaivite Sects* (California: University of California Press, 2017).

Luperini, Romano, "Symbol and Allegory: From Goethe to Lukács, from Marx to Benjamin", *Differentia: Review of Italian Thought*, vol. 5, no. 13, pp. 91–108.

Madhava Acharya, *The Sarva-Darśana-Samgraha, or, Review of the Different Systems of Hindu Philosophy*, trans. E.B. Cowell, and A.E. Gough (London: Kegan Paul, 1904).

Madhava-Vidyaranya, *Sankara-Dig-Vijaya: The Traditional Life of Sri Sankaracharya*, trans. Swamy Tapasyananda (Madras: Sri Ramakrishna Math, n.d.).

Mahadevappa, N.G., *Primer of Lingayatism* (Dharwad: Sharana Literature Publishers, 2022).

Mahapatra, Sitakant, *Bhima Bhoi* (New Delhi: Sahitya Akademi, 2017).

Mammata, *Kavyaprakasha of Mammata*, trans. Ganganath Jha (Varanasi: Bharatiya Vidya Prakashan, 1967).

McGreal, Ian Philip, *Great Thinkers of the Eastern World* (New York: Harper Collins, 1995).

Michael, R. Blake, *The Origins of Vīraśaiva Sects: A Typological Analysis of Ritual and Associational Patterns in the Śūnyasaṃpādane* (Delhi: Motilal Banarsidass Publishers, 1992).

Monius, Anne E., "The Many Lives of Daṇḍin: The Kāvyādarśa in Sanskrit and Tamil", *International Journal of Hindu Studies*, vol. 4, no. 2, pp. 195–223.

Muller-Ortega, Paul Eduardo, *The Triadic Heart of Siva: Kaula Tantricism of Abhinavagupta in the Non-Dual Shaivism of Kashmir* (Albany: State University of New York Press, 1989).

Murthy, P.N., trans., *Sri Yogavasishtam (Maharamayanam)* (Bombay: Bharatiya Vidya Bhavan, 2001).

Nagaraj, D.R., *Listening to the Loom: Essays on Literature, Politics and Violence*, ed. Prithvi Datta Chandra Shobhi (Ranikhet: Permanent Black, 2012).

Nagaraj, D.R., *The Flaming Feet and Other Essays: The Dalit Movement in India*, ed. Prithvi Datta Chandra Shobhi (Ranikhet: Permanent Black, 2010).

Nagaraj, D.R., "Introduction", in Ashis Nandy, *Exiled at Home* (New Delhi: Oxford University Press, 2005).

Nagaraj, D.R., "Critical Tensions in the History of Kannada Literary Culture", in Sheldon Pollock, ed., *Literary Cultures in History: Reconstructions from South Asia* (Berkeley: University of California Press, 2003).

Nagaraj, D.R., *The Flaming Feet* (Bangalore: South Forum Press and ICRA, 1993).

Nagendra, *Rasa Siddhanta* (Delhi: National Publishing House, 1969).

Nandimath, S.C., *A Handbook of Vīraśaivism* (Dharwar: L.E. Association, 1942).

Nandy, Ashis, "Foreword", in D.R. Nagaraj, *The Flaming Feet and Other Essays: The Dalit Movement in India*, ed. Prithvi Datta Chandra Shobhi (Ranikhet: Permanent Black, 2010).

Pande, Govind Chandra, *Studies in the Origins of Buddhism* (New Delhi: Motilal Banarsidass Publishers, 2015).

Pande, Govind Chandra, *Life and Thought of Shankaracharya* (New Delhi: Motilal Banarsidass Publishers, 2011).

Pande, Govind Chandra, *Foundations of Indian Cultures: Two Volumes* (New Delhi: Motilal Banarsidass Publishers, 2007).

Pandey, K.C., *Abhinavagupta* (Varanasi: Chowkhamba Sanskrit Series Office, 1963).

Pandit, Moti Lal, *An Introduction to the Philosophy of Trika Śaivism* (New Delhi: Munshiram Manoharlal Printers, 2007).

Pollock, Sheldon, *A Rasa Reader: Classical Indian Aesthetics* (Ranikhet: Permanent Black, 2016).

Pollock, Sheldon, *The Language of the Gods in the World of Men: Sanskrit, Culture, and Power in Premodern India* (Berkeley: University of California Press, 2006).

Pollock, Sheldon, ed., *Literary Cultures in History: Reconstructions from South Asia* (Berkeley: University of California Press, 2003).

Pollock, Sheldon, "Deep Orientalism? Notes on Sanskrit and Power Beyond the Raj", in Carol Appadurai, ed., *Orientalism and the Postcolonial Predicament: Perspectives On South Asia New Cultural Studies* (Philadelphia: University of Pennsylvania Press, 1993).

Pollock, Sheldon, "Areas, Disciplines, and the Goals of Inquiry", *The Journal of Asian Studies*, vol. 75, no. 4, pp. 913–28.

Pollock, Sheldon, "Cosmopolitan and Vernacular in History", *Public Culture*, vol. 12, no. 3, pp. 591–625.

Pollock, Sheldon, "The Cosmopolitan Vernacular", *The Journal of Asian Studies*, vol. 57, no.1, pp. 6–37.

Pollock, Sheldon, and Carol A. Breckenridge, "In Honor of D.R. Nagaraj", *Public Culture*, vol. 12, no. 3, p. 14.

Polt, Richard, *Heidegger: An Introduction* (London and New York: Routledge, 1999).

Prabhushankara, *Rastrakavi Kuvempu*, trans. H.S. Komalesha (New Delhi: Sahitya Akademi, 2023).

Quigley, Declan, *The Interpretation of Caste* (London: Oxford University Press, 1993).

Radhakrishnan, Sarvepalli, *The Brahma Sutra: The Philosophy of Spiritual Life* (London: George Allen and Unwin Ltd, 1960).

Raghavan, V., and Nagendra, ed., *An Introduction to Indian Poetics* (Madras: Macmillan, 1970).

Rājaśekhara, *Kāvyamīmāṁsā of Rājaśekhara*, trans. Sadhana Parashar (New Delhi: D.K. Printworld, 2013).

Ramanujan, A.K., "Why an Allama *Vachana* is not a Riddle: An Anthological Essay", in Vinay Dharwadker, ed., *The Collected Essays of A.K. Ramanujan* (New Delhi: Oxford University Press, 2014).

Rice, B.L., ed., *Epigraphia Carnatica*, vol. 10 (Mysore: Kuvempu Institute of Kannada Studies, 2019).

Rice, Edward P., *A History of Kanarese Literature* (Calcutta: Association Press, 1921).

Ricoeur, Paul, *On Translation*, trans. Eileen Brennan (London and New York: Routledge, 2006).

Sabara, *Śābara-Bhāṣya*, trans. Ganganatha Jha (Baroda: Oriental Institute, 1933).

Sanderson, Alexis, *Meaning in Tantric Ritual* (New Delhi: Tantra Foundation, 2012).

Sankaracarya, *Brahma Sūtra Bhāṣya of Sankaracarya*, trans. Swami Gambhirananda (Hollywood: Vedanta Press & Bookshop, 1972).

Schouten, J.P., *Revolution of the Mystics: On the Social Aspects of Vīraśaivism* (Delhi: Motilal Banarsidass Publishers, 1995).

Schrader, Friedrich Otto, *Introduction to the Pāñcarātra and the Ahirbudhnya Samhitā* (Madras: The Adyar Library and Research Centre, 1916).

Sharma, Peri Sarveswara, *Anthology of Kumarilabhatta's Works* (New Delhi: Motilal Banarsidass Publishers, 1980).

Sharma, T.R.S., *Reading Alfred Korzybski through Inter-Theoretic Explorations: Indian and Western* (New Delhi: Pencraft International, 2018).

Sharma, T.R.S., "Can Human Behaviour be Changed? For a Better World! Alfred Korzybski's General Semantics", *The Literary Criterion*, pp. 3–15.

Shastri, Pandit Madhusudan Kaul, ed., *Mālinivijayottaratantram* (Bombay: Tatva-Vevechaka Press, 1922).

Shivaprakash, H.S., "Fascination of the Difficult", in Shivaraja Byadarahalli, ed., *Ananya Pratibheya Pari* (Bengaluru: Ki. Ram. Prakashana, 2021).

Shivaprakash, H.S., "Introduction", in H.S. Shivaprakash, trans., *I Keep Vigil of Rudra: The Vachanas* (New Delhi: Penguin Random House, 2010).

Shri Purohit Swami, trans., *Avadhoota Gita* (New Delhi: Munshilal Manoharlal Publishers, 1988).

Shulman, David, *Tamil: A Biography* (London: The Belknap Press of Harvard University Press, 2016).

Shulman, David, *More than Real: A History of the Imagination in South India* (Cambridge: Harvard University Press, 2012).

Singh, Jaideva, trans., *Spandakarikas: The Divine Creative Pulsation* (Delhi: Motilal Banarsidass Publishers, 2007).

Singh, Jaideva, "Pratyabhijna Vimarshini", Glossary, sources unknown.

Skinner, Quentin, *Visions of Politics: Regarding Method*, vol. 1 (Cambridge: Cambridge University Press, 2002).

Skinner, Quentin, "Meaning and Understanding in the History of Ideas", *History and Theory*, vol. 8, no.1, pp. 3–53.

SNDP, "Kali Natakam – the Dance of Kali", https://www.sndp.org/html/kaliNatakam.html, accessed on 14 December 2024.

Snellgrove, D.L., *The Hevajra Tantra: A Critical Study* (London: Oxford University Press, 1959).

Sopa, Geshe Lhundub, "The Special Theory of Pratityasamutpada: The Cycle of Dependent Origination", *The Journal of the International Association of Buddhist Studies*, vol. 9. no. 1, pp. 105–19.

Srivijaya, *Srivijaya Kavirajamargam: The Way of the King of Poets*, trans. R.V.S. Sundaram, and Deven M. Patel (New Delhi: Manohar, 2017).

Stanford Encyclopedia of Philosophy, "Vasubandhu", https://plato.stanford.edu/entries/vasubandhu/index.html#ref-1, accessed on 17 February 2023.

Stock, Brian, *The Implications of Literacy: Written Language and Models of Interpretation in the Eleventh and Twelfth Centuries* (Princeton: Princeton University Press, 1983).

Stone, Matthew, *Levinas, Ethics and Law* (Edinburgh: Edinburgh University Press, 2018).

Subbanna, K.V., "The Kannada Cosmos Formed by Kavirajamarga", trans. M.R. Rakshith in N. Manu Chakravarthy, ed., *Community and Culture: Selected Writings by K.V. Subbanna along with Interviews and Tributes* (Heggodu: Akshara Prakashana, 2009).

Swami Lakshmanjoo, *The Mystery of Vibrationless Vibration in Kashmir Shaivism: Vasugupta's Spanda Karika & Kshemaraja's Spanda Sandoha* (California: Createspace Independent Publishing Platform, 2017).

Swami Lakshmanjoo, *Kashmir Shaivism: The Secret Supreme*, ed. John Hughes (Srinagar: Ishvar Ashram Trust, 2003).

Swami Lakshmanjoo, *Vijnana Bhairava: The Practice of Centring Awareness* (Varanasi: Indica Books, 2002).

Swami Vireswarananda, *Brahma Sutras* (Almora: Advaita Ashrama, 1936).

Thipperudraswamy, H., *Basaveshwara* (New Delhi: Sahitya Akademi, 2017).

Torzsok, Judith, "Women in Early Śākta Tantras: Dūtī, Yoginī and Sādhakī", *Cracow Indological Studies*, vol. 14 , pp. 339–67.

Tripathi, Radhavallabha, ed., *Kamasutram* (Text with Jayamangala Commentary) (New Delhi: New Bharatiya Book Corporation, 2019).

Vajpeyi, Ananya, "Let Poetry be a Sword", *The Caravan*, January 2011, pp. 114–15.

Wadiyar, Jaya Chamaraja, *Avadhuta: Reason and Reverence* (Bangalore: Indian Institute of World Culture, 1958).

Wainwright, William J., "Nontheistic Conceptions of the Divine", in William J. Wainwright, ed., *The Oxford Handbook of Philosophy of Religion* (New York: Oxford University Press, 2005).

White, David Gordon, *The Alchemical Body: Siddha Traditions in Medieval India* (Chicago: University of Chicago Press, 2007).

Wisdom Library, "Chapter XVII – Diction of a Play (lakṣaṇa)", https://www.wisdomlib.org/hinduism/book/the-natyashastra/d/doc210086.html#note-t-80442, accessed on 10 December 2024.

Yamunacharya, *Agama Pramanyam of Sri Yamunacharya*, ed. Pandit Shri Ram Mishra Shastri (Varanasi: Tara Yantralaya, 1937).

Yaravintelimath, C.R., *Vachana Lexicon* (Bangalore: Basava Samithi, 2022).

Yaravintelimath, C.R., "Introduction", in Allama Prabhu, *Lord of the Cave*, trans. C.R. Yaravintelimath (Bangalore: Basava Samithi, 2016).

Yogapedia, "Parashakti", https://www.yogapedia.com/definition/6171/parashakti, accessed on 23 November 2022.

YouTube, "Is there a Philosophy of 'Joy-full-ness'? Abhinavagupta's Reply by Mrinal Kaul", https://www.youtube.com/watch?v=SRsgfj_JaWQ, accessed on 5 January 2025.

YouTube, "The Viraktas of Vijayanagara", https://www.youtube.com/watch?v=A3l1Coo_Qws, accessed on 15 November 2024.

YouTube, "Webinar with Dr. Manu Devadevan on When Allama Prabhu Rejected Bhakti", https://www.youtube.com/watch?v=CjtDywc51jE, accessed on 5 January 2025.

Index

Sri Ramana Maharshi 54, 58,
    85–6
Srivijaya 48, 138–9, 382
sthala(s) 25, 29, 345
Stock, Brian 32, 233
sutaka (defilement) 109, 184, 223,
    227–8, 252, 268, 307, 383;
    notion of 109, 227

tantra 90, 101, 118, 125, 131,
    147, 152–3, 190, 198, 200,
    210, 213, 215, 219
tantrism 47, 50, 69, 87, 101, 122,
    124, 126, 128–9, 147, 153,
    159, 183, 188–93, 197–201,
    210–13, 219, 326, 364–5
tattva 50, 73, 77, 87, 125, 127,
    145, 163, 194–5, 205, 210
    216, 222, 236, 238, 265,
    370
tattvamasi 347–9
textual community (ies) 32, 50–1,
    232–3, 261–2, 303
Trika 47, 125, 166, 174, 190,
    209–11, 215
trinity 18, 94–6, 98, 100, 224;
    Brahmanical 95–6, 98

unfoldment (vikasikarana/vikasa-
    shila) 48, 93–4, 98, 101, 169,
    216
Untouchability 305
Untouchables 268, 287, 306,
    314–15
Upanishads, the 96, 117, 142,
    144, 252, 312, 329, 347, 350,
    383
Uttarapatha (northern path/left
    wing) 17, 45, 47, 50, 87,
    124–5, 126, 198–200, 202–5;

goddesses and gods in 126;
    philosophy of 45, 124–5
Uttar Pradesh 82, 307

vachanakara(s) 1, 14–15, 18–21,
    25–7, 38, 40–6, 48, 56, 58,
    73–4, 86, 88, 108–10, 114–15,
    128, 141, 145, 165, 173, 195,
    202, 217, 231, 239, 247–8,
    250, 257, 284, 287–8, 305,
    319, 331, 369
Vachana movement 14, 67, 73–4,
    140, 166, 174, 230, 233–4,
    260–1, 274, 306, 309
vachanas: archive 14, 28, 42;
    bedagina 25, 100; bedagu
    30–1, 100, 102, 241, 287,
    306, 314, 318, 333, 346, 348,
    350–1, 353; commentaries on
    28–9; literature 29, 42, 138,
    140; phenomenon 15, 18, 39;
    tradition 1, 39–40, 43, 57, 72,
    202; translations of 58–9
Vajrayana 67, 99, 316
Vaishnava(s) 30, 68, 94, 96,
    100–1, 128, 147, 151, 162,
    166, 186, 241, 259, 307, 322;
    literature 100–1; tradition 68,
    322
Vamadeva 199, 218
varna(s) 78, 105, 108, 225, 327
varnashrama 46, 80, 92, 94, 106,
    262, 294, 300, 314–15
varnaka 48, 165–6, 168, 207, 286,
    375, 379
vastuka 48–9, 165, 168, 207, 216,
    286, 375, 379
Vedanta 75, 80, 84, 94, 110, 252,
    303, 358, 364
vedapramanya 92, 94, 96, 105